Rhetoric, I shall urge, should be a study of misunderstandings and its remedies. We struggle all our days with misunderstandings, and no apology is required for any study which can prevent or remove them.

I. A. RICHARDS

First, we are concerned with the rhetorical climate, the impact of our times upon what people talk, and what people talk about.... Second, we are concerned with the responsible and effective practice of rhetoric in our times, with the character and behavior of listeners and speakers.

J. JEFFERY AUER

As the art of persuasion, the art of producing genuine conviction in an audience, rhetoric affect[s] the entire range of human action as nothing else in theory or in practice quite [does]. The study and use of rhetoric enable[s] one to move others, to get things done.

WALTER J. ONG

One fact that emerges from the history of rhetoric is that there is usually a resurgence of rhetoric during periods of violent social upheaval. Whenever the old order is passing away and the new order is marching—or stumbling—in, a loud, clear call goes up for the services of the person skilled in words.

EDWARD P. J. CORBETT

RHETORIC
IN THE
CLASSICAL
TRADITION

RHETORIC
IN THE
CLASSICAL
TRADITION

WINIFRED BRYAN HORNER

Texas Christian University

ST. MARTIN'S PRESS NEW YORK

To my children
Winifred, Richard, Elizabeth, and David
and to my husband, David

Senior Editor: Nancy Perry
Development Editor: Marilyn Moller
Project Editor: Julie Lasky
Production Supervisor: Christine Pearson
Text Design: Helen Granger/Levavi & Levavi
Cover Design: Katherine Urban
Cover Photo: Art Resource
    Detail from the ceiling of the Santa Costanza Cathedral, Rome, circa 350 A.D.
Graphics: G&H Soho

Library of Congress Catalog Card Number: 87-060578
Copyright © 1988 by St. Martin's Press, Inc.
All rights reserved.
Manufactured in the United States of America.
21098
fedcba

For information, write
St. Martin's Press, Inc.
175 Fifth Avenue
New York, NY 10010

ISBN: 0-312-00252-1

Acknowledgments

Ruth Adams and Frank Murray, "Vitamin E in the Hands of Creative Physicians," from *Vitamin E: Wonder Worker of the 70's?* Copyright 1971 by Larchmont Books, 6255 Barfield Road, Atlanta, Georgia, 30328.
The American Heritage Dictionary. Copyright © 1969 by Houghton Mifflin Company. Reprinted by permission from *The American Heritage Dictionary of the English Language.*
Aristides, "A Fat Man Struggles to Get Out" by Aristides. Reprinted from *The American Scholar*, Volume 54, Number 3, Summer, 1985. Copyright © 1985 by the author. By permission of the author.
Nan Desuka, "Why Handguns Must Be Outlawed." Reprinted by permission.

Acknowledgments and copyrights are continued at the back of the book on page 452, which constitute an extension of the copyright page.

Foreword

As an approach to the teaching of writing, classical rhetoric is fairly well known among those who have kept up with the books and articles published in the last twenty-five years or so. For about 2,500 years, classical rhetoric was in fact the *best*-known system for the teaching of oral and written composition in the Western World. Along about the middle of the nineteenth century, the classical system began to lose its preeminent position in the schools, supplanted by a system that was more concerned with the grammatical correctness of the written composition than with the substance and organization of its ideas. Handbooks of grammar, usage, and spelling replaced the full-blown rhetoric texts that dealt with the discovery and arrangement of ideas and with the style, the memorization, and the delivery of those ideas.

In the 1920s, a group of teachers at Cornell University was instrumental in reintroducing classical rhetoric to speech teachers in American universities, and in the mid-1960s, classical rhetoric suddenly reappeared in many freshman English composition courses. In that period, the classical system had to compete for a place in the curriculum with many other approaches to teaching composition. Since then, we have seen the publication of a number of books on the history of rhetoric and of many textbooks on its theory and practice. *Rhetoric in the Classical Tradition* has been designed for those college-level courses that are based on the principles and practices of classical rhetoric.

This rhetoric text differs from other recently published rhetoric texts with an orientation toward classical rhetoric in that it treats all five of the traditional canons of classical rhetoric: invention, arrangement, style, memory, and delivery. When the schools began to put more emphasis on the composition of written prose texts than on texts that were designed to be delivered orally, attention to the memorization and the vocalization of the text faded, if it did not entirely disappear, from the classroom and the textbooks. If a text was to be delivered to an audience in a written or printed form, what need was there for training in memorizing the text and in managing the voice and the appropriate gestures? Those became dispensable skills. So the typical post–World War II rhetoric text with a classical tinge to it dealt only with the first three of the traditional canons: invention, arrangement, and style.

Winifred Horner has found a way to restore attention to memory and delivery, even in a writing class. The invention of writing and printing made memory, in a certain sense, superfluous. If information and knowledge could be recorded in some graphic form, what need was there for us to store that information in our memories? After all, the written records could be stored in our file cabinets or in our libraries. But in Chapter 12, "Tapping Available Resources," Professor Horner shows us how we can resort to such repositories as books and data bases and libraries in addition to our own memory banks in order to discover or recover the facts, the information, and the knowledge we need to develop our written discourses. In Part V, which she entitles "Presentation," she shows us the written equivalent of the oral delivery system of the ancient Greeks and Romans. In dealing in this section with some of the special kinds of academic writing, Professor Horner shows us how to format and package these kinds of writing for delivery to our readers.

Other trappings of the classical system have been retained as well. Professor Horner reminds us that in the process of writing, we must keep our audience of potential readers constantly in mind. She shows us how to make effective use of appeals to the reason and the emotions of the audience and how to project an ingratiating image of ourselves as writers. She demonstrates how we can make use of the ancient stasis system in formulating a thesis for our paper, and then she instructs us in how to make systematic use of the classical "topics" to help us discover things to say in developing that thesis. She makes use of the Ciceronian conception of the basic parts of an oration to show us how to structure our composition. And she devotes two full chapters (10 and 11) to instructing us in the fine points of style, including a generous repertory of the figures of speech.

But there are also extensions of classical rhetoric in this book, with modern theories introduced to complement and sometimes to illuminate the classical system. Professor Horner shows us how the classical system can be used when we write not only persuasive essays but also expository essays. She gives us a short course in formal logic, introducing us to the essence of the Aristotelian syllogism, then showing us the simpler Toulmin model of deductive reasoning, and finally instructing us in how to detect fallacies, in our own reasoning and in the reasoning of others. And she constantly reminds us about how the electronic media have extended our resources for storing, retrieving, and transmitting information.

Winifred Horner's text may be the most sensible and the most fruitful adaptation of classical rhetoric available today for the undergraduate classroom. The essence of classical rhetoric is here, along with some of its special terminology. And the system is presented to modern students, not because it is venerable, but because it is useful. Whether explaining a concept or defining a term, Professor Horner is never condescending; she is careful to address the student as an intelligent and interested peer. Moreover, she has the gift of being able to simplify a subject without trivializing it.

Each chapter includes at least one full reading, and some have two or three, one for each of the major subdivisions. Even if a separate anthology of readings is not used with this text, there are enough readings here to give students the opportunity to apply to a particular piece of prose discourse the principles and concepts treated in the chapter. The critical apparatus and the suggestions for writing in each chapter are not just busywork; by inviting a realistic and meaningful response from the students, these exercises genuinely engage them in practicing what they have been taught.

Winifred Horner, the holder of the distinguished Radford Chair of Rhetoric at Texas Christian University, is a superb teacher and a masterful rhetorician. *Rhetoric in the Classical Tradition* demonstrates how well she herself can practice what she teaches.

EDWARD P. J. CORBETT
Ohio State University

Preface

This is a book about how to write—a composition textbook. More specifically, it is a book about language and all of its interactive processes—about reading, speaking, thinking, and learning as they affect and are affected by writing. Because people use language in manifold ways—to discover and define the world around them; to read, listen, and process information; and to communicate with other human beings—no single language process can or should be approached in isolation. All are part of the linguistic ability that enriches human experience and ensures the survival of culture.

Classical rhetoric, the systematic theory of language on which this book is based, has itself persisted through more than two thousand years. Over the millennia, communication theories have either adopted or rejected its tenets, building on its five-part foundation of invention, arrangement, style, memory, and delivery. For more than two thousand years rhetoric has survived distortions and reductions and has remained central to education and language studies. It is so deeply embedded in Western thought that it has touched every aspect of intellectual history and culture. And it continues to endure because it finds its source in the human spirit and its roots in the human mind.

Although classical rhetoric was developed in an oral culture, its primary concern is with symbol systems, spoken or written. The symbol systems may change as technology advances, but the process with which rhetoric deals is the same, and the relevance of rhetoric to the written culture of the twentieth century remains undisputed.

Classical rhetoric was largely concerned with the language of civil life, particularly the law courts. In Athens, where citizens could argue their own cases, eloquence in the assembly was the road to power. *Persuasion*, which in Greek translates as *belief*, conveyed more in ancient times than our modern use of the word, for it meant arguing for belief in any subject. But, again, the activity of persuasion remains vital to all human communication, even though the etymology of the word has been obscured with time.

Despite its continued relevance, however, classical rhetoric has been distorted and reduced in a number of ways since its inception. The seventeenth-century stylistic rhetorics excluded two of the six parts, invention and arrangement, and were dull lists of figures of speech. The eighteenth century reduced rhetoric to elocution—gestures and pronunciation. In the beginning of the twentieth century the full canon was even further reduced to mere correctness—spelling and punctuation. Moreover, because it is so difficult to talk about morals in a pluralistic society, there is a moral element lacking in modern rhetoric which has emptied rhetoric of much of its meaning. But without this ethical component, rhetoric—and for that matter, all human communication and interaction—is subject to abuse and misuse. When Quintilian spoke of the "good man" he was of course referring to a male citizen of Rome. Within this text the "good man" has become the good person, and Rome has become the world. In other words, students are urged to consider public issues in terms larger than themselves, to see themselves as part of a global community and to acknowledge their responsibilities to other members of that community. No true rhetoric based on the classical tradition can ignore this important ethical and moral component. The status of good citizen of a large and complex world involves a weighty moral responsibility, but it is a responsibility that cannot be ignored in modern times.

This book goes farther than writing texts of the last two hundred years in returning the last two parts of rhetoric, memory and delivery, to the full canon. Memory here is enlarged to mean more than what can be stored in one human brain. Classical rhetoricians called memory the treasure house of rhetoric, and today's treasure house has been enlarged to include our collective cultural memory—the information stored in libraries and computers. In this text, the section on memory treats the storage and retrieval of information—increasingly complex but important processes that every literate person must know.

Delivery, called *presentation* in this text, is the last part of classical rhetoric. It deals not with voice and gesture but with the common forms by which we communicate information in an academic setting. It is recognized that voice and gesture are superficial; good thinking and clear expression will always find appropriate ways of manifesting themselves. But other forms, like manners, are dictated by cultural mores and constantly change. Students need to be familiar with them, even though form, like voice and gesture, is ultimately only the visible sign of inner thought and expression.

Finally, this work is innovative in retaining the vocabulary of classical rhetoric—a violation of the rules for twentieth-century textbooks. This was done because a knowledge of classical vocabulary will increase the student's modern vocabulary immeasurably. Derivatives of ancient terms are mainstays of terminology in philosophy, psychology, sociology, history, religion, and, of course, language study. An acquaintance with them introduces the student to literally hundreds of words in modern English. The relationship between ancient and modern terminology will not only enhance the student's vocabulary but will give him or her a sense of human attitudes as they evolved over time. For instance, the fact that the word *delivery* was known as *actio* in Latin and as *hypocrisis* in Greek both imparts a historical sense to the term and enriches the student's understanding of its modern meaning.

After a very brief overview of classical rhetoric and its place in the ancient world, this book is divided according to the five parts of rhetoric. In the best classical tradition, Part One on invention is the longest and most detailed. Indeed, I have tried to represent the classical tradition as faithfully as possible while dealing with a history that encompasses hundreds of years, different cultures, and a number of philosophers. In drawing from Plato, I may do an injustice to Aristotle, and in quoting the *Ad Herennium*, I may ignore Quintilian's viewpoint. I have had to select and weave together theories that were never conceived in combination to make an understandable whole for today's student. Also, I have added later theories when they seemed to enlighten and enlarge classical rhetoric. Stephen Toulmin's argument theory makes the syllogism more understandable, so I have included it. I have introduced the idea of perspective to description following the work of Richard Young, Alton Becker, and Kenneth Pike. But the tradition has guided me, even though I have made some additions and emendations, leaving the "old, old track" to adapt to the exigencies of the twentieth century. In that respect I take as my inspiration the words of Quintilian:

> But rules are helpful all the same so long as they indicate the direct road and do not restrict us absolutely to the ruts made by others. For he who thinks it an unpardonable sin to leave the old, old track, must be content to move at much the same speed as a tight-rope walker. . . . The orator's task covers a large ground, is extremely varied and develops some new aspect almost every day, so that the last word on the subject will never have been said. I shall however try to set forth the traditional rules and to point out their best features, mentioning the changes, additions and subtractions which seem desirable (*Institutio Oratoria* II xiii 16–17).

This book is for the instructor and the student who believe that knowledge about language leads to skill in using language. It is for the person who believes that an acquaintance with classical rhetoric and the great philosophers who conceived it is part of literacy in its fullest sense. It is for the person who believes that writing is part of a full language process and cannot be learned apart from reading, speaking, listening, thinking, and learning. And finally it is for the person who, like the great philosophers, believes that learning any one of these language processes will not only enlarge knowledge of the others but will also ennoble the mind and lift the spirit.

I should like to acknowledge the help and support of my colleagues at Texas Christian University, especially Gary Tate, Neil Daniel, and Fred Erisman. My thanks as well to my former colleagues at the University of Missouri, Mary Lago, Luverne Walton, Kathy Smith, Donald Lance, and Gilbert Youmanns, and also Pushpajit Bhullar, who helped me with the chapter on the library. I should also like to acknowledge those people in the profession who have consistently supported my work: Linda Peterson; Lynn Bloom; Theresa Enos; Maxine Hairston; Andrea Lunsford; Richard Lloyd-Jones; Walter Ong; James J. Murphy; Donald Stewart; Richard Leo Enos, my first rhetoric professor; and Ed Corbett, my mentor in so many ways. And of course, I wish to recognize the help of all of my students from whom I learn so much, especially Mary Lina Berndt and Sherry Booth, my research assistants, and Kathy Raign, whose work on stasis theory changed the direction of this book. I should also like to thank Marilyn Keil, who by this time knows the book better than I, having entered its many drafts on the computer. I also want to thank my patient editors, Nancy Perry and Marilyn Moller, project editor Julie Lasky, and the reviewers who showed me ways to improve this book: Betsy Brown; Robert J. Connors, University of New Hampshire; Edward P. J. Corbett, Ohio State University; Sharon Crowley, Northern Arizona University; Ann B. Dobie, University of Southwestern Louisiana; Richard Leo Enos, Carnegie Mellon University; Carol Hartzog, University of California at Los Angeles; Howard Hinkel, University of Missouri; Charles Kneupper, University of Texas at Arlington; Linda Palmer, California State University at Sacramento; Laura Stokes, University of California at Davis; Josephine Tarvers, Rutgers University; William Woods, Wichita State University.

Finally, I should like to acknowledge my husband, David, whose continuing love and support helps me to write, grow, and be free.

WINIFRED BYRAN HORNER

Contents

PART V
PRESENTATION   377

Chapter 1

An Introduction to Classical Rhetoric

WHAT IS RHETORIC?
THE ANCIENT WORLD
CLASSICAL RHETORIC

Invention
Arrangement
Style
Memory
Presentation
Kinds of Rhetoric

A CLASSICAL EDUCATION
CLASSICAL RHETORIC FOR THE
TWENTIETH CENTURY

In the seven centuries from five hundred B.C. to the first century A.D. a golden age of art, architecture, and literature flourished in Athens and Rome. During those years the great Greek philosophers Socrates, Plato, and Aristotle, and the Latin rhetoricians Quintilian and Cicero produced rhetorical treatises that have been the basis for language and literature study ever since. Even today, modern ideas about the teaching of writing and the study of literature remain rooted in the precepts that these ancient scholars set forth. Their ideas have been enlarged and expanded but stand basically unchanged. Rhetoric was the art of persuasion, and, in their study of rhetoric, these scholars were in fact studying the human mind and the ways in which human beings acquire and process knowledge through language. Though occasions for language and language forms may change with time, the human mind remains the same. Whatever the century or culture, a writer, in using language, is basically processing knowledge, and a student, in learning to write, is at the same time learning to think. Although classical rhetoric was conceived in a primarily oral culture, the underlying principles remain valuable in a literate society. The classical orator and the contemporary writer share and rely on the same basic precepts.

WHAT IS RHETORIC?

Today rhetoric is defined in one modern dictionary as the art of speaking and writing effectively, but the term has disparaging connotations as well, often used to refer to empty or inflated language. In the classical world, however, the study of rhetoric embodied the principles and rules for effective communication.

In ancient Greece, the person who could use words to advantage was a person of wide influence. The effective orator possessed great power in the state. In the democratic city-state of Athens especially, the art of persuading others to one's own point of view was the road to wealth, power, and influence. Four centuries later, in the days of the Roman Republic, Marcus Tullius Cicero rose from an ordinary citizen to consul, the highest civilian position in the government, through his ability to speak eloquently before the Roman senate. There were, in fact, two roads to fame in the ancient world. One was through military might, the other through the ability to use words. Thus, it was nothing less than imperative for anyone who aspired to a position of influence to learn the art of speaking well—the art of rhetoric.

Skill with spoken and written language still brings power. It is still one road to influence that empowers us to share our vision and to persuade others, to hear other voices and understand their visions. In addition, it helps us to discover who we are and to explain that identity to others—to tell our stories and to make our ideas come alive. Through rhetoric we can move others to think and to act; we can change the world around us.

Rhetoric holds special importance in times of social upheaval. When societies are in flux, it is the clear and coherent voices that focus and direct action. Whereas historical events sometimes grow dim with the passage of time, well-spoken words can live on forever. Thus do the cadences of Abraham Lincoln's *Gettysburg Address* echo even today. John F. Kennedy's brief presidency may not have been marked by memorable deeds, but his words resound—and affect our society—as if they were spoken only yesterday: "Ask not what your country can do for you; ask what you can do for your country." Kennedy was not the first President to appeal for public service; his rhetorical skill makes his appeal so very effective.

Historically, those persons able to teach others how to speak and write effectively have been called rhetoricians and the art itself has been known as rhetoric. Aristotle defined it for his students as "the faculty of observing in any given case the available means of persuasion." For over two thousand years, the art of rhetoric has been central to education at all levels. It has, moreover, been not just the concern of the beginning student but has remained part of the learning and discovery experience of the most advanced students in their search for knowledge and the articulation of insights and ideas.

What distinguishes rhetoric from other studies of literature and linguistics is that it looks at all aspects of communication in terms of the message, the speaker, the audience, and the occasion. It also involves the emotional as well as the rational side of the human being as it takes in ethical, pathetic, and logical considerations. Rhetoric recognizes that carefully reasoned arguments may fail because they do not take into account the hopes and fears of the audience—those basic emotions that finally make us human. It allows for options and choices depending on the complex interactions between writer, audience, and occasion. Political speakers seeking votes address farmers at a rural Farm Bureau meeting on different issues, choose certain words, and offer different arguments than when they address parents at a suburban P.T.A. meeting. Their choice of issues, words, and arguments or proofs depends on the audience and the occasion.

The ability to use words and language is what defines humanness. Language researchers have tried to teach animals to speak, but they have never been able to bring them to the level that four-year-old children reach with apparent ease and without formal instruction. This ability to learn and use language distinguishes humans from other animals, but control over that ability—the ability to speak and write with purpose and clarity—often distinguishes one human being from another.

That ability is expressed in the Greek word *logos*, loosely translated as word or reason, a key concept in ancient rhetoric, carrying with it the mystical qualities often associated with human language. There is no exact translation, but *logos* combines the meanings of thought and expression. In the classical world, there was neither thought without expression nor expression without thought. Mental processes could not be separated from language, for to be human was to be at one and the same time a rational animal and a user of language. Thus, *logos*—thought and expression—not only defined the art of rhetoric, but was held to be the very essence of humanity.

In the ancient world, expression primarily took the form of the spoken word. In fact, Plato actually criticized writing by saying that people would grow lazy and use it as a substitute for memory. In not having to train and use their memories, he warned, students would lose a very important mental ability. His criticisms sound much like those levelled against calculators and computers today. The fact is, however, that writing enables us to store vast amounts of information. Our libraries hold far more than any one human mind. Plato might be reconciled to this modern reality by the fact that our minds are thus freed for other activities. In the twentieth century, calculators, tapes, microfilms, and the RAM of the computer are other ways that technological memory becomes more immediately available to more people in their daily working lives, freeing them in much the same way that the first writing once did.

Classical rhetoric was concerned more with spoken language and orators than with written language and writers, yet its terminology and principles apply to all language and all users of language. Classical rhetoric taught citizens how to persuade others: to argue their cases in the law courts, to deliberate issues in public assemblies, and to deliver appropriate ceremonial speeches such as funeral orations. Today, ordinary citizens are not often called upon to give ceremonial speeches or to make legal appeals, but they do indeed write to persuade in a number of different circumstances. A grant proposal, a job application, a request for a loan, a book review, or an essay on economic theory are all basically persuasive. Persuasion for ancient rhetoricians was a broad term and included all prose communication. It is as central to rhetorical study in the twentieth century as it was in the ancient world.

Finally, ancient rhetoricians were deeply concerned with moral values and the idea of the good person speaking well. They early recognized that rhetoric could be misused. Hence their insistence on the examination of values and questions of right and wrong. For the classical rhetorician the "good man" was initially a good citizen of the state—and good citizens knew rhetoric—how to present their own opinions in a persuasive manner and how to judge and evaluate the opinions of others. That was the duty of a citizen and training in rhetoric prepared the citizen for that duty. Today, rhetoric prepares the citizen of a larger world for just such duties. Through rhetoric, we must continue to examine moral values and to question right and wrong, especially in matters of human affairs. Rhetoric in the classical sense cannot be separated from this duty of world citizenship in the broadest sense of the word.

THE ANCIENT WORLD

Rhetoric was conceptualized five centuries before the birth of Christ in the law courts of Sicily, a large island-state off the southern coast of Italy, and from there found its way to the assemblies of the Greek cities. Greece at that time was not one united nation, but was divided into a number of powerful city-states, the most important of which were Athens, Sparta, Thebes, and Corinth. This network of city-states developed along the northern shores of the Mediterranean in what is now Greece, Italy, and Turkey. They came to be united because after expansion and colonization by the Greeks of the Greek mainland they all shared ties to the Hellenes, an ancient Greek tribe, and because they shared a number of religious shrines, such as the one at Delphi. These ties were developed and sustained through an oral and written communication network.

In the fifth century B.C came one of the great cultural periods in recorded history: the age of Pericles, an Athenian general who rose to prominence because of his political eloquence and military brilliance. Literature, art, sculpture, and architecture all thrived in Athens. The glory that was Greece was born during this period. Athenian thought prevailed in politics, and it was at this time in this city-state that the Western world's first democracy originated. Citizens argued their own cases before the assemblies and law courts, and there appeared a number of rhetoric handbooks, which set out rules and conventions that explained and prescribed ways of presenting a case. Most of these early handbooks are lost, but a great deal is known about them from the comments of later rhetoricians.

Athenian rhetoric was at that time closely associated with three great philosophers: Socrates, Plato, and Aristotle. Socrates (469–399 B.C.) was well known in Athenian circles for his love of inquiry—a method of question and answer dialogue—by which he led his students to seek understanding by exploring and questioning the world around them. This stance did not win approval with the more conservative elements of Athenian society, and Socrates was put to death, by being forced to drink hemlock, after being accused of corrupting the youth of Athens. Socrates himself never recorded his ideas; his lessons are known to us through the works of his greatest pupil, Plato.

Plato (429–347 B.C.) carried on the Socratic tradition and founded the Academy for the youth of Athens. Many of his works have come down to us. In the *Republic*, he describes the ideal state, and in his lesser known dialogues, the *Gorgias* (GOR-jus) and the *Phaedrus* (FAY-drus), he describes the ideal orator.

The philosophical/rhetorical tradition of Athens continued with one of Plato's pupils, Aristotle (384–322 B.C.). His *Rhetoric* is probably the most important early treatise on the subject. He founded the "peripatetic" school in the Athenian Lyceum, so called because of his way of teaching as he and his students strolled along the outdoor walkways. Aristotle's *Rhetoric* is a set of notes for the lectures that he delivered to his students. The *Rhetoric* is one of the first systematic treatments of the subject; in it Aristotle synthesized materials from other handbooks with his own brilliant insights into the practice and theory of rhetoric.

Aristotle was later tutor to Alexander the Great, who through his conquests carried the influence of Greek civilization across the known world. Thus, even after Greece fell as a political power and was replaced by the Roman Republic in the second century B.C., Hellenistic philosophy, art, and rhetoric prevailed.

The first full Latin rhetoric, the *Rhetorica ad Herennium* (re-TO-ree-ka ad he-RE-nee-um), usually called simply *Ad Herennium* was composed sometime between 86 and 82 B.C. by an unknown author who systematized and organized the Greek rhetorical tradition which was incorporated into the Roman schools of the first century B.C. As the empire expanded, this tradition and these rhetorical principles spread into western and southern Europe and dominated education well into the third or fourth century A.D.

The works of Marcus Tullius Cicero (106–43 B.C.) were the most important rhetorical documents in the Roman world. He was the great master of Latin prose, and his speeches are still read in Latin classes today. Although there is little that is original in his rhetorical theory, he pulled together a number of other theories and presented them clearly and concisely in works such as *De Inventione* (day in-ven-tee-ON-ay) and *De Oratore* (day o-ra-TO-ray). His works dominated Western education for centuries and kept Greek rhetoric alive in the Western world. In *De Oratore*, he describes the perfect orator as a person who possesses "knowledge of a vast number of things" and "has a certain portion of grace and wit, learning worthy of a well-bred man, and quickness and brevity in replying as well as attacking, accompanied with a refined decorum and urbanity" (1.5). In 43 B.C., Cicero's career came to an end when he was murdered by order of the emperor Marcus Antonius for opposing Julius Caesar.

Historically, political speeches and oratory decline during tyrannies and empires, but thrive in democracies, especially in times of revolution, unrest, and change. Such periods bring a need for voices able to speak to the hopes and desires of the restless populace, and rhetorical skills are therefore much sought after. Democracy also brings with it a certain freedom of speech and a call for participation in politics and society. So even while rhetoric was becoming established as the center of education during the period of the Roman Empire, oratory was in a period of decline since public speakers grew increasingly careful in their orations not daring to cross the will of the emperors. Not surprisingly, rhetorical emphasis shifted as well, with new stylistic gimmickry marking the speeches and writings of the period.

Two treatises, each quite different from the other, mark the closing of the ancient period of classical rhetoric: Quintilian's *Institutio Oratoria* (in-sti-TU-tee-o o-ra-TO-ree-a) and Longinus's (long-JI-nus) *On the Sublime.* Quintilian (A.D. 35–95) was the head of the Roman School of Oratory, and his book reflects his many years of teaching experience as he describes and prescribes educational and rhetorical principles. Like other classical authors, he maintains a strong moral tone as he outlines the education of the perfect orator, "the good man speaking well." Not only was Quintilian's work widely influential in his own time and for many centuries after, but it is still regarded as the best ancient summary of the classical tradition in a single work.

The second treatise, *On the Sublime*, was little known in its own time and in fact was not even recognized as important until the sixteenth century. In this short treatise Longinus, a Greek rhetorician and philosopher of the third century, in attempting to explain the lack of genius and creativity in his time, extols morality. Rather than blaming the death of democracy for the decline in great speakers—"the well-worn cliché that democracy is a good foster mother of greatness, that great speakers flourished when she flourished and died with her"—Longinus blames the love of wealth and pleasure for the decline of democracy and morality.

The sense of morality is a common thread through many of the rhetorical treatises, and, in both Greece and Rome, rhetorical skills stood at the heart of all education. In Greece, for example, boys (for there were few, if any, girls being educated) had musical and gymnastic training and had learned the basics of reading and writing by age fourteen. They then studied with a rhetorician to learn the art of oratory, which they might continue to study at intervals during the rest of their lives. They were being trained to be good citizens, to be able to express themselves effectively.

Women were largely excluded from this public life and their exclusion is apparent in the language of the treatises. Philosophers, orators, and rhetoricians were men and the pronoun "she" simply does not appear. Sensitive readers will be aware of this exclusion in the quotations from the ancient treatises.

CLASSICAL RHETORIC

The brief summary of classical rhetoric that follows includes the Latin and Greek vocabulary of rhetoric. We will see that most of these terms have a number of derivative words in modern languages that make up most of the vocabulary of language study, art, and philosophy not only in the English language, but in the French and the Italian as well. Knowing the basic vocabulary of classical rhetoric can increase your own vocabulary many times over. As long as vocabulary is considered a test for knowledge, a familiarity with such terms is important. It is also no small matter that knowing such root words can improve spelling and comprehension. In addition, comparing ancient words and meanings to modern ones can give you a sense of intellectual history. For example, the meaning of "rhetoric" in the ancient world as the most important of classical studies to its present dictionary definition which includes a reference to language marked by "undue use of bombast" indicates something about the misuse of rhetoric over a long history. Terms take on new meanings as attitudes change and rhetoric, as misused by charlatans and propagandists, altered its classical meaning.

Citizens were practicing the art of oratory long before ancient rhetoricians developed a theory and a vocabulary for rhetoric. By observing that certain orators were effective and others were not, these rhetoricians developed a set of precepts, or principles, for successful communication. It is these precepts that form the basis for their handbooks and their teaching. It is these principles that make up "the art of rhetoric."

The classical rhetoricians divided rhetoric into five parts: invention, arrangement, style, memory, and presentation. The following chart shows the English, Latin, and Greek terms for the five parts.

English	Latin	Greek
Invention	*inventio* (in-VEN-tee-o)	*heuresis* (hu-REE-sis)
Arrangement	*dispositio* (dis-po-ZI-tee-o)	*taxis* (TAK-sis)
Style	*elocutio* (e-lo-KU-tee-o)	*lexis* (LEK-sis)
Memory	*memoria* (me-MO-ree-a)	*mneme* (NE-may)
Delivery/Presentation	*actio* (AK-tee-o)	*hypocrisis* (hi-PO-kri-sis)

These five parts, or "faculties," are described in the *Rhetorica ad Herennium* in the following way:

> The speaker . . . should possess the faculties of Invention, Arrangement, Style, Memory, and Delivery. Invention is the devising of matter, true or plausible, that would make the case convincing. Arrangement is the ordering and distribution of the matter, making clear the place to which each thing is to be assigned. Style is the adaptation of suitable words and sentences to the matter devised. Memory is the firm retention in the mind of the matter, words, and arrangement. Delivery is the graceful regulation of voice, countenance, and gesture (1.2.3).

Although most scholars translate the fifth part as "delivery," this text uses the English word "presentation." Delivery suggests oral presentation exclusively, whereas the term "presentation" allows more easily for both written and oral forms. Modern English words such as "invention," "disposition," "elocution," "memory," and "action" are derived from the five terms. The Greek term *heuresis* gives us the modern word "heuristic," which refers to some device that guides us to discover. The other Greek terms provide the basis for the modern English words "taxonomy," a system of classification, and "mnemonic" devices, which in modern parlance are tricks to aid memory. It is interesting to note that the Greek word for delivery or presentation is the ancestor of our modern word "hypocrisy" and suggests something about oratorical excesses over the centuries since classical times.

Invention, the first part of rhetoric, by which arguments were devised, was considered the most important, and a number of treatises were written about that part of rhetoric alone. Reflecting that emphasis, over one-half of this text—Chapters 2 through 8—concern the processes of invention.

Invention

Aristotle defines rhetoric as "the faculty of observing in any given case the available means of persuasion," and invention is the process by which the orator or writer finds those means. One of the regular invention processes was initiated by Hermagores (her-MA-go-ris), who lived in the second century B.C. Although his works are lost to us, we know them well through references to them by later rhetoricians. He divided subjects into two types, those that refer to general cases and those that refer to specific cases. The first he called a thesis, the second a hypothesis—a different meaning from hypothesis in the modern sense. Hypothesis, in classical rhetoric, was exemplified by the specific question: "Should John marry Mary?" The thesis was the general question unlimited by specific persons, time, or place: "Should a man marry?" Later rhetoricians enlarged the concept in guiding students to the formation of a thesis through a series of questions:

> *an sit*: whether it is; *quid sit*: what it is; *quale sit*: what kind it is.

In the first two questions they examined the history of the subject and its essence; in the last they examined the qualitative values inherent in the subject. Through these questions they arrived at a thesis. We will discuss this system further in Chapter 2.

Aristotle offers two modes of invention: artistic and inartistic. The artistic proofs are constructed by the orator or writer and belong to the art of rhetoric. They comprise strategies of developing a subject by connecting it through such rhetorical devices as definition, comparison, induction, or deduction to subjects already known. Such strategies are developed at length in the first six chapters of this text. Inartistic proofs, on the other hand, are those considered to be outside the field of rhetoric and are merely to be used (such things as the written laws, witnesses, contracts, and, as was common in ancient times, examination under torture).

The idea of gaining proof from torture seems bizarre in the twentieth century. Today, you support arguments with such inartistic proofs as authority or statistics, both a far cry from torture. The artistic proofs, however—those that belong properly to the art of rhetoric—have endured through the ages. Artistotle delineates three types: *ethos, pathos,* and *logos*:

> There are, then, these three means of effecting persuasion. The man who is to be in command of them must, it is clear, be able (1) to reason logically [*logos*], (2) to understand human character and goodness in their various forms [*ethos*], and (3) to understand the emotions—that is, to name them and describe them, to know their causes and the way in which they are excited [*pathos*] (*Rhetoric* 1.1.1356a. 21–25).

With *ethos,* the speaker establishes good character and credibility and displays good will toward the audience. *Ethos* is the word from which we derive the term "ethical." With *pathos,* from which the word "pathetic" is derived, the speaker attempts to appeal to the audience's feelings. *Logos* refers to the proof contained in the words themselves. From this last term we get the English word "logic." Under *logos,* the classical rhetoricians included the strategies of logical proof adapted for rhetoric: induction and deduction. Rhetorical induction is argument by example and is, according to Aristotle, "the foundation of reasoning." Rhetorical deduction, on the other hand, is based on and uses the enthymeme, an abbreviated syllogism based on probabilities and matters in human affairs that present us with alternative possibilities.

Also included under rhetorical proof are what the classical rhetoricians called the *topoi* or topics, the "places" inside the mind where the orator could go to get good reasons for an argument. Aristotle lists twenty-eight topics. Often called "strategies" by modern rhetoricians, the list is traditionally shortened to include definition, classification and division, comparison and contrast, cause and effect. Students performed exercises in what they called their commonplace books writing on a single subject from the perspectives of these topics. The ancient rhetoricians, as have other rhetoricians through the ages, believed these strategies to be inherent in the human thinking and language process.

Topics also include the invalid or fallacious proofs—the ways that arguments can go wrong. Knowledge of fallacies is useful in refuting the arguments of others.

You will need to understand the special usage of certain terms in the study of rhetoric. For example, argument is now considered only in its limited meaning of disputation—you "have an argument." In rhetoric, the word is used in its broader meaning of proof of a position, development of a point, or support for a perspective. So a point may be developed by comparison—a rhetorical "argument from comparison." Another word that rhetoric uses in its special and original sense is "topic." In the rhetorical sense, as explained above, topics are strategies by which arguments might be developed, and include such things as definition and cause and effect. The careful distinctions in meaning are important since they rest on basic rhetorical concepts about language processing. These terms will become much clearer as they are discussed in detail in Chapters 2 through 8, which treat the whole subject of invention.

Arrangement

Classical rhetoricians were concerned with the appropriate way of ordering or arranging the parts of a speech. They did not always agree on the number of necessary parts. At one point, Aristotle suggests a beginning, middle, and end, but at another point maintained that a speech needed only two parts—a statement of the case and its proof.

Most ancient rhetoricians, however, use some variation of the seven divisions suggested in the *Ad Herennium*:

Opening (*Exordium*)

Statement of Background Facts (*Narratio*)

Exposition or Definition of Terms and Issues (*Explicatio* or *Definitio*)

Proposition or Thesis (*Partitio*)

Proof (*Amplificatio*)

Refutation of Opposing Arguments (*Refutatio* or *Reprehensio*)

Conclusion (*Peroratio* or *Epilogus*)

These seven divisions are discussed in detail in chapter 9.

Style

Aristotle defined good style as being clear and appropriate. He also urges that "naturalness is persuasive, artificiality is the contrary." Cicero listed four qualities of style in the *De Oratore*:

1. Correctness

2. Clarity

3. Appropriateness

4. Ornament

He maintains that correctness and clarity are such simple matters that orators are never praised for them, but he warns that they will be blamed for their omission. Appropriateness involves suiting the style to the occasion and the audience, and ornament included a study of the figures of speech, language devices such as metaphor, that enhance or change meaning. The ancient rhetoricians identified a large number of these. Trope, scheme, figure, or ornament are names used to denote the different kinds of figures of speech.

The classical rhetoricians also recognized that language was used differently on different occasions for different audiences. Thus, they identified three styles which they called the low style, the middle style, and the grand style. The low and middle styles were reserved for informal situations such as personal letters or extemporaneous speeches, while the grand style was used for large audiences and state or ceremonial occasions. Although the terms used to describe the styles have changed, a recognition of different styles for different audiences and different occasions is as important for the modern writer as for the ancient orator. Chapters 10 and 11 cover matters of clarity and appropriateness in style and review the more common figures of speech.

Memory

For the ancient orator, memory was an important part of the rhetorical art. Quintilian calls it "the treasurehouse of eloquence" (*Institutio Oratoria* 11.2.3).

One of the oldest full treatments of memory is in the *Ad Herennium*, whose unknown author devotes seven chapters of Book 3 to the subject. The author designates two kinds of memory: one natural, which is embedded in the mind, and the other the product of art, which is strengthened by training and discipline (3.16.28). Quintilian's final advice to the student is "to learn much by heart and to think much, and, if possible, to do this daily" (*Institutio Oratoria* 11.2.40).

Today, people are inclined to use aids to memory different from these, since they have at their disposal the technological resources of writing, print, microprints, and computers. As these systems become more and more sophisticated, storing information becomes more simple; retrieval, however, becomes a skill of its own. Chapter 12 reviews some of those retrieval methods.

Presentation

Even while complaining that "no systematic treatment of presentation or delivery has yet been composed," Aristotle insisted that "delivery is—very properly—not regarded as an elevated subject of inquiry." Though he in fact had very little to say about it, his followers had a great deal to say. The author of the *Ad Herennium* devotes a number of pages to it, even calling it "the faculty of greatest use to the speaker and the most valuable for persuasion" (3.11.19). In studying delivery, the ancients considered such things as gesture and voice.

In our concern with writing, we will primarily consider the appropriate formats that writing takes in the academic world, such as the research paper, responses to essay exams, and short papers on literature. Such matters of presentation are discussed in detail in Chapters 13 and 14.

Kinds of Rhetoric

Aristotle defined three categories of rhetoric, suggesting three kinds of orations for different audiences and occasions: deliberative, judicial, and epideictic. Deliberative, or political, oratory, he said, "urges us either to do or not to do something." Judicial, or forensic, oratory "attacks or defends somebody: one or the other of these two things must always be done by the parties in a case." Epideictic, or ceremonial, oratory "praises or censures somebody." The political orator is concerned with the future, the forensic orator with the past, and the ceremonial orator with the present. The orator, according to Aristotle, suited the speech to one of these purposes, depending on the audience and the occasion.

These parts and kinds of rhetoric which made up the art stood at the center of students' education from the fifth century B.C. to the first century A.D. shaping their practice and their morals; eloquence—speaking well—was the heart of their world. As Cicero said, looking back from the end of that period:

> That ancient learning, indeed, appears to have been at the same time the preceptress of living rightly and of speaking well; nor were there separate masters for those subjects, but the same teachers formed the morals and the language (*De Oratore* 3.15).

A CLASSICAL EDUCATION

Quintilian devotes the whole of the first book of the *Institutio Oratoria* to the education of the young student urging the student who complains to persevere and "to spend his time not, like so many in the theatre or in the Campus Martius, in dicing or in idle talk, to say naught of the hours that are wasted in sleep or long drawn banqueting, but in listening rather to the geometrician and the teacher of music. For by this he will win a richer harvest of delight than can ever be gathered from the pleasures of the ignorant" (*Institutio Oratoria* 1.12.18). As we have seen, in the ancient world education was largely concerned with the verbal arts, oratory in particular. The student first learned grammar, music, geometry, and gymnastics; then from the age of thirteen on studied rhetoric. The author of the *Ad Herennium* advises that the student can acquire the faculties of a good rhetorician by three means: theory, imitation, and practice.

> By theory is meant a set of rules that provide a definite method and system of speaking. Imitation stimulates us to attain, in accordance with a studied method, the effectiveness of certain models. Practice is assiduous exercise and experience (1.2.4).

Students of classical rhetoric first learned theories about language. They then studied good models of speeches and attempted to imitate them. Finally, they practiced their skills in the form of exercises.

This text follows the same progression in the examination of theory through models of good writing, both by students and by professionals, followed by practice exercises at the end of each chapter. Discussion of theory and analysis of models are reinforced and enhanced by the practice exercises. The exercises are composed of questions to consider, suggestions for writing, and exercises in revision. In many cases the revision exercises are designed to take place within a workshop atmosphere, to allow you to discuss your work with other students. Writing and rewriting can be productive in collaboration with other people and these exercises emphasize that part of the writing process. There are also suggestions that your instructor might wish to use in setting up workshops in the classroom.

The last section of the practice exercises deals with suggestions for writing in the "commonplace book." The commonplace book originated in the Renaissance and was widely used by students of rhetoric for many centuries. They recorded their ideas in these commonplace books, looking at subjects from many perspectives, using the "topics" or "commonplaces" discussed in Chapters 4 and 5. Today, it has evolved into the writer's notebook or journal. It is a place for recording ideas, for jotting notes, for writing what comes to mind, for copying something that appeals to you—words of a song or a well-turned phrase.

Many professional writers have kept notebooks to record their observations. Often just a jotted note will help the writer recall a scene or an idea. In the following excerpt, Joan Didion describes her methods.

"'That woman Estelle,'" the note reads, "'is partly the reason why George Sharp and I are separated today.' *Dirty crepe-de-Chine wrapper, hotel bar, Wilmington RR, 9:45 a.m. August Monday morning.*"

Since the note is in my notebook, it presumably has some meaning to me. I study it for a long while. At first I have only the most general notion of what I was doing on an August Monday morning in the bar of the hotel across from the Pennsylvania Railroad station in Wilmington, Delaware (waiting for a train? missing one? 1960? 1961? why Wilmington?), but I do remember being there. The woman in the dirty crepe-de-Chine wrapper had come down from her room for a beer, and the bartender had heard before the reason why George Sharp and she were separated today. "Sure," he said, and went on mopping the floor. "You told me." At the other end of the bar is a girl. She is talking, pointedly, not to the man beside her but to a cat lying in the triangle of sunlight cast through the open door. She is wearing a plaid silk dress from Peck & Peck, and the hem is coming down.

Here is what it is: the girl has been on the Eastern Shore, and now she is going back to the city, leaving the man beside her, and all she can see ahead are the viscous summer sidewalks and the 3 a.m. long-distance calls that will make her lie awake and then sleep drugged through all the steaming mornings left in August (1960? 1961?). Because she must go directly from the train to lunch in New York, she wishes that she had a safety pin for the hem of the plaid silk dress, and she also wishes that she could forget about the hem and the lunch and stay in the cool bar that smells of disinfectant and malt and make friends with the woman in the crepe-de-Chine wrapper. She is afflicted by a little self-pity, and she wants to compare Estelles. That is what that was all about.

Why did I write it down? In order to remember, of course, but exactly what was it I wanted to remember? How much of it actually happened? Did any of it? Why do I keep a notebook at all? It is easy to deceive oneself on all those scores.

Later in the same essay, Didion points out that the world is always seen from an individual's viewpoint—that her notebook is her attempt to make meaning of the world around her. Events need not be recorded exactly or completely or factually, but the notebook records events honestly from the writer's viewpoint, carrying "meaning only for its maker."

But our notebooks give us away, for however dutifully we record what we see around us, the common denominator of all we see is always, transparently, shamelessly the implacable "I." We are not talking here about the kind of notebook that is patently for public consumption, a structural conceit for binding together a series of graceful pensées; we are talking about something private, about bits of the mind's string too short to use, an indiscriminate and erratic assemblage with meaning only for its maker.

Transferring what has been recorded in a notebook to something for a reader is a reaching out, a decentering for the writer. What is personal and private becomes public and objective. What was just for the writer becomes a picture to describe or a story to be told for a particular reader in a special context.

The commonplace book is a record of your thoughts and can serve as a source of ideas for your own writing. If you are unaccustomed to keeping such a book, suggestions in each chapter for things that you might record in your commonplace book will help you get started. But it is important that you not feel constrained by these suggestions, because as you progress, the commonplace book, in becoming a record of your own thoughts and ideas, will become very much your own.

CLASSICAL RHETORIC FOR THE TWENTIETH CENTURY

There are important differences between classical rhetoric and the kind of speech-making and writing that we do today, together with underlying similarities. In the ancient world, law, business, and government were conducted orally. Little was written, and few even knew how to read. Silent reading was unknown. Students read their lessons aloud; libraries were noisy places. Most Romans had scribes who wrote and read for them, and Cicero once apologized to a friend for not having written sooner, giving as his excuse a sore throat. He followed the regular habit of dictating his correspondence. But writing and reading became more common in the life of the ordinary person through education and the invention of the printing press. The ways human beings use writing have continued to change through print, typewriters, and computers. In the ancient world, writing was used for records and important documents and letters. Before 1700, all examinations were oral. Today, writing is used in a number of diverse ways—we use it to discover and express ideas, to jog our memories, to report or pass on information. The ease of the physical act of writing through the typewriter and computer makes multiple drafts possible, and writing, revising, and rewriting, important tools in the process of invention. In the ancient world, on the other hand, writing on wax tablets or scrolls was physically difficult compared to the ease of speaking.

In spite of their differences, spoken and written language share the important characteristic of being symbol systems. Where spoken language uses sounds to make meaning, written language uses marks on a paper. Many of the same principles that underlie oratory underlie writing. Where the classical rhetorician uses the words "speaker" or "orator," composition texts substitute "writer" or "author." The precepts remain the same.

In the eighteenth century, when most persons in western Europe could read and write and the culture became predominantly literate, memory and presentation came to be regarded as unnecessary in the study of rhetoric. Orators did not have to memorize their speeches once they could write them down, and presentation, which included action and pronunciation, became unnecessary for written works.

In this text, however, these last two aspects are restored to twentieth-century rhetoric, adapted for use in a society where writing is deeply embedded in the culture. Where ancient rhetoricians saw memory as something existing within the human brain, this text enlarges the concept to include written materials held in libraries and computers—the cultural storehouses. You will learn methods of retrieving such information in Chapter 12.

Presentation has been restored in this text in a similar way, as the embodiment of the forms that writing assumes in a twentieth-century academic community. Just as tone of voice and physical stance are the outward form for the oration, so the research paper or lab report is the shape that a particular piece of writing may take. The basic rhetorical precepts underlie all language, spoken and written; the forms are secondary. The fifth part of rhetoric, therefore, consists of the formats you may choose to present ideas to an audience.

Another difference between ancient and modern rhetoric is that ancient rhetoric was solely concerned with civic life whereas modern writing has wide uses. Oratory included the speeches made in the senate and in the law court; the "good man" that Quintilian speaks of was the good citizen in the largest sense of the word. Over the centuries, the classical precepts have been adapted to many other kinds of discourse, such as reporting and exposition—fitting easily and usefully into new modes.

Another commonly held difference between ancient and modern rhetoric is that while classical rhetoric was concerned with persuasion alone, modern rhetoric has broadened its scope. Persuasion, in fact, underlies all of written and spoken communications in one sense or another. We attempt to persuade an audience to see something from our point of view or to take action that we consider appropriate. An application letter, a grant application, a research paper are all persuasive in that broad sense. This difference between classical and modern rhetoric is more apparent than real.

One final difference is that certain classical rhetoricians tended to view the rhetorical process as linear. First, the writer thought up the ideas, then arranged them, then "decorated" them with ornaments, then memorized and delivered the speech. Not all ancient rhetoricians shared this idea—Longinus, represents the philosophers who were aware of the organic nature of an oration and the recursiveness of the writing process:

> Among the factors which give most dignity to discourse is structure, which corresponds to the arrangement of the limbs of the body. One limb by itself, cut off from the others, is of no value, but all of them together complete and perfect the composition of the whole (*On the Sublime*, 40).

In order to study any organic whole it must be divided into parts so that each part can then be scrutinized. To return to the metaphor of the human body, the medical student must separate the heart from the arterial system in order to dissect and study it, the muscles from the bones in order to understand how they function. But in any organism no part truly functions except in relation to the whole. Just so, writing does not hold a simplistic linearity, rather it calls for constant revision and continual discovery. The thinking/writing process is recursive, doubling back on itself again and again throughout writing and revising. Writing provides far more freedom for revising and reworking than the ancient rhetoricians had in their orations. Although writing is ordinarily considered more permanent than speaking, it is much easier to destroy a piece of writing and rewrite a sentence or a paragraph than to take back words already spoken. Hastily spoken words can live forever in another person's mind, whereas a letter written in anger can be thrown away and forgotten. Finally, all writers have the option of discarding their work, of starting fresh, of revising and rewriting. In this way revising and writing become in themselves part of the ongoing discovery process.

Modern composition theory deals, in part, with the discovery of identity through expressive and personal writing. Classical rhetoric had no such goal. The forum and law courts were its context; to defend and persuade was its function. Ancient rhetoric was concerned with human transactions in the largest sense of the word—with moving an audience to action or new perspectives through language. All rhetoric, ancient and modern, is potentially empowering, giving power to find a voice, power to put ideas into words for an audience, power to gain willing belief and acceptance, and, therefore, power to affect, and perhaps even change the world.

The two passages that follow define rhetoric. In the first, Aristotle defines rhetoric in the fifth century B.C. In the second, Edward P. J. Corbett, Jr., explains rhetoric for the modern student.

Rhetoric may be defined as the faculty of observing in any given case the available means of persuasion. This is not a function of any other art. Every other art can instruct or persuade about its own particular subject-matter; for instance, medicine about what is healthy and unhealthy, geometry about the properties of magnitudes, arithmetic about numbers, and the same is true of the other arts and sciences. But rhetoric we look upon as the power of observing the means of persuasion on almost any subject presented to us; and that is why we say that, in its technical character, it is not concerned with any special or definite class of subjects (Aristotle *Rhetoric* 1.2.1355b.26–36).

Rhetoric is the art or the discipline that deals with the use of discourse, either spoken or written, to inform or persuade or move an audience, whether that audience is made up of a single person or a group of persons. Broadly defined in that way, rhetoric would seem to comprehend every kind of verbal expression that man engages in. But rhetoricians customarily have excluded from their province such informal modes of speech as "small talk," jokes, greetings ("Good to see you"), exclamations ("What a day!"), gossip, simple explanations or directions ("Take a left at the next intersection, go about three blocks to the first stoplight, and then . . ."). Although informative, directive, or suasory objectives can be realized in the stop-and-go, give-and-take form of the dialogue, rhetoric has traditionally been concerned with those instances of formal, premeditated, sustained monologue in which a single person seeks to exert an effect on an audience. This notion of "an effect on an audience"—a notion which gets at the very essence of rhetorical discourse—is implicit in such definitions of rhetoric as Marie Hochmuth Nichols's: "a means of so ordering discourse as to produce an effect on the listener or reader"; Kenneth Burke's: "the use of language as a symbolic means of inducing cooperation in beings that by nature respond to symbols"; or Donald Bryant's: "the function of adjusting ideas to people and of people to ideas." The classical rhetoricians seem to have narrowed the particular effect of rhetorical discourse to that of persuasion. Aristotle, for instance, defined rhetoric as "the faculty of discovering all the available means of persuasion in any given situation." But when one is reminded that the Greek word for *persuasion* derives from the Greek verb "to believe," one sees that Aristotle's definition can be made to comprehend not only those modes of discourse which are "argumentative" but also those "expository" modes of discourse which seek to win acceptance of information or explanation.

But whether we are seeking, as the eighteenth-century rhetorician

George Campbell put it, "to enlighten the understanding, to please the imagination, to move the passions, or to influence the will," we must adopt and adapt those strategies that will best achieve our end. *Strategies* is a good rhetorical word, because it implies the *choice* of available resources to achieve an end. It is no accident that the word *strategy* has military associations, for this word has its roots in the Greek word for *army*. Just as a general will adopt those resources, those tactics, which in his judgment are best calculated to discomfit the enemy, so the marshaller of language will seek out and use the best arguments, the best arrangement, and the best style to "win" his audience (Corbett, *Classical Rhetoric for the Modern Student*, 3–4).

Questions to Consider

1. Write a definition of rhetoric as you thought of it before you read this chapter. Compare yours with those of your classmates. How do they differ? How are they alike?

2. Examine the English, Latin, and Greek words on page 8. Can you think of modern English words that are derived from the Greek and Latin words? Are the meanings the same? Can you account for any differences in meaning between the ancient and modern words?

3. Following are two modern definitions of rhetoric. How are these definitions alike? How do they differ? How do they differ from Aristotle's definition quoted earlier in this book?

> Rhetoric, I shall urge, should be a study of misunderstandings and its remedies. We struggle all our days with misunderstandings, and no apology is required for any study which can prevent or remove them (I. A. Richards, *The Philosophy of Rhetoric*).

> First, we are concerned with the rhetorical climate, the impact of our times upon what people talk, and what people talk about. . . . Second, we are concerned with the responsible and effective practice of rhetoric in our times, with the character and behavior of our listeners and speakers (J. Jeffery Auer, *The Rhetoric of Our Times*).

Suggestions for Writing

1. Write a short paper giving your own definition of rhetoric.

2. Pick out the word "rhetoric" from a newspaper article, from a television news report, or from a recent conversation. How does the meaning differ from one of the definitions above? In a short paper, compare its modern meaning to the Aristotelian definition.

3. Look up Aristotle, or Plato, or Cicero, or Quintilian in the encyclopedia and write a report on his life and his philosophy.

4. Look up the author of any of the definitions of rhetoric above and identify the author, his dates, and his scholarly or philosophic contributions. Write a report for your classmates.

5. Look up the word "rhetoric" in any standard dictionary and write a paper comparing those definitions with any one of those given above.

Exercises in Revision

1. How does your definition of rhetoric differ from those of your classmates? Discuss those differences and try to arrive at a definition that you can agree on.

2. Compare the use of the word rhetoric that you found in newspapers with the ones that your classmates found. Are they similar or different in meaning?

3. Revise the paper that you wrote from one of the preceding suggestions using the findings and insights that you have gained from discussions with your classmates.

For a Commonplace Book

1. Ask several friends what they mean by rhetoric and record their answers.

2. Do you have any mnemonic devices that help you remember certain things? Record them in your commonplace book.

3. Notice when you hear a particularly effective phrase or word and record it in your commonplace book. Copy the words to one of your favorite songs or poems in your commonplace book.

PART I

INVENTION

> *"to seek out, hear, read, discuss, handle, and ponder everything that befalls in life . . . it is with this that the orator is concerned and this that forms the material with which he has to deal"*
>
> (QUINTILIAN *INSTITUTIO ORATORIA* 2.21.6).

Invention, the first part of rhetoric, meant for the classical rhetoricians finding rhetorical proof for their arguments and supporting material for their statements. Rhetorical argument arrives at probable conclusions, using good reasons similar to the kinds that we use in the deliberations that govern our important, everyday decisions. We act on the basis of the best reasons that we have available to us. We cannot know for certain which candidate to vote for, but we do decide and we do vote on the basis of probable premises—this candidate is likely to raise taxes; that one may cut student aid. These premises are not certain, they are probable, and we vote for one candidate on the basis of this kind of rhetorical proof. This section concerns ways of finding the best possible proofs for such deliberations and using them in writing.

The process of invention was the most important part of classical rhetoric, and the other parts depended heavily on the invention procedures. In writing, invention never ceases but underlies and informs the entire process of putting a paper together. Hermogenes (her-MA-ji-neez), one of the early rhetoricians, developed the *stasis* theory, a method by which the student questioned the issues involved in a subject and then generated a thesis or proposition from which to work. For many later rhetoricians this close examination of a subject—seeing it from all sides—was the first step in the invention process. Out of this close examination of the issues, the student developed a thesis or proposition. During this process, the student generated ways to develop and prove the thesis as well as ways to answer opposing arguments which in turn might alter or enlarge the thesis. Thus, the process was recursive as the student examined the issues and formed the thesis, then reexamined issues to check the thesis, thus perhaps revising the thesis. This process of formulating a thesis will be examined in Chapter 2.

Aristotle divided proofs for rhetorical arguments into two kinds— "artistic" and "inartistic." Artistic proofs were part of the *art* of rhetoric—proofs that depend on the skill of the orator; inartistic proofs, on the other hand, "are there at the outset—witnesses, evidence given under torture, written contracts, and so on" (*Rhetoric* 1.1.1355b38–40). The contemporary writer has better sources of information for the inartistic proofs in materials from authorities, statistics, and witnesses; these are treated in Chapter 7. Chapters 3, 4, and 5 will deal with the artistic proofs that can be constructed from the principles of rhetoric.

Aristotle taught his students that there were three kinds of artistic or rhetorical arguments that the orator could draw on. The first kind, he said, depends on establishing the character of the speaker (*ethos*); the second on putting the audience into a receptive frame of mind (*pathos*); the third on the proof provided in the speech itself (*logos*). Such proofs are equally important for the writer.

Of these Aristotle considered *ethos*, the character of the speaker or writer, to be the most effective kind of persuasion:

> Persuasion is achieved by the speaker's personal character when the speech is so spoken as to make us think him credible. We believe good men more fully and more readily than others; this is true generally whatever the question is, and absolutely true where exact certainty is impossible and opinions divided (*Rhetoric* 1.1.1356a 4–9).

So in judging what a person says, the reader or listener relies heavily on the character of the person who says it. For example, the success of contemporary advertising often relies on the image presented by the spokesperson for a given product: when a person who appears to be a doctor advises us to use a certain medication we are inclined to take the advice. When a politician who appears to be a person of character asks for our vote, we are inclined to vote for him or her. The importance of a good image in modern politics and advertising reinforces Aristotle's idea that the character the speaker projects is important in persuading an audience. In addition, in ordinary conversations and written exchanges, persons who project honesty win respect over persons who come across as deceitful or untrustworthy.

The second kind of proof, *pathos*, consists of appealing to the emotions of the audience. The writer who wishes to persuade the audience to a certain viewpoint or a certain action must have an audience that is sympathetic. If an audience does not have good feelings toward a writer, they may not pay much attention to what is being said. But if the writer is able to invoke a positive or friendly feeling in the readers, those readers will be receptive toward the writer's ideas. Aristotle further maintains that it is the responsibility of the speaker (or writer) to be aware of the feelings of the audience: to understand the nature of the audience, and to appeal to the needs, desires, goals, and hopes of that audience. So finally, the writer must know something about human nature in order to predict the audience's reactions. If a person is writing a letter to solicit money for a project, he or she will use different appeals when writing to a friend, a close relative, or a bank officer. Even though writing is usually a solitary activity, the skilled writer always writes with an audience in mind.

Writers who project themselves well (*ethos*) and appeal to their audience (*pathos*) must also consider the argument contained within the paper, itself (*logos*). This third kind of proof available to the orator or writer is in the words themselves. To Aristotle, such proof came "by means of the persuasive arguments suitable to the case in question" (Aristotle *Rhetoric* 1356a 20). The problem of finding proofs and supporting materials is as real for us as modern writers as it was for Aristotle's orators. The professor writing a scholarly paper, the business person writing a financial report, the student writing an essay exam, the engineer writing a feasibility report—all grope for ideas to make their cases convincing. Often in these situations the information does not lie in the library or in a textbook or in carefully taken notes; it may well lie in their own heads. Writers need to learn how to explore their own minds, to tap their own experiences and knowledge, to discover what they already know. The ancient rhetoricians systematized this search by referring to *topoi* (topics), "places" in the mind where this information is stored. Today, we refer to the topics as "strategies" for developing ideas. For example, you may choose to compare a subject to something you already know, or you may choose to define it. These strategies for developing ideas are covered in detail in Chapters 4 and 5. They serve as ways of stimulating thinking and writing and of discovering supporting material.

Aristotle insisted that the orator needed to know logic—induction (argument from the particular to the general) and deduction (argument from the general to the particular) before understanding the corresponding rhetorical forms of proof. Chapter 6 very briefly reviews the syllogism and induction and then moves on to a treatment of the corresponding kind of rhetorical proof involved in the enthymeme and the example.

Chapter 7 will cover the modern equivalent of inartistic proofs—supporting material from outside sources such as authorities or statistics. Finally, the last chapter in this section, Chapter 8, will discuss logical fallacies, the ways that our thinking and writing can go wrong.

Such discovery and invention procedures are basic to the ability to think and thus to express thoughts. Just as these strategies help us to think about a subject, so too do they provide ways of writing about that subject. Writing and thinking are inseparable activities. Good writing demands clear thinking just as clear thinking generates good writing. The activities are not inseparable but are, in fact, recursive, that is, as your ideas begin to crystallize, and you begin to write, new ideas will occur, which leads to revision, and so on. Although invention, which covers stasis and thesis and artistic proofs (*ethos, logos,* and *pathos*) and inartistic proofs (authorities and statistics), is presented here as the first task that the writer takes on, it does not stop when you write an introduction or any of the other parts of an essay described in Chapter 9. The invention process begins here, but it continues as you think, read, write, focus, arrange, and polish your paper.

Chapter 2

Formulating a Thesis

EXPLORING THE SUBJECT

    Fact
    Essence
    Quality

FINDING YOUR THESIS

    Narrowing Your Thesis
    Guiding Your Readers

USING TOPIC SENTENCES
ADLAI STEVENSON, "THE HARD KIND OF
    PATRIOTISM"

For classical rhetoricians, that part of the oration that states exactly what is to be proved is called the *proposition* or thesis. The second term is far more familiar today, as the "main idea" of an essay. Classical rhetoric, however, did not begin with a thesis as is sometimes suggested today but started instead with a subject and examined that subject from a number of different viewpoints. They looked at special incidents or cases, defined the terms and examined meanings associated with them, considered the moral implications, and only after a lengthy process of exploring the subject did they focus on a thesis.

Classical rhetoricians made a distinction between the hypothesis and the thesis. Hypothesis had a different meaning than the commonly accepted modern one of a provisional assumption. For the classical rhetoricians, the hypothesis concerned the specific case while the thesis concerned the general case. An example of this is, "Should Jane marry before she graduates?" as a hypothesis and "Should a woman marry before she graduates?" as the thesis. In this example, we move from the specific case of Jane to the more general question of all young women.

Thus, you may start with your own experience in connection with any subject and, in accordance with the principles of classical rhetoric, move from the specific experience to a generalization about it. For example, you may have been involved in an automobile accident where a drunken driver, who had no insurance, drove into the back of your car forcing you to be taken to the emergency room of a nearby hospital. That is an experience that you can write about vividly and well but how might you put it into a larger context? You might choose to move beyond the personal implications to exploring the larger issues of drunk driving, or required driver's insurance, or emergency medical care. The personal experience often provides the starting point for a subject. In the same way, when a general subject, such as the place of the humanities in higher education, is assigned you may move to your own personal experience with that subject—possibly the required liberal arts courses in your engineering program—and then return to the more general subject. The personal experience is important because it gives both you and your reader valuable insights into the larger issues involved.

The following passage is from an essay in support of gun control written by Senator Edward M. Kennedy shortly after the attempted assassination of President Reagan in 1981. He draws on his own family experience and then reminds his readers of other public figures who have been shot down in recent years. In doing so, he not only uses his personal experience, but reminds his readers of their experiences with violence before he moves on to his larger thesis of the necessity for gun control. He moves from the hypothesis of "Effective laws for gun control might have prevented the deaths of my brothers" to the generalized thesis "Effective laws for gun control might prevent violence in our society."

> The question is not whether we will disarm honest citizens, as some gun lobbyists have charged. The question is whether we will make it harder for those who break the law to arm themselves.
>
> Gun control is not an easy issue. But, for me, it is a fundamental issue. My family has been touched by violence; too many others have felt the same terrible force. Too many children have been raised without a father or a mother. Too many widows have lived out their lives alone. Too many people have died.
>
> We all know the toll that has been taken in this nation. We all know the leaders of our public life and of the human spirit who have been lost or wounded year after year: My brother, John Kennedy, and my brother, Robert Kennedy; Medgar Evers, who died so that others could live free; Martin Luther King, the apostle of nonviolence who became the victim of violence; George Wallace, who has been paralyzed for nearly nine years, and George Moscone,

the mayor of San Francisco who was killed in his office. Last year alone, we lost Allard Lowenstein and we almost lost Vernon Jordan. Four months ago, we lost John Lennon, that gentle soul who challenged us in song to "give peace a chance." We had two attacks on President Ford and now the attack on President Reagan.

It is unacceptable that all these good men have been shot down. They all sought, each in their own way, to make ours a better world. And, too often, too soon, their own world came to an end (Edward M. Kennedy, "The Need for Handgun Control").

It is a mistake to start with a thesis and then try to find reasons. Often such a paper will be a rationalization for a poorly examined or prejudiced viewpoint. Classical rhetoricians started with a subject often from a personal viewpoint, explored the issues involved and in the process focused on a main idea and formed a thesis. As you write and read that thesis may grow and change as your ideas form and focus.

EXPLORING THE SUBJECT

Long before speaking, the classical orator studied the subject, asking questions about the issues involved. You may do this by yourself, although often it is best to talk with other people, your friends or your classmates, in order to get new viewpoints and insights. In that kind of discussion you may develop new ideas as you express your own viewpoints and consider those of your friends. Quintilian suggests that you explore your subject by asking three questions:

An sit: Did it happen?

Quid sit: What is it?

Quale sit: What is its quality?

The first question is factual and explores whether something exists or actually happened. In the case of euthanasia, the question might be asked, "Does it exist?" Have life support systems been removed from terminally ill patients? Are there cases that can be cited? The second question is definitive and explores the essence of the subject, defining terms and exploring meanings. What is euthanasia? Is it murder or is it mercy killing? Is it a medical decision or a personal one? If it is mercy killing who makes the decision? What determines whether it is murder or mercy killing? The third question is qualitative and explores questions of good and bad, right and wrong. Is euthanasia beneficial or harmful? For the terminally ill patient? For the survivors? For the society? Is euthanasia necessary? What caused it? What are its effects? For the survivors? For the society? In classical rhetoric these questions were originally confined to legal issues, but in fact concern all human affairs as Quintilian reminds us.

You will note as you work with these questions that they are part of a recursive process (that as words such as euthanasia take on new or more precise meanings, the subject must be reexamined). Also you may have a firmly established opinion on a subject before you begin but as you examine the issues involved, you may find that your ideas will change and enlarge. Such questioning of your own ideas allows not only for papers that avoid simplistic approaches to a subject but for personal growth as well.

Fact

This first question explores whether something has happened or actually exists and if so under what circumstances. It looks for cases and incidents. You might pose the following factual questions in connection with your subject:

Did it happen? If so, where and when?

What were the circumstances?

Does it exist?

Can you cite incidents and cases?

Senator Kennedy, in the same essay cited previously on the kind of violence that results from the lack of effective gun control laws, reminds his readers of the recent wounding of President Reagan from an assassin's bullet and then continues to cite other cases of violence from handguns. The reader is left in no doubt about cases and incidents of "the clear and present danger."

The wounding of President Reagan has stunned the world and stirred a vast reaction. Yet he is only the most famous casualty of an endless guerrilla war inside this country waged with a growing arsenal of handguns in the wrong hands. Every day others less famous are wounded or killed; their families worry and suffer. They weep and, too often, they mourn.   1

Every 50 minutes an American is killed by a handgun; 29 Americans who are alive today will be shot dead tomorrow. In the streets of our cities, the arms race of Saturday-night specials and cheap handguns will take 10,000 lives this year and will threaten or wound   2 another 250,000 citizens. In the past year alone, we have seen a 13 percent rise in violent crime, the greatest increase in a decade.

Today the clear and present danger to our society is the midnight   3 mugger and the deranged assassin. And their weapons are as close as the nearest pawnshop. There are 55 million handguns in circulation. The lethal number rises by two and a half million each year. By the year 2000, there will be 100 million handguns in America.

After reading this introduction the reader knows at the outset that violence from handguns is a fact of American life.

Essence

The question of "what it is"—essence—is basic to any subject but definitions of complex subjects are seldom simple. They bring up aspects of a subject that cannot be ignored. Pornography has proved to be a knotty legal question because of the difficulty of arriving at an acceptable definition. In the following passage, the author wrestles with the question by comparing pornography to two closely related terms, obscenity and erotic art, pointing out differences and similarities in their purposes and their effects. He then clarifies the distinguishing characteristics of pornography.

I say pornography *and* obscenity because, though they have different dictionary definitions and are frequently distinguishable as "artistic" genres, they are nevertheless in the end identical in effect. Pornography is not objectionable simply because it arouses sexual desire or lust or prurience in the mind of the reader or spectator; this is a silly Victorian notion. A great many nonpornographic works—including some parts of the Bible—excite sexual desire very successfully. What is distinctive about pornography is that, in the words of D.H. Lawrence, it attempts "to do dirt on [sex] . . . [It is an] insult to a vital human relationship."

In other words, pornography differs from erotic art in that its whole purpose is to treat human beings obscenely, to deprive human beings of their specifically human dimension. That is what obscenity is all about. It is light years removed from any kind of carefree sensuality—there is no continuum between Fielding's *Tom Jones* and the Marquis de Sade's *Justine*. These works have quite opposite intentions. To quote Susan Sontag: "What pornographic literature does is precisely to drive a wedge between one's existence as a full human being and one's existence as a sexual being—while in ordinary life a healthy person is one who prevents such a gap from opening up." This definition occurs in an essay *defending* pornography—Miss Sontag is a candid as well as gifted critic—so the definition, which I accept, is neither tendentious nor censorious (Irving Kristol, "Pornography, Obscenity, and the Case for Censorship").

Some of the questions that you might pose about a subject either to yourself or to your classmates would include the following:

What is it?

What is it like?

What is it not like?

What is its purpose?

What is its effect?

What caused it?

What terms are associated with it?

What is the meaning of those terms?

Often questions that involve the essence of a subject—what something really is—are the most difficult to answer and the most important. The definitions of such subjects as euthanasia, pornography, and abortion can challenge our basic beliefs.

Quality

The third question concerns the quality of a subject and involves questions of right and wrong, good and bad. These questions were an important part of classical rhetoric and an essential consideration in almost every subject. Most questions involving human affairs finally involve such issues. Some of the questions suggested by quality are the following:

What are the consequences?

Is it good for me or bad?

Is it good for other people or bad?

Is it right or wrong for me?

Is it right or wrong for other people?

In an article arguing against the escalation of nuclear power and nuclear energy, Helen Caldicott suggests in vivid detail what the consequences might be for all people. She then concludes that from the perspective of a doctor and a mother nuclear power is bad. Finally, she argues that the nuclear phenomenon is wrong for all people because it is "our responsibility to continue creation."

> Look at the changing seasons—the spring and the flowers and the trees coming into leaf. Look at the fall of the year and the leaves turning gold. Look at our growing children. One child. One baby. We're a fantastic species. We're capable of such creativity, love and friendship.
>
> I've got three children. And I am a doctor who treats children, a great many of them having the commonest genetic disease of childhood—cystic fibrosis. I live with dying children. I live with grieving parents. I understand the value of every single human life.
>
> The ultimate in preventive medicine is to eliminate nuclear power and nuclear weapons. I look on this as a religious issue too. Because what is our responsibility to God but to continue creation? (Helen Caldicott, "What You Must Know About Radiation," from *Redbook*).

Questions of quality can only be answered within your own value system. Often the thesis evolves from these hard questions. Is handgun control right or wrong? Is abortion good or bad for me? For the society? The three questions of fact, essence, and quality are interdependent; questions of quality may well depend on answers to the questions of fact and essence—whether a thing is and what it is.

For the Roman citizen, good was defined in terms of good for the state. Questions of quality involved right and wrong, not for just the individual, but for the individual as a citizen of Rome. Right and wrong still involve more than good for a single individual; they involve the good of a larger community. Your value system depends on what you view as your community. Some persons may define their community as a religion, others as a country, or a family, or a philosophic or political ideology. But value systems depend on your seeing yourself as a member of a larger group. Questions of right and wrong or good and bad depend on moving beyond the "me" to the "us." For the classical orator the role of the "good man" was as a citizen of Rome; for the modern writer it may be as a citizen of the world within a worldwide brotherhood as Adlai Stevenson suggests in the essay that concludes this chapter.

> I can, therefore, wish no more for the profound patriotism of Americans than that they add to it a new dedication to the worldwide brotherhood of which they are a part and that, together with their love of America, there will grow a wider love which seeks to transform our earthly city, with all its races and peoples, all its

creeds and aspirations, into Saint Augustine's "Heavenly city where truth reigns, love is the law, and whose extent is eternity."

FINDING YOUR THESIS

As you explore your subject you will find yourself formulating possible theses or main ideas for your paper. The thesis was called by a number of names in classical rhetoric. Quintilian's word was *questio*, like modern "question," and it was often presented as a question for students to debate. In the modern essay the thesis sometimes takes the form of a question. Derivatives of the classical terminology—proposition, question, and thesis—often appear in writing and conversation as subjects are raised and matters are discussed. The terms are often used interchangeably and your main idea may be called a question, as Kennedy does in the passage cited earlier, or even stated as a question.

Trying out various thesis statements or propositions as you examine questions of fact, essence, and quality is an important part of examining your subject. Putting possible theses in writing will help you control and focus your material and may generate new ideas. Formulating and reformulating the thesis generates ideas, directs your choice of material, and assists in the selection of appropriate strategies for development. Your thesis will grow and evolve during the questioning and exploration of issues and the entire process of thinking and writing. Moving toward a thesis that seems workable for you helps you to narrow, direct, and focus the early stages of that process.

You might wish to think of a thesis as having the same logical structure as a sentence. It starts with a subject and is followed by a predicate that says something about the subject.

Subject: Justice

Predicate: can be difficult to determine.

A subject—justice, college, nuclear war, or child abuse—is not a thesis until something is "predicated" about it. It is still only a subject. So a thesis is a complete thought in the same way that a sentence is logically complete. Your initial thinking, reading, and research may be on a particular subject but as you question and explore issues you will begin, consciously or unconsciously, to formulate possible predicates about that subject. The distinction between a subject and a thesis is an important one, because the act of exploring the issues helps you to predicate something about your subject, thus formulating the thesis.

Narrowing Your Thesis

One of the seeming contradictions about a thesis is that the more narrow it is, the easier it is to find details and examples. Even though the thesis is a about a general rather than a specific subject the general subject needs to be limited. For example, justice is an infinitely broad subject and might be narrowed in any one of the following ways.

Justice as Set Forth in the Constitution

The Parole System: Justice for Whom?

The Jury: System of Justice

Justice in the Family: The Rights of Children

In the same way, each of the above subjects might be further narrowed.

Justice as Set Forth in the Constitution → The Fifth Amendment

The Parole System: Justice for Whom? → Parole for Convicted Murderers

A narrowed subject allows you to find those details that make writing effective.

With the above subjects there is still no predicate—thus, there is still no thesis. The predicate—what is said about the subject—must be narrowed in the same way that the subject is narrowed. For example, if the subject has been narrowed to the parole system, merely stating that it is bad or that it doesn't work is not enough. You will have to return to questioning the issues. How is it bad? What do you mean by "bad"? Have people released on parole continued to commit crimes? Does the system release people because space is needed in the prisons and not because the person is rehabilitated? So, in formulating a thesis, you find yourself circling back and exploring the issues through the classical questions of fact, essence, and quality.

Working toward precision in the language of your thesis helps to focus your thinking and writing. Words like "bad" and "good" don't provide a clear direction. The following thesis lacks precision in idea because of terms that need to be examined and questioned.

Certain things make the current parole system unfair.

Using the imprecise words "certain things" and "unfair" will lead to problems in a paper. You will need to examine these words. The questions of fact, essence, and quality need to be raised. What are those "certain things"? What does "unfair" mean? "Unfair" to whom? There are many directions that this thesis might take. The following is only one of them:

> The need for more space in prisons has caused many prisoners to be released on parole before they are ready.

Guiding Your Readers

The author of the *Ad Herennium* tells us to "make clear what points are agreed upon and what contested, and announce what points we intend to take up" (1.3.4). In an essay in favor of capital punishment, Ernst van den Haag opens with the following four sentences.

> Three questions about the death penalty so overlap that they must each be answered. I shall ask seriatim: Is the death penalty constitutional? Is it useful? Is it morally justifiable?

In this opening statement the author makes clear what the contested points are and the order in which he will address them.

Often the thesis is presented as a statement that appears within the essay or paper, but in classical rhetoric the thesis was the focus or direction that the writer or orator worked toward and worked from. Its formulation was more important than its statement in words or its placement in the text.

Often a paper will not actually contain a specific thesis statement, but always there must be a main idea that provides direction and exerts control over the material. With an "unstated" thesis, every detail must speak to the main idea so that the underlying proposition is quite clear. Many writers find it easiest to state the thesis in the paper itself, and most agree it is essential at some point to write it out as an aid to the thinking and writing that go into any piece of writing.

The thesis may appear in the first paragraph, the second paragraph, in the conclusion, or even, belying its common name, thesis statement, it may never be stated at all. Rather than a statement, it may be in question form that the essay answers as in the preceding passage, and it may be repeated a number of times in different words. Often writers pose the thesis in the first paragraph, where it stands as a clear guide to both the writer and the reader. Read the following paragraph and try to locate the thesis statement:

> A photographer once said "a powerful picture reaches into your heart and just rips it out." A visual moment, captured on film, can create a tremendous social and emotional impact. How can words

ever describe young John Kennedy, Jr., saluting the flag during his father's funeral procession? Could anything but a picture capture the emotion in Truman's face after his presidential victory? Almost all of us have seen the photograph of the naked screaming girl running from her burning village in Vietnam. The tragic moment, its stark message cemented on film, reveals more than words can ever convey. A single picture can hit the heart and make us feel as though we were actually there. Still ringing with truth is the old adage "a picture is worth a thousand words."

In this opening paragraph, the writer states the thesis in the second sentence directly after an opening quotation and then restates it through an "old adage" in the last sentence. In between, she engages the reader in a series of questions that recall powerful and familiar pictures. She follows the questions with a direct statement about another memorable photograph before restating her thesis. The thesis is stated twice within the short paragraph, but there is no feeling of redundancy because of the varied wording of the two statements.

> Thesis #1: A visual moment, captured on film, can create a tremendous social and emotional impact.

> Thesis #2: Still ringing with truth is the old adage "a picture is worth a thousand words."

Whether stated or unstated, at the beginning or end, in question or statement form, the thesis guides and controls your paper.

USING TOPIC SENTENCES

A topic sentence serves as a controlling idea for one segment of an essay and often indicates the kind of development the segment will take. Generally, these segments are paragraphs or groups of paragraphs set off by indentation, double spacing, or numbers that signal the reader that you are introducing a new idea. In the following paragraph the first sentence is the topic sentence that introduces the two subjects—cholesterol and saturated fat—which will be defined and described.

> But the primary culprits of heart disease are cholesterol and saturated fat in the diet. Together they contribute to high levels of blood cholesterol. Cholesterol is found in all foods of animal origin and, indeed, in every animal cell. It is an essential component of such substances as cell walls and hormones, but enough is manufac-

tured by the liver to provide the body with all it needs even if you never eat any food containing cholesterol. Saturated fat is found in meat and dairy products and is solid at room temperature. Beef fat and vegetable shortening are examples. Some vegetable oils—including palm oil, palm kernel oil and coconut oil—also are saturated fats, as is cocoa butter.

In this paragraph, the first sentence, the topic sentence, indicates that cholesterol and saturated fat are the primary causes of heart disease. The author then develops the idea by definition, one of the topics that will be explained in Chapter 4.

The following paragraph, introduced by the topic sentence, "There is no sharp line between art and play on the one hand . . . and work on the other," develops its idea through comparison and contrast—another topic explained in Chapter 4—with the conclusion that there is not necessarily any difference between the two except in the attitude of the person involved.

There is no sharp line between art and play on the one hand, which are supposed to be self-expressive, and work on the other. The difference lies in the inner stance. Games, if one hates them, as some who play professionally do, are work; work, if one can come to like it, may be play; "I do not know," said Havelock Ellis, who loved his work, "when I am working and when I am playing." Art has been defined as anything done with a passion for perfection in its execution, and on these terms there is no work that cannot be converted in some measure into art. (from Bland Blanchard, "The Pros and Cons of Conformity")

In the preceding passages the topic sentence comes at the beginning of the paragraph, but in the following example the paragraph builds to the topic sentence, which comes at the end.

When Phi Beta Kappa refused to grant new chapters to institutions whose aid to athletes was out of proportion to aid granted other students, faculty members from some liberal arts colleges objected to such a firm stand. They pointed out, with some justice, that the regulations were not being applied to existing Phi Beta Kappa chapters. With less justice and a shrinking sense of responsibility, they also argued that the liberal arts college breathed a purer air than that of the fieldhouse. Phi Beta Kappa has stood by its principles, but it is virtually the only organization within or related to the academic cosmos that has (Kenneth Eble, "Head, Heart and Hand Outstretched: Intercollegiate Athletics").

In this passage the author uses a single example that builds to his topic sentence stated in his last sentence, that academic organizations in general have not stood up for the principle of extending equal aid to gifted students and gifted athletes. When you are using a specific case, the topic sentence may be most effectively stated at the end of the paragraph connecting the specific case to the general idea.

As these examples illustrate, you may start your paragraph with a topic sentence, a clear statement of what you are going to say, or you may use an example, make a comparison, or discuss causes, and then end with a statement in the form of a topic sentence that draws a general conclusion. Some paragraph segments have no stated topic sentence, but they are governed by a main idea, and each sentence within the paragraph develops and adds to that idea. In the following passage the topic sentence is unstated, or at least only suggested. The writer speaks only of his own experience. Can you state the main idea of this paragraph in a concluding general statement about all writers?

> Until that night I had not understood what it meant to write. I had known that the writer's goal was to reveal truths in words manipulated so effectively as to cause a movement in the minds and hearts of those who read them. But I had not understood that it would cost anything. I had believed that I could do those things while remaining secure and safe in myself—I had even believed that writing fiction was a way to conceal my true feelings and weaknesses. That night I found out better. That night, I realized that no matter how good I became in the manipulation of symbols, I could never hope to move anyone without allowing myself to be moved, that I could reveal only slight truths unless I was willing to reveal the truths about myself. I did not enjoy the realization. For I was no fonder of self-revelation than my father, and though I knew I would love to do with written words what my father had done in speech, I was not sure I could pay the price. I was not sure I wanted to (David Bradley, "The Faith").

In this paragraph Bradley's main idea is that all writers must be deeply moved themselves before they can hope to move an audience. Every detail in the paragraph builds and sustains this point, as he speaks of his original desire to conceal his personal feelings through writing and the final realization that only through self-revelation can he truly move his readers.

In the same way your topic sentence focuses your writing and thinking on one main point that other sentences within the paragraph relate to and develop. It may help as you draft a paper to use a topic sentence as you initiate a new idea in order to guide your development. In later revisions such topic sentences may be eliminated or placed at the end of the paragraph depending on whether you wish to begin or conclude with your general idea. Even if you decide not to include a topic sentence in your paragraph it may help to write out the main idea of each segment of your essay in order to direct and focus your thinking and writing.

In the following essay Adlai Stevenson states his thesis and then leads the reader through a series of definitions and redefinitions to arrive at his conclusion. How does he answer the classical questions: whether it is, what it is, and what kind it is? What is his thesis? Where is it stated?

THE HARD KIND OF PATRIOTISM

ADLAI E. STEVENSON

It is not easy to be a patriot these days—not because it is difficult to love   1
one's country. The difficulty lies with loving one's country in the right
way.

The love itself is profound and instinctive, rooted in our childhood   2
discovery of all the infinite delights of being alive—for me, the vast skies,
the spring green of the corn, the fall colors and winter snow of the
Illinois prairie; for all of us, the shining Christmas trees, the colored
mesas and bright flowers of the desert, the rocky shores and pounding
seas "way down East," the aspens showering autumn gold on the slopes of
the Rockies.

It doesn't matter what your picture is. For all of us, it is "home," the   3
place where we spent the endless, dream-filled days of childhood, the
place that still nourishes our secret, life-giving imagination, the place we
love as we love bread, as we love the earliest image of maternal care, as we
love life itself. In doing so, we love what has largely made us what we are.
The difficulty is, as I have said, to love it in the right way.

I think the complexity of modern technological society makes the   4
loving difficult for everybody, but here in America we have some quite
special problems, which come not from our complex present but from
our historical inheritance.

Some states emerge from some pre-existing tribal unity, some grow up   5
within an already established culture, and some are forged by conquest,
with victor and vanquished settling down to a new synthesis.

None of these routes was followed by America. Our people have come   6
from every "tribal" group; they have largely had to create their own
civilization as they went along to absorb a continent. They have never
been conquered or had any sort of synthesis imposed upon them. Their

community had, in fact, a unique beginning—it was from the moment of its birth a land "dedicated to a proposition"—that men are born equal, that government is a government of laws, not men, and exists to serve them, that "life, liberty, and the pursuit of happiness" are man's inalienable right.

But consider the consequences of this astonishing start. We are Americans because we belong to a certain ideal, visionary type of political and social order. We can't point back to a long, shared civilization. It is true, most of us have Europe and the West behind us. But not all—and, anyway, it is a concept of the West that we create rather than inherit. And no one is standing on our necks keeping us down and together.   7

The result is a community, surely, whose instinctive, rooted, taken-for-granted unity has to be all the more dynamic. If we are not dedicated to our fundamental propositions, then the natural cement in our society may not be enough to take the strain.   8

I would agree that there are substitutes. When a President said that "the business of America is business," he told us something about the degree to which a standard of living can do stand-in duty for a way of life. But the question, "What manner of people are we?" cannot be everlastingly answered in terms of two-car families or split-level homes.   9

America is much more than an economic or geographical fact. It is a political and moral fact—the first community in which men set out in principle to institutionalize freedom, responsible government, and human equality. And we love it for this audacity! How easy it is, contemplating this vision, to see in it—as Jefferson or Lincoln saw in it—"The last, best hope of man." To be a nation founded on an ideal in one sense makes our love of country a more vital force than any instinctive pieties of blood and soil.   10

But it also demands a more complex and discriminating love. Will the fabric hold if the ideal fades? If the effort to realize our citizens' birthright of freedom and equality is not constantly renewed, on what can we fall back? As a going concern, we can no doubt survive many shocks and shames. It was Adam Smith who remarked that "There is a great deal of ruin in every state." But can we survive, as a confident and growing community, if the essentially liberal thrust of our origins is forgotten, if we equate liberty with passive noninterference, if we exclude large minorities from our standards of equality, if income becomes a substitute for idealism, consumption for dedication, privilege for neighborly good will?   11

Well, you may say, "Why be so concerned; after all, one of the most forceful elements of our free society is precisely our discontent with our own shortcomings. Because we are free, because we are not the victims of censorship and manipulated news, because no dictatorial government   12 imposes on us its version of the truth, we are at liberty to speak up against our shortcomings. We don't confuse silence with success. We know that 'between the idea and the reality . . . falls the shadow,' and we are determined to chase away that shadow in the uncompromising light of truth."

But *are we*? It is at this point that our patriotism, our love of country, has to be a discriminating, not a blind force. All too often, voices are raised, in the name of some superpatriotism, to still all criticism and to denounce honest divergencies as the next thing to treason. We have risen up from the pit of McCarthy's time, when honest men could lose their jobs for questioning whether there were 381 known Communists in the State Department. But the intolerant spirit which equates responsible criticisms with "selling the country short" or "being soft on communism" or "undermining the American way of life" is still abroad.   13

I can give you no comfort in suggesting there is an easy way around this type of criticism. Our position today *is* equivocal. We *are* in one sense a very conservative people—for no nation in history has had so much to conserve. Suggestions that everything is not perfect and that things must be changed *do* arouse the suspicion that something *I* cherish and *I* value may be modified. Even Aristotle complained that "everyone thinks chiefly of his own, hardly ever of the public interest." And our instinct is to preserve what we have, and then to give the instinct a colored wrapping of patriotism.   14

This is in part what the great Dr. Johnson meant when he said: "Patriotism is the last refuge of a scoundrel." To defend every abuse, every self-interest, every encrusted position of privilege in the name of love of country—when in fact it is only love of the status quo—that indeed is the lie in the soul to which any conservative society is prone.   15

We do not escape it—but with us, an extra edge of hypocrisy attaches to the confusion. For our basic reason for being a state is our attempt to build a dynamic and equal society of free men. Societies based on blood ties can perhaps safely confuse conservatism and patriotism. People with long backward-looking traditions can perhaps do so. Countries under the heel of dictators must do so. But if the world's first experiment in the open society uses patriotism as a cloak for inaction or reaction, then it will cease to be open—and then, as a social organism, it will lose its fundamental reason for existence.   16

Do not, therefore, regard the critics as questionable patriots. What were Washington and Jefferson and Adams but profound critics of the colonial status quo? Our society can stand a large dose of constructive criticism just because it is so solid and has so much to conserve. It is only if keen and lively minds constantly compare the ideal and the reality and see the shadow—the shadow of self-righteousness, of suburban sprawl, of   17 racial discrimination, of interminable strikes—it is only then that the shadow can be dispelled and the unique brightness of our national experiment can be seen and loved.

The patriots are those who love America enough to wish to see her as a 18 model to mankind. This is not treachery. This—as every parent, every teacher, every friend must know—is the truest and noblest affection. No patriots so defaced America as those who, in the name of Americanism, launched a witch-hunt which became a byword around the world. We have survived it. We shall survive John Birchism and all the rest of the superpatriots—but only at the price of perpetual and truly patriotic vigilance.

This discriminating and vigilant patriotism is all the more necessary 19 because the world at large is one in which a simple, direct, inward-looking nationalism is not enough.

We face in Communist hostility and expansionism a formidable force, 20 whether Mr. Khrushchev and Mr. Mao Tse-tung pull together or apart. They disagree so far only on whether capitalism should be peacefully or violently buried. They are both for the funeral. So long as this fundamental objective remains, we must regard the Communist Bloc as a whole with extreme wariness.

Even if the Communists are divided and confused everywhere—even if 21 they have scored of late none of the victories in Africa, East Asia, and the Middle East our doomsayers predicted—still the Communist Bloc is aggressive and powerful and determined to grow more so. Taken individually, the European states are all outnumbered. Even America has only a margin of superiority over the tough, austere Soviet Union. Even if the Russian forces in Cuba are not going to conquer the Americas, still their presence in this hemisphere endangers the peace.

So we have sensibly concluded in the NATO Alliance that our separate 22 sovereignties and nationalisms must be transcended in a common, overwhelming union of deterrent strength. Together our weight keeps the balance of power firmly down on our side, and it removes from each state the temptation of playing off one state against another and weakening the overall power in order to strengthen its own. This is the first reason for transcending narrow nationalism.

The second follows from our economic interdependence. The Atlantic 23 world has taken 70 per cent of world trade and absorbed 70 per cent of its own investments for the last seventy years. We are an interwoven international economy. Bank rates in Britain affect investments in New York. Restrictions here affect carpet makers in Belgium. French farmers affect everybody. We can only avoid the mismanagement of this community if we pursue joint policies. My friend Jean Monnet has outlined the essential list: expansion of demand, currency stability, investment overseas, trade with the developing nations, reserves for world trade. Without joint policies here, we could easily slip back to the debacle of the period between the great civil wars of Europe of 1914 and 1939.

In this context, separate, divisive nationalism is not patriotism. It 24 cannot be patriotism to enlarge a country's illusory sense of potency and influence, and reduce its security and economic viability. True patriotism demands that, in some essential categories, purely national solutions be left behind in the interest of the nation itself. It is this effort to transcend narrow nationalism that marked the supremely successful Marshall Plan. It marks the great enterprise of European unification—after so many tribal wars. It could mark the building of an Atlantic partnership as a secure nucleus of world order.

So our vision must be of the open society fulfilling itself in an open 25 world. This we can love. This gives our country its universal validity. This is a patriotism which sets no limits to the capacity of our country to act as the organizing principle of wider and wider associations, until in some way not yet foreseen we can embrace the family of man.

And here our patriotism encounters its last ambiguity. There are mis- 26 guided patriots who feel we pay too much attention to other nations, that we are somehow enfeebled by respecting world opinion. Well, "a decent respect for the opinions of mankind" was the very first order of business when the Republic was created; the Declaration of Independence was written, not to proclaim our separation, but to explain it and win other nations to our cause. The founding fathers did not think it was "soft" or "un-American" to respect the opinions of others, and today for a man to love his country truly, he must also know how to love mankind. The change springs from many causes. The two appalling wars of this century, culminating in the atom bomb, have taught all men the impossibility of war. Horace may have said: "It is sweet and fitting to die for one's country." But to be snuffed out in the one brief blast of an atomic explosion bears no relation to the courage and clarity of the old limited ideal.

Nor is this a simple shrinking from annihilation. It is something much 27 deeper—a growing sense of our solidarity as a human species on a planet made one and vulnerable by our science and technology.

For, on this shrunken globe, men can no longer live as strangers. Men 28 can war against each other as hostile neighbors, as we are determined not to do; or they can coexist in frigid isolation, as we are doing. But our prayer is that men everywhere will learn, finally, to live as brothers, to respect each other's differences, to heal each other's wounds, to promote each other's progress, and to benefit from each other's knowledge. If the evangelical virtue of charity can be translated into political terms, aren't these our goals?

Aristotle said that the end of politics must be the good of man. Man's 29
greatest good and greatest present need is, then, to establish world peace.
Without it, the democratic enterprise—one might even say the human
enterprise—will be utterly, fatally doomed. War under modern conditions is bereft of even that dubious logic it may have had in the past. With
the development of modern technology "victory" in war has become a
mockery. What victory—victory for what or for whom?

Perhaps younger people are especially sensitive to this growing convic- 30
tion that nowadays all wars are civil wars and all killing is fratricide. The
movement takes many forms—multilateral diplomacy through the
United Nations, the search for world peace through world law, the universal desire for nuclear disarmament, the sense of sacrifice and service of
the Peace Corps, the growing revulsion against Jim Crowism, the belief
that dignity rests in man as such and that all must be treated as ends, not
means.

But whatever its form, I believe that, far from being in any sense an 31
enemy to patriotism, it is a new expression of the respect for life from
which all true love springs. We can truly begin to perceive the meaning of
our great propositions—of liberty and equality—if we see them as part of
the patrimony of all men. We shall not love our corner of the planet less
for loving the planet too, and resisting with all our skill and passion the
dangers that would reduce it to smoldering ashes.

I can, therefore, wish no more for the profound patriotism of Ameri- 32
cans than that they add to it a new dedication to the world-wide brotherhood of which they are a part and that, together with their love of
America, there will grow a wider love which seeks to transform our
earthly city, with all its races and peoples, all its creeds and aspirations,
into Saint Augustine's "Heavenly city where truth reigns, love is the law,
and whose extent is eternity."

The next five chapters of this book discuss strategies that classical
rhetoric uses to develop ideas. They called these strategies proofs or
arguments. The word argument was not used in its modern sense of
disagreement. Both argument and proof were ways of supporting or
developing a thesis. The thesis in classical rhetoric is the pivotal point
toward which a writer works in exploring a subject—finding direction
out of chaos—and the point through which and from which strategies
and arguments come.

Aristotle divides proof into two kinds—artistic and inartistic. The
artistic proofs, those arguments most appropriate for rhetoric, are covered in Chapter 3 as the appeal of the speaker and the appeal to the

audience. Chapters 4, 5, and 6 cover the strategies derived from the classical topics and induction and deduction and their rhetorical equivalents, the enthymeme and the example. Chapter 7 describes logical fallacies, ways that our arguments can go wrong.

Questions to Consider

1. Using the questions of conjecture, essence, and quality, what can you ask about the following subjects?

A. higher education

B. divestiture in South Africa

C. college athletics

D. nuclear energy

E. foreign policy in Central America

2. What disagreements do you have with other people on these subjects? On what are the disagreements based? How can you answer to their arguments?

3. What kinds of theses can you derive from your discussion?

4. Are there questions that you cannot answer and that may force you to go to outside sources? List those questions.

5. Evaluate the following theses. What kinds of questions do you need to ask to focus or direct your ideas? Can you form new theses on the basis of your examination of the issues?

A. The 1984 presidential election was a disaster.

B. Students should be required to take a physical education class.

C. The grading system is not fair.

D. *Gone with the Wind* is the best movie ever produced.

E. Solar energy—yes or no?

F. In my opinion, the textbook we are using in Calculus I is worthless.

6. The following paragraph is neither unified nor well developed. Eliminate any sentences that do not contribute to the writer's main idea and suggest ways in which this idea could be developed.

I am sick and tired of being bombarded with a steady stream of commercials every time I turn on my TV, and I know that I'm not alone. After all, as a student, I don't have much time to watch TV, and I don't care to spend what time I do have being lectured about products and services. My economics class takes up most of my time. I spend nearly three hours a day studying it. I'm also taking four other courses, including English, history, math, and political science. Not only do these commercials frequently insult our intelligence, but many are deliberately deceptive as well. Did you ever read the claims on a bottle of shampoo? Perhaps advertisers could sell their product more effectively if they announced at the beginning of a program that they would not interrupt it with their commercials. Such a gesture of goodwill would surely encourage my undying gratitude—and my willingness to purchase their products.

Suggestions for Writing

1. Choose an essay or column from the editorial section of your newspaper with which you do not agree. Identify the thesis or main idea. In a short paper, explain why you do or do not agree with the author's main idea.

2. Form a thesis that represents your own point of view (after asking the questions of conjecture, essence, and quality). Write an essay supporting your thesis.

3. Examine a paper of your own. Identify the main idea and the thesis if it is stated. Is the thesis clear and precise? Is it sufficiently narrowed? Rewrite your paper after rethinking your thesis.

Exercises in Revision

1. Exchange essays you wrote before reading this chapter with another member of your class. Ask each other the following questions:

A. Can you determine what the main idea is?

B. Is it stated in the essay?

C. Is it clear to the reader?

D. Are all the points made in the essay pertinent to the thesis?

2. Using the same essay, identify the subject of the essay. Ask each other the questions of fact, essence, and quality listed on pp. 30, 31, and 32.

3. Select an essay with which you are familiar or one from this book. You might use the Adlai Stevenson essay at the end of this chapter. Into what major sections is the essay divided? How are those sections indicated? By indentation? By topic sentences? Can you identify such defined sections in one of your own essays?

For a Commonplace Book

1. Make a list of five subjects that you would like to write about.

2. Formulate a thesis about one of your favorite songs, books, or movies.

Chapter 3

Establishing Credibility and Appealing to Your Audience

Of the modes of persuasion furnished by the spoken word there are
three kinds. The first kind depends on the personal character of the
speaker; the second on putting the audience into a certain frame of
mind; the third on the proof, or apparent proof, provided by the
words of the speech itself (*Rhetoric* 1.2.1356a1–5).

Aristotle is describing the three kinds of rhetorical proof available to
the orator, *ethos, pathos*, and *logos*, described briefly in the introduction to
this section. Two thousand years later a modern rhetorician, Wayne
Booth, voices the same idea in connection with writing.

The common ingredient that I find in all of the writing I admire—
excluding for now novels, plays, and poems—is something that I
shall reluctantly call the rhetorical stance, a stance which depends

on discovering and maintaining in any writing situation a proper balance among the three elements that are at work in any communicative effort; the available arguments about the subject itself [*logos*], the interest and peculiarities of the audience [*pathos*], and the voice, the implied character, of the speaker [*ethos*].

The vocabulary is different but the ideas remain the same for oratory and for writing, for the fifth century B.C. and for the twentieth century.

ETHOS: ESTABLISHING CREDIBILITY

In writing, as in speech, the strength of the argument rests to a great degree on the credibility that the author establishes. The author's good character adds weight to the words, provides support for the statements, and lends proof to the arguments. Establishing this character depends, in turn, on the words, examples, statements, and arguments that the writer offers.

In orations, speakers literally and physically stand behind what they say, but in writing, the author may be physically separated from the reader. In conversations, there is constant interaction—questions and interruptions—between the speaker and hearer. In writing, the reader usually cannot question the author. We read letters from friends who are thousands of miles away and all we have in this case are the words on the page. But through their writings, these persons are very real and very much present. Through the words on the page, writers establish who they are and what they believe.

Authors can establish their credibility by demonstrating three qualities through the words on the page: intelligence, virtue, and goodwill. Intelligence can be indicated by experience or special knowledge of the subject, although the best evidence may well lie in careful, well-reasoned arguments. Virtue and goodwill can be shown by identifying with the values and interests of the audience. Note the interaction between *ethos* and *pathos* here as the author's credibility depends on the audience's belief in his or her goodwill.

One of the most successful users of *ethos* was Martin Luther King, Jr. His voice and his moral stature were eloquent weapons in the fight for civil rights and integration in the 1960s. The following excerpts are from his "Letter from Birmingham Jail." The letter was in answer to a statement from eight fellow clergymen from Alabama who criticized him for his "unwise and untimely" activities in connection with his participation in a demonstration for human rights in Birmingham, for which he was subsequently jailed.

My Dear Fellow Clergymen:

While confined here in the Birmingham city jail, I came across your recent statement calling my present activities "unwise and untimely." Seldom do I pause to answer criticism of my work and ideas. If I sought to answer all the criticisms that cross my desk, my secretaries would have little time for anything other than such correspondence in the course of the day, and I would have no time for constructive work. But since I feel that you are men of genuine good will and that your criticisms are sincerely set forth, I want to try to answer your statement in what I hope will be patient and reasonable terms.

In this opening paragraph, King establishes his *ethos*: He underscores his concern for constructive rather than destructive activities, which must always be the concern of people of character and virtue. He appeals to the goodwill of his readers by making it clear that he is answering their particular criticisms because he knows that even though they have criticized his actions as "unwise and untimely" he also understands that they are "men of genuine good will" and that their criticisms are "sincerely set forth." His final sentence—that he will try to answer their statement in "patient and reasonable terms"—establishes him as a person of intelligence and common sense. This opening paragraph, in answer to a statement criticizing his actions, predisposes his readers to accept at the outset that he is a reasonable person writing without malice.

In the next paragraph, he gives the reasons for his being in Birmingham, since his critics had also blamed him for being an "outsider." He carefully explains that he has organizational ties in Birmingham and had been asked by the Alabama Christian Movement for Human Rights to engage in a "nonviolent direct-action program if such were deemed necessary." The third paragraph, however, outlines the real reasons for his being there:

But more basically, I am in Birmingham because injustice is here. Just as the prophets of the eighth century B.C. left their villages and carried their "thus saith the Lord" far beyond the boundaries of their home towns, and just as the Apostle Paul left his village of Tarsus and carried the gospel of Jesus Christ to the far corners of the Greco-Roman world, so am I compelled to carry the gospel of freedom beyond my own home town. Like Paul, I must constantly respond to the Macedonian call for aid.

Notice here how King places his actions in a larger moral context—a fight against injustice: "I am in Birmingham because injustice is here."

He then compares himself to religious figures from history who carried Christianity "far beyond the boundaries of their home towns" to the "far corners" of the known world. He proclaims himself a person of virtue not only in responding to the call of the Alabama Christian Movement for Human Rights, but in maintaining that he "must constantly respond to . . . [a] call for aid." And King speaks to the shared values of his audience, since he knows that his readers, who are themselves clergymen, understand and are particularly sympathetic to the religious commitments he cites.

He continues to establish the intellectual thrust of his argument by allusions to outside authorities such as the theologian Reinhold Niebuhr, and the medieval philosopher St. Thomas Aquinas, and by a number of Biblical references. In addition, writing from what must have been an emotional viewpoint, he still maintains a reasoned and careful argument.

> In any nonviolent campaign there are four basic steps: collection of the facts to determine whether injustices exist; negotiation; self-justification; and direct action.

Such carefully controlled steps in an emotionally packed situation mark King as a person of intelligence and common sense.

After a carefully reasoned series of arguments supporting his position, the conclusion once more reminds the audience of King's motives and morals:

> Never before have I written so long a letter. I'm afraid it is much too long to take your precious time. I can assure you that it would have been much shorter if I had been writing from a comfortable desk, but what else can one do when he is alone in a narrow jail cell, other than write long letters, think long thoughts, and pray long prayers?
>
> If I have said anything in this letter that overstates the truth and indicates an unreasonable impatience, I beg you to forgive me. If I have said anything that understates the truth and indicates my having a patience that allows me to settle for anything less than brotherhood, I beg God to forgive me.
>
> I hope this letter finds you strong in the faith. I also hope that circumstances will soon make it possible for me to meet each of you, not as an integrationist or a civil-rights leader but as a "fellow clergyman and a Christian brother." Let us all hope that the dark clouds of racial prejudice will soon pass away and the deep fog of misunderstanding will be lifted from our fear-drenched communities, and in some not too distant tomorrow the radiant stars of

love and brotherhood will shine over our great nation with all their scintillating beauty.

> Yours for the cause of Peace and Brotherhood,
> Martin Luther King, Jr.

He reiterates the virtue of his cause by calling on God's forgiveness if he has settled "for anything less than brotherhood," and he emphasizes the reasonableness of his cause by asking his readers' forgiveness if he has "said anything that understates the truth." Finally, he establishes his goodwill toward his audience by hoping that his letter is not too long for their "precious time," and reminds them of their Christian brotherhood by his hope that they will meet soon as fellow clergymen. He emphasizes their common cause by repeating the word brother or brotherhood four times in the last two paragraphs. He leaves his readers with the firm impression that he is a person of intelligence, virtue, and goodwill arguing a just cause. And it is in his words, sentences, and allusions that King establishes his character.

Ways of Establishing Credibility as a Writer

You can establish your good character and credibility in the same way that Martin Luther King, Jr., does. Remember that what you say and how you say it tell your audience who you are, giving them a sense of your intelligence and common sense, virtue and good character, and above all basic goodwill toward them, your readers. Following are some questions that can help you to establish your credibility systematically:

Intelligence and Common Sense

1. Have I used arguments that sound reasonable to me?

   Would the arguments that I use be convincing to me? Are they based on ideas that make sense to my audience? Do the ideas follow each other in a logical way?

2. Have I overstated my case using inappropriate exaggeration?

   Have I exaggerated any of the statements that I make? Have I used words that are too strong? Have I used examples or details that are outlandish? Have I carefully qualified my assertions?

3. Have I allowed for doubts and uncertainties?

   Few stands or viewpoints are unequivocally one-sided. Do I allow for doubts—my own and those of other people? Do I acknowledge and honestly talk about those doubts and uncertainties?

4. Have I acknowledged other viewpoints?

Every subject has a number of different viewpoints, some of which may be shared by members of the audience. Do I recognize those differing viewpoints as valid and worthy of discussion?

Virtue and Good Character

1. Have I compared myself and my case to persons of known integrity?

   If I know certain persons or situations that my audience thinks of as honest and sincere, how can I connect my ideas with those persons or situations?

2. Can I put the issue within a larger moral framework?

   If I am discussing women's rights, for example, can I put that issue within the larger one of human rights, thereby adding to the significance of the question that I am discussing?

3. Have I stated my beliefs, values, and priorities in connection with this issue?

   If I am discussing women's rights, for example, have I made it clear that I believe in the rights of all human beings? If I am discussing the right to vote, have I made it clear that I believe in the tenets of a democratic form of government?

Goodwill

1. Have I acknowledged and given careful consideration to the audience's viewpoint?

   If I am advocating a certain candidate for office do I acknowledge that the audience might have some good reason for supporting another candidate?

2. Have I reviewed our points of agreement?

   If I am trying to persuade my audience to vote for a bond issue to support schools, do I point out that good education is our investment in the future, and that in a democracy equal educational opportunities should be open to all children?

3. Have I reminded my audience of our common interests and concerns?

   For example, in connection with a school bond issue, have I reminded my audience that better schools will bring in new business and in many ways improve the quality of life in the community?

4. Have I demonstrated that I respect and acknowledge my audience's intelligence, sincerity, and common sense?

For example, have I made an effort to present sound arguments not based on prejudice or banalities? Have I avoided trivialities? Have I answered doubts and questions that my audience might have? Have I presented my ideas clearly and in an organized fashion? Finally, is the essay free of mechanical errors in spelling and punctuation and in a form that is easy to read and that will not offend the intelligence of my audience or detract from what I am saying?

Ethical Concerns

A serious concern of rhetoricians and philosophers from ancient times to the present is that rhetoric can be misused by the unscrupulous and that the appearance of good character may in fact be only an appearance. The classical rhetoricians, and especially Quintilian, believed that an orator should not only appear to be "a good man," but should be one. Persons skilled in the use of words can use them to their advantage for both good and evil ends. The political speaker who wins votes by sounding persuasive and appearing to be of good character may turn out to be a liar; the advertiser who makes unrealistic promises about a product may be a charlatan. But Aristotle defends rhetoric against such misuse:

> And if it be objected that one who uses such power of speech unjustly might do great harm, that is a charge which may be made in common against all good things except virtue, and above all against the things that are most useful, as strength, health, wealth, generalship (*Rhetoric* 1.1.1355b1–6).

Rhetoric can always be used for evil ends; thus the true integrity of the writer or orator becomes paramount. There is no way to guard against an evil person using rhetoric for bad purposes, therefore, as readers and listeners you need to measure the person who speaks or writes as carefully as possible. Your character as the writer is an important element in what you say and you should remember that your readers will respond to the image you present of yourself.

The final question, then, for both classical orators and modern writers remains:

Have I presented myself as a person of good character?

Am I using rhetoric for a good purpose?

In Chapter 8, a review of fallacies introduces errors in reasoning as well as some of the false appeals that might be used by persons who misuse rhetoric for less than good purposes.

PATHOS: APPEALING TO YOUR AUDIENCE

Pathos, according to Aristotle, is an important method of persuasion:

> Persuasion may come through the hearers, when the speech stirs their emotions. Our judgments when we are pleased and friendly are not the same as when we are pained and hostile (*Rhetoric* 1.1.1356a13–16).

As a writer you should write to a particular audience in a particular situation. In ordinary verbal exchanges, we are acutely aware of our audience; we constantly interact with our listeners. Good writing creates a similar interaction between the author and the readers. As writers therefore, we must have an idea about what motivates and moves our readers. We must recognize and appeal to their hopes, their values, their fears, and their desires. We must anticipate their questions as well as their doubts, and we must respond to both in our writing. Rhetoric recognizes the whole person—the rational as well as the emotional side of being human.

Notice how Martin Luther King, Jr., in this paragraph from "Letter from Birmingham Jail" demonstrates what segregation might do to all of those persons that his readers hold most dear—mothers and fathers, sisters and brothers, and finally children. By demonstrating how the family can be hurt by segregation, King appeals to his readers' emotions—how segregation affects them:

> Perhaps it is easy for those who have never felt the stinging darts of segregation to say, "Wait." But when you have seen vicious mobs lynch your mothers and fathers at will and drown your sisters and brothers at whim; when you have seen hate-filled policemen curse, kick and even kill your black brothers and sisters; when you see the vast majority of your twenty million Negro brothers smothering in an airtight cage of poverty in the midst of an affluent society; when you suddenly find your tongue twisted and your speech stammering as you seek to explain to your six-year-old daughter why she can't go to the public amusement park that has just been advertised on television, and see tears well up in her eyes when she is told that Funtown is closed to colored children, and see ominous clouds of inferiority beginning to form in her little mental sky, and see her beginning to distort her personality by developing an unconscious bitterness toward white people. . . .

For the reader who has not felt segregation, how does King make him or her feel those "stinging darts"? If he had only described the lynchings, the hate-filled policemen, the poverty, without asking the reader to consider their mothers, fathers, sisters and brothers in those situations, would the effect have been the same? What effect does the "you" in "you seek to explain to your child" have on the reader?

In another essay, "A Hanging," George Orwell makes an eloquent argument against capital punishment. At the time that this essay was written, 1945, there appeared many well-reasoned arguments against capital punishment citing impressive facts and figures demonstrating that capital punishment was not a deterrent to crime. But Orwell's poignant and moving essay describing a hanging in painful and minute detail moves the reader in a way that facts and statistics never can. Orwell appeals to his readers' emotions by making the scene so real that you, the reader, feel as though you are there—walking beside the doomed man.

> It is curious, but till that moment I had never realized what it means to destroy a healthy, conscious man. When I saw the prisoner step aside to avoid the puddle I saw the mystery, the unspeakable wrongness, of cutting a life short when it is in full tide. This man was not dying, he was alive just as we are alive. All the organs of his body were working—bowels digesting food, skin renewing itself, nails growing, tissues forming—all toiling away in solemn foolery. His nails would still be growing when he stood on the drop, when he was falling through the air with a tenth-of-a-second to live. His eyes saw the yellow gravel and the grey walls, and his brain still remembered, foresaw, reasoned—reasoned even about puddles. He and we were a party of men walking together, seeing, hearing, feeling, understanding the same world; and in two minutes, with a sudden snap, one of us would be gone—one mind less, one world less.

In the line, "This man was not dying, he was alive just as we are alive," Orwell involves the reader in the hanging by his use of the present tense and the pronoun "we." Later the reader is drawn into the scene by the phrase "one of us would be gone."

Orwell could not have known every one of his many readers at the time. They may have been friendly or hostile and have had any number of assumptions or biases. This anonymity, however, does not allow the writer to proceed without any thought of that audience. You must determine who the audience is you are writing for and then anticipate and respond to expected reactions. Since your readers cannot respond in person, you must be constantly sensitive to their possible questions and doubts and answer to them.

Analyzing an Audience

The first and most obvious step is to identify and get acquainted with your readers. Knowing their values will help you choose ways for establishing your own integrity; knowing your reader's hopes and fears will help you recognize and acknowledge them in a sympathetic way. Determine who your audience is and consider which of these questions is relevant given your subject:

Is the audience male or female or both?

What is their age?

Are they married, single, divorced, or widowed?

What nationality are they?

Do they belong to a particular ethnic group?

What is their political and religious affiliation?

What is their educational background?

Once you have thought about the answers to these questions, ask yourself the following questions:

What information does my audience have about my subject?

What information do I need to give them?

What interest do they have in my subject?

How can I interest them in my subject?

What values do we share?

On what do we agree?

What might be our points of disagreement?

What are their hopes and goals?

What do they fear?

Recall how well Martin Luther King, Jr., held these ideas in mind. He knew that his audience was well aware of his work and his ideas, but he felt that he needed to inform them of his reasons for being in Birmingham. King knew that his fellow clergymen were interested in the cause of desegregation and he reminds them of their shared values in their religious beliefs. King was aware of his audience's position on the issue as he wrote, and his feeling for them is evident in his writing.

In the following section we'll look at some of the audiences commonly encountered by writers together with some of the ways that writers might deal with their expected reactions.

The Friendly Audience The easiest kind of audience to address is the one that shares your own interests and beliefs or one that is already interested in your subject, such as a campus activist group or a social organization with which you are associated. When a dean writes to the college president urging a change in the curriculum, the dean can assume that they both share a concern for the education of the student. Their priorities, however, may differ. The president's concern may be primarily financial; the curriculum dean's may be staffing the courses, even though they share a deep concern for education. When an engineer writes to the president of the company suggesting a change in the design of a product, he or she can assume that the president will also be interested in producing a better product or cutting costs. It is important to understand when an audience is friendly and open to ideas and when it is not.

Politicians who address a group of people who have paid a hundred dollars a plate to attend a dinner can assume that they are speaking to a friendly audience that supports their views. An elected official in his or her inaugural address can safely assume that a majority of those who voted are friendly.

In the same way, you may assume that certain audiences will share your beliefs and you may wish to remind them of these commonalities. In the essay at the end of the preceding chapter, Adlai Stevenson reminded his readers of their shared love for their country. He recounted those things from his childhood that made him love his country, and then followed with the things that "all of us" love, in order to establish an identity relationship with his readers.

> It is not easy to be a patriot these days—not because it is difficult to love one's country. The difficulty lies with loving one's country in the right way.
>
> The love itself is profound and instinctive, rooted in our child-hood discovery of all the infinite delights of being alive—for me, the vast skies, the spring green of the corn, the fall colors and winter snow of the Illinois prairie; for all of us, the shining Christmas trees, the colored mesas and bright flowers of the desert, the rocky shores and pounding seas "way down East," the aspens showering autumn gold on the slopes of the Rockies.

In his *Gettysburg Address*, Lincoln reminded his audience of their common ancestry—"Fourscore and seven years ago, our forefathers. . . ." If both the writer and reader hold certain beliefs effective arguments can be built on a basis of shared assumptions, such as one or more of the following:

Everything in the Bible is true.
Less government is better government.
Taxes should be increased.
Premarital sex is immoral.
The justice system is unfair.
Abortion is murder.
Welfare needs reform.
Taxation unjustly penalizes the middle class.

If you as a writer know that your audience believes any one of the above generalizations how, then, might you appeal to their emotions while presenting your viewpoint? One of the ways of testing your audience is to read something that you have written and put yourself in the role of the reader. For example, "We all believe in the necessity of developing nuclear energy sources" might be a shared belief with nuclear engineers, but not with an audience of environmentalists. Similarly, how would you as a reader react to the statement that "Education is our number one priority" if you were a legislator? A teacher? A student? An employee of a defense industry? In order to understand your audience, it is sometimes helpful to read your own paper, putting yourself in the role of the reader in order to develop the reader-ear.

The audience is seldom a complete mystery. It is thus important to try to perceive and be aware of their interests and beliefs and to tailor your arguments and appeals to those common beliefs. As you write you might keep the following questions in mind:

How can I remind the audience of our common beliefs and values?

How can I make clear the connection between those shared beliefs and values and the subject of this paper?

In the following essay written for the *New York Times*, how successfully does the author answer those questions?

The great tradition of American churchmen from William Ellery Channing and Ralph Waldo Emerson and Theodore Parker to Washington Gladden, James Cardinal Gibbons, and Reinhold Niebuhr, is that of the moral crusader. They preached public morality, not public religion. No one can question the right of, or the duty of, churchmen of all denominations today to preach morality and religion; it is when they connect morality with a particular brand of religious faith and this, in turn, with political policies that they venture into troubled waters (Henry Steele Commager, "Public Morality, Not Religion").

The General Audience Many times writing is directed to an audience that is so general that their attitudes, beliefs, and interests are unknown. For example, even in essays that assume an audience of your classmates, you cannot know their religion, their political loyalties, or their finances. Consequently, writers are very careful not to say or imply anything that would irritate or offend their readers needlessly. In writing to a general audience, you should avoid anything that might be taken as a slur against a regional, ethnic, social, racial, religious, or political group. Under any circumstances, you might wish to avoid controversial issues unless such issues are an important part of your message. Usually they only distract. As you write, keep in mind the following questions:

> Are there any statements that might offend readers within certain racial, ethnic, social, sexual, political, or religious groups?
>
> Are such statements necessary for this subject?
>
> Can I avoid or soften such statements?

The following essay by Bruno Bettelheim appeared in a general circulation magazine, *Harper's*, in 1985. How well does he avoid offending parents? How does he soften his statements?

> Many parents wonder what is the best way to teach their children discipline. But the majority of those who have asked my opinions on discipline have spoken of it as something that parents impose on children, rather than something that parents instill in them. What they really seem to have in mind is punishment—in particular, physical punishment.
>
> Unfortunately, punishment teaches a child that those who have power can force others to do their will. And when the child is old enough and able, he will try to use such force himself—for instance, punishing his parents by acting in ways most distressing to them. Thus parents would be well advised to keep in mind Shakespeare's words: "They that have power to hurt and will do none . . . They rightly do inherit heaven's graces." Among those graces is being loved and emulated by one's children.

The Professional Audience A common occurrence in college and professional writing is that you may be writing for an audience that does not necessarily share common interests or beliefs but shares certain knowledge with you. This audience may share an understanding of specialized terminology that is obscure to readers outside the field of study. Below is a report written by an engineering student for her professor:

> All fluids possess a definite resistance to change of form. This property, a sort of internal friction, is absolute viscosity. Kinematic viscosity is the ratio of absolute viscosity to the density of the fluid. To understand viscosity quantitatively, one can start with the Hagen-Poiseuille equation. The pressure drop required to cause a Newtonian fluid to flow in the laminar region is expressed by the following equation. . . .

This student is well aware that her professor knows the meaning of such terms as *viscosity, Hagen-Poiseuille equation, Newtonian fluid,* and *laminar region.* There is no need to define these terms within the context of the course for which this report is written. If the audience were made up of laypersons, all of these terms would need careful and extensive definitions. In the following essay, describing a cat at play, Konrad Lorenz is writing for a general audience—not a technical one. Note the difference in the vocabulary.

> If we now improve on our plaything by attaching a thread to it and letting it dangle from above, the kitten will exhibit entirely different prey-catching movements. Jumping high, it grabs the prey with both paws at once, bringing them together in a wide, sweeping movement from the sides. During this movement, the paws appear abnormally large, for all the digits with their extended claws are widely spread, and the dewclaws are bent at right angles to the paw. This grasping movement, which many kittens delightedly perform in play, is identical to the last detail with the movement used by cats to grab a bird just leaving the ground.

Lorenz is constantly aware of his readers and the extent of his readers' knowledge of the subject and senses when a definition or an explanation is in order and when it would be boring and unnecessary.

Once you have determined your audience, ask yourself the following questions as you write:

> What background information do my readers need?
>
> What specialized technical terms need defining?

The Hostile Audience More often than you might imagine, you will be called on to write to an audience who may not share your interests and on a subject where there is basic disagreement. In this case, it is important that you address both the points of disagreement and areas of agreement. The following letter of complaint was written to request a refund on a dress that contained a flaw in the material:

Jones Dress Shop
1245 Memphis Street
Daringer, Ohio 43210

Dear Manager:

Recently I purchased a dress at your shop when I was attending a meeting in Daringer. I did not open the box until I returned to Dallas. Then I discovered that the dress had a flaw in the material in the back of the skirt. The flaw is noticeable and makes the dress virtually unwearable. I bought the dress very hurriedly and did not notice the problem when I tried it on in the store. There was no damage to the box in transit, so I presume the dress must have been in that condition when I bought it. I am sure that you will agree with me that the dress is not wearable, and I hope that you will be willing to return my money.

I have never bought anything from your store before, but it was highly recommended by a friend who lives in Daringer. I hope that you will be able to refund my money when the dress arrives.

Thank you for your kindness in this matter.

Sincerely,

Notice that this writer forestalls the manager's argument that the dress might have been damaged after it left the store, and also appeals to the manager's integrity in standing behind the good reputation of the store within its community. This writer has been very sensitive to the reader's reactions to her request.

Another example of writing to the hostile and unbelieving audience—in this case a less identifiable one—is an excerpt from Charles Darwin's *The Descent of Man*, written over a hundred years ago, when the idea that humans are descended from apes was a new and startling discovery, one most of his readers found unpleasant and unacceptable. Darwin fully expected disbelief and criticism from his audience. How does he forestall those reactions in the following passage?

The main conclusion arrived at in this work, namely, that man is descended from some lowly-organized form, will, I regret to think be highly distasteful to many persons. But there can hardly be a doubt that we are descended from barbarians. The astonishment which I felt on first seeing a party of Fuegians on a wild and broken shore will never be forgotten by me, for the reflection at once rushed into my mind—such were our ancestors. These men were absolutely naked and bedaubed with paint, their long hair was tangled, their mouths frothed in excitement, and their expression was wild, startled, and distrustful. They possessed hardly any arts, and, like wild animals, lived on what they could catch; they had no government, and were merciless to everyone not of their own small tribe. He who has seen a savage in his native land will not feel much shame, if forced to acknowledge that the blood of some more humble creature flows in his veins. For my own part, I would as soon be descended from that heroic little monkey, who braved his dreaded enemy in order to save the life of his keeper; or from that old baboon who, descending from the mountains, carried away in triumph his young comrade from a crowd of astonished dogs—as from a savage who delights to torture his enemies, offers up bloody sacrifices, practices infanticide without remorse, treats his wives like slaves, knows no decency, and is haunted by the grossest superstitions.

Man may be excused for feeling some pride at having risen, though not through his own exertions, to the very summit of the organic scale; and the fact of his having thus risen, instead of having been aboriginally placed there, may give him hopes for a still higher destiny in the distant future. But we are not here concerned with hopes or fears, only with the truth as far as our reason allows us to discover it. I have given the evidence to the best of my ability; and we must acknowledge, as it seems to me, that man with all his noble qualities, with sympathy which feels for the most debased, with benevolence which extends not only to other men but to the humblest living creature, with his godlike intellect which has penetrated into the movements and constitution of the solar system—with all these exalted powers—man still bears in his bodily frame the indelible stamp of his lowly origin.

In this preface, Darwin anticipates the objections that his readers will have to his proposition that humans are descended from apes. He attempts to answer those objections in several ways. First he reminds his readers that it is a commonly accepted fact that humans are descended from barbarians and then asserts that he has more respect for animals— "that heroic little monkey"—than he has for savages. He concludes, therefore, that he would just as soon have animals as his ancestors as he would murderous, unkempt savages. Finally, he praises the accomplishments of the human race while restating his unpopular thesis for which, he asserts, he has given the evidence.

In the same way, you may try to foresee the objections that a hostile audience will have to the ideas in your paper and attempt to acknowledge and answer them in the same way that these writers have done. Test your readers' possible reactions by asking yourself the following questions:

What are the points of disagreement?

How have I acknowledged them and tried to address them?

What are our areas of agreement?

How can I build on them?

The Multiple Audience The general or unknown audience is certainly a multiple audience, but often writing will be directed to two or three specific audiences whose individual special interests are well-known. For example, you may be writing a proposal for the president of a company, but you must also address the interests and concerns of a number of other audiences. The financial vice-president will be concerned with its economic feasibility; the chief engineer with its technical aspects. You may send a letter of application to the personnel manager, but it will also be read by the head of the department to which you are applying, and probably by other persons concerned with your possible employment. A letter to the editor is ostensibly addressed to the editor of the newspaper, but the audience consists of the readers of the paper. A job-performance evaluation may be addressed to a particular employee, but it will probably be read by his or her supervisors. Just because a letter or a report or a proposal is addressed to only one person, that is no guarantee that only one person will read it. You need to be aware of these multiple audiences and learn to respond to a multiplicity of interests and concerns. Consider these questions as you write:

Who will read this essay, report, letter, application?

What kinds of questions and needs can I assume these readers will have?

Are there conflicts among these interests and if so, how can I address or resolve such conflicts?

The Instructor Audience You are dealing with a very special audience when writing for an instructor. In writing to a newspaper or to a friend, you probably write to inform or to persuade or to amuse. When applying for a job, you write a letter to inform a possible employer of your credentials and to persuade him or her of their worth, thereby furnishing the employer with information he or she does not already have. When you write a paper on the Civil War for a history professor, however, you know that your professor knows more than you now know about the Civil

War. You are not writing to inform the instructor about the war; your purpose is to demonstrate your knowledge about the war. This important fact affects your writing and you should shape your essay accordingly: you need to include dates, important events, and key terms. (See Chapter 14 which covers the essay exam.)

Similarly, when writing for your writing instructor, you are not simply giving the instructor information on a subject, rather you are demonstrating your ability to formulate ideas, synthesize and organize material, write clearly and coherently, and handle the conventions of edited American English. Keep in mind the following questions as you write:

> How can I demonstrate that I know the material well enough to synthesize it and to interpret it in order to apply it to special cases, and to extend it to new ones?

> Have I demonstrated such mastery by clear definitions, use of key terms including important factual matter, and presentation of the subject in a clear and coherent manner?

Shaping an Audience

Occasionally, it is possible to shape or at least direct an audience by announcing forthrightly certain expectations you have of them as readers. You may also ask them indirectly to laugh or to cry or just to consider your words very carefully. Sometimes readers can be told directly the role that they are expected to play. In an appeal for funds, the following writer requests the reader to assume a listening stance:

> I know that you receive numerous requests for donations to worthy causes. I am asking you, nevertheless, at least to read through this letter and seriously consider the following unusual circumstances.

In the preface to the 1973 edition of *Coming of Age in Samoa*, anthropologist Margaret Mead reminds her audience that they must read the book in the context in which it was written almost fifty years before.

> It seems more than ever necessary to stress, shout as loud as I can, this is about the Samoa and the United States of 1926–1928. When you read it, remember this. Do not confuse yourselves and the Samoan people by expecting to find life in the Manuan Islands of American Samoa as I found it. Remember that it is your grandparents and great-grandparents I am writing about when they were young and carefree in Samoa or plagued by our expectations from adolescents in the United States.

Readers usually respond willingly when they are asked to assume a certain role. Through a sort of cooperative principle, they are willing to play by the rules that the writer sets out for them particularly if the author has established goodwill toward them. They are pretty good-natured about being ready to laugh or cry or "seriously consider"—they usually want to become the readers that the writer tells them to become—but it is up to the writer to make the reader's role quite clear. When you expect your readers to play a certain role, consider the following questions as you write:

What role do I wish the reader to play?

How have I made that role clear to the reader?

How can I make clear how I wish the reader to respond and react?

Before you begin to write, try to find out as much as you can about your audience. Build their confidence and trust by establishing your *ethos* and speak to those readers as if they were sitting on the other side of your desk, as Virginia Woolf does in the following essay. First delivered orally to the Women's Service League, the address was written ahead of time and later widely anthologized. In it Woolf addresses not only the immediate audience to whom she was speaking but also a readership that has transcended the particular time and place.

Woolf was a well-known writer at the time of this address and was well aware that her words would be distributed in print. How does she move from her own "story" to the experience of her immediate audience and then to the larger audience that she knew she was addressing?

PROFESSIONS FOR WOMEN

VIRGINIA WOOLF

When your secretary invited me to come here, she told me that your 1
Society is concerned with the employment of women and she suggested that I might tell you something about my own professional experiences. It is true I am a woman; it is true I am employed; but what professional experiences have I had? It is difficult to say. My profession is literature; and in that profession there are fewer experiences for women than in any other, with the exception of the stage—fewer, I mean, that are peculiar to women. For the road was cut many years ago—by Fanny Burney, by Aphra Behn, by Harriet Martineau, by Jane Austen, by George Eliot—

many famous women, and many more unknown and forgotten, have been before me, making the path smooth, and regulating my steps. Thus, when I came to write, there were very few material obstacles in my way. Writing was a reputable and harmless occupation. The family peace was not broken by the scratching of a pen. No demand was made upon the family purse. For ten and sixpence one can buy paper enough to write all the plays of Shakespeare—if one has a mind that way. Pianos and models, Paris, Vienna and Berlin, masters and mistresses, are not needed by a writer. The cheapness of writing paper is, of course, the reason why women have succeeded as writers before they have succeeded in the other professions.

But to tell you my story—it is a simple one. You have only got to figure 2 to yourselves a girl in a bedroom with a pen in her hand. She had only to move that pen from left to right—from ten o'clock to one. Then it occurred to her to do what is simple and cheap enough after all—to slip a few of those pages into an envelope, fix a penny stamp in the corner, and drop the envelope into the red box at the corner. It was thus that I became a journalist; and my effort was rewarded on the first day of the following month—a very glorious day it was for me—by a letter from an editor containing a cheque for one pound ten shillings and sixpence. But to show you how little I deserve to be called a professional woman, how little I know of the struggles and difficulties of such lives, I have to admit that instead of spending that sum upon bread and butter, rent, shoes and stockings, or butcher's bills, I went out and bought a cat—a beautiful cat, a Persian cat, which very soon involved me in bitter disputes with my neighbours.

What could be easier than to write articles and to buy Persian cats with 3 the profits? But wait a moment. Articles have to be about something. Mine, I seem to remember, was about a novel by a famous man. And while I was writing this review, I discovered that if I were going to review books I should need to do battle with a certain phantom. And the phantom was a woman, and when I came to know her better I called her after the heroine of a famous poem, The Angel in the House. It was she who used to come between me and my paper when I was writing reviews. It was she who bothered me and wasted my time and so tormented me that at last I killed her. You who come of a younger and happier generation may not have heard of her—you may not know what I mean by the Angel in the House. I will describe her as shortly as I can. She was intensely sympathetic. She was immensely charming. She was utterly unselfish. She excelled in the difficult arts of family life. She sacrificed herself daily. If there was chicken, she took the leg; if there was a draught she sat in it—in short she was so constituted that she never had a mind or a wish of her own, but preferred to sympathize always with the minds and wishes of others. Above all—I need not say it—she was pure. Her purity was supposed to be her chief beauty—her blushes, her great grace. In those days—the last of Queen Victoria—every house had its Angel. And when I came to write I encountered her with the very first words. The shadow of her wings fell on my page; I heard the rustling of her skirts in the room. Directly, that is to say, I took my pen in hand to review that novel by a famous man, she slipped behind me and whispered: "My dear, you are a young woman. You are writing about a book that has been written by a man. Be sympathetic; be tender; flatter; deceive; use all the arts and wiles of our sex. Never let anybody guess that you have a mind of your own. Above all, be pure." And she made as if to guide my pen. I now record the one act for which I take some credit to myself, though the credit rightly belongs to some excellent ancestors of mine who left me a certain sum of money—shall we say five hundred pounds a year?—so that it was not necessary for me to depend solely on charm for my living. I turned upon her and caught her by the throat. I did my best to kill her. My excuse, if I were to be had up in a court of law, would be that I acted in self-defence. Had I not killed her she would have killed me. She would have plucked the heart out of my writing. For, as I found, directly I put pen to paper, you cannot review even a novel without having a mind of your own, without expressing what you think to be the truth about human relations, morality, sex. And all these questions, according to the Angel in the House, cannot be dealt with freely and openly by women; they must charm, they must conciliate, they must—to put it bluntly—tell lies if they are to succeed. Thus, whenever I felt the shadow of her wing or the radiance of her halo upon my page, I took up the inkpot and flung it at her. She died hard. Her fictitious nature was of great assistance to her. It is far harder to kill a phantom than a reality. She was always creeping back when I thought I had despatched her. Though I flatter myself that I killed her in the end, the struggle was severe; it took much time that had better have been spent upon learning Greek grammar; or in roaming the world in search of adventures. But it was a real experience; it was an experience that was bound to befall all women writers at that time. Killing the Angel in the House was part of the occupation of a woman writer.

But to continue my story. The Angel was dead; what then remained? 4 You may say that what remained was a simple and common object—a young woman in a bedroom with an inkpot. In other words, now that she had rid herself of falsehood, that young woman had only to be herself. Ah, but what is "herself"? I mean, what is a woman? I assure you, I do not know. I do not believe that you know. I do not believe that anybody can know until she has expressed herself in all the arts and professions open to human skill. That indeed is one of the reasons why I have come here— out of respect for you, who are in process of showing us by your experiments what a woman is, who are in process of providing us, by your failures and successes, with that extremely important piece of information.

But to continue the story of my professional experiences. I made one 5
pound ten and six by my first review; and I bought a Persian cat with the
proceeds. Then I grew ambitious. A Persian cat is all very well, I said; but
a Persian cat is not enough. I must have a motor car. And it was thus that I
became a novelist—for it is a very strange thing that people will give you
a motor car if you will tell them a story. It is a still stranger thing that
there is nothing so delightful in the world as telling stories. It is far
pleasanter than writing reviews of famous novels. And yet, if I am to obey
your secretary and tell you my professional experiences as a novelist, I
must tell you about a very strange experience that befell me as a novelist.
And to understand it you must try to imagine a novelist's state of mind. I
hope I am not giving away professional secrets if I say that a novelist's
chief desire is to be as unconscious as possible. He has to induce in
himself a state of perpetual lethargy. He wants life to proceed with the
utmost quiet and regularity. He wants to see the same faces, to read the
same books, to do the same things day after day, month after month,
while he is writing, so that nothing may break the illusion in which he is
living—so that nothing may disturb or disquiet the mysterious nosings
about, feelings round, darts, dashes and sudden discoveries of that very
shy and illusive spirit, the imagination. I suspect that this state is the same
both for men and women. Be that as it may, I want you to imagine me
writing a novel in a state of trance. I want you to figure to yourselves a girl
sitting with a pen in her hand, which for minutes, and indeed for hours,
she never dips into the inkpot. The image that comes to my mind when I
think of this girl is the image of a fisherman lying sunk in dreams on the
verge of a deep lake with a rod held out over the water. She was letting
her imagination sweep unchecked round every rock and cranny of the
world that lies submerged in the depths of our unconscious being. Now
came the experience, the experience that I believe to be far commoner
with women writers than with men. The line raced through the girl's
fingers. Her imagination had rushed away. It had sought the pools, the
depths, the dark places where the largest fish slumber. And then there
was a smash. There was an explosion. There was foam and confusion. The
imagination had dashed itself against something hard. The girl was
roused from her dream. She was indeed in a state of the most acute and
difficult distress. To speak without figure she had thought of something,
something about the body, about the passions which it was unfitting for
her as a woman to say. Men, her reason told her, would be shocked. The
consciousness of what men will say of a woman who speaks the truth
about her passions had roused her from her artist's state of unconscious-
ness. She could write no more. The trance was over. Her imagination
could work no longer. This I believe to be a very common experience with

women writers—they are impeded by the extreme conventionality of the other sex. For though men sensibly allow themselves great freedom in these respects, I doubt that they realize or can control the extreme severity with which they condemn such freedom in women.

These then were two very genuine experiences of my own. These were 6 two of the adventures of my professional life. The first—killing the Angel in the House—I think I solved. She died. But the second, telling the truth about my own experiences as a body, I do not think I solved. I doubt that any woman has solved it yet. The obstacles against her are still immensely powerful—and yet they are very difficult to define. Outwardly, what is simpler than to write books? Outwardly, what obstacles are there for a woman rather than for a man? Inwardly, I think, the case is very different; she has still many ghosts to fight, many prejudices to overcome. Indeed it will be a long time still, I think, before a woman can sit down to write a book without finding a phantom to be slain, a rock to be dashed against. And if this is so in literature, the freest of all professions for women, how is it in the new professions which you are now for the first time entering?

Those are the questions that I should like, had I time, to ask you. And 7 indeed, if I have laid stress upon these professional experiences of mine, it is because I believe that they are, though in different forms, yours also. Even when the path is nominally open—when there is nothing to prevent a woman from being a doctor, a lawyer, a civil servant—there are many phantoms and obstacles, as I believe, looming in her way. To discuss and define them is I think of great value and importance; for thus only can the labour be shared, the difficulties be solved. But besides this, it is necessary also to discuss the ends and the aims for which we are fighting, for which we are doing battle with these formidable obstacles. Those aims cannot be taken for granted; they must be perpetually questioned and examined. The whole position, as I see it—here in this hall sur- rounded by women practising for the first time in history I know not how many different professions—is one of extraordinary interest and impor- tance. You have won rooms of your own in the house hitherto exclusively owned by men. You are able, though not without great labour and effort, to pay the rent. You are earning your five hundred pounds a year. But this freedom is only a beginning; the room is your own, but it is still bare. It has to be furnished; it has to be decorated; it has to be shared. How are you going to furnish it, how are you going to decorate it? With whom are you going to share it, and upon what terms? These, I think are questions of the utmost importance and interest. For the first time in history you are able to ask them; for the first time you are able to decide for yourselves what the answers should be. Willingly would I stay and discuss those questions and answers—but not tonight. My time is up; and I must cease.

Although a famous writer at the time of this address, Woolf acknowledges the help of those women writers who had come before her and made her way easier. She also modestly admits, somewhat ironically, that writing is an easier profession for women because the family peace is undisturbed and writing materials are cheap. She then moves to her "simple story." Her introduction is disarming, and she establishes her goodwill with the audience by her unassuming approach. Woolf begins by telling "her story," and it is not until she mentions the "Angel in the House" that one begins to see how this story concerns every woman who tries to enter traditionally male professions. She enlarges the scope of her concern by connecting her position as a writer to other women in other professions:

> Outwardly, what is simpler than to write books? Outwardly, what obstacles are there for a woman rather than for a man? Inwardly, I think, the case is very different; she has still many ghosts to fight, many prejudices to overcome. Indeed it will be a long time still, I think, before a woman can sit down to write a book without finding a phantom to be slain, a rock to be dashed against. And if this is so in literature, the freest of all professions for women, how is it in the new professions which you are now for the first time entering?

In the last paragraph, she relates her experiences as a writer to those of her audience and then to all professional women. ". . . if I have laid stress upon these professional experiences of mine, it is because I believe that they are, though in different forms, yours also." Her words continue to speak eloquently to all women.

Questions to Consider

1. Make a list of all the similarities you can think of between the activities of speaking and writing; then list the differences. (Some have already been mentioned in this chapter.) Discuss how those similarities and differences can affect your writing.

2. Discuss your impression of the writer's *ethos* conveyed by the appearance of the following paragraph. How and to what extent does that impression interfere with your acceptance of the writer's point? What does this exercise suggest about the value of editing and proofreading your written work carefully?

Their are a number of resons that I fell my final grade in compostion should be changed from a D to a C. First, on my out of class writting asisgnments, I recieved the folowing grads: D−, D, D, C, C−, D+, C, C+. These grades average out to a B and show you my steady progress in the coarse. Secondly, on my in-class writing asignments, I recieved a D, a C−, and a C+. This also shows my progress in the coarse. finally, my mideterm and fianl exam grades also a C. As a result, I believe I desreve as a final grade a C and not a D.

3. For each of the following paragraphs, first describe what impression the writer conveys of his or her intelligence, virtue, and goodwill and how that impression is conveyed; then identify how that writer appears to perceive his or her audience. Support your assertions with evidence from the texts.

a. Looking back at my social life over the past ten years, I can safely say that I've dated my fair share of nerds. But I'm beginning to believe that there's something to be said for the man who's not the least bit concerned about what's in, what's hot, and what's not. I wouldn't mind meeting someone now who doesn't feel compelled to jog, can function without being wired to a Walkman, and never uses the words "sushi" and "bar" in the same sentence. Yes, for just the sheer novelty of it, I'd like to meet a man unenthused about personal computers, complex carbohydrates, or Trivial Pursuit. In short, someone who is decidedly un-hip.

b. Let me describe the actual process of how to get rich. In the first place, you will have a much easier time if you know something valuable before you set off. A good grasp of investment banking (more precisely, the "deal business") would suffice, or a degree in engineering plus a few years operating in a manufac- turing company, or field and money-raising experience in oil or hard-rock geology, or a thorough knowledge of some aspect of finance, such as consumer credit or leasing, or of a consumer business, such as bottling or mail order sales. You must have a business sense and entrepreneurial flair. Ask a seasoned friend how he sizes you up. You also need six months' or a year's eating money, preferably borrowed from older family members.

c. I think the observable reluctance of the majority of Americans to assert themselves in minor matters is related to our increased sense of helplessness in an age of technology and centralized political and economic power. For generations, Americans who were too hot, or too cold, got up and did something about it. Now we call the plumber, or the electrician, or the furnace man. The habit of looking after our own needs obviously had something to do with the assertiveness that characterized the American family familiar to readers of American literature. With the technifica- tion of life goes our direct responsibility for our material en- vironment, and we are conditioned to adopt a position of help- lessness not only as regards the broken air conditioner, but as regards the overheated train. It takes an expert to fix the former, but not the latter; yet these distinctions, as we withdraw into helplessness, tend to fade away.

4. Before you can appeal to your readers emotionally, you need to know who they are and how they may respond to your message. Imagine yourself writing a letter in one of the following hypothetical situations and characterize the audience as friendly, professional/technical, hostile, or general. Then consider what strategies you might incorporate to make the audience receptive to your message.

A. You are writing a letter to your parents asking them to send you $100 for some purpose of your own choosing.

B. You are writing to Brent Mussberger, your fifth cousin twice removed, to get for you two tickets to the Superbowl.

C. You are writing a letter to a company complaining about one of their products and demanding they take some action.

D. You are writing a letter trying to convince a prospective employer to hire you for what you consider to be your ideal job.

E. You are writing a "Dear John" or "Dear Jane" letter.

F. You are writing a letter to the editor of your hometown newspaper about the choice of columnists run in the Sunday edition.

Suggestions for Writing

1. Write one of the letters proposed in exercise 4 above, carefully presenting your "case" in accordance with your perception of your audience, your purpose, and the character or *ethos* you want to promote.

2. Choose an article from a magazine you read regularly and analyze it to determine what image the writer creates of his or her intelligence, virtue, or goodwill. Then write a paragraph identifying and supporting your conclusions.

3. Examine the same article again, but this time analyze it to determine the writer's perception of his or her audience. (The publication in which the article appears may afford some clue.) Then write a paragraph identifying and supporting your conclusions.

4. Advertisements frequently make use of popular, well-known personalities to endorse a particular cause or product. Why? Choose one of these advertisements and consider what character traits the spokesperson represents and how such traits may help him or her to sell the product. Write a page or two summarizing your conclusions.

5. Compare an article in a popular magazine to one in an academic journal. In a short paper, compare the different audiences and the different *ethos* projected by the authors.

Exercises in Revision

1. Write a page or two in which you try to persuade a close friend or relative to buy something from you that you currently own. Then rewrite it and try to sell that article to a complete stranger. Consider how and why the two versions differ and write a page summarizing your conclusions.

2. Analyze the writing submitted by members of your workshop in response to the assignments suggested above, considering the following questions:

A. What impression does the writer convey of his or her intelligence, virtue, and goodwill? How or by what means is that impression conveyed?

B. How does the writer appear to perceive his or her audience? How is that perception conveyed?

C. Is the writer's *ethos* and *pathos* appropriate for his or her subject, purpose, and audience? Why, or why not?

For a Commonplace Book

1. Review the description of the commonplace book in Chapter 1 and write a page or two about how you expect to use it.

2. As a short exercise to demonstrate how you alter your language in accordance with your relationship with your audience, indicate in writing how you would customarily tell a person to stop annoying you if that person were a parent, a stranger, a roommate, your best friend, a child, your son or daughter, or a teacher. Then write a page in which you account for the different ways you would express that message.

Chapter 4

Discovering Ideas: Definition and Classification

Lines of argument that could be effectively used in persuasion were called *topoi* (TO-poy) or "topics" and are more familiar to us as the strategies of definition, classification, comparison, and cause and effect. Note that in classical rhetoric "argument" is not used in the modern sense of disagreement—having an argument—but as a method of proof or a strategy for persuasion.

The ancient rhetoricians knew a great deal about how the mind worked merely from their study of language. They knew that to explain an elephant to someone unfamiliar with the animal, it helps first to put it into a class such as "animal" and then explore similarities—"with four legs and a tail like a dog"—and differences—"but larger with a long nose called a trunk." They recognized these types of explanation as regular processes of thinking and speaking and concluded that they would be even more useful if each one were assigned to a particular "place" in the memory. These would be places where an orator could go to find ideas— a sort of rhetorical file cabinet for such things as definition, classification, comparison—useful starting places for arguments on any subject. The Greeks called them *koinoi topoi* (KOY-noy TO-poy), common places. English rhetoricians called them topics, and modern composition textbooks often refer to them as strategies or rhetorical modes. With some additions, deletions, and rearrangements, this system of classical topics is presented in the next two chapters as a method of invention in writing. The strategies may be regarded as ways of inquiring into a subject or arguing a position.

Although these strategies will be discussed and practiced one at a time, they are seldom used in isolation. In an extended definition, the writer may well compare and contrast ideas, and use cause and effect to clarify ideas. And certain words may have to be defined within an extended classification. The writing exercises at the end of the chapters will call for definition or comparison or classification because they are just that— exercises. You must learn to play the scales on the piano before you can play a sonata, to dribble the ball before you can play basketball. So you practice with definition exercises or comparison exercises before you try to write the paper that gracefully combines all of the strategies.

DEFINITION

Definition comes from the Latin word *definere* (day-FEN-uh-ray) meaning "to set bounds to." Thus when we define a term, we are marking the limits of its meaning; we are building a fence to mark the border between what it means and what it does not mean. Definition can be an effective strategy for persuading a reader or proving a point. For example, if an exam is defined as diagnostic rather than qualifying, an argument can be made for allowing a student who takes such an exam to have entrance into a particular program where a so-called qualifying exam might bar his or her entrance.

A definition may be one sentence, one paragraph, an article, or a book, depending on the approach and the nature of what is being defined. Definitions are seldom straightforward and may even be persuasive in transmitting the writer's perspective. Some terms are almost impossible to define without some "viewpoint." Try defining feminism, liberalism, or democracy without injecting your own opinions. Legal judgments have depended on definitions of such terms as equal opportunity, spouse, and minority. One company that had employed only men for a number of years defined benefits in terms of "the wife." The husband of one of the first women employees sued for medical benefits, and the judge ruled in his favor saying that in this case the term "wife" had to be defined as spouse. And the complex questions surrounding abortion and euthanasia depend largely on the legal and medical definitions of life and death.

Defining a concept or an object is one of the most basic language or thought processes. Exploring a definition helps us to think and rethink an idea as we work through the thinking and writing process. The person who cannot define a concept probably does not understand it. That is why definitions are so often an important part of examinations; they test your knowledge and understanding of that knowledge. The kind of definition most commonly called for on an examination is what Aristotle named the "essential definition."

The Essential Definition

This most basic definition is often called the one-sentence definition because it can logically be contained in a single sentence. You may already know it by that name. It is composed of three parts:

1. the term to be defined

2. the class

3. the difference between the term and other members of the class.

Classical rhetoricians called these parts the *definiendum* (day-fi-nee-EN-dum) or term, the *genus* (JE-nus) or class, and the *differentia* (di-fe-REN-shee-a) or differences. A typical definition might be:

A mammal is an animal that nourishes its young with milk secreted from mammary glands.

1. mammal = term

2. animal = class

3. that nourishes its young with milk secreted from mammary glands = difference

In this definition, a mammal is put in the class of animals and then differentiated from other members of that class—from other animals. This difference defines, limits, and sets the boundary for the meaning of the word *mammal*.

In the essential definition, the connecting verb between the term and the class is usually a form of *to be*, indicating that the term is the same as or equal to the class plus the difference. The definition can be thought of as a mathematical equation, where the term is A, the class is B, and the difference is C.

$$\text{Term} = \text{class} + \text{difference}$$

$$A = \quad B + C$$

Most definitions require more than one difference to set the term off from other members of its class. Take the example of the beagle.

Term   = Class   +   Differences

A beagle is a dog that is small.
　　　　　　　　　　　short haired.
　　　　　　　　　　　white with large black or brown spots.
　　　　　　　　　　　used for hunting.

These differences still do not define the beagle as separate from any other hunting dog, say the bassett; such a difference must be pointed out. This may be done in two ways. You may say that the beagle is very much like the bassett except that it is smaller. Or you may define the beagle by saying what it is and by adding, "but it is not a bassett," if your reader is familiar with a bassett. In making ideas clear to the reader, it is always important to be aware and to stay within the reader's knowledge and experience in defining new terms.

Note that the larger the class, the more members it contains and therefore the more members from which the term must be differentiated. So if beagle had been put into the class of animal, it would have had to be differentiated from all other animals rather than only from all other dogs. The definition of beagle could be made simpler by putting it into an even smaller class such as hound dog or hunting dog. Thus if hound dog were used, the difference of short hair would not have to be used since all hound dogs have short hair.

Term   = Class   +   Differences

A beagle is a hound dog that is small.
　　　　　　　　　　　~~short haired.~~
　　　　　　　　　　　white with large black or brown spots.
　　　　　　　　　　　used for hunting.

Similarly, if beagle is put into the even smaller class of hunting dogs, another difference can be eliminated.

Term   = Class   +   Differences

A beagle is a hunting dog that is small.
~~short haired~~.
white with large black or brown spots.
~~used for hunting~~.

When a term is put in the class of "things" as in "A bed is a thing used for . . . ," a bed must be distinguished from all other "things" in the world. The smaller the class in which the defining term is placed, the easier it is to differentiate it.

There are several ways in which a term can differ from other terms in its class. Differences between an object or concept and other members in its class can be made on the basis of:

1. its form

2. its function

3. its properties

4. its causes or its effects

So in the following definition:

A chair used for seating for one person is a piece of furniture with four legs and a back.

In this definition, the term is put in the class of furniture and then differentiated on the basis of its form and its function.

Term = Class   +   Differences

Chair   furniture   four legs and back (form)
                    used for seating (function)

Note that a chair is differentiated from other pieces of furniture such as a stool by its form (having a back), and such as a bed by its function (used for seating). A beagle is differentiated by its coloring and short hair—its properties—and a tornado could well be differentiated from other storms by the kind of atmospheric conditions that *caused* it and its devastating *effects*. Not all of these differences (form, function, properties, cause and effect) will apply in all cases, but they furnish a quick review of the possibilities.

The essential definition is central to our way of understanding meaning and our way of knowing. It can also frame our way of writing about a subject and explaining meaning to a reader.

Checking the Validity of a Definition

There are a number of ways that definitions can go wrong. What follows is a list for checking the validity of your own and other people's definitions. Ask yourself as you write:

1. Is my definition so narrow that it leaves out concepts that properly belong within the term?

If you define a storm as a "weather phenomenon characterized by high wind," you exclude electrical storms that may have little or no wind involved in them. This definition narrows the term *storm* so that it includes only storms accompanied by high wind.

2. Is my definition so broad that it includes concepts that do not properly belong in the term?

The definition "a frog is a small animal that is tailless and moves by hopping," would include not only frogs but also a number of other small animals like grasshoppers and toads that hop and have no tails. Adding that the frog is smooth-skinned and largely aquatic would exclude toads and grasshoppers and clear up the problem in this definition.

3. Is the definition circular in that the term is defined by using the same or similar words?

The following definition is not helpful: "Denticulate means minutely dentate." A reader who is seeking the meaning of *denticulate* would probably not know the meaning of *dentate*. A more understandable definition would be "characterized as having small tooth like projections as in a denticulated leaf."

4. Is the definition expressed in words that are clearly understood by the audience?

Defining an elephant to a young child as a mammal would hardly be helpful, or defining a beagle as a hound dog would not be informative to a person who does not know what a hound dog is. It is essential to keep the reader's realm of knowledge and experience in mind when forming your definition. You might wish to review some of the special audiences outlined in Chapter 3 and consider how definitions might differ for these audiences.

5. Does the definition contain emotional language?

Such a definition as, "a frog is a disgusting creature," tells the reader a great deal about your feelings, but not much about frogs. Someone unfamiliar with frogs would know much more about them after reading the following definition.

A frog is a chiefly aquatic creature with a smooth, moist skin, webbed feet for swimming, and long hind legs for leaping.

When to Define

Your awareness of your readers will determine what terms need to be defined. Keep in mind the specialized audiences outlined in Chapter 3. As a general guide, two categories of terms may need definition: specialized terms and emotionally loaded words.

1. Specialized Terms: New or highly technical terminology should be defined for the general reader, but the need for such definitions when addressing a more specific audience is determined by the audience. If you are sure the reader knows the terminology, such definitions are unnecessary. So for a livestock farmer, the terms *steer* and *heifer* do not have to be defined, but for the general reader, they might have to be explained.

Such definitions can often be inserted between commas, immediately after the word, as in this example.

The steers, the castrated male cattle, sold on the market for about $10.00 per 100 pounds more than the heifers, the young females.

2. Loaded Words: A definition is also needed for a term loaded with emotional overtones. Words often have two kinds of meaning: *denotative*, the *explicit* meaning of a word, and *connotative*, the *implicit* meaning. The prefix *de* means "from"; the prefix *con* means "with." So *de* indicates the meanings that come "from" the term itself; *con* indicates the meanings associated "with" the term.

For instance, the word *pig* is defined denotatively by the *American Heritage Dictionary* as "any of several mammals of the family Suidae, having short legs, cloven hoofs, bristly hair, and a cartilaginous snout used for digging," but its connotative meaning of dirty, obese, and gross is well known. Similarly, "home" and "apple pie" have positive connotative meanings associated with them quite aside from their denotative meanings.

A word is a symbol that denotes or indicates something. When I say or write the word *chair*, I can point to the piece of furniture that *chair* stands for, but I can also describe the emotions that the words *love* and *jealousy* stand for. We know that words have connotative meanings that cling to them like lipstick on a glass rim, and we must take these into account when defining words or describing meanings.

For example, the *American Heritage Dictionary* gives the following definition for *cult*:

> A system of religious worship and ritual, especially one focusing upon a single deity or spirit.

This meaning appears to differ very little from that of *religion*: "an integrated system of the expression of man's belief in a superhuman power" and, in fact, the definition of "cult" uses the word *religious*. Nevertheless many people feel that cults are "bad" while religions are "good." Thus, the word *cult* denotes much the same thing that *religion* denotes, but the connotations are vastly different. So also being *persistent* is generally considered good, but being *stubborn* is seen in a negative light, although both refer to tenacity in pursuing a goal. Being *assertive* is good, but being *aggressive* is not. Denotations are more likely to be dictionary definitions, while connotations reflect a culture's attitudes. Dictionary definitions may occasionally suggest connotations, but ordinarily we learn connotations through reading and knowing the culture.

The terms *communism, democracy*, and *socialism*, call up strong feelings—both negative and positive. If these words are to be used in any kind of clear way, they need to be defined and possibly delineated from the common meaning as well. For example, here is a paragraph in which the author states which definition of *communism* she is using.

> By communism, I do not mean the Marxist-Leninist doctrine espoused by the Soviet Union, but that form of communism characterized by the absence of classes and by common ownership of the means of production and subsistence.

The author needs to explain such a definition in order to dispel connotations as much as possible and to call up a more fundamental meaning than the one understood by most people.

3. Stipulative Definition: Words often have two or more definitions. For example, the *American Heritage Dictionary* gives four current meanings for the word *religion*. (The examples are my own.)

1. The expression of man's belief in and reverence for a superhuman power recognized as the creator and governor of the universe:

   The religions of the world have many things in common.

2. Any particular integrated system of this expression:

   She belongs to the Presbyterian religion.

3. The spiritual or emotional attitude of one who recognizes the existence of a superhuman power or powers:

   Their religion obliges them to donate their money to the poor.

4. Any objective attended to or pursued with zeal or conscientiousness:

   Making money is their religion.

These four definitions are closely related in meaning but also significantly different. For example, I might describe John's religion as a system, i.e., Presbyterian (meaning #2), or I might describe John's religion as his spiritual or emotional attitudes (meaning #3). These would be quite different. In a long paper, there is the danger of using the word *religion* with both meanings. Therefore, with a term that has a number of meanings, you must stipulate the particular meaning that you are using.

In this study, I use the word *religion* to mean a particular system integrating belief in and reverence for a superhuman power.

With this definition stipulated near the beginning of the paper, the reader will not be confused about the meaning of the word. Thus, when you make a statement about "the religions in the United States," your reader knows that you mean religious systems such as Presbyterianism or Catholicism.

Stipulative definitions must be within the realm of the ordinary meanings listed in the dictionary and commonly accepted by your reader. The following definition, for example, would not be workable because it is not a meaning that the ordinary reader would accept:

By religion I mean a set of superstitious practices and beliefs.

Extending a Definition

Sometimes a definition can follow all the rules for correctness yet still be unclear. It is often difficult for the reader to absorb a short definition, especially when it is highly specialized. Consequently, the writer may choose a number of ways to extend the definition to make it more understandable for the reader, staying aware of the audience—their knowledge and their prejudices—as the following discussion will demonstrate. A long example or several shorter ones may follow an essential definition. You may develop a full essay by extending a definition in one or all of the following ways.

With Example Nine out of ten people when asked to define *euphemism* will do it as follows:

A euphemism is when you say "passed away" for "died."

Definitions that use "is when," although generally unacceptable in formal writing, are usually ones that employ examples. It is very helpful to clarify definitions by examples, but such definitions are in no way complete or truly informative. Such a definition for "euphemism" would serve to remind the person who had only temporarily forgotten what a euphemism is, but for the person who had never heard of a euphemism, the definition would fail. A better definition would be:

A euphemism is the substitution of an agreeable word or phrase for one that is unpleasant.

Notice that the second definition, although logically correct, is still in the realm of the abstract. For a person who does not know what a euphemism is, the second definition may be as confusing as the first. An example would clarify the issue.

A euphemism is the substitution of a pleasant word or phrase for one that is disagreeable; for example, in the use of "passed away" for "died."

The definition now becomes clear. In writing, examples are an excellent way of clarifying a difficult concept. Your instructor may often specify on an exam that you use examples to clarify your definitions, as in this instruction:

Define the term *dialect*. Make your definition clear by at least two examples.

This is the instructor's way of determining whether you are just parroting memorized words and phrases or whether you really understand the concept. In a paper, a definition with an example may be only a sentence, as in the definition of euphemism, or it may be extended to a paragraph or an entire paper.

Note how in the following paragraph the definition of justice depends on several well-chosen examples:

> Justice is a condition where all persons, no matter who they are, are treated equally. Justice is a fair trial for all. It is not a multi-millionaire hiring a team of defense lawyers to tie up the court with their appeals while the person on welfare cannot afford to feed his or her family much less hire a lawyer to appeal the sentence. Justice is knowing who you are will not affect the job you get. Justice is not women receiving less pay than men or blacks receiving no jobs at all. Justice is honesty in the people you have to trust. It is not fearing that all judges are on the take or all politicians are dishonest. Justice is knowing you will have the freedom to be who you want to be no matter who you are.

This student starts with two sentences that tell what justice is, followed by an example of what it is not. Another sentence follows giving another example of what justice is. The writer moves on to two more examples then concludes with a definition that builds on the previous examples. The examples of injustice contribute to the reader's understanding of justice.

With Synonym One of the most common ways terms are defined in the dictionary is by synonym. This is helpful as long as the synonym is more familiar to the reader than the original term. Most of us have had the experience of looking up a word in the dictionary, then having to look up the synonym, and finding the original word listed as a synonym for the synonym, a circular and fruitless search for meaning. In using synonyms to clarify definitions, be sure that your reader is familiar with the synonym. Often such synonyms are enclosed in commas and inserted directly after the original word, as in this example:

He suffered from an efflorescence, a rash, on his skin.

With Etymology Another way to clarify a term is to explain its historical roots, its etymology. For example, the word *sincere* comes from two words that meant "without" and "wax" and was originally used in connection with marble statues. It was common practice in Greek statues to fill with wax those dents made when the sculptor's chisel slipped. So a statue that had no wax-filled indentations was considered superior because it was pure marble and therefore *sincere*. Thus the English word *sincere* means genuine. Another word that takes on clearer meaning through an examination of its roots is "sophomore" which comes from two Greek roots, *soph* meaning wise and *more* meaning fool. From the same roots we also get "sophisticated" and "moron."

Such *etymologies* may necessitate a trip to the dictionary for most of us, but such histories can often be enlightening.

Using Definition in Writing

Any or all of the methods of definition may be used in combination as the organizing principle of a full-length essay. A full definition of a complex concept might require a combination of all of the methods. Thus, an opening paragraph might provide the essential definition. A second paragraph might describe the particular class, and the third and fourth paragraphs might compare and contrast the concept with other members in its class. Additional paragraphs might discuss its history or *etymology*, its connotations, and common synonyms. Examples could be used in any or all of these paragraphs.

In organizing an extended definition paper any of the following methods of definition can be used, singly or in combination.

1. Essential definition

   a. Put term in a class; describe the class.
   b. Compare and contrast with other members of the class.

2. Synonym

3. Etymology

4. Connotations

5. Example

Usually the essential definition comes first, followed by synonyms. Then a discussion of the etymology of the term might enlighten the meaning as well as lead into a discussion of connotations. An example is almost a necessary part of any definition and might be as brief as a paragraph or as extended as two or three pages depending on the complexity of the term.

In defining any term you might ask yourself the following questions:

What do I mean by X?

What is the dictionary meaning of X?

What is the history of the word X?

Are there older meanings of X?

What are some synonyms of X?

What are the connotations of X?

What is an example of X?

What is the smallest class that I can put X in?

How does X differ from other things in this class? In its form? In its function? In its properties? In its causes and effects?

Gary Goshgarian in the following essay presents an extended definition of science fiction.

ZEROING IN ON SCIENCE FICTION

GARY GOSHGARIAN

For the sake of argument, let's say you don't know a thing about science   1
fiction but want to. It makes sense to begin your research at your local
bookstore. Toward the rear of the store, just past a sign saying WESTERNS
and pressed between sections labeled MYSTERIES and THE OCCULT you find a
collection of titles labeled SCIENCE FICTION. You're standing before a rack
six rows high and twenty feet long—a small galaxy of paperback SF books
from A to Z. You randomly select a few and read the publishers' blurbs
hoping to get some idea of what SF is all about, hoping to see what all
these books have in common. And that's where your troubles begin.

At one end you find Isaac Asimov's *Caves of Steel*, which is about a man   2
and a robot who in some distant future solve a murder; at the other end is
Roger Zelazny's *Lord of Light*, in which Hindu deities are reincarnated as
people. A little confused, you pull out *Frankenstein*, a classic SF tale about
a scientist who creates a human monster in his laboratory, then *Rosemary's
Baby*, a recent best-seller about a woman who gives birth to a little devil.
Even more confused, you begin yanking books off the shelves wondering
if you're going to discern a common denominator, or at least some clear
categories. *A Clockwork Orange*: a gang of ultra-violent youths who rule the
night streets of an iron-gray society. *The Fires of Azeroth*: the people of
three planets experience an Armageddon. *Starship Troopers*: a young
soldier of the twenty-second century discovers courage in interplanetary
battles. *War of the Worlds*: beings from Mars invade the earth. *Clash of the
Titans*: Perseus, son of Zeus, slays Medusa and saves Andromeda. They
can't all be "science fiction," can they? Some sound rational and scientific, while others sound magical and mystical. Some seem to describe

worlds and events that are probable, while others clearly deal with matters impossible. Some appear to have messages, while others appear to be pure escapism.

What you need, of course, is a reasonable definition of science fiction, 3 one that distinguishes it from the non-SF sometimes mistakenly shelved with it. The best place to begin defining is with the name, *science fiction*. The second word first. *Fiction* signals a kind of literature. In form, then, SF should have the basic fictional ingredients of a story—plot, character, setting, action, point of view. In function, SF, like all forms of literature, should tell us something about the human experience. Now to the second word, the qualifier, *science*. This crucial word separates SF from other fiction genres like fantasy, westerns, and the occult. What makes SF is the science, real or imaginary; without it there is no science fiction. Putting the two halves together produces a general formula that should subsume most SF material—"most" because no literary definition is totally inclusive or exclusive. *Science fiction is the branch of literature that imaginatively speculates on the consequences of living in a scientific or technological world.*

A closer look at the definition will help outline some SF prerequisites. 4 The word *speculates* implies the future. Therefore, a writer who "imaginatively speculates" is one who creates experiences and conditions that have not yet occurred in the real world. Certainly humans have experienced love, hate, and fear before, and any nonhistorical fiction may presume some general future time. But—and this is where SF differs from non-SF—the future experiences and conditions in science fiction are categorically scientific or technological. In other words, SF is about being human in some imagined technological future. The definition does not specify locale, so SF stories can be set on earth, in space, or on worlds galaxies away. Nor does the definition specify *whose* technology. In *War of the Worlds*, by H. G. Wells, the know-how of bug-eyed Martians transports them millions of miles to earth and then nearly devastates the planet with deadly gases and heat rays.

It is the science and scientific rationale of SF that separate it from 5 fantasy, with which it is often confused. The SF author explains even the most fantastic events with science or pseudoscience to make the improbable seem plausible. A fantasy writer, on the other hand, breaks the laws of nature by crediting fantastic events to magic or supernatural powers. The world of SF is a world that could be; the world of fantasy is a world that could never be. Two rival classics, one SF and one fantasy, underscore the distinction. Perhaps the first SF novel was Mary Shelley's *Frankenstein*, published in 1819 at the beginning of the modern scientific age. As everyone knows, it is the tale of a young scientist named Frankenstein who discovers a means of animating a composite corpse. Once alive, the monstrous creation responds to its creator's rejection by destroying Frankenstein's friends and relatives. Nearly eighty years after the publication of *Frankenstein*, Bram Stoker wrote *Dracula* about a 400-year-old vampire who thrives on the blood of innocents. Both novels center on human monsters, both contain scientists, both are steeped in brooding Gothic atmosphere. So why is *Frankenstein* SF and *Dracula* fantasy? It is a matter of strategies. Frankenstein's monster is born of scientific experimentation in a laboratory, the product of some future breakthrough in biology and chemistry that seemed plausible at the time Shelley wrote. Dracula, however, is a creature from outside the natural order; neither his existence nor his ability to take the form of bats and wolves could be or can be explained scientifically.

Distinct as they are, fantasy and science fiction sometimes overlap in a   6 hybrid category called *fantasy science fiction*. Here an odd juxtaposition of impossibility and plausibility, the magical and the scientific, flying unicorns and atomic-powered space ships, creates a tension that highlights the limitations of both human sciences and human perceptions of nature. A whole body of fantasy SF known as *sword and sorcery* deals with the high adventures of superhumans who are pitted against fiendish warlords in some faraway world. Two of the most famous writers of such space opera are Fritz Leiber, known for his famous Gray Mouser series, and Edgar Rice Burroughs, who wrote a dozen Martian adventure novels. (Burroughs, of course, is also the creator of Tarzan.) What qualifies their stories as fantasy SF is the scientific hardware, the machinery that transports characters to Burroughs's Barsoom or Leiber's Lankhmar, where the extraordinary events occur.

Just as science and logic distinguish SF from fantasy, so the degree of   7 scientific emphasis distinguishes *hard science fiction* from *soft science fiction*. Hard SF, which flourished in the 1930s and 1940s, stresses scientific knowledge and gadgetry. To create the illusion of a scientifically credible future, hard SF writers draw on known principles and innovations to stock their stories with hard details and jargon. Their protagonists, usually scientists and engineers, romp among the stars seeking a logical solution to some problem. In a sense, the true heroes of hard SF are Yankee ingenuity and modern science. A prime example is Asimov's *Caves of Steel*—a detective story celebrating the cooperation of humans and machines. The book's positive attitude toward the scientific pursuit of truth and invention is characteristic of the form.

Soft SF focuses not so much on the benefits of scientific advancement   8 as on its social and moral consequences. Drawing on sociology, psychology, philosophy, archaeology, and political science, soft SF dramatizes how a technological culture may change the quality of human life, altering morality, evolution, and the environment. Though a soft SF story is always set in the future, its writer draws on some current trend or innovation, thus gaining the opportunity for social commentary and criticism. Such is the case with Anthony Burgess's *A Clockwork Orange*, in which Alex, a juvenile thug, is conditioned by experimental psychologists to become incapable of violence. Science succeeds in rendering Alex nonviolent, but it does not make him morally good. In fact, it dehumanizes him because he can no longer defend himself against the hostile world he inhabits. In the end, the government is forced to recondition Alex back to his old anti-social self, just as the harsh, loveless state conditioned him to violence from his birth. And Burgess thus poses the question of whether humans are creatures of free will or just mechanically conditioned organisms, clockwork oranges. The special advantage of soft SF is that it can raise such moral questions out of the context of daily existence. How will humans live in a world that is run by machines? That is grossly overpopulated? That is polluted by chemicals? That is out of fuel? That is a radioactive wasteland? That has lost its ancient gods?

In attempting to understand what SF is all about, you should not get too caught up in classing a story as fantasy SF or hard SF or soft SF. The categories are just not that neat, and elements of each will share the same page. What is true of SF—and of no other kind of fiction—is that it deals with unfamiliar situations brought about by science. But it is important to recognize that, like all literature, science fiction is about humanity— not robots, Martians, and star ships. Such marvels may cram the pages, but they are there only to test the limits of human experience. 9

Goshgarian begins by pointing out the need for what he calls a "rational definition," which, interestingly enough, turns out to be Aristotle's essential definition in extended form. He puts science fiction into the class of fictional literature, and then briefly describes the features of that class—plot, character, setting, action, point of view. He also qualifies science fiction by saying "most" science fiction since "no literary definition is totally inclusive or exclusive." That is, no definition of literature can include everything that it should include and exclude all those works that it should exclude. He further limits the class of fiction by putting *science* in front of it: "Science fiction is the branch of literature that imaginatively speculates on the consequences of living in a scientific or technological world." This definition would have been better if he had omitted the word *scientific*, which makes the definition circular. He then distinguishes science fiction from fantasy, another member of the class of fictional literature. Fantasy credits fantastic events to magic or supernatural powers while science fiction, he asserts, credits them to science or pseudoscience. He follows this with examples of fantasy and of science fiction to clarify the distinction. Note that he uses the almost universally familiar *Dracula* and *Frankenstein* as his examples. He then continues by pointing out the characteristics of a hybrid class that he calls "fantasy science fiction," and closes his discussion with the distinction between two subcategories—hard science fiction and soft science fiction. In his last paragraph, he states that what distinguishes science fiction from all other members of the class of fiction "is that it deals with unfamiliar situations brought about by science," but, like other members of the class of literature, "science fiction is about humanity—not robots."

CLASSIFICATION

Classification is a familiar activity in ordering our lives. We are constantly classifying and dividing the objects around us. Sorting the laundry, setting up a filing system, designing a curriculum is our way of dividing up the world for our own purposes. It is our way of making order out of seeming disorder. The Post Office divides the mail according to geographic areas using zip codes to make delivery simpler. And as we classify and divide, we discover more about that world. So classification and division help us to think as we write and to write as we think—a recursive and ongoing process. Argument or proof through classification and division is an effective means of persuasion. For example, classifying a murderer as a juvenile is a strong argument for a less severe sentence.

Classification and division are basic to our ways of knowing and our systems of knowledge. For the ancients, classification was a science, and our modern word *taxonomy* (the science, laws, or principles of classification), comes from two Greek words: *tassein* meaning "to arrange or set in order" and *onoma* meaning "distribution." Knowledge is organized through our systems of classification and division. In classification, individual objects are put in a class, while in division, a class is separated into smaller subclasses, or *species*. Science fiction and fantasy can both be classed as fictional literature, and, on the other hand, fictional literature may be divided into a number of species including science fiction and fantasy. One of the best known systems of taxonomy is in the field of biology. Organisms are classified beginning with the broadest and most inclusive category, descending in order to the smallest and most exclusive.

Genus and Species

Genus (JEE-nus) is the Latin word for class and has been taken into the English language. When a genus is divided, the subclasses are known as species. The genus of apples can be divided into several different species—Jonathan, Red Delicious, Pippin, and so on. From that fact it can be argued that what is true of the genus of apples must be true of the various species. So if all apples are round and edible, then it follows that Jonathan, Red Delicious, and Pippin apples must also be round and edible. So each species will demonstrate the characteristics of the *genus*.

Let us take an example from everyday conversation. If we are at an Italian restaurant I may ask you what *manicotti* is, and you may reply by telling me that it is a kind of noodle stuffed with cheese and meat. I am familiar with the characteristics of noodles in general, so by putting *manicotti* into the class of noodles you are giving me quite a bit of information about *manicotti*. Classifying does the same thing for the reader. By putting a subject into a class you draw on the reader's knowledge about other members of the class on the assumption that what is true for one member of the class is also true for other members of the class. For example, classifying abortion or euthanasia as murder could be a compelling argument against legalizing them. But you must persuade the reader that the classification is valid for the argument to succeed. Again, you need always to be aware of your audience.

In addition to using classification as an argument, you can also use it as an organizing principle and divide a class into a number of subclasses, then discuss each one in turn. The student writer of the following example, entitled "Fishermen," divides trout fishermen into two groups: "occasional trout fishermen" who are "out for a good time" and "those who have made it a science." This division helps the student organize the material in a way that the reader can understand.

> Fishing is the most rewarding sport I have ever participated in. It is an activity that anyone, regardless of age or sex, can take part in. I am primarily a trout fisherman. Trout fishermen fall into one of two categories: occasional trout fishermen who are out with the intention of just having a good time and those who have made it a science and go after the big ones. I fall into the latter category.
>
> Most occasional trout fishermen have two objectives: enjoying their weekend or holiday and catching a few fish. Weather is important to this faction of anglers. It can't be too cold, too hot, or raining. Therefore, most people do their angling in the spring or the fall. Atmosphere also plays a large role. Having your family, girlfriend, or best buddy with you is almost a necessity. A typical day on the stream may go something like this: 7:00 A.M. to 9:00 A.M. you fish. 9:00 A.M. to 10:00 A.M. you eat breakfast. 10:00 A.M. to 1:00 P.M. you fish some more. 1:00 P.M. to 3:00 P.M. you eat lunch and take a nap. 3:00 P.M. to 5:00 P.M. you get in your final fishing for the day (if you woke up from your nap). Then it is time for dinner, horseshoes, badminton, marshmallow roasting, and various other activities. Maybe you had a good day on the stream and caught your limit. Maybe the day wasn't so good and you only caught two small ones, broke your line seven times, and slipped into the stream. Fishing wasn't so good but you still had a good time. Tomorrow you may just take it easy, go for a walk in the woods, or go on a picnic.

Scientific fishermen, commonly referred to as lunkermen, are a totally different breed of angler. The lunkerman has only one thing on his mind: catching a trout that weighs three pounds or more. Most trout streams are clear and you can see the fish in the water. A lunkerman can tell how much a fish weighs before he catches it. He would rather not go to the trouble of taking the fish off his hook if it doesn't weigh at least three pounds. Being seen with a sub-lunker category of fish on his stringer would be total embarrassment for a lunkerman. I have gone for weeks without catching a trout, even though I had fished everyday. It is a sure bet that when I did catch one it was a lunker. Weather makes no difference to a lunkerman. I have fished in weather ranging from 0 to 105 degrees. Rain is a welcome occurrence, for most people leave the stream and it gives you a better shot at the big ones. A lunkerman will fish from the beginning of the season to the close, which is March 1st to October 31st. A lunkerman fishes by himself. No girlfriends, families, or buddies accompany him on his trips. It has to be just you against the elusive big ones. A lunkerman never stands still unless he has a big one spotted. The rest of the time you can see him roaming the banks, his eyes fixed on the water, searching for a prospective catch. Another tactic I use to spot lunkers that gives you a different perspective and light angle on the water is climbing trees that hang over the streams. A true lunkerman takes no time out during the fishing day to eat, rest, or anything else. It is a constant struggle between the elements and the fisherman.

All of a lunkerman's experiences and emotions emerge as the lunker takes the lure into his mouth, which is the beginning of a two or three hour battle of natural instinct against human logic and talent. I have always given the pursued an advantage by using lightweight line and equipment. Against such odds I usually lose more than I win, but the thought that I might get revenge the next day keeps me going back time after time. Fishing is a way to pleasure for most anglers; to some it is a religion.

This student divides the class of trout fishermen into two species: the occasional fisherman and the scientific fisherman. The former he defines as having two objectives: "enjoying their weekend or holiday and catching a few fish." He describes the feature of the scientific fisherman, on the other hand, as having "only one thing on his mind: catching a trout that weighs three pounds or more." Then for each of these categories of fishermen he describes in some detail a typical day of fishing and concludes by restating the characteristics of each of the species of fishermen: "Fishing is a way to pleasure for most anglers; to some it is a religion."

Using Classification and Division in Writing

How classification and division are used depends basically on purpose—and that purpose depends on the material, the occasion, and the reader. You may use classification and division in any one of the following ways:

> To inform: The material may be too complex for the reader to understand unless you divide it into more manageable subclasses.

> To argue a point: By putting certain groups into the class of terrorists, they then take on all the attributes of the class of terrorists.

> To persuade: You may persuade someone to support a candidate by putting that candidate into the class of liberals or conservatives.

> To amuse: By dividing a class into subclasses that are not the usual or expected ones the writer can sometimes create humorous effects.

In some cases you may want to make your purpose clear to the reader by stating it, as in this example:

> In order to understand how the publishing industry functions it is important to understand the various ways that it markets its books.

A classification or division introduced into an essay with no purpose attached may be confusing as in the following example.

> Computers can be divided into three classes: home computers, small office computers, and industrial computers.

An explicitly stated purpose might be helpful. This statement tells your reader not only how you are going to classify and divide the class of computers, but why:

> In order to understand how computers are used in the university setting, we might divide them into four types: home computers, small office computers, school computers, and industrial computers.

The Dividing Principle

Ancient logicians talked about *partitio* as the logical division of a subject into its parts, and recognized that there had to be only one dividing principle when a class is divided into a number of subclasses. In the biologist's taxonomy, the basis of division is usually a complex set of characteristics that have been determined only after long studies of animals and plants. But the categories continually shift and change as the taxonomy process itself brings about new discoveries and increasing knowledge. The discovery of viruses created just such a problem in zoology. It is still not determined whether a virus belongs in the class of animal or plant life. Light presents a similar problem to physicists. Is it finally a particle or a wave? Increasing knowledge will determine such classifications. Such principles of division in the field of biology furnish a basis for continual research and scholarly discussion with ongoing revision of categories or bases of division, just as working out classes and subclasses allows writers to discover and invent their subjects.

In simple divisions, the reason for only one dividing principle might be more obvious than in long complex divisions. In the following faulty division, the class of apples is divided into three categories on the basis of not one but two principles: color and taste.

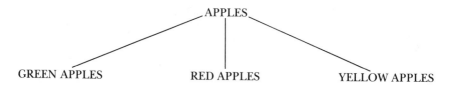

This division is faulty because sour apples can contain some green apples, and green apples can contain some sour apples. A logical division is one in which each class is divided on the basis of only one dividing principle. To make the apple division logical, the class of apples must be divided either on the basis of color or on the basis of taste, as in these examples:

DIVIDING PRINCIPLE = *COLOR*

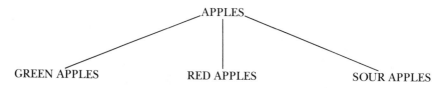

DIVIDING PRINCIPLE = *TASTE*

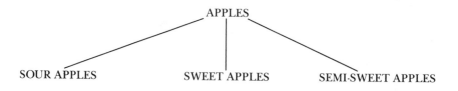

The basis of division will change each time a class is divided into smaller subclasses. For example, you might use color to divide the class of apples and taste to divide the subclass of red apples. The important thing to remember is not to use more than one basis of division at each rank in the division process.

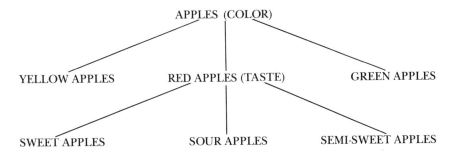

The choice of a principle of division in either case would depend on your purpose in making the division—whether choosing apples for a certain recipe, or selecting ones to eat, or to make a table arrangement. Your intention governs the selection of a division principle.

Thus in making a division, you are dealing with a class, a series of subclasses, a basis of division, and a purpose in division. So in dividing apples by color, these four elements could be outlined this way:

1. class = apples

2. subclasses = red apples, yellow apples, green apples

3. basis of division = color

4. purpose of division = to make an attractive table decoration

Elaborating on Classifications and Divisions

Classification, grouping concepts together, and division, dividing a class into subclasses, can be effective rhetorical arguments and may serve as organizing principles for a subject as well. Thus classification and division are not only aids to the thinking and writing process, but can serve as ways of clarifying a subject for a reader. What follows are two ways that you can clarify your subjects for an audience through classifications and divisions.

With Example Examples are a way of bringing material into the world of people and objects with which the reader is familiar. Classes often are far removed from persons and specific objects. The category of students is more difficult to grasp than any single member of the class such as freshmen. It is easier to understand the study of history than the class of social sciences in general. It is easier to know about Sue or Jim than to understand the whole category of college freshmen in general.

One of the best ways to explain the characteristics of a class is to refer to a single example within that class. In the following paragraph, a student is describing a familiar but complex principle of psychology. Note how she skillfully follows each definition with an example of what the id, the ego, and the superego might say.

> There are three parts of your conscience which tend to control your actions. They are the id, ego, and superego. The id is mainly a pleasure principle. For example, if you see something in the store you want, the id would say, "Go on and take it; they won't miss a little thing like that," but your ego would tell you, "Don't do it; you know you're not a thief!" There will always be a battle between these two, but the overpowering one, if you don't shut it out, is the superego which says, "It's simply wrong to steal."

Note how much less clear and interesting the paragraph is when the examples are omitted.

> There are three parts of your conscience which tend to control your actions. They are the id, ego, and superego. The id is mainly a pleasure principle. There is always a battle between the id and the ego. The overpowering one is the superego.

By Naming In the process of forming subclasses, you may wish, in addition to describing each one, to name each one. Such names serve not only your own convenience, but also can suggest to your reader your attitude toward your subject—serious, humorous, technical, ironic. For example, when the writer divides spoken language into cultivated speech, common speech, and folk speech, the names tell the reader something about the writer's attitude toward the subject. There are times when attempts are made to get away from an expression of these attitudes in naming subclasses as the Post Office does by using zip codes for geographical areas. But, in writing, naming your classes and subclasses can effectively establish your attitude toward your subject.

You might ask yourself the following questions when trying to classify or divide a subject.

> What class of things does X belong to?
>
> What are some other members of this class?

What are some examples of X?

For what purposes might I want to divide X into parts?

On the basis of each of these purposes, into how many parts might I divide X?

What is the dividing principle for this division?

How might I name these parts? What attitude am I expressing by these names?

The following essay by Russell Lynes is a good example of an essay that uses classification as an organizing principle and uses naming effectively.

ON WEEKEND GUESTS

RUSSELL LYNES

What makes a good guest is a subtle complex of personality, manners, 1 and delicacy of feeling, coupled with one's own state of forbearance at the moment when the guest appears. There are friends one can always depend on, but they are likely to be old friends for whom no amount of trouble is a burden and whose awareness of one's shortcomings is equaled by their readiness to accept them.

But not all guests can be old friends; they are merely the certain islands 2 of calm and delight in a summer filled with potential catastrophe. Let us consider those other guests, most of whom we have invited in overexpansive moments to share our hospitality.

The standard weekend guests are a couple, but there the standard stops 3 and the variations set in. We cannot discuss all of the variations, but let us take a few common ones and face up to this problem now that summer is well under way and it is too late to do anything about it.

Age makes less difference in guests than you would think; it is "habit 4 patterns" (as the psychologists call the ruts of behavior) that are important to consider in dealing with guests. If, for example, you have invited what seemed to you on urban acquaintance a lively, active couple, you may as well resign yourself to their spending most of the weekend asleep. Being lively in the city is an extremely enervating business, and your couple will make up for it over the weekend. There is no use leaving the lawnmower conspicuously displayed; these are not the kind of people who are going to volunteer to push it. The chances are that they will arrive late for dinner on Friday, completely equipped for tennis, golf, and swimming, and it will take the whole family to stow them and their tack in the guest room. By nine o'clock one of them will say: "Oh, this country air. I can hardly keep my eyes open." And by nine-thirty they'll both be asleep upstairs.

On Saturday morning it becomes obvious that these active urban types are country sluggards. They emerge dressed like manikins from a resort shop—the man in slacks and loafers and plaid shirt and his wife in shorts and sandals and halter—in the clothes, in other words, that people who spend much time in the country haven't time for—and they wear dark glasses. If you are sensible, you have been up for a good while yourself and got the lawn mowed (your guests love to lie in bed and listen to the reassuring whir of a lawnmower) and had your breakfast. You have made a list of the things you want to do without regard to what your friends want to do. If they feel like it they'll patter along when you go to town to shop; if they don't, they are perfectly happy sitting in reclining chairs, their faces lifted like platters to the sun.

You need not worry about all the sports equipment they brought with them. That was a gesture. They won't begin to bustle until late afternoon when it is cocktail time. Then they will replace their shorts with something longer, and emerge after they have used up all the hot water, ready to use up all the gin.

The chances of what may then happen are about equally divided; they may drink so fast and furiously (they feel so full of health from a day in the sun) that they will again be ready for bed by nine-thirty. If this happens, Sunday's performance will echo Saturday's. If, however, they decide to make an evening of it, they won't appear until just before lunch on Sunday, by which time you can have had at least a half a day to yourself. The rest of the day you may as well throw away.

By contrast, let us look at a quite different sort of couple from the city. It would be risking too much to say that the opposite type, the kind of couple who reflect the cares and the harrying tempo of urban life and have a peaked air about them, are invariably the active ones over a weekend in the country, but there is some truth in it. They are likely to arrive somewhat bedraggled, usually by train, with the hot sooty look of people emerging from a couple of hours on a local in which the air conditioning has broken down. The first breath of clear country air brightens their gray faces; they stand on the platform and look around them as though refreshing their memories of what a tree looks like. They have a small suitcase each and carry no athletic equipment. If everything about the landscape enchants them as you drive them home, you should be warned that you are in for an active two days.

This sort of couple has a good deal in common with puppies. You throw out any kind of suggestion, and they scamper after it and bring it back and drop it at your feet. Everything is grist for their mill, but they have forgotten to bring the mill. If you suggest tennis, they'd just love tennis, but, of course, they have no rackets and no sneakers, and after you have ransacked the house and tried your own, your wife's and your children's sneakers on them and have concluded that you are in for a game of patball, they settle down to beat the pants off you with rackets that you have long since given up as warped and worthless.

You can save up the lawn for this type. One will surely cut it for you 10 while the other weeds the flowers, or they may work in shifts. You will have difficulty keeping them out of the kitchen, if you are the sort who thinks of the kitchen as your private sanctum, because they will insist on helping with the dishes. The only real trouble you will encounter arises if you are so misguided as to leave them to their own devices to entertain themselves. Their puppy eyes will look at you as though you ought to be throwing a ball for them. You even have to suggest to them that it is time to go to bed. When you put them on the train on Sunday evening, you will notice that for all the healthful paces through which they have put you and themselves, they will have that same gray and harried look they had when they arrived.

These two kinds of couples are, of course, merely composites of many 11 other species. But what of the couples who do not seem to make pairs and who go their separate ways? And what of those couples of which you like one member and can't abide the other? For our purposes they have to be considered as individuals. There are those who think that the state of being a guest relieves them of all responsibility and those who consider guesthood a perpetual challenge. In either case the extremes are difficult to cope with.

The range of individual guests is, of course, endless, and perforce we 12 must confine ourselves to those whose eccentricities have some chance of seeming to be part of larger and more universally recognized patterns. You can make your own synthesis (nobody is anybody these days who doesn't at least try to make a synthesis) and match them as you please.

Some guests want to be left alone, and some say they want to be ("Don't 13 bother about me. Just go about your business. I'll find plenty to do.") and are miserable if they are.

The first of these lone wolves can be the pleasantest of all guests if they 14 are resourceful, can take care of themselves happily, and at the same time pervade your household with the warm feeling that they enjoy just being in it. At their best they don't mind being interrupted in their own pursuits if there is some activity in which you want them to join. At their worst they make you feel that all they want out of you is a bed and three meals a day and a chance to ignore you. These are the men and women who come for the weekend to get away from people (including you) and to have a little quiet. They think they have discharged all of their responsibilities if they bring a box of chocolates that they have bought in the railroad station. They are so well able to take care of themselves that they make you feel as though you were in their employ.

A guest of the second type (who really does not want to be left alone 15 but protests that he does) offers an acute problem of tact. He appears at breakfast with a small stack of books, a magazine, and some writing paper, bright-eyed and presumably equipped for the day. He quickly sets the books aside and takes your morning paper. (The sort of person who has a number of books from which to choose is rarely a reader. He is always looking for a chance to find time to sit down with a good book, but curiously he never seems to find it. He won't find it over the weekend either.) After his third cup of coffee, you may get back the paper, and your friend will wander off to find a place to read one of the books. In half an hour or less he'll be hovering around again. "Too nice a day to sit and read," he'll say, and that is your signal to quit whatever you are doing and invent something to keep him busy. His resources and imagination were exhausted by picking out which books in your library he would fondle.

If this type stretches your tact, then you should be especially warned of 16 the guest who makes an elaborate show of being tactful about you. He acts as though he knows that he is too much trouble and that everything you do for him is a great nuisance. He is constantly leaping out of his chair to perform some little service for you or for your wife, to get out the ice, to find the children's ball in the bushes, or to fetch the wood for the fireplace, all of which would be ingratiating if it weren't done half-apologetically. You soon find yourself wanting to tell him to sit down and relax, but instead you respond with an elaborate display of tact on your own part. He is wearisome because he is so hard to live up to.

Even so he is preferable to the intentionally tactless guest who thinks 17 that to make light of your shortcomings as a host is a demonstration of easy fellowship and poise. He laughs at the way you lay a fire, and insists on taking your effort apart and stacking the kindling in his way. He reminds you that the leaky faucet in the bathroom could be fixed with a five-cent washer and fifteen minutes' work, and that you have put the wrong kind of composition shingles on your house; he could have got a much better brand for you wholesale at half the price you paid. He follows you wherever you go all weekend long; he stands in the kitchen door while you are getting drinks or a meal. If you play golf with him he tells you how to correct your slice, and if he sees you chopping wood he will observe that you are lucky you haven't cut your leg off long since, handling an axe the way you do. When he is not telling you how you ought to live, his conversation is almost entirely about the remarkable place at which he spent last weekend, with friends who did everything in such style. He is unaware that the walls of most country places are excellent conductors of sound, and you have no respite from him for some time after he has presumably gone to bed. If he is married, you can listen to him telling his wife that you would have a nice little place if you only knew how to take care of it.

Even the careless guest is preferable to the tactless type, though he too 18 offers some minor aggravations. He strews the place with his belongings, he breaks a blade of the lawnmower on a rock anyone ought to be able to see, and he invariably is inspired to take a dip in the lake or river or ocean just as you are about to produce lunch or supper. When he does ultimately appear to be fed he will have deposited his wet bathing suit over the back of a piece of upholstered furniture. There is no malice in his soul, though, and it is possible to love him.

It is impossible, on the other hand, to love the belligerently indolent 19 guest who frustrates all attempts to make his visit pleasant or interesting. That is not to say that a host should force entertainment on anyone who doesn't want it, for a good host knows when to put enticements in his guest's way and when not to. But the belligerently indolent guest has a gift for making it quite obvious to his host that he expects to be enter-tained, yet displays a distinct distaste for any diversion that may be suggested to him. This is a common characteristic in children, and in adults it is, I believe, an indication of retarded maturity. I have often seen adults behave like a child I know who continually asks, "What'll I do now?" When a suggestion is made to him he has a pat reply. "Would you like to go swimming?" you ask him, and the reply is invariably, "Not particularly." "Well then," you say, trying again, "how would you like to play catch?" "Not particularly," he says, and so it goes. When such guests, children or adults, do finally submit themselves to some plan you have suggested, they give you the uncomfortable sensation that they wish you had been bright enough to invent something really entertaining.

If this kind of guest is tiring because he is a constant challenge to your 20 ingenuity, the opposite type, the ebullient guest, who sets out to give his host and hostess a rousing good time, takes the least planning and is the most exhausting. He arrives full of ideas, of projects for excursions, of resolve to get you out and give you some real exercise, and unless you want to be rude to him (which is necessary in extreme cases) it is best just to put yourself in his hands.

There are a number of common manifestations of the ebullient guest, 21 each requiring a special defensive operation and its own system of logistics. I happen to have a house in the Berkshires. These gentle hills were at one time (especially in the environs of Stockbridge and Lenox) remarkable for the size and extravagance of the summer estates which graced their slopes. There is a legend in the Berkshires that a young man who was at Yale just before the turn of the century sent his mother a telegram in which he said, "Bringing some '97 friends for weekend," and his mother wired back, "Terribly sorry have room for only seventy-six." Most of the big estates are now hotels, or schools, or church institutions, and the Berkshires have become a hotbed of summer culture. We have music festivals at Tanglewood that rival Salzburg and Glyndebourne in fame. We have dance festivals at a place called Jacob's Pillow, and we have enough summer theaters to give several platoons of Broadway stars their annual breath of fresh air. We used to frequent these places; in fact months before the music festival our friends could be seen conspicuously angling for invitations. We finally grew tired of running a lodging house for our music- and dance-minded acquaintances, and we ourselves took to angling for invitations elsewhere during that part of the summer. It was the ebullient guests who wanted to be sure that we got our dosage of culture who finally drove us to take umbrage.

Umbrage is one way to cope with the ebullient. Another way is to lend   22 your guest the family car, and if necessary your wife, and let them go on an excursion of their own making. A third method is to buy two tickets to the festival or the dance or the theater and say that they are all you could get (which could easily be true) and insist that the guests use them. This is both a generous gesture and assurance of a few hours' respite.

There is one kind of ebullience, however, which I have frequently   23 encountered and have never been able to discover an answer to. It is found in a single guest or in a couple who seem to know a great many more people in the vicinity to which you have invited them than you do. The minute they get in the house they start calling up their friends. By the end of fifteen minutes they have invited themselves and you to one house for lunch, another for drinks, and have possibly even got you committed to appear at the Saturday night country club dance. You may, on the other hand, find yourself giving a cocktail party for a lot of people you scarcely know and have been successfully avoiding for years. Short of cutting the telephone wires before your guests arrive, I know of no way to keep their socially manic behavior in control.

Lynes initially divides the class "weekend guests" into old friends and acquaintances. He then divides the acquaintances into couples and individuals on the basis of "habit patterns." With this dividing principle in mind, he subdivides the couples into active and passive and the individuals into lone wolf, lonesome, tactful, tactless, careless, indolent, ebullient. This division not only organizes the classes that Lynes wants to discuss, it also makes that organization clear to the reader. Through his subclasses and their names, he leads his reader into the connotations that the names imply.

The following diagram represents the organization of the essay:

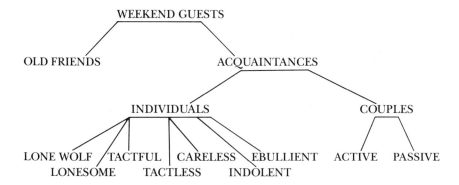

In this essay, Lynes's purpose of amusing the reader is reinforced by the names he gives to his subclasses and the variety of examples that he uses. How would his treatment of the subject of guests have been different if he had been writing an etiquette book, an entertainment guide, or a recipe book?

Definition and classification are basic thought and language processes and are often used in conjunction with each other and with the topics of comparison and cause and effect that are treated in the next chapter.

Questions to Consider

1. Evaluate the following essential definitions using the checklist provided in this chapter on pp. 83–84.

A. Nuclear power is a very dangerous form of energy.

B. A typewriter is a machine used for writing.

C. Inarticulate means not articulate.

D. Baseball is a popular game played in the United States.

E. Abortion is murder.

F. A nihilist is one who espouses the philosophy of nihilism.

G. A bicycle is a vehicle you ride for pleasure.

H. Religion is the opiate of the people.

I. English 1 is where you learn to write essays.

J. Christmas is a thing we celebrate every year on December 25.

2. Anticipate for what audience you might need to define the following words; then create an accurate essential definition for each.

A. a fast break

B. bar mitzvah

C. RAM (random access memory)

D. Big Mac

E. *logos*

3. Consider for what purpose, in what context and to whom you might want to provide a definition of the following concepts:

A. a conservative point of view

B. humor

C. insanity

D. soul

4. With your classmates, compose a list of all the television shows you can think of, and then consider all of the ways you could classify them according to various principles of division, such as genre (e.g., detective shows, game shows, talk shows), times of the day they are shown, days of the week they are shown, network on which they are shown, and so on. Which principles of division do you find most workable in planning a paper on television shows?

5. Make a list of all of the ways you use classification in a single day. You'll probably be surprised by its length.

Suggestions for Writing

1. Greeting cards are well known for providing sentimental definitions of family members to commemorate holidays and birthdays. (Remember the cards beginning with "What is a Mother"?) Write a page or two developed by definition in which you explain the meaning of one of the following terms: mother, father, sister, brother, grandmother, grandfather, husband, or wife. Try to avoid the sentimental language that characterizes greeting cards, and don't be afraid to interject some humor into your definition.

2. Choose a technical term or concept related to a hobby or profession and write a page or two in which you define that term or concept in such a way that a layperson can understand it. Be sure to take advantage of all the possible ways of defining a term: essential definition, etymology, negative definition, examples, and synonyms.

3. Write a page in which you provide an explanation of the etymology of your last name. If you don't know what the etymology is, make one up that seems plausible.

4. Choose a familiar class of literature—such as fiction, poetry, biography, or nonfiction—and in a page or two, further divide that class into additional subclasses according to some consistent principle and for some particular purpose of your own choosing. Be sure that each subclass is distinct, well defined, and that you give examples.

5. Following the example of Lynes's essay on kinds of guests, identify, define, and illustrate kinds of students, teachers, or friends. Again, don't be afraid to use humor to make your point.

6. Write a page or two classifying kinds of graffiti you find on your campus (or even at a more specific location) into at least three types. Be sure your principle of division is clear and consistently applied, and remember to illustrate each type with specific examples.

Exercises in Revision

1. Examine the writing that uses definition submitted by members of your workshop group and apply the questions provided in this chapter to determine any weaknesses. Then make suggestions for the writers to rewrite the definitions to eliminate these weaknesses.

2. Examine the writing submitted by members of your workshop group that uses classification and division to determine whether the purpose of the classification is clear, the principle of division is consistently applied, and each class is well illustrated. Based on your group's suggestions for improvement, rewrite your classification exercise to eliminate the weaknesses.

3. Make a list of the weaknesses you perceive in the examples of the writing submitted by members of your workshop group in response to the assignment in exercise 2; then classify those weaknesses according to some consistent principle and, as a group, write a paragraph in which you identify the kinds of problems and illustrate them with specific examples taken from the original writings.

4. Focus on a major strength in a piece of writing from a magazine with which you are familiar, and then write a paragraph in which you define this strength using essential definition.

For a Commonplace Book

Try to find examples in your own reading of articles using the topics of definition and classification. You might want to refer to your textbooks from other courses. Record in your commonplace book the purpose for which the authors use these topics.

Chapter 5

Discovering Ideas: Comparison and Contrast, Cause and Effect

This chapter will treat four more of the topics, further strategies for supporting a position or arguing a case: comparison and contrast; and cause and effect.

COMPARISON AND CONTRAST

One of the most familiar phrases in an essay exam is "Compare and contrast. . . ." Ordinarily, comparison asks for a demonstration of likenesses, and contrast for differences. Keeping in mind two questions—How is X similar to Y? How is X different from Y?—is a good way to start generating an answer to such a question. Pointing out the similarities or differences between two concepts is not only a way of describing a subject but also a way of arguing a position. Comparing the ingestion of drugs to swallowing poison could be a deterring argument.

Comparison and contrast were of concern not only to classical rhetoricians but also to students of logic, and Aristotle treats the topics not only in his rhetoric but also at great length in his logical treatises, which orators were expected to know. Consequently, this section begins with a short description of logical comparison and contrast.

Logical Comparison

Rhetorical comparisons rely on carefully reasoned logical arguments. There are two general principles that underlie logical comparisons:

1. Compare only objects or persons that belong to the same class.

All members of the same class share certain features. For example, there are certain features that are common to all religions—that is, features that distinguish the class of religions from other classes, such as governments or political parties. Thus, since all religions share a belief in some kind of afterlife, Catholicism and Presbyterianism could be compared on the basis of these beliefs. Similarly the differences in their beliefs could be contrasted.

One common way of denying the validity of a logical comparison is with the remark "That's like comparing apples and oranges." This often-repeated phrase is in actuality denying the logic of the comparison, implying that apples and oranges are different classes of fruit so that a logical comparison is not possible.

2. Base your comparison on specific points of similarity. Make clear to your reader the basis of comparison.

In the following introductory paragraphs to an essay entitled "The Reciprocity of Words and Numbers," Joan Baum sets up a comparison between learning math and learning to write based on the kinds of skills involved in each. She maintains that both are "deliberate, self-conscious acts," requiring definition of key terms, arrangement of terms, and uniformity of order and tone. She makes clear to the reader in these beginning paragraphs that her comparison is based on the skills involved.

Both mathematics and writing are deliberate, self-conscious acts. They share a sense of discipline. The ordering of words on a sheet of ruled paper, or of numbers in an equation, belongs to a common process of "composition": the putting of parts in their proper places.

To write an essay or to solve an algebraic problem, a student must define key terms, must understand guidelines for ordering terms in a series, and must strive for uniformity of order and tone. Factoring a quadratic equation and developing a paragraph both require consistent procedures toward the end of working out the main idea. Indeed, math and writing require such similar skills, in many respects, that the two otherwise disparate fields could reinforce each other—particularly in teaching.

Rhetorical Comparison and Contrast

The writer may make effective use of comparison and contrast to clarify an idea or to make it more vivid or emphatic. These rhetorical comparisons often bend the rules for logical comparisons. They may compare objects or persons that are not in the same class—objects that appear to be unlike—to emphasize and explore interesting points of similarity. So although monasteries and prisons or oak trees and grandparents are not in the same class such comparisons may add vividness to a single shared characteristic. The following example shows the effective use of such a comparison:

> Grandparents are like the oak tree in my backyard. I used to sit underneath it when I was frightened or lonely and it was always there—the trunk strong and straight to support me and the leaves cool and thick to shelter me.

Although rhetorical comparisons can never be used as proof for a position, they can be used with great effectiveness to make a point more clear or accessible to your reader. Probably the most familiar of the rhetorical comparisons is analogy, discussed later in this chapter.

Sometimes rhetorical comparisons can compare apparently dissimilar ideas, bringing the reader to see the similarities and explore an idea from a different perspective. This kind of comparison is often used in poetry and can be extended far beyond a single word or line. A poem that compares a number of apparently dissimilar concepts is Robert Burns's "My Luve Is Like a Red, Red Rose." In the first stanza, Burns compares his love to a rose and a melody.

> My Luve is like a red, red rose
> That's newly sprung in June;
> My Luve is like the melodie
> That's sweetly played in tune!

The effectiveness of such unlike comparisons is that the reader searches out similarities when the two ideas are brought together. Why is the poet's love like a rose—sweet smelling and beautiful and possibly with thorns? Why is the rose red? Why is his love like the melodie "that's sweetly played in tune"? The reader's mind wanders through the possibilities of similarities, searching for the meaning Burns is trying to express by this unusual comparison.

Two of the best known figures of speech, metaphor and simile, depend heavily on the topic of comparison. Chapter 11 describes these figures in detail.

Demonstrating from Similar Cases Writers often clarify or argue points by demonstrating similarities between two ideas. In the following essay, Thomas De Quincey, a nineteenth-century essayist, shows the similarities between the biblical David and Joan of Arc. David was the biblical hero who slew the mighty Goliath, and Joan of Arc was the saint who led the armies of France to victory over their enemies.

> What is to be thought of her? What is to be thought of the poor shepherd girl from the hills and forests of Lorraine, that—like the Hebrew shepherd boy from the hills and forests of Judea—rose suddenly out of the quiet, out of the safety, out of the religious inspiration, rooted in deep pastoral solitudes, to a station in the van of armies, and to the more perilous station at the right hand of kings? The Hebrew boy inaugurated his patriotic mission by an act, by a victorious act, such as no man could deny. But so did the girl of Lorraine, if we read her story as it was read by those who saw her nearest. Adverse armies bore witness to the boy as no pretender; but so they did to the gentle girl. Judged by the voices of all who saw them from a station of good will, both were found true and loyal to any promises involved in their first acts.

Notice how the repetition of parallel phrases reinforces the similarities:

> the shepherd girl from the hills and forests of Lorraine
>
> the shepherd boy from the hills and forests of Judea
>
> But so did the girl of Lorraine
>
> but so they did to the gentle girl

The paragraph concludes by pointing out their basic similarities of character—"both were found true and loyal"—with the author qualifying this view as one voiced by "all who saw them from a station of good will."

This powerful opening paragraph is followed by the differences in Joan of Arc's and David's subsequent fortunes:

Enemies it was that made the difference between their subsequent fortunes. The boy rose to a splendour and a noonday prosperity, both personal and public, that rang through the records of his people, and became a byword among his posterity for a thousand years, until the sceptre was departing from Judah.

The phrase "on the contrary" marks the beginning of the contrast demonstrating the difference in the fate of the girl:

The poor forsaken girl, on the contrary, drank not herself from that cup of rest which she had secured for France. She never sang together with the songs that rose in her native Domremy as echoes to the departing steps of invaders. She mingled not in the festal dances at Vaucouleurs which celebrated in rapture the redemption of France. No! for her voice was then silent; no! for her feet were dust.

In the second part of the paragraph the essayist contrasts their fates as David rose to a position of power while Joan of Arc was burned at the stake. By first pointing out similarities, he makes the difference between their ultimate fates more striking.

Often writers using rhetorical comparison may compare two situations or ideas that seem at first to be widely dissimilar, as in the following essay by Dina Ingber, "Computer Addicts."

It is 3 A.M. Everything on the university campus seems ghostlike in the quiet, misty darkness, everything except the computer center. Here, twenty students, rumpled and bleary-eyed, sit transfixed at their consoles, tapping away on the terminal keys. With eyes glued to the video screen, they tap on for hours. For the rest of the world, it might be the middle of the night, but here time does not exist. As in the gambling casinos of Las Vegas, there are no windows or clocks. This is a world unto itself. Like gamblers, these young computer "hackers" are pursuing a kind of compulsion, a drive so consuming it overshadows nearly every other part of their lives and forms the focal point of their existence. They are compulsive computer programmers.

This writer demonstrates the similarities between the gambling casino and the computer center—"As in the gambling casino there are no windows or clocks." She then shows the similarities between the compu-

ter programmers and the gamblers—"Like gamblers, these young computer 'hackers' are pursuing a kind of compulsion, a drive so consuming it
overshadows nearly every other part of their lives and forms the focal
point of their existence." She concludes by classifying both gamblers and
computer "hackers" as "compulsive." Although the reader ordinarily
does not think of computer students working late in the night as "compulsive," the author is able to demonstrate that quality in them by
comparing their activities and behavior to that of compulsive gamblers.

Analogy is a special kind of comparison in which a similarity or concept
is compared with a more familiar one with which it shares some characteristics. An analogy rests on the probability that if situations are similar
in a number of significant respects, the chances are that they will be alike
in other respects. If you were explaining a proposal for a parking garage
on the university campus you might choose to compare the local parking
situation to that of another university that had successfully built such a
garage. But the basis for an effective analogy is that the two situations
must be similar in a number of respects. Thus, if the university is a large
urban school, it would hardly be convincing to compare the parking
situation to that of a small college in a small town. So if the parking
situation at X University is similar to that at Y University in points A
(number of cars), and B (location of university), it will also be similar in
point C (need for parking garage).

> If parking situation at X University = parking situation at Y Univer-
> sity in A and B, then parking situation at X = parking situation at Y
> in C.

In an analogy, you emphasize the established similarities in order to
make the similarity of the point to be established convincing to the
reader. The author of the *Ad Herennium* stresses that part of the effectiveness of the rhetorical analogy lies in the fact that "it permits the hearer
himself to guess what the speaker has not mentioned" (4.54.67–68).

In the following excerpt William F. Buckley sets up an analogy between
teenage sex and drugs to explain what he sees as the ill effects of teenage
sex:

> Teenage sex is most usefully thought of as a drug. That is to say, sex
> gives pleasure; as drugs gives pleasure; and sex is somewhere be-
> tween a habituate and an addiction, which is true of many drugs.
> Alcohol, which is a drug of sorts, is innocently consumed in moder-
> ation, and the point is therefore to instruct potential victims on
> where the point of moderation lies. The analogous question in sex
> is to instruct those who are unaware or uncaring of the implication
> of wanton sex of its limitations. Just as the drug taker who overdoes

it can damage himself physically, so the human animal who looks on sex merely as one of the smorgasbord of pleasures available to the pleasure-seeker needs to be instructed in the discipline of sensible self-limitation. The 15-year-old girl who has had no instruction at all in the subject is really quite helpless, particularly inasmuch as the routine inducements are to libertinism, rather than to self-restraint, even as you will find more advertisements to buy this or that alcoholic drink than you will find warnings against buying it. What happens, then, is that the 15-year-old girl runs a number of risks. One is that of finding herself, though unprepared, pregnant. Other risks include diseases and emotional derangements. Insufficient attention, it seems to me, is paid to the question whether the male (or female) animal whose sex life is undisciplined is happier than his/her complement. I see no evidence that this is so.

The analogy in Buckley's article runs as follows:

Sex is like drugs in the following ways:

1. They both give pleasure.

2. They both are "somewhere between a habituate and an addition."

3. Both are all right in moderation.

4. Both are damaging unless there is "sensible self-limitation."

Therefore there should be instruction in the proper use of drugs and sex and of the damaging effects of overuse.

An analogy can never be mistaken for positive proof, since two objects or situations may be similar in many respects and still be different in one. But analogies can be effective in rhetorical argument where probabilities are sought or when you want to explain more clearly an obscure concept.

Demonstration from Differences Cicero tells us that it "is the same mental process that finds differences and similarities" (*Topica* 11. 46). Often in writing about similarities, we may also discover the differences. In the following paragraph, the student effectively shows differences between an ordinary New Year's celebration and one spent under the strain of illness, thus emphasizing the effects of her father's illness on her family. Can you rewrite this paragraph without the contrasting statements as a straight narrative? What is the effect of such a revision?

Although the new year brings happiness and joy to some, it also brings worry and frustration to others. Traditionally the celebration of bringing in the new year means lots of friends getting together to watch football games on television and drink beer. Instead of celebration and happiness, my family and I sat in a hospital lobby waiting to hear news about my father. This time of year usually means extra time for the working person to relax and enjoy a few more days of vacation. Our time was spent either traveling on the highway to get to the hospital or sitting in a small enclosed room waiting for the return of my father after another series of tests. After the holidays, when everyone returns to the old routine of working or going back to school, one breathes a sigh of relief and goes about his business. We too breathed a sigh of relief after Dad's operation was a success and the doctor was sure that he had done his job to perfection.

This student uses the same methods for emphasizing the differences that De Quincey used in his introduction in the Joan of Arc essay. Through repetition of words and balanced phrases, she emphasizes two sharply different ways of spending New Year's day.

> a. happiness and joy to some
> b. worry and frustration to others
>
> a. lots of friends watching football games on TV
> b. my family and I waiting to hear news about my father
>
> a. extra time to relax and enjoy
> b. our time was spent sitting in a small enclosed room waiting
>
> a. after the holidays, one breathes a sigh of relief
> b. we too breathed a sigh of relief after Dad's operation

Using Comparison and Contrast in Writing

A series of similarities or differences can be arranged in a number of ways. Two objects or concepts may be compared point-by-point or compared in blocks pertaining to the whole subject. So, in comparing tennis shoes with jogging shoes, the writer might choose the point-by-point method and first compare the soles of each, then the uppers, then the arch supports, then the heels, or the writer might choose the block method and describe the parts of tennis shoes in one paragraph and the parts of jogging shoes in the second paragraph.

The student describing her New Year's day in the hospital waiting room clearly uses the point-by-point pattern. Each sentence describing the traditional celebration is contrasted with her family's activities in the sentence immediately following. This method heightens the contrast. Another student uses the block pattern to present a rather jaundiced view of Christmas at his grandmother's house.

> Christmas Day is supposed to be a time for relatives to get together and have fun, but for our family, Christmas day is the same every year. Most families have fun when they go to their grandmother's house. The younger children may go outside and play. While the teenagers either play cards or sit around the fire talking, the adults try to get caught up with the family gossip. But our Christmas day is just the opposite. We go to our grandmother's house and sit around for hours with nothing to do. There are no young children in the family, so the sound of children's laughter is not heard. The teens are snobbish and self-centered and sit around wishing they were home. The adults assemble in groups according to level of income and tell each other how poor they are. Christmas day at Grandmother's house should be a day of celebration, but for our family, we might as well all stay home.

After the first sentence that sets the tone and delineates the differences, the next three sentences describe what most families do on Christmas. The remaining sentences describe what his family does. Even though this student describes first one kind of Christmas and then another, he sets up his points of difference carefully. He makes a general statement about each kind of Christmas celebration, then describes what the children do, followed by what the teens do, and concludes with what the adults do.

Developing similarities and differences can be a voyage of discovery on the page and in your mind as you write. Choosing ideas to compare with your main idea is determined not only by your subject but also by your audience. Ask yourself if your reader is familiar with the subject of your comparison. If you are telling a reader about Joan of Arc by comparing her to David, is your reader familiar with David? If you are comparing or contrasting two ideas, have you consistently developed the similarities or differences? Finally, have you used balanced words and phrases to reinforce points of similarity and difference?

In exploring similarities and differences in connection with your subject, you might ask yourself the following questions.

What is X like?

How many points of similarity can I show?

Have I made the point of this comparison clear to my reader?

What is X not like?

How many kinds of differences can I show?

What does this contrast demonstrate to the reader?

You may wish to make a complex concept clear to a reader by comparing it to something that is more familiar; you may argue from analogy that if something works in one situation it will also work in a closely similar one; you may use comparison to fill out a definition or contrast to make a subject more vivid. In all of these situations, comparison and contrast can serve the writer.

In the following excerpt from *Life on the Mississippi*, Mark Twain shows two views of the Mississippi: through the eyes of a casual observer and through the eyes of an experienced riverboat pilot.

FROM *LIFE ON THE MISSISSIPPI*:

MARK TWAIN

Now when I had mastered the language of this water, and had come to   1
know every trifling feature that bordered the great river as familiarly as I
knew the letters of the alphabet, I had made a valuable acquisition. But I
had lost something, too. I had lost something which could never be
restored to me while I lived. All the grace, the beauty, the poetry, had
gone out of the majestic river! I still keep in mind a certain wonderful
sunset which I witnessed when steamboating was new to me. A broad
expanse of the river was turned to blood; in the middle distance the red
hue brightened into gold, through which a solitary log came floating
black and conspicuous; in one place a long slanting mark lay sparkling
upon the water; in another the surface was broken by boiling, tumbling
rings, that were as many-tinted as an opal, where the ruddy flush was
faintest, was a smooth spot that was covered with graceful circles and
radiating lines, ever so delicately traced; the shore on our left was densely
wooded, and the somber shadow that fell from this forest was broken in
one place by a long, ruffled trail that shone like silver; and high above the
forest wall a clean-stemmed dead tree waved a single leafy bough that
glowed like a flame in the unobstructed splendor that was flowing from
the sun. There were graceful curves, reflected images, woody heights, soft
distances; and over the whole scene, far and near, the dissolving lights

drifted steadily, enriching it every passing moment with new marvels of coloring.

I stood like one bewitched. I drank it in, in a speechless rapture. The world was new to me, and I had never seen anything like this at home. But as I have said, a day came when I began to cease from noting the glories and the charms which the moon and the sun and the twilight wrought upon the river's face; another day came when I ceased altogether to note them. Then, if that sunset scene had been repeated, I should have looked upon it without rapture, and should have commented upon it, inwardly, after this fashion: "This sun means that we are going to have wind tomorrow; that floating log means that the river is rising, small thanks to it; that slanting mark on the water refers to a bluff reef which is going to kill somebody's steamboat one of these nights, if it keeps on stretching out like that; those tumbling 'boils' show a dissolving bar and a changing channel there; the lines and circles in the slick place show the river is shoaling up dangerously; that silver streak in the shadow of the forest is the 'break' from a new snag, and he has located himself in the very best place he could have found to fish for steamboats; that tall dead tree, with a single living branch, is not going to last long, and then how is a body ever going to get through this blind place at night without the friendly old landmark?"

No, the romance and beauty were all gone from the river. All the value any feature of it had for me now was the amount of usefulness it could furnish toward compassing the safe piloting of a steamboat. Since those days, I have pitied doctors from my heart. What does the lovely flush in a beauty's cheek mean to a doctor but a "break" that ripples above some deadly disease? Are not all her visible charms sown thick with what are to him the signs and symbols of hidden decay? Does he ever see her beauty at all, or doesn't he simply view her professionally, and comment upon her unwholesome condition all to himself? And doesn't he sometimes wonder whether he has gained most or lost most by learning his trade?

In this excerpt, the author traces a number of objects that casual observers might notice as they view the sunset—a "solitary log," a "slanting mark," "boiling, tumbling rings," "graceful circles," "silver streak," and a "dead tree," all of which made the "grace, the beauty, the poetry . . . of the majestic river." In the following paragraph, he views the same objects, this time from the steamboat pilot's point of view and realizes that, as a pilot, he has "lost something which could never be restored." In the third paragraph Twain compares the steamboat pilot to the doctor who views his patient with the same pragmatic eye as the pilot does the river. In these paragraphs, through an exploration of differences between the riverboat pilot and the casual observer and similarities between the pilot and the doctor, Twain argues his position that in mastering his trade, he had made a "valuable acquisition," but in doing so, he had lost something of great value. In this excerpt the vivid contrast emphasizes what he has lost by learning his trade and the comparison of the riverboat pilot with the doctor drives his point home.

CAUSE AND EFFECT

Cicero distinguishes between kinds of causes: "ones that produce the effect without aid from another source, and others which require assistance" (*Topica.* 15, 59). In this discussion we call the first kind "necessary" and the second kind "sufficient" causes. Though the classical rhetoricians considered cause and effect as two separate topics, Cicero wrote that "a knowledge of causes produces a knowledge of results," so they are often treated together. Exploring causes and effects of events, concepts, and issues is an important kind of perspective to add to your writing. Often such discussions answer the reader's question of "Why?" When readers have the answer to this question, they will better understand the argument you present—by seeing why you make certain claims.

Kinds of Causes

Causes are often difficult to ascertain. It may be easy to understand that the rain caused the weather to cool off, but the cause of a backache may be difficult even for a well-trained doctor to determine and the causes for winning an election or an aircraft explosion are even more elusive. It helps in determining causes to distinguish the various kinds of causes.

Necessary Causes A necessary cause is one without which the effect could not have occurred. It is always associated with the result. We can be certain in the case of a necessary cause that if the effect is present the cause is also present. Certain bacteria or viruses are the necessary causes of certain diseases. The diseases cannot occur without the presence of the virus or bacteria.

Sufficient Causes A sufficient cause is one that could produce the effect. Sometimes this kind of cause is called the precipitating cause. An effect may have any number of sufficient causes, any one of which might produce the effect. Though a virus is the necessary cause of a particular disease, an overall run-down or weakened physical condition may well allow the virus to invade the system and would thus be sufficient cause. Often we can only speculate about sufficient causes. If the conditions are right for a riot, any one of a number of causes may be sufficient to trigger the riot—unemployment, political unrest, poverty, hot weather—especially if one or two other sufficient causes are also present.

Immediate and Remote Causes Since many events have a long chain of causes leading up to them, you often need to distinguish the immediate causes from the remote causes. Smoking, for example, may have caused the cancer that caused the heart failure that caused the death. In this case, the immediate cause was heart failure; the remote causes were cancer and smoking. An examination of immediate causes only furnishes a limited picture. It is usually necessary to trace at least part of the chain of remote causes to understand fully a subject or an event.

Note how H. D. F. Kitto in the following excerpt explores a chain of causes, beginning with the climate, that account for Greek culture.

We ought not to leave this matter of the Greek climate without considering its effect on Greek, especially on Athenian, life.

In the first place, it enabled the Greek to live with extremely little apparatus. In Greece one can lead an active life on much less food than harsher climates make necessary; but there is also the fact that the Greek—the Greek *man*—could and did spend most of his leisure hours out of doors. That in itself meant that he had more leisure; he did not need to work in order to buy settees and coal.—After all, the reason why we English have invented "le confort anglais" is that we cannot be comfortable and warm except indoors. The leisure which the Athenian enjoyed is popularly attributed to the existence of slavery. Slavery had something to do with it, but not so much as the fact that three-quarters of the things which we slave for the Greek simply did without.

So, spending out of doors the leisure which he earned largely by doing without things which we find or think necessary, the Greek, whether in town or village, was able to sharpen his wits and improve his manners through constant intercourse with his fellows. Few people have been so completely sociable. Talk was the breath of life to the Greek—as indeed it still is, though somewhat spoiled by a serious addiction to newspapers. What society but Athens could have produced a figure like Socrates—a man who changed the current of human thought without writing a word, without preaching a doctrine, simply by talking in the streets of a city which he never left but twice—for the battlefield? In what other society is one so little conscious of a chasm between the educated and the uneducated, between those with taste and the vulgar? The real education of the Athenian, and of many another Greek, was given in the places of assembly—in the hours of talk in market place, colonnade, or gymnasium, in the political assembly, in the theater, at the public recitals of Homer, and at the religious processions and celebrations. For it was perhaps the greatest boon conferred upon Attica by her climate that her big assemblies could be held in the open air. However democratic the instincts of the Athenian might be, Athenian democracy could not have developed as it did—nor for that matter Athenian drama—if a roof and walls had been necessary. In our conditions of shelter, privacy, and admission fees, the life of the well-to-do must be potentially richer than the life of the poor, and only six hundred can have direct access to the business of the nation. In Athens all these things could be open to all because they could be open to the air and the sun. To explain Athenian culture simply as the product of the Athenian climate would be foolish, though not unfashionable; nevertheless it is demonstrable that in a different climate it could not have developed as it did.

Kitto states that the leisure that the Athenian enjoyed was due to the warm climate, and the leisure, in turn, caused him "to sharpen his wits and improve his manners through constant intercourse with his fellows." This constant intercourse resulted in the "hours of talk." The gentle climate also allowed crowds to assemble out of doors instead of being confined to buildings. This open-air assembly allowed for development of Athenian culture. Thus, we have the following chain of causes:

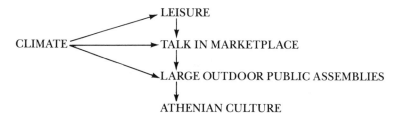

Kitto concludes that "to explain Athenian culture simply as the product of the Athenian climate would be foolish." In other words, the Greek climate was not a necessary cause, but allowed other possibilities that, in turn, encouraged the development of the Athenian culture.

Rhetorical Cause and Effect

Writers may explore an idea by defining it, putting it in a class, comparing or contrasting it with another idea, or by looking at its causes and effects. There are a number of ways to use cause and effect to approach an idea. You can explore the idea in terms of its causes, in terms of its effects, or in terms of itself as a cause or an effect of another event or idea. Thus, high unemployment in a certain area might be caused by the closing of a local business. Its effects might be riots and other disturbances. From another viewpoint, a writer writing about riots might see unemployment as a cause or in writing about the closing of a local business might see unemployment as an effect. Often ideas and events are related one to the other in a chain of causes and effects. You may choose to focus on one event or issue within the chain.

1. From cause to effect: In this form of reasoning, you proceed from a known cause to a probable effect. Thus if it is raining, it can be predicted that the picnic will be postponed. The known cause is rain; the probable effect about which there is speculation is the postponement of the picnic.

2. From effect to cause: In this type of reasoning you move from a known effect to the cause that produced it. Most medical diagnoses follow this procedure. The patient goes to the doctor with a backache, a headache, or a sore throat and the doctor in his or her diagnosis tries to determine the cause. The effect is known; the cause is speculative.

3. From effect to effect: In this type of reasoning you assume that whatever produced one effect will also regularly produce other effects. If the patient has a sore throat, that patient may well develop a fever; both effects caused by a virus. Similarly, if there are street riots caused by high unemployment, use of drugs and criminal activities may also ensue.

In this selection from his essay "Politics and the English Language," George Orwell explores the causes and effects of what he calls "the decline of a language."

Now, it is clear that the decline of a language must ultimately have political and economic causes: it is not due simply to the bad influence of this or that individual writer. But an effect can become a cause, reinforcing the original cause and producing the same effect in an intensified form, and so on indefinitely. A man may take to drink because he feels himself to be a failure, and then fail all the more completely because he drinks. It is rather the same thing that is happening to the English language. It becomes ugly and inaccurate because our thoughts are foolish, but the slovenliness of our language makes it easier for us to have foolish thoughts. The point is that the process is reversible. Modern English, especially written English, is full of bad habits which spread by imitation and which can be avoided if one is willing to take the necessary trouble. If one gets rid of these habits one can think more clearly, and to think clearly is a necessary first step towards political regeneration: so that the fight against bad English is not frivolous and is not the exclusive concern of professional writers.

In this essay, Orwell first states that there must be political and economic causes for the decline of a language; it cannot be caused simply by individual writers. He then moves on to the assertion that the decline of the language can not only be an effect but can also act as a cause for "foolish thoughts." He concludes by saying that eliminating the "bad habits" of language users will cause persons to "think more clearly," which is a "necessary first step towards political regeneration." Thus he moves from effect to cause and from cause to effect in this chain of reasoning that introduces his discussion.

It is seldom enough to think of a subject in terms of only one cause or one effect. In the same way that Orwell moves through a chain of causes and effects, you will need to explore causes in terms of their causes, and effects in terms of multiple effects. In this way your subject becomes the center of a web of careful reasoning.

Using Cause and Effect in Your Writing It is not always easy to determine true causes or to predict effects when causes are known. In the following fable, "The Rabbits Who Caused All the Trouble," James Thurber pokes fun at the attributing of false causes to events.

Within the memory of the youngest child there was a family of rabbits who lived near a pack of wolves. The wolves announced that they did not like the way the rabbits were living. (The wolves were crazy about the way they themselves were living, because it was the only way to live.) One night several wolves were killed in an earthquake and this was blamed on the rabbits, for it is well known that rabbits pound on the ground with their hind legs and cause earthquakes. On another night one of the wolves was killed by a bolt of lightning and this was also blamed on the rabbits, for it is well known that lettuce-eaters cause lightning. The wolves threatened to civilize the rabbits if they didn't behave, and the rabbits decided to run away to a desert island. But the other animals, who lived at a great distance, shamed them, saying, "You must stay where you are and be brave. This is no world for escapists. If the wolves attack you, we will come to your aid, in all probability." So the rabbits continued to live near the wolves and one day there was a terrible flood which drowned a great many wolves. This was blamed on the rabbits, for it is well known that carrot-nibblers with long ears cause floods. The wolves descended on the rabbits, for their own good, and imprisoned them in a dark cave, for their own protection.

When nothing was heard about the rabbits for some weeks, the other animals demanded to know what had happened to them. The wolves replied that the rabbits had been eaten and since they had been eaten the affair was a purely internal matter. But the other animals warned that they might possibly unite against the wolves unless some reason was given for the destruction of the rabbits. So the wolves gave them one. "They were trying to escape," said the wolves, "and, as you know, this is no world for escapists."

Moral: Run, don't walk, to the nearest desert island.

In this fable the wolves attribute a number of false causes to events that obviously have other causes. Earthquakes are not caused by rabbits pounding on the ground with their hind legs, nor is lightning caused by lettuce-eaters. Such natural events have other more complex causes. In your own writing you need to question the validity of causes very carefully. Ask yourself these questions as you write:

1. Could this cause produce this effect? Is it a sufficient cause?

2. Is there another cause that may have produced the effect?

When causes are unknown, superstitions may develop to explain events that have no ready explanations. The person who believes an illness is caused by the breaking of a mirror is dealing with an insufficient cause, as is the person who attributes success in a project to the "stars." As the following essay by Lewis Thomas demonstrates, human beings want very much to understand causes for both good and bad events—in the former case so that they can duplicate the effect and in the latter case so that they can prevent the effect. So persons seek and attribute causes—sometimes simple and often outlandish ones—for a backache, a lack of success, the hiccups, failure on an examination, and other events that may have a complex set of direct and indirect causes. Often ignorance of real causes and a desire to find good reasons encourage persons to attribute false or insufficient causes.

In the following essay, Lewis Thomas explores true causes of certain diseases and demonstrates what happens when magic is substituted to bring results when real causes are unknown. It is a careful study of false causes, insufficient causes, confusion of cause with effect, and the substitution of magic for true cause in the history of medicine.

ON MAGIC IN MEDICINE

LEWIS THOMAS

Medicine has always been under pressure to provide public explanations   1
for the diseases with which it deals, and the formulation of comprehen-
sive, unifying theories has been the most ancient and willing preoccupa-
tion of the profession. In the earliest days, hostile spirits needing exor-
cism were the principal pathogens, and the shaman's duty was simply the
development of improved techniques for incantation. Later on, especially in the Western world, the idea that the distribution of body
fluids among various organs determined the course of all illnesses took
hold, and we were in for centuries of bleeding, cupping, sweating, and
purging in efforts to intervene. Early in this century the theory of autointoxication evolved, and a large part of therapy was directed at emptying
the large intestine and keeping it empty. Then the global concept of focal
infection became popular, accompanied by the linked notion of allergy
to the presumed microbial pathogens, and no one knows the resulting
toll of extracted teeth, tonsils, gallbladders, and appendixes: the idea of
psychosomatic influences on disease emerged in the 1930s and, for a
while, seemed to sweep the field.

Gradually, one by one, some of our worst diseases have been edited out   2
of such systems by having their causes indisputably identified and dealt
with. Tuberculosis was the paradigm. This was the most chronic and
inexorably progressive of common human maladies, capable of affecting
virtually every organ in the body and obviously influenced by crowding,
nutrition, housing and poverty; theories involving the climate in general,
and night air and insufficient sunlight in particular, gave rise to the spa
as a therapeutic institution. It was not until the development of today's
effective chemotherapy that it became clear to everyone that the disease
had a single, dominant, central cause. If you got rid of the tubercle bacil-
lus you were rid of the disease.

But that was some time ago, and today the idea that complicated   3
diseases can have single causes is again out of fashion. The microbial
infections that can be neatly coped with by antibiotics are regarded as
lucky anomalies. The new theory is that most of today's human illnesses,
the infections aside, are multifactorial in nature, caused by two great
arrays of causative mechanisms: 1) the influence of things in the environment and 2) one's personal life-style. For medicine to become effective in
dealing with such diseases, it has become common belief that the environ-

ment will have to be changed, and personal ways of living will also have to be transformed, and radically.

These things may turn out to be true, for all I know, but it will take a long time to get the necessary proofs. Meanwhile, the field is wide open for magic. 4

One great difficulty in getting straightforward answers is that so many of the diseases in question have unpredictable courses, and some of them have a substantial tendency toward spontaneous remission. In rheumatoid arthritis, for instance, when such widely disparate therapeutic measures as copper bracelets, a move to Arizona, diets low in sugar or salt or meat or whatever, and even an inspirational book have been accepted by patients as useful, the trouble in evaluation is that approximately 35 percent of patients with this diagnosis are bound to recover no matter what they do. But if you actually have rheumatoid arthritis or, for that matter, schizophrenia, and then get over it, or if you are a doctor and observe this to happen, it is hard to be persuaded that it wasn't *something* you did that was responsible. Hence you need very large numbers of patients and lots of time, and a cool head. 5

Magic is back again, and in full force. Laetrile cures cancer, acupuncture is useful for deafness and low-back pain, vitamins are good for anything, and meditation, yoga, dancing, biofeedback, and shouting one another down in crowded rooms over weekends are specifics for the human condition. Running, a good thing to be doing for its own sake, has acquired the medicinal value formerly attributed to rare herbs from Indonesia. 6

There is a recurring advertisement, placed by Blue Cross on the op-ed page of *The New York Times*, which urges you to take advantage of science by changing your life habits, with the suggestion that if you do so, by adopting seven easy-to-follow items of life-style, you can achieve eleven added years beyond what you'll get if you don't. Since today's average figure is around seventy-two for all parties in both sexes, this might mean going on until at least the age of eighty-three. You can do this formidable thing, it is claimed, by simply eating breakfast, exercising regularly, maintaining normal weight, not smoking cigarettes, not drinking excessively, sleeping eight hours each night, and not eating between meals. 7

The science which produced this illumination was a careful study by California epidemiologists, based on a questionnaire given to about seven thousand people. Five years after the questionnaire, a body count was made by sorting through the county death certificates, and the 371 people who had died were matched up with their answers to the questions. To be sure, there were more deaths among the heavy smokers and drinkers, as you might expect from the known incidence of lung cancer in smokers and cirrhosis and auto accidents among drinkers. But there was 8 also a higher mortality among those who said they didn't eat breakfast, and even higher in those who took no exercise, no exercise at all, not even going off in the family car for weekend picnics. Being up to 20 percent overweight was not so bad, surprisingly, but being *underweight* was clearly associated with a higher death rate.

The paper describing these observations has been widely quoted, and   9
not just by Blue Cross. References to the Seven Healthy Life Habits keep turning up in popular magazines and in the health columns of newspapers, always with that promise of eleven more years.

The findings fit nicely with what is becoming folk doctrine about   10
disease. You become ill because of not living right. If you get cancer it is, somehow or other, your own fault. If you didn't cause it by smoking or drinking or eating the wrong things, it came from allowing yourself to persist with the wrong kind of personality, in the wrong environment. If you have a coronary occlusion, you didn't run enough. Or you were too tense, or you *wished* too much, and didn't get a good enough sleep. Or you got fat. Your fault.

But eating breakfast? It is a kind of enchantment, pure magic.   11

You have to read the report carefully to discover that there is another,   12
more banal way of explaining the findings. Leave aside the higher deaths in heavy smokers and drinkers, for there is no puzzle in either case; these are dangerous things to do. But it is hard to imagine any good reason for dying within five years from not eating a good breakfast, or any sort of breakfast.

The other explanation turns cause and effect around. Among the   13
people in that group of seven thousand who answered that they don't eat breakfast, don't go off on picnics, are underweight, and can't sleep properly, there were surely some who were already ill when the questionnaire arrived. They didn't eat breakfast because they couldn't stand the sight of food. They had lost their appetites, were losing weight, didn't feel up to moving around much, and had trouble sleeping. They didn't play tennis or go off on family picnics because they didn't *feel* good. Some of these people probably had an undetected cancer, perhaps of the pancreas; others may have had hypertension or early kidney failure or some other organic disease which the questionnaire had no way of picking up. The study did not ascertain the causes of death in the 371, but just a few deaths from such indiscerned disorders would have made a significant statistical impact. The author of the paper was careful to note these possible interpretations, although the point was not made strongly, and the general sense you have in reading it is that you can live on and on if only you will eat breakfast and play tennis.

The popular acceptance of the notion of Seven Healthy Life Habits, as   14
a way of staying alive, says something important about today's public attitudes, or at least the attitudes in the public mind, about disease and

dying. People have always wanted causes that are simple and easy to comprehend, and about which the individual can *do* something. If you believe that you can ward off the common causes of premature death— cancer, heart disease, and stroke, diseases whose pathogenesis we really do not understand—by jogging, hoping, and eating and sleeping regularly, these are good things to believe even if not necessarily true. Medicine has survived other periods of unifying theory, constructed to explain all of human disease, not always as benign in their effects as this one is likely to be. After all, if people can be induced to give up smoking, stop overdrinking and overeating, and take some sort of regular exercise, most of them are bound to feel the better for leading more orderly, regular lives, and many of them are surely going to look better.

15 Nobody can say an unfriendly word against the sheer goodness of keeping fit, but we should go carefully with the promises.

16 There is also a bifurcated ideological appeal contained in the seven-life-habits doctrine, quite apart from the subliminal notion of good luck in the numbers involved (7 come 11). Both ends of the political spectrum can find congenial items. At the further right, it is attractive to hear that the individual, the good old freestanding, free-enterprising American citizen, is responsible for his own health and when things go wrong it is his own damn fault for smoking and drinking and living wrong (and he can jolly well pay for it). On the other hand, at the left, it is nice to be told that all our health problems, including dying, are caused by failure of the community to bring up its members to live properly, and if you really want to improve the health of the people, research is not the answer; you should upheave the present society and invent a better one. At either end, you can't lose.

17 In between, the skeptics in medicine have a hard time of it. It is much more difficult to be convincing about ignorance concerning disease mechanisms than it is to make claims for full comprehension, especially when the comprehension leads, logically or not, to some sort of action. When it comes to serious illness, the public tends, understandably, to be more skeptical about the skeptics, more willing to believe the true believers. It is medicine's oldest dilemma, not to be settled by candor or by any kind of rhetoric; what it needs is a lot of time and patience, waiting for science to come in, as it has in the past, with the solid facts.

In his introduction, Thomas makes us question the commonly held contemporary belief that illness is caused by "the influence of things in the environment and one's personal life-style" by citing the past beliefs in spirits, distribution of bodily fluids, and autointoxication as causes that have been proven false. He points out the difficulty of proving with any

certainty that the accepted contemporary causes are necessary or sufficient causes of illness. He then cites a study by California epidemiologists, which purported to prove that eating breakfast could avert illness
and lead to a long life. He shows the confusion between cause and effect
in this commonly held belief by suggesting that those who did not eat
breakfast were already sick and simply did not feel like eating. By analyzing the causes of illness listed in the "Seven Healthy Life Habits" and
separating true causes—such as heavy smoking and drinking—from false
causes, Lewis proves his point that as in the past, we must wait for science
to come in "with the solid facts."

In discovering causes and effects connected with your subject you
might ask the following questions.

What is the cause of X?

Is there more than one cause of X?

Which causes are necessary? Which are sufficient?

Which causes are immediate? Which are remote?

What are the effects of X?

What comes before X? Are these causes?

What comes after X? Are these effects?

The topics covered in these last two chapters are important tools in
logos, one of the three parts of rhetorical proof. In the next chapter,
logical and rhetorical induction and deduction together with the syllogism will be examined—completing this discussion of artistic proofs that
involves *ethos, pathos*, and *logos*.

Questions to Consider

1. As a class, make a list comparing your expectations of your freshman year with what you are discovering to be the reality. How might you use those similarities and differences to advise a friend in a letter or a phone call who is planning to attend your school?

2. Identify the following causes of the proposed effects as either necessary or sufficient:

A. *Causes*:
   You did not study for the exam.
   You did not take the exam.
   You took the exam but answered fewer than half of the questions.
   You arrived late to the exam.
   Your notes were stolen the night before the exam.
   Effect: You failed the exam.

B. *Causes*:
   You cannot find the key.
   The car is out of gas.
   The battery is dead.
   The fuel line is frozen.
   The temperature outside is 95°F.
   The right-front tire is flat.
   Effect: Your car won't start.

3. The important thing to remember about the topics is that they can be used to generate ideas. Consider, for example, the different essays that could result from applying each of the topics discussed in Chapters 4 and 5 to this idea:

Many students have difficulty writing in college.
Definition: How do you define "writing in college?" What, precisely, are the difficulties? Who are these students?
Classification: What kinds of difficulties do they experience? What kinds of students experience such difficulties?
Comparison: How is college writing similar to other writing? How is it different? How do the difficulties students experience in college writing compare with the difficulties they experienced in high school?

Cause and Effect: Why do the students experience such difficulties? What are the effects of experiencing such difficulties—in college or after graduation?

Try applying these topics to other statements as a means of generating ideas. For example:

A. Many people are offended by pornographic magazines.

B. Violence occurs in many families every day in the United States.

C. Many women are now choosing to have their babies outside of the hospital.

Suggestions for Writing

1. Write a page or two in which you compare your language habits in two different contexts. Consider, for example, how the language you speak compares with the language you write; do you use the same kinds of words, the same sentence patterns? Or, consider how the language you use at home compares with the language you use in the classroom or how your private voice compares with your public voice.

2. Find an advertisement for a product you now own. Then write a page or two in which you compare or contrast its claims with what you have found to be true about the product. Based on your experience with the product, what can you conclude about the truthfulness of the advertisement?

3. Compare a photograph taken recently of yourself with a photograph taken years ago. In an essay identify and explain those similarities and differences that you find significant.

4. Write an essay in which you explain why writing is difficult for you.

5. Write a paragraph or two in which you explain how your life would change were you to win the Publishers' Clearing House Sweepstakes and receive $1,000,000.

6. Using Thurber's fable appearing in this chapter as an example, write a fable of your own to explain and justify some truth, using causes that are obviously false. Be sure to sum up the point of your fable in a closing moral.

Exercises in Revision

1. Evaluate a piece of writing submitted by a member of your workshop group; then write a paragraph in which you explain why you have evaluated the writing as you did. Discuss your conclusions with the author.

2. Compare an early draft of one of your writing exercises with a revision, and make a list of all of the similarities and differences between the two versions. Is the revision a significant improvement over the draft? Why, or why not?

3. Examine the writing used in 1 and 2 employing the topic of comparison submitted by members of your workshop group. Using the questions provided in this chapter, determine whether their comparisons are valid. If not, suggest appropriate revisions.

4. Examine the writing used in 1 and 2 employing the topic of cause and effect submitted by members of your workshop group. Using the questions provided in this chapter, offer suggestions for improvement as needed.

For a Commonplace Book

Try to find examples in your own reading of articles using the topics of comparison and cause and effect. Determine the author's purpose in using those topics and record your conclusions in your commonplace book.

Chapter 6

Finding Good Reasons

T his chapter continues with *logos*, the third artistic or rhetorical proof. Whereas *ethos* depends on the character of the speaker or writer and *pathos* on putting the audience into a certain frame of mind, *logos* is proving the case. The modern word, logic, the study of the principles of reasoning, comes from the Greek word *logos*.

Classical rhetoricians and philosophers make a distinction, however, between logical and rhetorical proof. Logic has to do with universal and certain truths; rhetoric with probable truths. It is the same kind of distinction we often make today between the kind of truth demonstrated in a science laboratory and the kind of probable truth arrived at in a discussion of philosophy or history. Today, important decisions, both at the national level and at the professional and personal level, are, in fact, based on probabilities derived from commonly held generalities or from similar cases. We can only arrive at probable causes for the Vietnam War, but the more that can be learned about those probable causes the more that can be learned about the prevention of similar wars in the future. So human beings continue to work in the area of probabilities, seeking out good reasons as much as they are able so they may better understand human affairs and make more informed decisions. The kind of reasoning, *logos*, that informs such decisions is the province of rhetoric. In order to understand rhetorical reasoning, however, you will need some background in logic. Consequently, this chapter starts with a brief description of logical reasoning.

LOGICAL REASONING

In logical reasoning, an argument is judged by two standards: truth and validity. In this context, these two terms have very different meanings. An argument is *true* if the material on which it is based is generally accepted as true and *valid* if the reasoning follows a logical sequence.

The word *truth* describes the matter or content of the statements or assertions upon which an argument is built. It would be difficult to find a single belief that is held as truth by all cultures, religions, and nationalities. But persons belong to groups and cultures that hold beliefs as truths, and it is on these shared beliefs that arguments can be based. For example, in our culture, murder is considered a criminal act, and honesty is generally considered the best policy. On the other hand, there is great division on whether taxes should be increased or on whether there is indeed life after death. Consequently, the contemporary writer bases arguments on beliefs that are accepted as true by particular audiences. As a result, a knowledge of audience is paramount in selecting and shaping appropriate arguments.

In the following argument, readers will not accept the first statement as true, so the conclusion is untrue.

All human beings have four legs, and John is a human being, so John has four legs.

However, even though the conclusion is untrue the argument is valid. The word *validity* describes the form of the argument or the way in which the individual statements in the argument are related to one another—whether they in fact follow from one another. An argument is valid if the reasoning is sound, if one statement logically follows another in a reasonable sequence. The preceding argument is valid because it follows that if all human beings *did* have four legs, and if John *is* a human being, then John must have four legs. The conclusion is untrue because the first statement is untrue, but the statements logically follow one from the other, so the argument is valid though untrue.

Deduction and Induction

There are generally two ways to approach an argument, by deduction and by induction. In *deduction*, the argument moves from a general statement to a particular instance; in *induction*, it moves from a particular instance to similar instances and then to a general truth. A customer, in shopping at the grocery store, may taste one or two cherries, reason that if one is sweet, the other cherries must also be sweet and conclude, or induce, from that sample that all the cherries in the bin are sweet. That customer is making an induction about all the cherries on the basis of only one or two sample cherries. A person who knows two persons with red hair who are short tempered may assume that all red heads have short tempers. It is from this kind of thinking that many prejudices about persons and groups arise. Since the customer cannot sample all the cherries and since the person cannot know all members of a group, the generalizations they presume may be incorrect. This is a common type of cognitive process and represents the way the child learns and develops language. The child who has eaten chocolate bars makes the assumption that all chocolate is sweet and delicious, but that child's first encounter with unsweetened baking chocolate will be a surprise.

Deduction is the reverse of this process—it is reasoning from a general truth about a group to an assumption about one of its members. So the person who thinks that all children love candy may deduce from that belief that Tommie likes candy. Some of these assumptions are based on well-founded ideas; others are not. Not all cherries are sweet, nor do all children love candy. On the other hand, since everyone in your Biology I class has taken high school chemistry as a prerequisite, you can safely assume that your classmate John has taken high school biology.

Logicians have studied these two processes in great detail, and an elaborate discussion of them is not necessary here. But since they are so common to our language processes, we will look at some of the general principles.

Deduction

The primary form of deductive thinking is represented in the syllogism, from a Greek word that means "to reason together." The original root is from *logos*, Greek for *word*, demonstrating once again the close connection between language and reason. Aristotle, who first formulated the syllogism in his logical treatises, recognized that to argue well, a person needs to understand the rudiments of the syllogism before learning to use the enthymeme (EN-thuh-meem), the abbreviated rhetorical form of the syllogism. The syllogism is a useful way to structure an argument as well as an analytical tool to demonstrate errors in your own and other people's arguments.

There are three general types of syllogism: the categorical, the disjunctive, and the hypothetical.

The Categorical Syllogism A categorical syllogism is made up of three parts: a *major premise* that states a generalization, a *minor premise* that states a particular case, a *conclusion* that follows from these two statements. What follows is the classic example of the syllogism:

> Major Premise: All men are mortal.
>
> Minor Premise: Socrates is a man.
>
> Conclusion: Therefore Socrates is mortal.

The categorical syllogism has to do with categories or whole classes and operates on the assumption that what is true of a class will also be true of its members. You might wish to review this point as it was taken up under classification in Chapter 4. Categorical syllogisms are characterized by having a word such as *all* or *every* in the major premise:

> *All* A's are B's.
>
> *All* men are mortal.

The categorical syllogism can be represented in a sort of shorthand in the following manner:

> All A's are B's.
>
> C is an A.
>
> Therefore C is a B.

Note that the categorical syllogism has only three terms (A, B, and C) and that each term is used twice and only twice in the syllogism. The conclusion of a deductive argument or syllogism is signalled by such words as *so, therefore, thus,* and *consequently.* The following is an example of a categorical syllogism in sentence form: Murder is wrong and euthanasia is murder; therefore euthanasia is wrong.

This argument can be broken down into the following syllogism.

Major Premise: Murder is wrong.

Minor Premise: Euthanasia is murder.

Conclusion: Consequently, euthanasia is wrong.

In these examples, we have seen that two positive premises—"All A's *are* B's," "C *is* an A"—yields a positive conclusion—"Therefore C *is* a B." If, however, one of the premises is negative, the conclusion will be negative, as in these examples:

No A's are B.

C is an A.

Therefore C is not a B.

No burglars are honest.

John is a burglar.

Therefore John is not honest.

The third possible categorical syllogism, one with two negative premises, yields *no conclusion*, as in these examples:

No A's are B.

C is not an A.

No conclusion possible.

No men are mortal.

Socrates is not a man.

No conclusion possible.

Deductive reasoning seldom appears in conversation or in writing as a well-formed three-statement syllogism with a major premise, a minor premise, and a conclusion. In conversation we might hear one of the following remarks: "Jane is good at math. I bet she can play the piano, too." Syllogistic reasoning lies behind such a statement. The unstated major premise is the assumption that people who are good at math can also play the piano. This kind of abbreviated syllogism, in which one premise is stated and one is implied, is called the *enthymeme*, which will be discussed in detail later in this chapter.

In his treatise on rhetoric, Cicero states that both the major premise and the minor premise of a deductive argument must be supported by proof "by which the brief statement . . . of the premise is supported by reasons and made plainer and more plausible" (*De Inventione* 1.27.67). If you were to use the following syllogism to generate an essay, such proof of the premises might make up the major part of the argument.

Adults make their own financial decisions.

College students are adults.

College students should make their own financial decisions.

The major premise would have to be supported by proof that adults do indeed make their own financial decisions. The minor premise, that college students are adults, could be supported by pointing out that they drive cars, are subject to service in the armed forces, vote in elections, and often hold jobs to contribute to their own support. If the major and minor premises in this syllogism are supported logically by examples, then the conclusion that college students should make their own financial decisions follows.

The Disjunctive Syllogism The disjunctive syllogism has to do with what the classical rhetoricians called contraries and contradictions. It is represented in statements and comments marked by such words as *either*, *or*, and *neither*, *nor*. This kind of syllogism contains two alternatives in its major premise connected by *or* or *nor*:

George is either lying or he is stupid.

George is not stupid.

Therefore, he is lying.

Major Premise: either X or Y

Minor Premise: not Y

Conclusion: Therefore X

The major premise of the disjunctive syllogism must state *all* of the available possibilities. In other words, George is lying or is stupid; there is no possibility that George is mistaken or misinformed. The minor premise must eliminate *one* of the alternatives in the first statement for the conclusion to be valid. The minor premise in a disjunctive syllogism cannot introduce a new element. In other words George *must be* either lying or stupid.

There must, then, be a clear connection between the major and minor premises before a conclusion is possible. No conclusion can be drawn from the first two statements in the following example:

> Bill either must make an A on the biology exam, or he will flunk the course.
>
> Bill hates biology, so he will flunk the course.

There is no direct connection between hating biology and flunking the exam, nor does it follow the rules of the syllogism because Bill's feelings about biology are not stated in the major premise.

A conclusion can be drawn, however, in the following example:

> Bill either must make an A on the biology exam, or he will flunk the course.
>
> Bill did not make an A on the biology exam, so he will flunk the course.

There is a direct connection between the premises here because the minor premise eliminates one of the alternatives given in the major premise, making an A on the exam.

The Hypothetical Syllogism The hypothetical syllogism is based on the classical topic of antecedents and consequents and is closely connected to the topic of cause and effect discussed in Chapter 5. It is the formal statement of sequential events that follow one another, characterized primarily by the words *if, when,* or *provided that.* A consequent is what necessarily follows from something else, which is called the antecedent. The major premise states a condition, the antecedent, that must be fulfilled for an event, the consequent, to occur. One event will follow another, but the causal relation is not definite. For example:

> If government officials are not adequately paid, then bribery will become common.

The necessary condition, the antecedent, is the *if* clause and comes before the consequent, the *then* clause.

> Antecedent: *If* government officials are not adequately paid
>
> Consequent: *Then* bribery will become common.

The minor premise either affirms the antecedent (*if* clause) or denies the consequent (*then* clause).

> Affirms the antecedent: Government officials are not adequately paid.

or

> Denies the consequent: Government officials are adequately paid.

If the minor premise affirms the antecedent, the conclusion then affirms the consequent.

> Major Premise: If government officials are not adequately paid, then bribery will become common.
> Minor Premise: Government officials are not adequately paid.
> Conclusion: Therefore, bribery will become common.

This relationship can be represented as follows:

> Major Premise: If A, then B
> Minor Premise: Affirm A
> Conclusion: Therefore B

If the minor premise denies the consequent, the conclusion then denies the antecedent.

> Major Premise: If government officials are not adequately paid, then bribery will become common.
> Minor Premise: Bribery will not become common.
> Conclusion: Government officials are adequately paid.

This relationship can be represented as follows:

> Major Premise: If A, then B
> Minor Premise: Deny B
> Conclusion: Therefore deny A

Hypothetical statements occur frequently in writing as in the following example. They can be used as a basis for lengthy and complicated arguments, or they can be used as simple statements.

> If he's guilty he will be condemned, but he hasn't been condemned so he must be not guilty.

The Declaration of Independence written primarily by Thomas Jefferson, a student of logic and rhetoric, is a carefully reasoned argument based on syllogistic reasoning that has endured over time. It is based on premises that have served as the founding principles for the United States and other democracies.

THE DECLARATION OF INDEPENDENCE

THOMAS JEFFERSON

When in the course of human events, it becomes necessary for one people to dissolve the political bands which have connected them with another, and to assume among the Powers of the earth, the separate and equal station to which the Laws of Nature and of Nature's God entitle them, a decent respect to the opinions of mankind requires that they should declare the causes which impel them to the separation. 1

We hold these truths to be self-evident, that all men are created equal, that they are endowed by their Creator with certain unalienable Rights, that among these are Life, Liberty and the pursuit of Happiness. That to secure these rights, Governments are instituted among Men deriving their just powers from the consent of the governed. That whenever any Form of Government becomes destructive of these ends, it is the Right of the People to alter or to abolish it, and to institute new Government, laying its foundation on such principles and organizing its powers in such form, as to them shall seem most likely to effect their Safety and Happiness. Prudence, indeed, will dictate that Governments long established should not be changed for light and transient causes; and accordingly all experience hath shown, that mankind are more disposed to suffer, while evils are sufferable, than to right themselves by abolishing the forms to which they are accustomed. But when a long train of abuses and usurpations pursuing invariably the same Object evinces a design to reduce them under absolute Despotism, it is their right, it is their duty, to throw off such government, and to provide new Guards for their future security. Such has been the patient sufferance of these Colonies; and such is now the necessity which constrains them to alter their former Systems of Government. The history of the present King of Great Britain is a history of repeated injuries and usurpations, all having in direct object the establishment of an absolute Tyranny over these States. To prove this, let Facts be submitted to a candid world. 2

He has refused his Assent to Laws, the most wholesome and necessary   3
for the public good.

He has forbidden his Governors to pass Laws of immediate and press-   4
ing importance, unless suspended in their operation till his Assent
should be obtained; and when so suspended, he has utterly neglected to
attend them.

He has refused to pass other Laws for the accommodation of large   5
districts of people, unless those people would relinquish the right of
Representation in the Legislature, a right inestimable to them and formidable to tyrants only.

He has called together legislative bodies at places unusual, uncomfort-   6
able, and distant from the depository of their Public Records, for the sole
purpose of fatiguing them into compliance with his measures.

He has dissolved Representative Houses repeatedly, for opposing with   7
manly firmness his invasions on the rights of the people.

He has refused for a long time, after such dissolutions, to cause others   8
to be elected; whereby the Legislative Powers, incapable of Annihilation,
have returned to the People at large for their exercise; the State remaining in the mean time exposed to all the dangers of invasion from without,
and convulsions within.

He has endeavoured to prevent the population of these States; for that   9
purpose obstructing the Laws of Naturalization of Foreigners; refusing to
pass others to encourage their migration hither, and raising the conditions of new Appropriations of Lands.

He has obstructed the Administration of Justice, by refusing his Assent   10
to Laws for establishing Judiciary Powers.

He has made Judges dependent on his Will alone, for the tenure of   11
their offices, and the amount and payment of their salaries.

He has erected a multitude of New Offices, and sent hither swarms of   12
Officers to harass our People, and eat out their substance.

He has kept among us, in time of peace, Standing Armies without the   13
Consent of our Legislature.

He has affected to render the Military independent of and superior to   14
the Civil Power.

He has combined with others to subject us to jurisdictions foreign to   15
our constitution, and unacknowledged by our laws; giving his Assent to
their acts of pretended Legislation:

For quartering large bodies of armed troops among us: 16

For protecting them, by a mock Trial, from Punishment for any Mur-   17
ders which they should commit on the Inhabitants of these States:

For cutting off our Trade with all parts of the world: 18

For imposing Taxes on us without our Consent: 19

For depriving us in many cases, of the benefits of Trial by Jury: 20

For transporting us beyond Seas to be tried for pretended offenses: 21

For abolishing the free System of English Laws in a Neighbouring 22 Province, establishing therein an Arbitrary government, and enlarging its boundaries so as to render it at once an example and fit instrument for introducing the same absolute rule into these Colonies:

For taking away our Charters, abolishing our most valuable Laws, and 23 altering fundamentally the Forms of our Governments:

For suspending our own Legislatures, and declaring themselves in- 24 vested with Power to legislate for us in all cases whatsoever.

He has abdicated Government here, by declaring us out of his Protec- 25 tion and waging War against us.

He has plundered our seas, ravaged our Coasts, burnt our towns and 26 destroyed the Lives of our people.

He is at this time transporting large Armies of foreign Mercenaries to 27 compleat works of death, desolation and tyranny, already begun with circumstances of Cruelty & perfidy scarcely paralleled in the most barbarous ages, and totally unworthy the Head of a civilized nation.

He has constrained our fellow Citizens taken Captive on the high Seas 28 to bear Arms against their Country, to become the executioners of their friends and Brethren, or to fall themselves by their Hands.

He has excited domestic insurrections amongst us, and has endeav- 29 oured to bring on the inhabitants of our frontiers, the merciless Indian Savages, whose known rule of warfare, is an undistinguished destruction of all ages, sexes and conditions.

In every stage of these Oppressions We Have Petitioned for Redress in 30 the most humble terms: Our repeated petitions have been answered only by repeated injury. A Prince, whose character is thus marked by every act which may define a Tyrant, is unfit to be the ruler of a free People.

Not have We been wanting in attention to our British brethren. We 31 have warned them from time to time of attempts by their legislature to extend an unwarrantable jurisdiction over us. We have reminded them of the circumstances of our emigration and settlement here. We have appealed to their native justice and magnanimity and we have conjured them by the ties of our common kindred to disavow these usurpations, which would inevitably interrupt our connections and correspondence. They too have been deaf to the voice of justice and of consanguinity. We must, therefore acquiesce in the necessity, which denounces our Separation, and hold them, as we hold the rest of mankind, Enemies in War, in Peace Friends.

We, therefore, the Representatives of the United States of America, in 32 General Congress, Assembled, appealing to the Supreme Judge of the world for the rectitude of our intentions, do, in the Name, and by Authority of the good People of these Colonies, solemnly publish and declare, That these United Colonies are, and of Right ought to be Free and Independent States; that they are Absolved from all Allegiance to the British Crown, and that all political connection between them and the State of Great Britain, is and ought to be totally dissolved; and that as Free and Independent States, they have full power to levy War, conclude Peace, contract Alliances, establish Commerce, and to do all other Acts and Things which Independent States may of right do. And for the support of this Declaration, with a firm reliance on the protection of Divine Providence, we mutually pledge to each other our lives, our Fortunes and our sacred Honor.

The argument in this document is based on a number of truths that the authors feel to be "self-evident." These include such by now familiar ideas as "all men are created equal," and that all persons have the right to "Life, Liberty and the pursuit of Happiness." The purpose of governments, the document affirms, is to insure these rights. The hypothetical argument begins in the second paragraph:

> . . . whenever any Form of Government becomes destructive of these ends, it is the Right of the People to alter or to abolish it, and to institute new Government. . . .

The authors then continue by presenting the minor premise, a long list of "facts" that demonstrate how the government has been "destructive of these ends," thus affirming the antecedent. This then affirms the consequent, their right "to alter or to abolish it." Therefore it is the right of the people "to alter or abolish it, and to institute new Government."

The syllogism would take the following shape:

> Major Premise: If a government becomes destructive, then the people have a right to alter or abolish it and institute a new government.
>
> Minor Premise: The government has become destructive.
>
> Conclusion: Therefore the people have a right to alter or abolish it and institute a new government.

The Toulmin Model

Another way of looking at deductive reasoning is through a structural model developed in this century by Stephen Toulmin, a philosopher and rhetorician. This model has many similarities to the syllogism, but it offers a different way of looking at the classical model. The Toulmin model has three primary elements—*data, warrant,* and *claim*—related to each other in the following way:

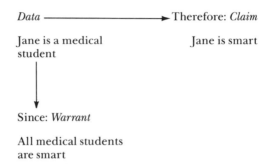

In this argument the *data* is the evidence; the *warrant* is the supporting argument; and the *claim* is the conclusion. This argument can also be expressed in the form of a syllogism:

All medical students are smart.
Jane is a medical student.
Therefore Jane is smart.

In ordinary conversation or in writing this argument would probably be expressed in one of the following ways:

Jane has got to be smart. She is a medical student.

Jane is a medical student, so you know she must be smart.

Both of these statements omit the assumed major premise that all medical students are smart. The Toulmin model also allows for other elements in the structure of the argument: the *backing,* the *rebuttal,* and, most important, the *qualifier.*

The *backing* provides additional reasons, or supporting arguments for the warrant, and is characterized by the word *because.* The *rebuttal* allows for exceptions, limitations, or special circumstances which may limit the claim and is characterized by the word *unless.* The *qualifier* marks the limitations of the claim and is characterized by the word *probably.* With these added features, the above argument would be structured in the following way:

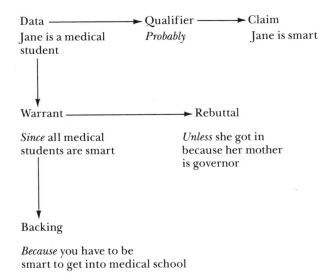

Stated in sentence form the above argument would read like this:

> Jane is a medical student, so she is *probably* smart, *since* she is a medical student, and *because* you have to be smart to get into medical school, *unless* she just got in because her mother is the governor.

The sentence might be broken into two or more sentences, and either the warrant or backing might be omitted as understood, just as the major or minor premise might be omitted as understood in the syllogism. It is interesting to note that the sentence has a logical structure and that the relations of the parts of the argument are indicated by the conjunctions, *since, because,* and *unless.* Such words do more than just connect two ideas; they in fact demonstrate the *logical* connections between ideas. The backing, rebuttal, and qualifier in the Toulmin model make the syllogism less rigid and therefore more useful in your reading and writing.

The syllogism, in not allowing for the qualifier, backing, and rebuttal is more appropriate for formal logic, while the Toulmin model is a way of adapting the syllogism to rhetoric. Rhetoric deals with probabilities, and therefore the qualifier is appropriate to problematic arguments.

Induction

In modern logic, induction is the kind of argument that makes a general assumption about a class of objects based on an examination of a number of samples. It is characterized by movement from particular instances to a general truth. Inductive inferences and arguments are invaluable in the natural and social sciences and in practical affairs as well. They are also the way we grow, learn, think, and communicate with persons around us. A child tastes an apple, so he assumes that all round red objects are edible and therefore takes the next logical step and tries to eat his round red ball. One man is a "Daddy," so all men are "Daddy's." As we grow and mature, our sampling is larger, and our generalizations more reliable, but we continue to make inductions on the basis of our necessarily limited experience.

Modern logicians distinguish two kinds of induction—perfect induction and scientific induction. In *perfect* induction all the members of a class are examined in connection with one particular trait or characteristic. Thus, if all of the test scores of the students in the tenth grade at a particular school are examined, a perfect inductive statement can be made about the test scores for that group. *Scientific* induction, on the other hand, allows for representative sampling. It assumes that fairly solid assumptions can be made if the following general criteria are observed in selecting samples:

1. A large number of samples is examined. A general conclusion cannot be made about all test scores if only one student's score is examined. A sufficiently large proportion of these scores must be sampled before the induction has any reliability.

2. Samples are representatively selected. If the level of students in a tenth-grade class is to be induced from a number of samples, it would be unwise to examine only the IQ scores of those students who sit in the front row. They may be there because they are more interested in the subject matter, or the teacher may have put them there because they are difficult students. Samples must be representatively selected.

3. Allowance is made for atypical examples. Atypical examples should be accounted for in the final induction as exceptions to the generalization. A student who has only been in the class for two days should probably not be included in the sampling or, if included, should be accounted for.

In their ordinary thinking, persons are inclined to make generalizations hastily and to hold tenaciously to beliefs based on an extremely limited number of samples. Exposure to a limited variety of people appears to lead to strongly held prejudices.

Forming generalizations from experience is a sign of linguistic growth, but recognizing the limitations of these generalizations is a sign of maturity. As experience broadens and takes in more of the world, almost all generalizations tend to have exceptions. As a child I may believe that all flowers are yellow, since only jonquils grow in my yard, but as I see flowers beyond my yard and my own neighborhood my generalization must be reevaluated. The same holds true for generalizations about races, religions, and cultures.

RHETORICAL REASONING

In determining proof, the classical student of logic attempted to determine truth by means of what the ancient philosophers called "dialectic," a search for truth through a dialogue among philosophers. The student of logic also used induction and deduction, which included the syllogism. The rhetorician, on the other hand, attempted to determine probable truths dealing in the realm of human affairs where truth is always contingent. In rhetorical proof, Aristotle tells us, the example substitutes for induction and the enthymeme for deduction and the syllogism. According to Aristotle, the enthymeme, the shortened syllogism which draws a probable conclusion, is better suited to rhetoric; the enthymeme is for Aristotle at the heart of rhetoric because it dealt with problematic issues.

The Enthymeme

The enthymeme may differ from the syllogism in two important ways:

1. *One of the premises is implied but not stated.*

In ordinary discourse, either spoken or written, the full syllogism with the major premise, the minor premise, and the conclusion is seldom stated. So in the following statement the major premise is omitted or understood:

Jane must have stolen the money. She is a Johnson.

The unstated premise is that all the Johnsons steal money. The full syllogism would be:

All the Johnsons steal money.
Jane is a Johnson.
Therefore, Jane must have stolen the money.

Stated without the major premise, this line of reasoning is called an enthymeme. Unstated major premises must be examined with care since they often rest on belief systems that underlie linguistic assumptions. Many prejudices are unstated but form the underlying major premise on which attitudes about racial, ethnic, political, or religious groups are based. If Margery is wearing a white laboratory coat, and it is assumed that she is a nurse rather than a doctor, the unstated (mistaken) assumption is that all nurses are women or that no women are doctors. It is important to examine these unstated premises with care.

> 2. *The enthymeme is based on probable premises and arrives at probable conclusions.*

This characteristic of the enthymeme makes it an important tool in the field of rhetoric. Rhetoric does not deal only with scientific truth in the modern sense; it deals with probabilities and the kind of decisions and judgments that are made every day. An example might be: "If you go to college you'll get a good job." A college degree does not insure a higher standard of living, but a degree carries a high probability for better employment. Such judgments are woven into the fabric of peoples' lives.

In his famous essay criticizing James Fenimore Cooper, Mark Twain uses an enthymeme with an unstated major premise for his argument.

FENIMORE COOPER'S LITERARY OFFENSES

MARK TWAIN

The Pathfinder and The Deerslayer stand at the head of Cooper's novels as artistic creations. There are others of his works which contain parts as perfect as are to be found in these, and scenes even more thrilling. Not one can be compared with either of them as a finished whole.

The defects in both of these tales are comparatively slight. They were pure works of art.—Prof. Lounsbury.

The five tales reveal an extraordinary fullness of invention. . . . One of the very greatest characters in fiction, Natty Bumppo. . . .

The craft of the woodsman, the tricks of the trapper, all the delicate art of the forest were familiar to Cooper from his youth up.—Prof. Brander Matthews.

Cooper is the greatest artist in the domain of romantic fiction yet produced by America.—Wilkie Collins.

It seems to me that it was far from right for the Professor of English in   1
Yale, the Professor of English Literature in Columbia, and Wilkie Collins
to deliver opinions on Cooper's literature without having read some of it.
It would have been much more decorous to keep silent and let persons
talk who have read Cooper.

Cooper's art has some defects. In one place in *Deerslayer*, and in the   2
restricted space of two-thirds of a page, Cooper has scored 114 offenses
against literary art out of a possible 115. It breaks the record.

There are nineteen rules governing literary art in the domain of   3
romantic fiction—some say twenty-two. In *Deerslayer* Cooper violated
eighteen of them. These eighteen require:

1. That a tale shall accomplish something and arrive somewhere. But   4
the *Deerslayer* tale accomplishes nothing and arrives in the air.

2. They require that the episodes of a tale shall be necessary parts of
the tale and shall help to develop it. But as the *Deerslayer* tale is not a tale,
and accomplishes nothing and arrives nowhere, the episodes have no
rightful place in the work, since there was nothing for them to develop.

3. They require that the personages in a tale shall be alive, except in the
case of corpses, and that always the reader shall be able to tell the corpses
from the others. But this detail has often been overlooked in the *Deerslayer* tale.

4. They require that the personages in a tale, both dead and alive, shall
exhibit a sufficient excuse for being there. But this detail also has been
overlooked in the *Deerslayer* tale.

5. They require that when the personages of a tale deal in conversation,
the talk shall sound like human talk, and be talk such as human beings
would be likely to talk in the given circumstances, and have a discoverable meaning, also a discoverable purpose, and a show of relevancy, and
remain in the neighborhood of the subject in hand, and be interesting to
the reader, and help out the tale, and stop when the people cannot think
of anything more to say. But this requirement has been ignored from the
beginning of the *Deerslayer* tale to the end of it.

6. They require that when the author describes the character of a
personage in his tale, the conduct and conversation of that personage
shall justify said description. But this law gets little or no attention in the
Deerslayer tale, as Natty Bumppo's case will amply prove.

7. They require that when a personage talks like an illustrated, gilt-edged, tree-calf, hand-tooled, seven-dollar *Friendship's Offering* in the beginning of a paragraph, he shall not talk like a Negro minstrel in the end
of it. But this rule is flung down and danced upon in the *Deerslayer* tale.

8. They require that crass stupidities shall not be played upon the
reader as the "craft of the woodsman, the delicate art of the forest," by
either the author or the people in the tale. But this rule is persistently
violated in the *Deerslayer* tale.

9. They require that the personages of a tale shall confine themselves to possibilities and let miracles alone; or, if they venture a miracle, the author must so plausibly set it forth as to make it look possible and reasonable. But these rules are not respected in the *Deerslayer* tale.

10. They require that the author shall make the reader feel a deep interest in the personages of his tale and in their fate; and that he shall make the reader love the good people in the tale and hate the bad ones. But the reader of the *Deerslayer* tale dislikes the good people in it, is indifferent to the others, and wishes they would all get drowned together.

11. They require that the characters in a tale shall be so clearly defined that the reader can tell beforehand what each will do in a given emergency. But in the *Deerslayer* tale this rule is vacated.

In addition to these large rules there are some little ones. These require 5 that the author shall

12. *Say* what he is proposing to say, not merely come near it.

13. Use the right word, not its second cousin.

14. Eschew surplusage.

15. Not omit necessary detail.

16. Avoid slovenliness of form.

17. Use good grammar.

18. Employ a simple and straightforward style.

Even these seven are coldly and persistently violated in the *Deerslayer* 6 tale.

Cooper's gift in the way of invention was not a rich endowment; but 7 such as it was he liked to work it, he was pleased with the effects, and indeed he did some quite sweet things with it. In his little box of stage properties he kept six or eight cunning devices, tricks, artifices for his savages and woodsmen to deceive and circumvent each other with, and he was never so happy as when he was working these innocent things and seeing them go. A favorite one was to make a moccasined person tread in the tracks of the moccasined enemy, and thus hide his own trail. Cooper wore out barrels and barrels of moccasins in working that trick. Another stage property that he pulled out of his box pretty frequently was his broken twig. He prized his broken twig above all the rest of his effects, and worked it the hardest. It is a restful chapter in any book of his when somebody doesn't step on a dry twig and alarm all the reds and whites for two hundred yards around. Every time a Cooper person is in peril, and absolute silence is worth four dollars a minute, he is sure to step on a dry twig. There may be a hundred handier things to step on, but that wouldn't satisfy Cooper. Cooper requires him to turn out and find a dry twig; and if he can't do it, go and borrow one. In fact, the Leatherstocking Series ought to have been called the Broken Twig Series.

I am sorry there is not room to put in a few dozen instances of the 8 delicate art of the forest, as practised by Natty Bumppo and some of the other Cooperian experts. Perhaps we may venture two or three samples. Cooper was a sailor—a naval officer; yet he gravely tells us how a vessel, driving towards a lee shore in a gale, is steered for a particular spot by her skipper because he knows of an *undertow* there which will hold her back against the gale and save her. For just pure woodcraft, or sailorcraft, or whatever it is, isn't that neat? For several years Cooper was daily in the society of artillery, and he ought to have noticed that when a cannon-ball strikes the ground it either buries itself or skips a hundred feet or so; skips again a hundred feet or so—and so on, till it finally gets tired and rolls. Now in one place he loses some "females"—as he always calls women—in the edge of a wood near a plain at night in a fog, on purpose to give Bumppo a chance to show off the delicate art of the forest before the reader. These mislaid people are hunting for a fort. They hear a cannon-blast, and a cannon-ball presently comes rolling into the wood and stops at their feet. To the females this suggests nothing. The case is very different with the admirable Bumppo. I wish I may never know peace again if he doesn't strike out promptly and *follow the track* of that cannon-ball across the plain through the dense fog and find the fort. Isn't it a daisy? If Cooper had any real knowledge of Nature's ways of doing things, he had a most delicate art in concealing the fact. For instance: one of his acute Indian experts, Chingachgook (pronounced Chicago, I think), has lost the trail of a person he is tracking through the forest. Apparently that trail is hopelessly lost. Neither you nor I could ever have guessed out the way to find it. It was very different with Chicago. Chicago was not stumped for long. He turned a running stream out of its course, and there, in the slush in its old bed, were that person's moccasin-tracks. The current did not wash them away, as it would have done in all other like cases—no, even the eternal laws of Nature have to vacate when Cooper wants to put up a delicate job of woodcraft on the reader.

We must be a little wary when Brander Matthews tells us that Cooper's 9 books "reveal an extraordinary fullness of invention." As a rule, I am quite willing to accept Brander Matthews' literary judgments and applaud his lucid and graceful phrasing of them; but that particular statement needs to be taken with a few tons of salt. Bless your heart, Cooper hadn't any more invention than a horse; and I don't mean a high-class horse, either; I mean a clotheshorse. It would be very difficult to find a really clever "situation" in Cooper's books, and still more difficult to find one of any kind which he has failed to render absurd by his handling of it. Look at the episodes of "the caves"; and at the celebrated scuffle between Magua and those others on the tableland a few days later; and at Hurry Harry's queer water-transit from the castle to the ark; and at Deerslayer's half-hour with his first corpse; and at the quarrel between Hurry Harry and Deerslayer later; and at—but choose for yourself; you can't go amiss.

If Cooper had been an observer, his inventive faculty would have   10
worked better; not more interestingly, but more rationally, more plausibly. Cooper's proudest creations in the way of "situations" suffer notice-
ably from the absence of the observer's protecting gift. Cooper's eye was
splendidly inaccurate. Cooper seldom saw anything correctly. He saw
nearly all things as through a glass eye, darkly. Of course a man who
cannot see the commonest little everyday matters accurately is working at
a disadvantage when he is constructing a "situation." In the *Deerslayer* tale
Cooper has a stream which is fifty feet wide where it flows out of a lake; it
presently narrows to twenty as it meanders along for no given reason, and
yet when a stream acts like that it ought to be required to explain itself.
Fourteen pages later the width of the brook's outlet from the lake has
suddenly shrunk thirty feet and become "the narrowest part of the
stream." This shrinkage is not accounted for. The stream has bends in it,
a sure indication that it has alluvial banks and cuts them; yet these bends
are only thirty and fifty feet long. If Cooper had been a nice and
punctilious observer he would have noticed that the bends were oftener
nine hundred feet long than short of it.

Cooper made the exit of that stream fifty feet wide, in the first place,   11
for no particular reason; in the second place, he narrowed it to less than
twenty to accommodate some Indians. He bends a "sapling" to the form
of an arch over this narrow passage and conceals six Indians in its foliage.
They are "laying" for a settler's scow or ark which is coming up the
stream on its way to the lake; it is being hauled against the stiff current by
a rope whose stationary end is anchored in the lake; its rate of progress
cannot be more than a mile an hour. Cooper describes the ark, but pretty
obscurely. In the matter of dimensions "it was little more than a modern
canal-boat." Let us guess, then, that it was about one hundred and forty
feet long. It was of "greater breadth than common." Let us guess, then,
that it was about sixteen feet wide. This leviathan had been prowling
down bends which were but a third as long as itself, and scraping between
banks where it had only two feet of space to spare on each side. We
cannot too much admire this miracle. A low-roofed log dwelling occupies
"two-thirds of the ark's length"—a dwelling ninety feet long and sixteen
feet wide, let us say—a kind of vestibule train. The dwelling has two
rooms—each forty-five feet long and sixteen feet wide, let us guess. One
of them is the bedroom of the Hutter girls, Judith and Hetty; the other is
the parlor in the daytime, at night it is papa's bedchamber. The ark is
arriving at the stream's exit now, whose width has been reduced to less
than twenty feet to accommodate the Indians—say to eighteen. There is a
foot to spare on each side of the boat. Did the Indians notice that there
was going to be a tight squeeze there? Did they notice that they could
make money by climbing down out of that arched sapling and just
stepping aboard when the ark scraped by? No; other Indians would have
noticed these things, but Cooper's Indians never notice anything. Cooper

thinks they are marvelous creatures for noticing, but he was almost always in error about his Indians. There was seldom a sane one among them.

The ark is one hundred and forty feet long; the dwelling is ninety feet 12 long. The idea of the Indians is to drop softly and secretly from the arched sapling to the dwelling as the ark creeps along under it at the rate of a mile an hour, and butcher the family. It will take the ark a minute and a half to pass under. It will take the ninety foot dwelling a minute to pass under. Now, then, what did the six Indians do? It would take you thirty years to guess, and even then you would have to give it up, I believe. Therefore I will tell you what the Indians did. Their chief, a person of quite extraordinary intellect for a Cooper Indian, warily watched the canalboat as it squeezed along under him, and when he had got his calculations fined down to exactly the right shade, as he judged, he let go and dropped. And *missed the house*! He missed the house and landed in the stern of the scow. It was not much of a fall, yet it knocked him silly. He lay there unconscious. If the house had been ninety-seven feet long he would have made the trip. The fault was Cooper's not his. The error lay in the construction of the house. Cooper was no architect.

There still remained in the roost five Indians. The boat has passed 13 under and is now out of their reach. Let me explain what the five did— you would not be able to reason it out for yourself. No. 1 jumped for the boat, but fell in the water astern of it. Then No. 2 jumped for the boat, but fell in the water still farther astern of it. Then No. 3 jumped for the boat, and fell a good way astern of it. Then No. 4 jumped for the boat, and fell in the water *away* astern. Then even No. 5 made a jump for the boat—for he was a Cooper Indian. In the matter of intellect, the difference between a Cooper Indian and the Indian that stands in front of the cigar shop is not spacious. The scow episode is really a sublime burst of invention; but it does not thrill, because the inaccuracy of the details throws a sort of air of fictitiousness and general improbability over it. This comes of Cooper's inadequacy as an observer.

The conversations in the Cooper books have a curious sound in our 14 modern ears. To believe that such talk really ever came out of people's mouths would be to believe that there was a time when time was of no value to a person who thought he had something to say; when it was the custom to spread a two-minute remark out to ten; when a man's mouth was a rolling mill, and busied itself all day long in turning four-foot pigs of thought into thirty-foot bars of conversational railroad iron by attenuation; when subjects were seldom faithfully stuck to, but the talk wandered all around and arrived nowhere; when conversations consisted mainly of irrelevancies, with here and there a relevancy, a relevancy with an embarrassed look, as not being able to explain how it got there.

Cooper was certainly not a master in the construction of dialogue. 15 Inaccurate observation defeated him here as it defeated him in so many other enterprises of his. He even failed to notice that the man who talks corrupt English six days in the week must and will talk it on the seventh, and can't help himself. In the *Deerslayer* story he lets Deerslayer talk the showiest kind of book talk sometimes, and at other times the basest of base dialects. For instance, when some one asks him if he has a sweetheart, and if so, where she abides, this is his majestic answer: "She's in the forest—hanging from the boughs of the trees, in a soft rain—in the dew on the open grass—the clouds that float about in the blue heavens—the birds that sing in the woods—the sweet springs where I slake my thirst—and in all the other glorious gifts that come from God's Providence!"

And he preceded that, a little before, with this: "It consarns me as all   16 things that touches a fri'nd consarns a fri'nd."

And this is another of his remarks: "If I was Injin born, now, I might tell   17 of this, or carry in the scalp and boast of the expl'ite afore the whole tribe; or if my inimy had only been a bear!"—and so on.

We cannot imagine such a thing as a veteran Scotch commander-in-   18 chief comporting himself in the field like a windy melodramatic actor, but Cooper could. On one occasion Alice and Cora were being chased by the French through a fog in the neighborhood of their father's fort:

> "*Point de quartier aux coquins!*" cried an eager pursuer, who seemed to direct the operations of the enemy.
>
> "Stand firm and be ready, my gallant 60ths!" suddenly exclaimed a voice above them; "wait to see the enemy; fire low, and sweep the glacis."
>
> "Father! Father!" exclaimed a piercing cry from out the mist; "it is I! Alice! thy own Elsie! spare, O! save your daughters!"
>
> "Hold!" shouted the former speaker, in the awful tones of parental agony, the sound reaching even to the woods, and rolling back in solemn echo. "'Tis she! God has restored me my children! Throw open the sallyport; to the field, 60ths, to the field; pull not a trigger, lest ye kill my lambs! Drive off these dogs of France with your steel."

Cooper's word sense was singularly dull. When a person has a poor ear   19 for music he will flat and sharp right along without knowing it. He keeps near the tune, but it is *not* the tune. When a person has a poor ear for words, the result is a literary flatting and sharping; you perceive what he is intending to say, but you also perceive that he doesn't *say* it. This is Cooper. He was not a word musician. His ear was satisfied with the *approximate* word. I will furnish some circumstantial evidence in support of this charge. My instances are gathered from half a dozen pages of the tale called *Deerslayer*. He uses "verbal" for "oral"; "precision" for "facility"; "phenomena" for "marvels"; "necessary" for "predetermined"; "unsophisticated" for "primitive"; "preparation" for "expectancy"; "rebuked" for "subdued"; "dependent on" for "resulting from"; "fact" for "condition"; "fact" for "conjecture"; "precaution" for "caution"; "explain" for "determine"; "mortified" for "disappointed"; "meretricious" for "factitious"; "materially" for "considerably"; "decreasing" for "deepening"; "increasing" for "disappearing"; "embedded" for "enclosed"; "treacherous" for "hostile"; "stood" for "stooped"; "softened" for "re-placed"; "rejoined" for "remarked"; "situation" for "condition"; "dif-ferent" for "differing"; "insensible" for "unsentient"; "brevity" for "ce-lerity"; "distrusted" for "suspicious"; "mental imbecility" for "imbecility"; "eyes" for "sight"; "counteracting" for "opposing"; "funeral obsequies" for "obsequies."

There have been daring people in the world who claimed that Cooper 20 could write English, but they are all dead now—all dead but Lounsbury. I don't remember that Lounsbury makes the claim in so many words, still he makes it, for he says that *Deerslayer* is a "pure work of art." Pure, in that connection means faultless—faultless in all details—and language is a detail. If Mr. Lounsbury had only compared Cooper's English with the English which he writes himself—but it is plain that he didn't; and so it is likely that he imagines until this day that Cooper's is as clean and compact as his own. Now I feel sure, deep down in my heart, that Cooper wrote about the poorest English that exists in our language, and that the English of *Deerslayer* is the very worst that even Cooper ever wrote.

I may be mistaken, but it does seem to me that *Deerslayer* is not a work 21 of art in any sense; it does seem to me that it is destitute of every detail that goes to the making of a work of art; in truth, it seems to me that *Deerslayer* is just simply a literary *delirium tremens*.

The unstated major premise in the essay can be reconstructed as the following:

> In literary works of art the author should demonstrate certain qualities that include a gift for invention, careful observation, real-istic dialogue, and a good sense of words.

This premise is never stated in so many words in the essay, but the whole essay develops the minor premise:

> James Fenimore Cooper does not demonstrate such qualities.

After an introduction that lists eighteen violations Cooper has made of "the rules governing literary art in the domain of romantic fiction," Twain begins his real argument in paragraph 7.

> Cooper's gift in the way of invention was not a rich endowment. . . .

He begins his support of the second point of the minor premise—that Cooper was not an observer—in paragraph 10.

> If Cooper had been an observer, his inventive faculty would have
> worked better. . . . Cooper's proudest creations in the way of "situa-
> tions" suffer noticeably from the absence of the observer's protect-
> ing gift. Cooper's eye was spendidly inaccurate. Cooper seldom saw
> anything correctly. He saw nearly all things as through a glass eye,
> darkly.

The third point in the minor premise—that Cooper's dialogue is not
realistic—is stated in paragraph 15.

> Cooper was certainly not a master in the construction of dialogue.
> . . . In the *Deerslayer* story he lets Deerslayer talk the showiest kind of
> book talk sometimes, and at other times the basest of base dialects.

Twain makes the final point in the minor premise in paragraph 19.

> Cooper's word sense was singularly dull.

The minor premise then leads to the conclusion stated in the final
paragraph that *Deerslayer* is not a literary work of art.

> I may be mistaken, but it does seem to me that *Deerslayer* is not a
> work of art in any sense . . . it seems to me that *Deerslayer* is just
> simply a literary *delirium tremens*.

Note that the minor premise is not stated in its entirety at any one point
in the essay and that each part of that premise is supported with copious
examples. In demonstrating the inaccuracy of Cooper's dialogue he
makes the following observation and gives an example to support this
observation:

> In the *Deerslayer* story he lets Deerslayer talk the showiest kind of
> book talk sometimes, and at other times the basest of base dialects.
> For instance, when some one asks him if he has a sweetheart, and if
> so, where she abides, this is his majestic answer: "She's in the
> forest—hanging from the boughs of the trees, in a soft rain—in the
> dew on the open grass—the clouds that float about in the blue
> heavens—the birds that sing in the woods—the sweet springs where
> I slake my thirst—and in all the other glorious gifts that come from
> God's Providence!"
>   And he preceded that, a little before, with this: "It consarns me as
> all things that touches a fri'nd consarns a fri'nd" (15–16).

In paragraph 19, he supports his statement about Cooper's lack of word sense:

> He was not a word musician. His ear was satisfied with the *approximate* word. I will furnish some circumstantial evidence in support of this charge. My instances are gathered from half a dozen pages of the tale called *Deerslayer*. . . .

He then cites thirty examples of inaccurate word usages. Twain's copious support of his points through examples taken from the text itself lead the reader to the inevitable conclusion.

The full syllogism including implied major premise is the following:

> Major Premise (Implied but unstated): In a literary work of art, the author must demonstrate a gift for invention, careful observation, realistic dialogue, and a good sense of words.

> Minor Premise (Stated in first sentences of paragraphs 7, 10, 14, and 19): James Fenimore Cooper does not demonstrate a gift for invention, careful observation, realistic dialogue, and a good sense of words in *Deerslayer*.

> Conclusion (Stated in last paragraph): *Deerslayer* is not a literary work of art.

The Maxim

A maxim is the statement of a general truth and can serve as either a premise or a conclusion of an enthymeme. Maxims are truths, such as proverbs, that are generally held to be true by certain cultures or groups within a culture. In order to use maxims successfully, the writer needs to be sensitive to the beliefs and values of the audience. In writing for a group of educators the following maxims might be appropriate:

> Education is important.

> Reading and writing are central to education.

> An educated person has more chances of succeeding in life than the uneducated person.

Statements such as these need no proof or support for such an audience. They would be easily accepted. In other cases certain maxims might need support with a group of educators:

It is better to "mainstream" exceptional students.

Students who have high IQ's should be put in accelerated classes.

Some maxims would be accepted by most persons in this culture:

It is wrong to steal.

Persons who work hard will succeed.

When you feel that a maxim is not readily acceptable for your audience, then you will need to support it with examples, details, by definition or comparison, by cause or classification. For example, the statement "it is better to mainstream exceptional students" might be supported by specific cases where mainstreaming has been successful, or by defining more precisely either "mainstreaming" or "exceptional students," or by discussing the effects of mainstreaming on both ordinary students and exceptional students.

In speaking of a popular audience, Aristotle tells us common maxims should be used since familiar maxims carry credibility. He also adds that people in general take pleasure in hearing what they already know to be true. Certainly maxims are useful, but hackneyed maxims or clichés should be avoided. Note in the following excerpt from "The Declaration of Independence" how the authors use a series of maxims—self-evident truths—to lend moral character to a revolutionary document and to unite the audience in a common cause.

We hold these truths to be self-evident, that all men are created equal, that they are endowed by their Creator with certain unalienable Rights, that among these are Life, Liberty and the pursuit of Happiness. That to secure these rights, Governments are instituted among Men deriving their just powers from the consent of the governed. That whenever any Form of Government becomes destructive of these ends, it is the Right of the People to alter or to abolish it, and to institute new Government, laying its foundation on such principles and organizing its powers in such form, as to them shall seem most likely to effect their Safety and Happiness.

In the case of this document, maxims are well used and serve the case effectively. They offer proof through *ethos* by establishing the intelligence and virtue of the writers; they offer proof through *pathos* by appealing to the audience's sense of self, as well as their belief in liberty, and equality; and, finally, they offer proof through *logos* by setting up the major premise of the argument. However, you must guard against maxims that are so overused that they lose meaning, or arguments that are based on unexamined assumptions or premises. Particularly in academic writing, such assumptions are bound to be challenged.

The Example

In rhetorical induction, the argument is based on examples of similar cases. Aristotle maintained that it is better to use the argument based on the enthymeme first and follow it by examples. We noted how Mark Twain did that very effectively in his essay on *Deerslayer*. Aristotle insists that examples can be as persuasive as the deductive argument.

There are two main kinds of examples, those based on past fact and those based on similar cases. Aristotle justified those grounded in past fact by pointing out that the future will probably be like the past. So we use examples of past fact to prove present or future fact. David Hume, an eighteenth-century philosopher, illustrates the point.

> That a stone will fall, that fire will burn, that the earth has solidity, we have observed a thousand and a thousand times; and when any new instance of this nature is presented, we draw without hesitation the accustomed inference.

Examples based on similar cases are known as illustrative examples. In the following essay, Loren Eiseley shows through a number of similar cases how human animals and other animals all have a deep feeling of place.

THE BROWN WASPS

LOREN EISELEY

There is a corner in the waiting room of one of the great Eastern 1 stations where women never sit. It is always in the shadow and overhung by rows of lockers. It is, however, always frequented—not so much by genuine travelers as by the dying. It is here that a certain element of the abandoned poor seeks a refuge out of the weather, clinging for a few hours longer to the city that has fathered them. In a precisely similar manner I have seen, on a sunny day in midwinter, a few old brown wasps creep slowly over an abandoned wasp nest in a thicket. Numbed and forgetful and frost-blackened, the hum of the spring hive still resounded faintly in their sodden tissues. Then the temperature would fall and they would drop away into the white oblivion of the snow. Here in the station it is in no way different save that the city is busy in its snows. But the old ones cling to their seats as though these were symbolic and could not be given up. Now and then they sleep, their gray old heads resting with painful awkwardness on the backs of the benches.

Also they are not at rest. For an hour they may sleep in the gasping 2 exhaustion of the ill-nourished and aged who have to walk in the night. Then a policeman comes by on his round and nudges them upright.

"You can't sleep here," he growls. 3

A strange ritual then begins. An old man is difficult to waken. After a 4 muttered conversation the policeman presses a coin into his hand and passes fiercely along the benches prodding and gesturing toward the door. In his wake, like birds rising and settling behind the passage of a farmer through a cornfield, the men totter up, move a few paces and subside once more upon the benches.

One man, after a slight, apologetic lurch, does not move at all. Tuber- 5 cularly thin, he sleeps on steadily. The policeman does not look back. To him, too, this has become a ritual. He will not have to notice it again officially for another hour.

Once in a while one of the sleepers will not awake. Like the brown 6 wasps, he will have had his wish to die in the great droning center of the hive rather than in some lonely room. It is not so bad here with the shuffle of footsteps and the knowledge that there are others who share the bad luck of the world. There are also the whistles and the sounds of everyone, everyone in the world, starting on journeys. Amidst so many journeys somebody is bound to come out all right. Somebody.

Maybe it was on a like thought that the brown wasps fell away from the 7 old paper nest in the thicket. You hold till the last, even if it is only to a public seat in a railroad station. You want your place in the hive more than you want a room or a place where the aged can be eased gently out of the way. It is the place that matters, the place at the heart of things. It is life that you want, that bruises your gray old head with the hard chairs; a man has a right to his place.

But sometimes the place is lost in the years behind us. Or sometimes it 8 is a thing of air, a kind of vaporous distortion above a heap of rubble. We cling to a time and place because without them man is lost, not only man but life. This is why the voices, real or unreal, which speak from the floating trumpets at spiritualist seances are so unnerving. They are voices out of nowhere whose only reality lies in their ability to stir the memory of a living person with some fragment of the past. Before the medium's cabinet both the dead and the living revolve endlessly about an episode, a place, an event that has already been engulfed by time.

This feeling runs deep in life; it brings stray cats running over endless 9 miles, and birds homing from the ends of the earth. It is as though all living creatures, and particularly the more intelligent, can survive only by fixing or transforming a bit of time into space or by securing a bit of space with its objects immortalized and made permanent in time. For example, I once saw, on a flower pot in my own living room, the efforts of a field mouse to build a remembered field. I have lived to see this episode repeated in a thousand guises, and since I have spent a large portion of my life in the shade of a nonexistent tree, I think I am entitled to speak for the field mouse.

One day as I cut across the field which at that time extended on one 10 side of our suburban shopping center, I found a giant slug feeding from a runnel of pink ice cream in an abandoned Dixie cup. I could see his eyes telescope and protrude in a kind of dim, uncertain ecstasy as his dark body bunched and elongated in the curve of the cup. Then, as I stood there at the edge of the concrete, contemplating the slug, I began to realize it was like standing on a shore where a different type of life creeps up and fumbles tentatively among the rocks and sea wrack. It knows its place and will only creep so far until something changes. Little by little as I stood there I began to see more of this shore that surrounds the place of man. I looked with sudden care and attention at things I had been running over thoughtlessly for years. I even waded out a short way into the grass and the wild-rose thickets to see more. A huge black-belted bee went droning by and there were some indistinct scurryings in the under-brush.

Then I came to a sign which informed me that this field was to be the 11 site of a new Wanamaker suburban store. Thousands of obscure lives were about to perish, the spores of puffballs would go smoking off to new fields, and the bodies of little white-footed mice would be crunched under the inexorable wheels of the bulldozers. Life disappears or modifies its appearances so fast that everything takes on an aspect of illusion—a momentary fizzing and boiling with smoke rings, like pouring dissident chemicals into a retort. Here man was advancing, but in a few years his plaster and bricks would be disappearing once more into the insatiable maw of the clover. Being of an archaeological cast of mind, I thought of this fact with an obscure sense of satisfaction and waded back through the rose thickets to the concrete parking lot. As I did so, a mouse scurried ahead of me, frightened of my steps if not of that ominous Wanamaker sign. I saw him vanish in the general direction of my apartment house, his little body quivering with fear in the great open sun on the blazing concrete. Blinded and confused, he was running straight away from his field. In another week scores would follow him.

I forgot the episode then and went home to the quiet of my living 12 room. It was not until a week later, letting myself into the apartment, that I realized I had a visitor. I am fond of plants and had several ferns standing on the floor in pots to avoid the noon glare by the south window.

As I snapped on the light and glanced carelessly around the room, I 13
saw a little heap of earth on the carpet and a scrabble of pebbles that had
been kicked merrily over the edge of one of the flower pots. To my
astonishment I discovered a full-fledged burrow delving downward
among the fern roots. I waited silently. The creature who had made the
burrow did not appear. I remembered the wild field then, and the flight
of the mice. No house mouse, no *Mus domesticus*, had kicked up this little
heap of earth or sought refuge under a fern root in a flower pot. I
thought of the desperate little creature I had seen fleeing from the wild-
rose thicket. Through intricacies of pipes and attics, he, or one of his
fellows, had climbed to this high green solitary room. I could visualize
what had occurred. He had an image in his head, a world of seed pods
and quiet, of green sheltering leaves in the dim light among the weed
stems. It was the only world he knew and it was gone.

Somehow in his flight he had found his way to this room with drawn 14
shades where no one would come till nightfall. And here he had smelled
green leaves and run quickly up the flower pot to dabble his paws in
common earth. He had even struggled half the afternoon to carry his
burrow deeper and had failed. I examined the hole, but no whiskered
twitching face appeared. He was gone. I gathered up the earth and
refilled the burrow. I did not expect to find traces of him again.

Yet for three nights thereafter I came home to the darkened room and 15
my ferns to find the dirt kicked gaily about the rug and the burrow
reopened, though I was never able to catch the field mouse within it. I
dropped a little food about the mouth of the burrow, but it was never
touched. I looked under beds or sat reading with one ear cocked for
rustlings in the ferns. It was all in vain; I never saw him. Probably he
ended in a trap in some other tenant's room.

But before he disappeared I had come to look hopefully for his eve- 16
ning burrow. About my ferns there had begun to linger the insubstantial
vapor of an autumn field, the distilled essence, as it were, of a mouse
brain in exile from its home. It was a small dream, like our dreams,
carried a long and weary journey along pipes and through spider webs,
past holes over which loomed the shadows of waiting cats, and finally,
desperately, into this room where he had played in the shuttered daylight
for an hour among the green ferns on the floor. Every day these invisible
dreams pass us on the street, or rise from beneath our feet, or look out
upon us from beneath a bush.

Some years ago the old elevated railway in Philadelphia was torn down 17
and replaced by a subway system. This ancient El with its barnlike
stations containing nut-vending machines and scattered food scraps had,
for generations, been the favorite feeding ground of flocks of pigeons,
generally one flock to a station along the route of the El. Hundreds of
pigeons were dependent upon the system. They flapped in and out of its

stanchions and steel work or gathered in watchful little audiences about the feet of anyone who rattled the peanut-vending machines. They even watched people who jingled change in their hands, and prospected for food under the feet of the crowds who gathered between trains. Probably very few among the waiting people who tossed a crumb to an eager pigeon realized that this El was like a food-bearing river, and that the life which haunted its banks was dependent upon the running of the trains with their human freight.

I saw the river stop. 18

The time came when the underground tubes were ready; the traffic 19 was transferred to a realm unreachable by pigeons. It was like a great river subsiding suddenly into desert sands. For a day, for two days, pigeons continued to circle over the El or stand close to the red vending machines. They were patient birds, and surely this great river which had flowed through the lives of unnumbered generations was merely suffering from some momentary drought.

They listened for the familiar vibrations that had always heralded an 20 approaching train; they flapped hopefully about the head of an occasional workman walking along the steel runways. They passed from one empty station to another, all the while growing hungrier. Finally they flew away.

I thought I had seen the last of them about the El, but there was a 21 revival and it provided a curious instance of the memory of living things for a way of life or a locality that has long been cherished. Some weeks after the El was abandoned workmen began to tear it down. I went to work every morning by one particular station, and the time came when the demolition crews reached this spot. Acetylene torches showered passersby with sparks, pneumatic drills hammered at the base of the structure, and a blind man who, like the pigeons, had clung with his cup to a stairway leading to the change booth, was forced to give up his place.

It was then, strangely, momentarily, one morning that I witnessed the 22 return of a little band of the familiar pigeons. I even recognized one or two members of the flock that had lived around this particular station before they were dispersed into the streets. They flew bravely in and out among the sparks and the hammers and the shouting workmen. They had returned—and they had returned because the hubbub of the wreckers had convinced them that the river was about to flow once more. For several hours they flapped in and out through the empty windows, nodding their heads and watching the fall of girders with attentive little eyes. By the following morning the station was reduced to some burned-off stanchions in the street. My bird friends had gone. It was plain, however, that they retained a memory for an insubstantial structure now compounded of air and time. Even the blind man clung to it. Someone had provided him with a chair, and he sat at the same corner staring sightlessly at an invisible stairway where, so far as he was concerned, the crowds were still ascending to the trains.

I have said my life has been passed in the shade of a nonexistent tree, 23 so that such sights do not offend me. Prematurely I am one of the brown wasps and I often sit with them in the great droning hive of the station, dreaming sometimes of a certain tree. It was planted sixty years ago by a boy with a bucket and a toy spade in a little Nebraska town. That boy was myself. It was a cottonwood sapling and the boy remembered it because of some words spoken by his father and because everyone died or moved away who was supposed to wait and grow old under its shade. The boy was passed from hand to hand, but the tree for some intangible reason had taken root in his mind. It was under its branches that he sheltered; it was from this tree that his memories, which are my memories, led away into the world.

After sixty years the mood of the brown wasps grows heavier upon one. 24 During a long inward struggle I thought it would do me good to go and look upon that actual tree. I found a rational excuse in which to clothe this madness. I purchased a ticket and at the end of two thousand miles I walked another mile to an address that was still the same. The house had not been altered.

I came close to the white picket fence and reluctantly, with great effort, 25 looked down the long vista of the yard. There was nothing there to see. For sixty years that cottonwood had been growing in my mind. Season by season its seeds had been floating farther on the hot prairie winds. We had planted it lovingly there, my father and I, because he had a great hunger for soil and live things growing, and because none of these things had long been ours to protect. We had planted the little sapling and watered it faithfully, and I remembered that I had run out with my small bucket to drench its roots the day we moved away. And all the years since it had been growing in my mind, a huge tree that somehow stood for my father and the love I bore him. I took a grasp on the picket fence and forced myself to look again.

A boy with the hard bird eye of youth pedaled a tricycle slowly up 26 beside me.

"What'cha lookin' at?" he asked curiously. 27

"A tree," I said. 28

"What for?" he said. 29

"It isn't there," I said, to myself mostly, and began to walk away at a 30 pace just slow enough not to seem to be running.

"What isn't there?" the boy asked. I didn't answer. It was obvious I was 31 attached by a thread to a thing that had never been there, or certainly not for long. Something that had to be held in the air, or sustained in the mind, because it was part of my orientation in the universe and I could not survive without it. There was more than an animal's attachment to a

place. There was something else, the attachment of the spirit to a grouping of events in time; it was part of our morality.

So I had come home at last, driven by a memory in the brain as surely 32
as the field mouse who had delved long ago into my flower pot or the
pigeons flying forever amidst the rattle of nut-vending machines. These,
the burrow under the greenery in my living room and the red-bellied
bowls of peanuts now hovering in midair in the minds of pigeons, were
all part of an elusive world that existed nowhere and yet everywhere. I
looked once at the real world about me while the persistent boy pedaled
at my heels.

It was without meaning, though my feet took a remembered path. In 33
sixty years the house and street had rotted out of my mind. But the tree,
the tree that no longer was, that had perished in its first season, bloomed
on in my individual mind, unblemished as my father's words. "We'll plant
a tree here, son, and we're not going to move any more. And when you're
an old, old man you can sit under it and think how we planted it here, you
and me, together."

I began to outpace the boy on the tricycle. 34

"Do you live here, Mister?" he shouted after me suspiciously. I took a 35
firm grasp on airy nothing—to be precise, on the bole of a great tree. "I
do," I said. I spoke for myself, one field mouse, and several pigeons. We
were all out of touch but somehow permanent. It was the world that had
changed.

In the opening paragraphs, Eiseley uses the example of old men
waiting to die, sitting in the waiting room of one of "the great Eastern
stations." He uses a similar example of dying brown wasps who creep
"slowly over an abandoned wasp nest in a thicket" to make the main
point of his essay, which he then states in paragraphs 7 and 8:

> You want your place in the hive more than you want a room or a
> place where the aged can be eased gently out of the way. It is the
> place that matters, the place at the heart of things. It is life that you
> want, that bruises your gray old head with the hard chairs; a man
> has a right to his place. . . . We cling to a time and place because
> without them man is lost, not only man but life.

Eiseley points out that all living creatures must immortalize a bit of space
and make it permanent in their minds—a bit of space to which they can
return. He cites similar cases in paragraph 9:

> This feeling runs deep in life; it brings stray cats running over
> endless miles, and birds homing from the ends of the earth.

The essay develops a series of illustrative examples of creatures who have been similarly displaced but who keep the memory of a place in their hearts. There is the field mouse building a remembered field in a flower pot, a slug on the concrete parking lot of a suburban shopping center feeding from "a runnel of pink ice cream in an abandoned Dixie cup," the flock of pigeons circling the construction workers demolishing the abandoned station where they had been accustomed to feeding from the hands of passengers. Eiseley uses these similar cases as illustrative examples of living creatures' need for a remembered place. His last example, in paragraph 33, is his own experience of returning to the place where he and his father planted a tree that has long since disappeared but which continues to live in his own mind.

> But the tree, the tree that no longer was, that had perished in its first season, bloomed on in my individual mind, unblemished as my father's words. "We'll plant a tree here, son, and we're not going to move any more. And when you're an old, old man you can sit under it and think how we planted it here, you and me, together."

Illustrative examples serve other kinds of proof as well. In the discussion of argument from definition in Chapter 3, we examined the importance of using examples.

In this chapter, we discussed separately logical proof and rhetorical proof, but in fact, the line is not so clear-cut. Rhetorical proof with its enthymeme and example is in fact built on the bedrock of logical deduction and induction and in order to understand one you must know the other. Today, we are inclined to think of rational proof as the only intellectually legitimate kind although we often fail to be persuaded by it. Rhetoric affirms the importance of ethical persuasion (*ethos*) and the appeal to the emotions of the audience (*pathos*) in addition to reason (*logos*), and in doing so affirms both the rational and the emotional side of the human being, recognizing the importance of speaking and writing to the whole person. Rhetoric also recognizes the limitations of strict logic in the important deliberations of human affairs and the need for arriving at probable and contingent truths when certainties are neither possible nor desirable.

This chapter concludes the section on artistic proofs (Chapters 3–6). The next chapter will consider the resources available to you in the inartistic proofs through such things as outside authorities and statistics.

Questions to Consider

1. Examine the following statements to determine whether they are maxims and, if so, to what audience they might be most acceptable.

A. Honesty is the best policy.

B. A freshman writing course is the most difficult course students take during their first year of college.

C. Those who can't do teach.

D. Thou shalt not kill.

E. All people are created equal.

F. Exercise is good for you.

G. Premarital sex is a sin.

H. Children should be seen and not heard.

I. They who live by the sword shall die by the sword.

J. Love is blind.

2. Which of the following syllogisms are valid, or true, or both?

A. All vegetables are green.
Beets are a vegetable.
Therefore, beets are green.

B. Your mother has either blue eyes or brown eyes.
She does not have brown eyes.
Therefore, she has blue eyes.

C. No human being is immortal.
God is not a human being.
Therefore, God is immortal.

D. Either you completed your high school education or you dropped out.
You completed your high school education.
Therefore, you did not drop out.

E. If you do not take the exam, you cannot pass it.
You do not take it.
Therefore, you cannot pass it.

    F. If you do not take the exam, you will not pass it.
You take the exam.
Therefore, you will pass it.

  3. Identify the missing premises in the following enthymemes:

    A. I failed that course because the instructor didn't like me.

    B. What was Jim's car doing on the wrong side of the road anyway? If he hadn't been drunk, he never would have had that accident.

    C. I'm not surprised he made the team. After all, his father is the superintendant of schools.

    D. If I'd only taken my boss to lunch more often, I could have gotten that raise.

  4. For additional practice in analyzing arguments, rewrite each of the following arguments in the form of major premise, minor premise, and conclusion. Then, in each case determine whether the argument is both true and valid. (This exercise is taken from Richard B. Angell's *Reasoning and Logic* [New York: Appleton-Century-Crofts, 1964], p. 49.)

    A. All bats are birds, for all birds have wings and all bats have wings.

    B. All gulls are birds, for all birds have wings and all gulls have wings.

    C. No pole vaulters can clear eighteen feet. Therefore no pole vaulters are good pole vaulters. For any good pole vaulter could clear eighteen feet.

    D. Any pole vaulter who can clear eighteen feet is a good pole vaulter. But no pole vaulters can clear eighteen feet, thus there are no good pole vaulters.

    E. People should never kill innocent creatures. Hence people should never kill animals, for animals are human.

Suggestions for Writing

  1. Write a paper in which you try to persuade a friend to join a demonstration in favor of nuclear disarmament.

2. Apply one or more of the "rules governing literary art" that Twain mentions in the essay reprinted in this chapter to a modern film or work of fiction; argue in a page or two that the work either fulfills or fails to fulfill the rule(s) you have chosen and discuss the effects.

3. Choose a popular maxim or proverb (you may use one from the list provided above) and write a 2–3 page paper in which you prove how it may not always be true under certain circumstances.

Exercises in Revision

1. Examine the logical and rhetorical proofs presented in the papers written by members of your workshop group in response to one of the assignments suggested above, to determine their truth and validity. For those that are invalid or untrue, suggest possible revisions.

2. Exchange essays written by members of your workshop group in response to one of the assignments suggested above and write a brief response indicating whether the writer managed to persuade you to accept his or her point of view and why or why not. Give your response to the author to help with subsequent revision.

For a Commonplace Book

Listen in your conversations with friends, family, and classmates for the use of logical and rhetorical proofs in discussions and arguments. Record in your commonplace book any examples you encounter and analyze their validity, truth, and persuasiveness.

Chapter 7

Using Outside Evidence

Aristotle spoke of inartistic proofs as those that already exist and "have merely to be used." He used the word *art*, to mean "system" or "method," so artistic proofs are those derived from rhetorical skill or method, those available to writers and speakers from within their own minds. Inartistic proofs, on the other hand, come from outside sources. For the ancient rhetoricians, this included evidence from witnesses who described or narrated events; evidence given under torture, which was legal in their day; evidence from written contracts; and authority. Aristotle did not treat inartistic proofs very fully in his *Rhetoric*, and this text departs from ancient instruction at this point. Because of print and other highly developed technologies much of the evidence in modern writing comes

174

from a rich source of outside authorities and complex statistics. The first outside resource for most writers, however, is often their own "witnessing" of people or events. So in this chapter on inartistic proofs, the first subjects covered are narration and description, followed by a discussion of the use of statistics, a modern form of inartistic proof, and the use of authority.

DESCRIPTION

In descriptions, writers tell their readers what they see or hear in a particular situation. They may describe a person, a place, or an idea as they see it or experience it. It is always a view from the writer's own perspective.

Descriptions are usually controlled by the writer's overall purpose; if not, the description may be hopelessly detailed or unfocused. You might describe the desk at which you are working, but without a purpose or point, you would have to describe everything on it. If, however, you start with the point that the desk is so cluttered that work is difficult, you would select the details with that main idea in mind. Thus, you might include in your description the pile of books in one corner, the telephone, the telephone book, the class notebooks, the letters from friends, the pile of bills. But the color of the desk, the shape of the desk, and the kind of finish would not be relevant for the purpose of your description.

Using the Senses

In addition, effective descriptions rely on impressions about persons and places that come through one or more of the five senses—taste, smell, sight, sound, and touch. Thus you, in turn, in describing an object may do so in terms of how it looks, smells, and tastes.

A doctor learns to use all five senses in examining a patient, a botanist in studying a plant, a farmer in evaluating crops. So skilled writers become accustomed to observing the world with alertness, tapping all their senses to pass on their observations to others.

In the following description, a student has taken an ordinary baseball and made it vivid in terms of all of the senses through which she has experienced that baseball. In her description, she passes on those rich sensory experiences to help her reader "feel" the baseball.

She picked up the baseball that he had carelessly tossed on the couch as he passed through the living room on his way to the kitchen. She listened for the rattle of the cookie jar lid as she picked up the ball from where it had rolled between the cushions. It was still warm and damp from his hands and had the aroma of small boys and sunshine and outdoors and sweat. She looked at the frayed seams and heard the *swock* sound as she tossed it gently from hand to hand. Feeling its hardness, and smelling its boyness, she was suddenly overcome with a feeling of love for her young son.

This student uses the sound of the cookie jar lid, the "swock" of the ball; the smell of "small boys and sunshine and outdoors and sweat"; the feel of the ball "still warm and damp from his hands"; the sight of the ball's frayed seams. Each of these sensory images contributes to the feeling the writer wishes to pass on to her readers—her "love for her young son."

What follows is an excerpt from a description of a Christmas in Wales, "Memories of Christmas," by one of the great poets in the English language, Dylan Thomas. Note how the scene is described in terms of tastes, smells, feelings, as well as sights and sounds. How many different sensory experiences does Thomas include?

One Christmas was so much like another, in those years, around the sea-town corner now and out of all sound except the distant speaking of the voices I sometimes hear a moment before sleep, that I can never remember whether it snowed for six days and six nights when I was twelve or whether it snowed for twelve days and twelve nights when I was six; or whether the ice broke and the skating grocer vanished like a snowman through a white trap-door on that same Christmas Day that the mince-pies finished Uncle Arnold and we tobogganed down the seaward hill, all the afternoon, on the best tea-tray, and Mrs. Griffiths complained, and we threw a snowball at her niece, and my hands burned so, with the heat and the cold, when I held them in front of the fire, that I cried for twenty minutes and then had some jelly.

All the Christmases roll down the hill towards the Welsh-speaking sea, like a snowball growing whiter and bigger and rounder, like a cold and headlong moon bundling down the sky that was our street; and they stop at the rim of the ice-edged, fish-freezing waves, and I plunge my hands in the snow and bring out whatever I can find; holly or robins or pudding, squabbles and carols and oranges and tin whistles, and the fire in the front room, and bang go the crackers, and holy, holy, holy, ring the bells, and the glass bells shaking on the tree, and Mother Goose, and Struwelpeter—oh! the baby-burning flames and the clacking scissorman!—Billy Bunter and Black Beauty, Little Women and boys who have three helpings, Alice and Mrs. Potter's badgers, penknives, teddy-bears—named after a Mr. Theodore Bear, their inventor, or father, who died recently in the United States—mouth-organs, tin-soldiers, and blanc-mange, and Auntie Bessie playing "Pop Goes the Weasel" and "Nuts in May" and "Oranges and Lemons" on the untuned piano in the parlor all through the thimble-hiding musical-chairing blind-man's bluffing party at the end of the never-to-be-forgotten day at the end of the unremembered year.

In goes my hand into that wool-white bell-tongued ball of holidays resting at the margin of the carol-singing sea, and out come Mrs. Prothero and the firemen.

This description uses infinite detail that captures the sights, sounds, smells, touch, and taste of Christmas to build a rich and unforgettable description. Such piling up of specific detail—"mouth organs, tin-soldiers, and blanc-mange, and Auntie Bessie playing 'Pop Goes the Weasel'"—together with a wide variety of sensory images help to make the description more vivid.

Using Perspective

Every object, scene, or person can be viewed from different perspectives. So a chair viewed from the back is different when viewed from the front. A flower is different when seen from the side and from above. A hotel dining room will appear different if viewed from the perspective of a busboy or a guest. And a political demonstration is a different matter when viewed from the perspective of the demonstrators, or the police, or the objects of the protest, or the community. A writer's skill is often evidenced in the ability to see something from a new and interesting angle and to transfer that particular insight to a reader. A good writer is one who can offer the reader a new outlook on the well known and familiar. Richard Young, a contemporary rhetorician, developed the tagmemic theory of invention using terminology and concepts from modern physics and linguistics. Using particle, wave, and field—terms used to describe relationships between objects in space—Young transferred these notions to perspectives in rhetoric. He suggests three possible ways of viewing an object, event, or idea.

Particle: View the unit as an isolated, static entity.

Wave: View the unit as a dynamic, changing object or event.

Field: View the unit as part of a pattern or system.

Young emphasizes that the unit is not either particle, wave, or field but may be viewed from any one of these perspectives. He used a house as an example. Viewed as particle, the house is seen as isolated from other houses in the neighborhood and considered at a single point in time. Its features are described and it is treated as static in time and space with emphasis on the house itself. Viewed as wave, it is seen as dynamic and changing. The house might be described as it was when new and then as it changed over time as it began to deteriorate and decay. Viewed in the field perspective, the house is looked at in terms of its relation to other houses and to its neighborhood. Its place in a larger pattern or system is emphasized.

In the following description of his grandmother, Randall Freisinger, a poet, looks at his grandmother from all three perspectives. In the particle perspective, he describes her as she lies in her casket. In the wave perspective, he traces her changing from a child to an old woman, and in the field perspective, he describes her relationship with her family and the people around her.

Particle: View the unit as a static, isolated object or event.

Grandmother was dead dead dead, and, as such, a paradox to those of us who had heeded the dubious motive of obligation to sit with her one last time. Tucked away in her casket in a small niche out of the main current so as not to intrude, she remained the center of gravity in that convention of cross-purposes. She attracted and repelled. She kept us rooted in the moment, yet planted in the past. By breaking her jaw and manipulating wires, the morticians had massaged her flaccid face into a smile, more precisely a smirk, one which bespoke some grim joke which I deemed to be on all of us and which I regarded with grave sobriety. More clinical than kin, I touched her hands. They were cold, numb as stone. The ring finger on her left hand showed a bruise. Someone at the nursing home had stripped her of her wedding ring, and her swollen flesh had resisted the outrage. She was laid out in her wedding dress, which was over sixty years old. My wife had ironed it the day before, crying at the discovery of a small slit in the bodice which Grandmother had made in order to nurse her first child. Grimly propped there, she did not look like a bride or a breast feeder of children. She looked old and tired, used up and finished. The putty and powder and paint could not conceal her deadness. And in her deadness she had achieved a permanence which I did not want to understand. Outside it was cold. Everyone moved gladly toward the cars, talking, lighting cigarettes, thinking of tomorrow and beyond. Inside, Grandmother smiled, like Raphaels in darkened galleries hung.

In the first sentence the repetition of the word "dead" gives the impression of the grandmother as a static entity isolated and tucked away in her casket. The words *grimly propped, old and tired, used up and finished*, and the final *in her deadness* all give the feeling of lifelessness, the static finality of his grandmother in her casket.

Wave: View the unit as a changing, dynamic object.

Grandmother lay in her casket the day of her funeral as if sculpted from stone, as if she had been made for not other worlds than the grave that awaited her just a short distance from the chapel. But I knew otherwise. The incredible gallery of pictures she left in her attic traces a life which, though plain by most measures, was rich with change. There is the family portrait of 1904 revealing a pouty little girl of five, stiff in her high-necked frock and wearing pretty ribbons in her elegantly curled hair. When I first saw that picture, the boy in me found it hard to accept that she had ever been so young. In 1912 she is sixteen, still pouty, but showing a sensuousness of face which still attracts me, and which must surely have stirred my grandfather, for a 1913 photo records their public wedding in the town square on Market Day in Nelson, Nebraska. There is also their formal wedding picture, Grandfather in a handsome suit and owning a wonderful head of hair, Grandmother in her wedding dress, the bodice not yet slit for nursing her first child. A 1914 snapshot captures her in a stylish hat. With arms smartly crossed, her spectacles perched on the bridge of her nose, somehow she looks like an expatriate poet or painter, though to my knowledge she had no artistic inclinations. She smiles easily, a smile so unlike the one forced upon her at the end. A 1920 pose with her two daughters shows her gaining weight, but she is still voluptuous, a flower suggestively placed in the V of a low-cut dress. Then the 1950s. Now stout, thick of ankle, standing in a field in Raytown, Missouri, another fashionable hat on her head, this time graced by an outlandish plume. But for all the outlandishness, she is the grandmother I first remember, the old but wonderfully gentle woman who bought me my first bicycle, without my parents' knowledge, consent, or approval, and then made sure I was allowed to ride it. A few years later a picture dated June, 1956 catches her in the chicken yard of their small farm. How she warred against those chickens! Out of the house she would storm like Attila, Scourge of God and chickens, grabbing her unfortunate victim as she flew to the fray. Then, with astonishing resolution, she would place its squawking head under her boot, twist and lift, and cast the incredulous torso flap into the tall grass to earn the awfullest chicken truth. I never understood that schizophrenic dimension to her: how she who could hug my fears away could inflict such premeditated hun-like ferocity on chickens with whom I daily played. Even the day of her funeral I'm not sure I forgave her that behavior. Other pictures survive, and they, too, passed through my mind the day we buried her—her standing like a gun moll beside the Hudson in which we travelled to Arizona one summer; her and Grandfather with their 50th Anniversary cake. But one image particularly stands out, and it is on no film but that of my memory: how she stood at Grandfather's grave Christmas Day, 1976, stared at the recently turned earth and the struggling sod, and smiled as unearthly a smile as I have ever seen. She was so weak that she buckled in the wind that day, but she examined the grave, then the plot reserved for her, and she smiled. She heard something that day that only mortals on the sad heights hear. And she made a promise. Two months later she was gone.

In this description, the author abandons the picture of his grandmother lying dead in the coffin and sees her from a different perspective, as a dynamic woman in a series of pictures left in the attic that "were rich in change." He sees her in photographs as a girl of five, a young woman of sixteen, a bride, a matron in one of her "outlandish hats," a woman "warring with chickens," and finally the poignant picture of her at "Grandfather's grave" with "an unearthly smile." This is a description of a woman seen from the "wave" perspective in the dynamic changes of a rich, full, and remembered life.

Field: View the unit as part of a larger pattern or system.

Because I was so close to my grandmother, I reacted painfully every time I visited her in the nursing home, and I took the insults to her body and spirit personally. But she was only one of many old people in one of thousands of nursing homes, most of whom suffer for the values of a culture that celebrates throw-away cans and disposable lives. We as a society are engaged in a race, the finish line for which is not especially clear, and if we are to arrive with the greatest possible speed, we must discard those who would slow us down. That was the problem with my grandmother, and that is the problem today with old people across this land. They slow us down. We must take time out to feed them like children, wipe and change them like children, and hardest of all, love them like children. This is so hard because they are, after all, *not* children. They are dreck, human junk, and our culture has little patience with junk. If you are reasonably affluent and socially mobile, if you like to travel and entertain in your home, what do you do with an eighty-year-old mother or grandmother who nightly wets her bed, who falls when she stands but persists in standing, who, in her arteriosclerotic fogs, has grown mean and selfish, so grossly egocentric that she vilifies your every attempt at kindness? What do you do? You park her, and then pray for salvage. You visit her when you can, though it is terribly inconvenient and horribly depressing. And when you come, you see her parked there, next to prune-faced ladies with goiters big as cantaloupes, next to loud and smelly men who shit in their pants and spit their food at the aides, next to ancient heaps, their sex no longer discernible, who weave and chant like crazed mystics or slump in their wheelchairs like unstrung marionettes. You see how little dignity is left to any of them, and you leave as quickly as is inhumanly possible, each time guilty, glad, and afraid. Guilty because you are a collaborator. Glad because that is one more visit you won't have to make. Afraid because one day it could all happen to you.

From this "field" perspective, Freisinger writes about his grandmother from still another viewpoint, as one of many elderly persons living in the nursing home. He describes the relation of his grandmother and that of other old people to their culture, to their families, and finally to himself when he leaves the nursing home feeling guilty, glad, and finally afraid because one day it could all happen to you.

Description, which the Greeks called *ecphrasis* (ek-FRA-sis), was an important exercise in the classical schools. Quintilian includes it with the figures of speech, which we will discuss in Chapter 11. Description is characterized by several rhetoricians as "bringing before the eyes what is to be shown." Some ancient rhetoricians did not make it a separate exercise since they felt that it was included not only in the topics but also in narration. Neither narration nor description can be separated from each other or from the topics. In telling a story, you may want to describe a person or a place connected with the incident: also you may make a description of a person more vivid by showing that person in action—by telling a story. In the same way, in defining Nazism you could make it more real with a narration from *The Diary of Anne Frank* or a description of the Auschwitz concentration camp. Narration and description serve all parts of rhetoric.

NARRATION

The *narratio* (na-RA-tee-o) for ancient rhetoricians was that part of the oration that stated the facts of the case in the precise order in which they occurred. It is discussed in that context in Chapter 9. In the classical world, people argued their own cases in the courts of law and defended themselves and their ideas before the assembly. As a result, much of classical rhetoric dealt with how to argue legal cases and the question of whether or not an event took place. In *narratio* they explored the event in much the same way that a modern journalist reports a news story. They were concerned with the elements of actor, action, time, place, cause, manner, and starting point. The following article is a report by Lenny Schulman of a project called "Apparitions and Amtrak" that appeared in *Time* magazine. Notice how carefully the writer brings in all of the elements of narration in reporting the story.

IN NEW MEXICO: VISIONS ALONG THE AMTRAK LINE

LENNY SCHULMAN

Along a railroad track in a ravine in Canyoncito, N. Mex., just north of the Lamy train station, there have been occasional sightings of curious apparitions. On this gloomy Sunday, passengers on the *Southwest Chief* have been warned to keep their eyes open. Their train will be passing through Canyoncito between 2 and 3 in the afternoon.   1

Canyoncito is on wild, beautiful land 15 miles southeast of Santa Fe. The landscape is dotted with adobe ranch houses and corrals. Chamizas with yellow flowers, delicate violet asters, sage, piñons and cacti grow everywhere.   2

In the ravine the sky is overcast, and rain appears imminent. Two women emerge from a red Datsun pickup parked under the railroad trestle. A golden retriever stands guard by their side. Victoria Cross, 36, pulls on a long, flowing green-velvet mask that is sewn to a wrangler's hat. The mask has many gourds hanging from it. Sherie Hartle, 35, is putting on a white mask that resembles a death's-head. The masks are frightening; they are right out of a peyote dream.   3

Vicki and Sherie are in the process of transforming themselves into the "curious apparitions" that passengers on the *Southwest Chief* have been warned about. The performance that is about to begin is part of a project called "Apparitions and Amtrak," funded in part by a grant from the New Mexico Arts Division and the National Endowment for the Arts.   4

Vicki, who moved to Santa Fe 14 years ago, makes almost all of the masks and costumes used in the performance. She describes her favorite apparitions this way: "The Jester is a bedspread, some socks and curtains, beads and bells. Buttonface is pajamas, a favorite shirt, lots of buttons, a vegetable steamer, socks and an old cloth flag I used to fly in Arroyo Hondo. The apparitions are gentle reminders to the Amtrak passengers that dreams are important aspects of our lives."   5

Today Vicki is the Mexican Hat. Sherie, a massage therapist when she is 6
not performing, will be the Winter One. Vicki's trunk, overflowing with
costumes and masks, stands in the ravine about ten feet from the Galisteo
creek. Sherie, doing a little dance in her robe and mask, suddenly slips on
a flat, wet rock and falls hard on her back. "I'm O.K.! I'm O.K.!" she
shouts through her mask, and she gets back up.

Suddenly an old Subaru cuts down into the ravine, and Ifan Evans, 47, 7
who is driving, brings the car to a sharp halt just a few feet from the
creek. Four people all seem to exit the car at the same time, and there is
much hugging and kissing. But there is little time to waste.

"What time is the train due?" Dianne Porter, 40, an "environmental 8
visionary" who works in the Marcy Street Card Shop, asks Vicki. "In
about 15 minutes. We have to hurry."

Dianne chooses a costume for herself and her daughter Bridey, 9. 9
Dianne will be Spiral Head, and Bridey will be the Summer Bird. Vicki
chooses the Baby Raven for Veva Burns, Bridey's friend, who is also nine.

Dianne adjusts Bridey's costume, and then she and Bridey and Veva go 10
under the trestle and climb a steep incline that is strewn with boulders.
The footing is slippery; they go cautiously and emerge on a concrete
platform that is five feet from the railroad tracks.

Meanwhile, Ifan Evans, the Jester, puts on a Pinocchio mask, says 11
goodbye to Vicki and Sherie and walks away down a path. Ifan carries a
tall staff with a long, flowing pink pennant attached to it. On the way, he
meets Thor Sigstedt, who is with his children Dylan, 5, and Tara, 7.

Thor, 34, owns the land here, about 40 acres of it. He has long, sandy 12
hair and a kind, weathered face. "We're not going to take part today, but
we'll watch from up there." Thor points to a spot farther up the hill by
two tall ponderosa pines. Behind these hills are the Sangre de Cristo
mountains.

They say goodbye, and Ifan continues his walk down the path until he 13
comes to a barbed-wire corral. There, a tan pony and a gray mule stand
quietly. A heavenly silence seems to enfold the land. Ifan walks to the
corral, and the mule comes over to better observe this strange man. They
stare at each other for several minutes, and then Ifan nods to the mule
and walks on. Ifan, today, will be a solitary apparition in the dreamscape.

Ifan says of his performing, "It's a reminder of who I am inside. When I 14
climb under one of these masks, sound changes—I'm different. It reminds me that I'm more than just a squash player, more than an escapee
from New York. It's telling me of something I should do, or used to do."

Vicki is the first to hear the train whistle blow. "The train! The train is 15
coming!" she shouts.

"How do you know?" Veva calls down to her. 16

"I heard it. I heard the whistle." 17

Vicki starts to perform a mad Apache war dance, spinning and turning 18 in small, violent circles. Twenty feet in front of Vicki, high on the concrete platform, Bridey, Veva and Dianne are shrieking with excitement. As the train comes into view, they begin to spin and dance as if possessed. Bridey calls out to her mother as the train pulls onto the trestle, "Stop! Stop! You'll make it rain! You'll make it rain!"

It's all over in a minute. The engineer waves. These are friendly   19 apparitions; they wave back. Several passengers sight the dancers and flash broad smiles. As the last car crosses the trestle, the sun comes out for the first time all day, and at the same time, it begins to rain. "You made it rain! You made it rain!" Bridey shouts. "You made lightning!"

Vicki, who has been dancing as if in a hallucinatory trance the whole   20 time the train was passing, is now screaming at the top of her lungs, "Where's Sandino? Where's my dog? Is he still alive?"

Time stands still in Canyoncito for a few precious seconds until Bridey   21 calls down to Vicki, "He's O.K., he's O.K. I see him. He's coming back—he ran after the train." Enter Sandino, performance star. He comes zooming down from an overpass, jumps a steep embankment, caroms mightily through the creek, stutter-steps around some sage and leaps onto Vicki. Vicki hugs her dog. The train is gone; the land is quiet again.

Schulman establishes time by the phrase "on this gloomy Sunday" and "between 2 and 3 in the afternoon." The author documents place in the first paragraph and uses description in the second paragraph to make the setting more vivid.

> Canyoncito is on wild, beautiful land 15 miles southeast of Santa Fe. The landscape is dotted with adobe ranch houses and corrals. Chamizas with yellow flowers, delicate violet asters, sage, piñons and cacti grow everywhere.

The first two actors are introduced in the third paragraph, Victoria Cross, 36, and Sherie Hartle, 35. The starting point of the action is also introduced as they "emerge from a red Datsun pickup" and pull on their masks, which are colorfully described. Not until the second sentence in the fourth paragraph is the cause for these actors and this action explained.

> The performance that is about to begin is part of a project called "Apparitions and Amtrak," funded in part by a grant from the New Mexico Arts Division and the National Endowment for the Arts.

Another cause in the form of personal motivation is described later in the article. Locate this cause for one performer's action. How does this information enhance the narrative?

There is a series of paragraphs that give the starting point of the action for each of the actors, Vicki, Dianne, Bridey, Ifan Evans, and Thor. Then the action—as the train approaches—is described in terms of sound and vivid colors and finally in the dog who runs wildly after the train.

> He comes zooming down from an overpass, jumps a steep embankment, caroms mightily through the creek, stutter-steps around some sage and leaps onto Vicki. Vicki hugs her dog. The train is gone; the land is quiet again.

As the performance ends, the action stops abruptly after "the train is gone."

This report combines all of the elements of actor, action, time, place, cause, manner, and starting point in narrating this event. Schulman also uses description to enliven the narrative by giving a vivid backdrop to the action.

Narration is also useful in lab reports, progress reports, and minutes where a detailed narration of what happened is required. The essential elements are still actor, action, time, place, cause, manner, and starting point.

Narration is most familiar to us in short stories and novels, but telling a story about what happened can serve any writer well and is not just a tool of the fiction writer. Accounts of familiar people and the narration of familiar events can make an abstract or complex idea more accessible to a reader. Good narrative makes a point, although in story-telling that point is often not stated. But most stories in essay writing are told to support an idea or to illustrate a point.

In the following excerpt from "How Women's Diets Reflect Fear of Power" the author, Kim Chernin, uses narrations drawn from her own experience to support two points that she is making.

> My experience of obsession began in 1957, when I was 17 years old. I was on vacation in Berlin, sitting at the table with my German landlords. I remember the day vividly: The wind was blowing; the curtain lifted on the window and a beam of sunlight crossed the room and stopped at the spout of the teapot. I felt that I was about to remember something and then, unaccountably, I was moved to tears. But I did not cry, I ate. Then, while no one was looking, I stuffed two rolls into my pocket, stood up from the table and left the room. Once out of the house, I began running, from street stall to street stall, buying cones of roasted chestnuts and pounds of chocolate.
>
> Today, I can sit down at a meal without computing calories. My body, my hunger, my food, the things that once seemed like enemies, now have begun to look like friends. But for 20 years after

that day in Berlin, compulsive eating was my routine, alternating with an equally compulsive addiction to dieting. My weight ranged from 90 to 130 pounds, and I became familiar with all those extravagant hopes and dismal failures experienced by every woman who tries to diet. Until I changed.

There were two moments of breakthrough. The first occurred when I was 26 years old. I had awakened around midnight, wondering how I could possibly be hungry, since I had eaten a great deal that day. Yet when I opened the refrigerator, I realized almost immediately that I wasn't interested; in fact, I wasn't really hungry. I was actually restless, frightened and confused. I didn't know if I wanted to continue at the university, if I wanted to marry the man who wanted to marry me, if I would be able to earn a living. I understood that food was not what I was hungering for.

Many of life's emotions—from loneliness to rage, from a love of life to a first falling in love—can be felt as appetite. And some would explain the obsession with weight in these easy, familiar terms. But there are deeper levels of understanding to plumb. That night, for example, standing in front of the refrigerator, I realized that my hunger was for larger things, for identity, for creativity, for power, for a meaningful place in society. The hunger most women feel, which drives them to eat more than they need, is fed by the evolution and expression of self.

My second moment of insight into the meaning of this obsession occurred almost 10 years later. I was again lying in bed. My attention was vaguely focused upon my round body. I fantasized my body's transformation to a consummate loveliness, the flesh trimmed away, stomach flat, thighs like those of the adolescent boy I had seen that day running in the park.

Such fantasies of transformation had occupied me often before, but this time I recognized that they were prompted by a bitter contempt for the female nature of my own body. The physical ideal for a woman in America today, I realized, was a man's body. The very curves and softness I had been trying to diet away were the natural qualities of a woman's body. Hips rounding, belly curved, thighs too large for an adolescent boy—what had driven me to deny this evidence of my woman's body?

The stories drawn from her past experience begin with "There were two moments of breakthrough" in the third paragraph. To what realizations did these incidents bring her? What are the points that she is supporting? Would they have been as convincing without the narrative? How do the different elements of actor, action, time, place, cause, manner, and starting point figure in these stories?

In the introduction to this essay Chernin also uses a detailed narrative and then follows it with two paragraphs of statistics.

The locker room of the tennis club. A tall woman enters, removes her towel; she throws it across a bench, faces herself squarely in the mirror, climbs on the scale, looks down.

"I knew it," she mutters.

"Up or down?" I ask, hoping to suggest that there might be lands and cultures where gaining weight would not be considered a disaster.

"Two pounds," she says, ignoring the suggestion. "Two pounds!"

Then she turns, grabs the towel and swings out at the mirror, smashing it violently, the towel splattering water over the glass.

"Fat pig!" she shouts at her image in the mirror. "You fat, fat pig!"

The Harvard Medical School Health Letter estimates that some 20 million Americans are on a "serious" diet at any given moment. According to the sociologist Natalie Allon, these dieters are spending $10 billion dollars a year in the process, much of it at hundreds of spas and health farms that charge from $185 to $3,000 a week. Diet books enrich their authors—"Never-Say-Diet Book," for example, out just a year, has spent 35 weeks of that time on the best-seller list and sold 560,000 copies.

Two facts make the current obsession with weight extraordinary. One is the scope of it. Throughout history, there have been dieters, including Roman matrons, who were willing to starve themselves. But there has never been a period when such large numbers of people have spent so much time, money and emotional energy on their weight. Weight Watchers, for example, holds more than 12,000 individual classes every week and has enrolled 13 million members since its founding in 1963.

How effective would Chernin's introductory narration have been without the statistics? How effective would the statistics have been without the narrative? How do they complement one another?

Chapter 9 discusses further the use of narration as anecdote in introductory paragraphs.

STATISTICS

Statistics make up a special kind of evidence derived from numerical data and generally carry great weight in an argument. As illustrated in Chernin's article, however, many times figures alone cannot convince, but they can be used effectively to support an assertion. You must exercise special care in using statistics by explaining terms, by giving reliable sources, and by relating the statistic to the point you are making. A statistic by itself means very little.

The terminology used in statistics can be confusing to your reader and may need an explanation. In the following example, the writer explains the meaning of "the ninety-seventh percentile."

> She was in the ninety-seventh percentile on the test; that is, out of a hundred students ninety-seven scored lower and only three made higher grades.

Terminology

To begin with, it is important that you review some of the common terminology used with statistics, such as *average* or *mean, median, mode* or *norm, percentage,* and *percentile.* These terms have precise and important meanings. Although based on mathematical computations, they are widely used in writing.

Average or *mean* is the number obtained by dividing the sum of a set of quantities by the number of quantities in the set. So in a group of children aged 10, 6, 4, 3, 2, the total (25) divided by the number of children (5) would produce the average age or mean of the children as 5, although none of the children is actually 5 years old.

The *median* is the middle number in a set of quantities above and below which lie an equal number of quantities. So in the same group of children the median age would be 4. The *mode* is the number that occurs most frequently in a number of quantities. So in a group of children aged 6, 4, 3, 3, 3, 3, 1, the age 3 is the mode.

The words *percentage* and *percentile* are similar in meaning; both are used to indicate quantity with relation to a whole. Both depend on numbers compared to 100 as the denominator. So if 65 out of a 100 students made a B on the test, the fraction would be 65/100 and the percentage of students making a B would be 65 percent.

A percentile starts with any number on the scale one to a hundred and delineates the numbers higher and lower than the percentile number listed. For example, if someone is in the ninety-seventh percentile on the scores of a test, it means that out of a hundred students, 3 made higher grades and 97 made lower grades.

A *correlation* is a particular kind of statistical probability based on two events that frequently occur together. If there is a high incidence of cancer among persons who smoke, there may be high correlation between cancer and smoking. When correlations are high enough, there is a strong suspicion of cause and effect. Then correlations must be tested. In the case of smoking, it was not until laboratory rats were forced to inhale cigarette smoke that a cause and effect relationship, rather than a high correlation, could be established. Two events that have a high correlation may, in fact, be two effects of a common cause rather than a cause and effect relationship. For example, smoking and cancer might both be caused by stress, as demonstrated by this diagram:

SMOKING AND CANCER AS CORRELATION

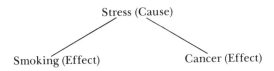

Stress (Cause)

Smoking (Effect) Cancer (Effect)

The following diagram shows a direct cause/effect relationship between smoking and cancer.

SMOKING AND CANCER AS CAUSE AND EFFECT

Smoking (Cause)

Cancer (Effect)

You may use correlations in your writing but such statistical relationships should be carefully distinguished as correlations not cause and effect.

Because such terms are commonly used in statistical material, you need to understand their precise meanings before you use statistics in your writing and be able to make those meanings clear to your reader.

You must also understand what the names of the units used in the statistical evaluation mean. For instance, in the following example, all of the figures in the paragraph depend on the meaning of the term *poverty threshold*:

> Of all the families below the Census Bureau's poverty threshold in 1982, a startling 46% were headed by women. Of all the families headed by women in 1982, more than one-third lived in poverty. Nationwide, the bureau reported an 8.1% rise in the poverty population during 1982, to 34.4 million. That increased the poverty rate to 15%, the highest such rate since 1966. The poverty threshold in 1982 for a family of four was $9,862; figures for 1983 aren't yet available.

Poverty threshold is defined in the last sentence as an income level of $9,862 for a family of four. In 1982, a family of four that had an income less than that figure would be classified as living in poverty. But notice that in the following paragraph that occurs later in the same article the author questions the definition given to poverty, which, in turn, throws all of the statistics into question.

> Thomas Moore, the director of domestic studies at the Hoover Institution at Stanford University, argues that poverty statistics overstate the number of poor people because researchers don't add in such noncash benefits as food stamps or Medicaid when calculating family incomes.

Definitions of terms are pivotal in your argument. Be sure to explain terms to your reader unless you feel confident that he or she understands them. Here again, an awareness of audience is essential.

Using Statistics in Writing

When you use figures to support your arguments you must use them with care in order to convince the careful reader. The reader may question such things as the source, the date of the figures, and other matters. All figures and statistics should include the following information.

The source of the figures In addition to citing the source of the figures, you need to use sources that are well known to be reliable.

The following passage is taken from the 1981 testimony of Edward C. Melby, Professor of Medicine and Dean of the College of Veterinary Science at Cornell University. He was speaking before a congressional committee considering legislation to restrict animal-based research. As President of the Association for Biomedical Research he is defending the use of animal-based research.

> In the underdeveloped countries, many infectious diseases still account for tremendous morbidity and mortality. According to the 1980 World Health Organization Summary Reports, 200,000,000 people are affected by schistosomiasis; 100,000,000 by leishumaniasis with 400,000 new cases developing annually; 300-400,000,000 cases of malaria which kills in excess of 100,000,000 children each year, and, 100,000,000 humans are affected by trypanosomiasis. It is estimated that the morbidity from these four diseases alone is four times the entire population of the United States. At the present time, there are no alternatives to the use of animals in demonstrating the host response to these infectious agents.

This passage carries great reliability. Dr. Melby, through his professional position, has the highest credibility. In addition, he carefully cites the source and date for his figures—the World Health Organization Summary Reports of 1980—a source that is known and respected by his hearers and would be readily available to anyone wishing to check his figures.

The date of the figures In most cases, recent evidence, just because it is more recent, will refute older evidence. Any figures that are outdated can be reasonably doubted if they are being applied to prove a current fact. In the preceding excerpt, Dr. Melby is careful to use statistics from the most recent reports of the World Health Organization Summary Reports.

The method by which the figures were gathered Election polls that sample the population to predict the outcome of an election are good evidence of the way results can be skewed by poor sampling. Naturally the whole population cannot be questioned, so it is imperative that the sample be selected so that it represents a fair cross-section. For example, if the polling were done by telephone only during the day, the population polled would probably contain a large percentage of persons who are not employed. Such a group would not be representative. Randomly selected samples are a must in any statistic that works from a sample of the total population, and you may make the statistic more believable if you describe the method by which it was gathered.

The percentage base Has the price of wheat gone up 50 percent or gone down 10 percent? It all depends upon the year used as the base. Twenty-three percent of the students ate a hot lunch. Which students? Fifth graders at a certain school? All the students at a certain school? All students in the city grade schools? High schools? Public and private schools? Or is the statistic based on only a sample of any one of these populations? The percentage is meaningless unless you clarify the percentage base—23 percent of *what*.

AUTHORITY

In supporting an argument, writers lean heavily on the observations and opinions of other people. But before accepting other persons' ideas, you will want to evaluate those observations and opinions, as well as the persons making them. Judgments depend on the *ethos* of the person and are a special kind of opinion, arrived at by an authority on the basis of expert knowledge.

It is important to distinguish between ordinary opinions and judgments made by an authority. Certain persons are recognized as authorities because of their special knowledge of a subject and thus their opinions carry weight and are termed judgments. Journals recognized in special fields carry articles by authorities and most college campuses have professors who are authorities in particular areas. Footnotes, endnotes, and citations are a way such authorities are acknowledged. Documentation carries the basic kind of information that readers wish to know such as *who* said it, *when* it was said, and *under what circumstances* it was said. Thus the author (who), the title of the book or article (the circumstances), and the date (when) are always included either in the text or in the citation.

> In a recent address to the Iowa Farm Bureau on Russian agriculture, William Green remarked that. . . .

We furnish this same kind of information in informal conversations in a less formal way.

> Yesterday when we were drinking coffee in the Union, Bill said that John is a good tennis player, and he ought to know. He's been playing with him almost every day this summer.

In using outside authority, the writer, like the speaker in the above example of conversation, may wish to include within the text not only the name of the authority but the basis for his or her authority if the person is not well known:

> Jane Smith, a zoologist from the Animal Science Institute, said recently at a dinner for visiting zookeepers that pandas seldom mate in captivity.

Or the authority may be indicated more informally, as in this example:

> My roommate, who went to the University of Illinois last year, said that freshmen there could not get parking stickers for on-campus parking.

In this case, the writer has established the roommate's authority on the subject of parking at the University of Illinois.

Using Authority in Writing

Often writers misuse authority, creating doubts in the minds of readers. You can check your use of authority by considering the following questions before you accept an authority cited in a piece of writing or choose an authority to cite in your own:

1. Is the person an authority in the field in which she or he is being cited as an authority?

Advertisements often make use of the transfer of authority to sell a product. John McEnroe may be an authority on tennis, but he can hardly be expected to be an authority on deodorants or toothpaste. You need to make sure that the reader understands that the authority is being cited as an authority in the field in which she or he is knowledgeable.

2. Is the authority biased or prejudiced?

When someone is prejudiced, that person has pre-judged the case and his or her opinion does not carry the appropriate authority. You might ask yourself the following questions when evaluating the use of authority in your reading: Does the authority speak with any ulterior motive for gain? Is a person being paid to promote a certain product? Has a person been promised a job or a promotion for supporting a certain political candidate? The opinions of people who stand to gain because of those opinions must be evaluated carefully and used with reservations in your own writing.

3. Is the authority being quoted out of context?

Book jackets often use short quotations taken out of context from reviews of the book. Such quotes can be extremely misleading. A recent book jacket quoted a review as saying the book was "one of the best." The original full quote was "one of the best of a bad collection." When you cite an authority, be sure you scrupulously maintain that person's meaning.

Do not overlook using yourself as an authority. You may well be an authority on dorm food if you have been living in a dormitory, or on rugby if you are playing on a rugby team. You must, however, be sure to establish the grounds for your authority—establish your *ethos*.

I have been playing all sorts of sports since I was four years old, and tennis is a sport that requires hours of practice.

When using yourself as an authority there is no need to acknowledge the source, but when using outside authority such documentation is necessary. It is sometimes difficult, however, to determine how much of the information—the author, the title, the date, the publication information—should be included in the text itself and how much should be added in parentheses or included in a footnote or an endnote. Documentation will be covered in more detail in Chapter 13 on the research paper, but since it is an important part of using authorities effectively it is first treated here.

It may be helpful to identify the context—the article or book from which you are drawing your idea—by mentioning the subject of the article.

> In a 1975 article in which he advocated reform of the traditional English curriculum, John O. Hagan gave English teachers a new perspective on their mission by pointing out that they are basically teachers of reading and writing.

In this excerpt, the author puts the quote in the context of an article "advocating reform of the English curriculum," giving the words a more meaningful context than just the title of the article and the name of the journal, which would then be mentioned in a reference citation.

Often the date is not necessary within the text although it must be provided in the formal citation.

> Ronald F. Reid's article on the history of the Boylston Professorship of Rhetoric and Oratory at Harvard and William Riley Parker's account of how English departments came into being in American universities in the last quarter of the nineteenth century supply additional details about the formation of the curricula in literature and composition.

The author did not think that the dates of these articles were significant enough to include in the text, probably because of the historical subject matter, so he dropped that information to the citation. This excerpt refers to two articles giving the authors and the subjects of the articles, rather than merely the titles, and introduces a section drawing from them and describing the curricula in literature and composition. The endnote citation gives details of publication information and dates.

It is not necessary to identify the authority whom you are quoting if that person is already well known to a specialized readership. In this reference, the writer uses a quotation from Joan Kramer, a person well known to her readers, to support a point that she is making.

> Joan Kramer's research makes clear that bluegill and bass must be carefully balanced in farm ponds in order to guarantee the "survival of both."

In the following article, authority is used extensively to support the use of vitamin E. Sometimes the authority is used well; and sometimes not. As you read, try to identify undocumented use of authority.

VITAMIN E IN THE HANDS OF CREATIVE PHYSICIANS

RUTH ADAMS
FRANK MURRAY

1 Of all the substances in the medical researcher's pharmacopoeia, perhaps the most maligned, neglected and ignored is vitamin E. In spite of this apparent ostracism in the United States, however, some of the world's leading medical authorities are using alpha tocopherol—more commonly known as vitamin E—to successfully treat and cure a host of mankind's most notorious scourges.

2 For those medical researchers who are at work trying to treat and prevent heart attacks—our No. 1 killer—and to help many more thousands who are dying of related circulatory disorders, vitamin E is playing a major role. And for many athletes, vitamin E (in the form of wheat germ oil, specially formulated oils for stamina and endurance, vitamin E capsules and perles, etc.) has long been as indispensable as calisthenics.

3 "There are over 570,000 deaths from heart attacks each year," says a publication of the American Heart Association, "many thousands of them among people in the prime of life—and growing indications that heart disease may be a disease of prosperity."

4 In scientific minds, vitamin E may be related to fertility and reproduction, said an article in *Medical World News* for April 18, 1969. But a famous ball player, Bobby Bolin of the San Francisco Giants, credits the vitamin with keeping his pitching arm in condition. He developed a sore shoulder in 1966, resulting in a poor pitching season for two years. He began to take vitamin E. The article said that he expected to be a "regular starter" at the beginning of the 1969 season, and that vitamin E was responsible for the good news.

5 It isn't surprising that many athletes have discovered the benefits of taking vitamin E regularly. The vitamin is in short supply in most of our diets. Vitamin E is an essential part of the whole circulatory mechanism of the body, since it affects our use of oxygen. When you have plenty of vitamin E on hand, your cells can get along on less oxygen. This is surely an advantage for an athlete, who expends large quantities of oxygen. And, according to recent research at the Battelle Memorial Institute,

which we will discuss in greater detail in a later section of this book, vitamin E, along with vitamin A, is important to anyone who lives in the midst of constant air pollution.

From *The Summary*, a scientific journal published by the Shute Institute 6 in Canada, a publication we will frequently refer to, we learn additional facts about vitamin E. Dr. Evan Shute, who heads the clinic, and Dr. Wilfrid E. Shute, his brother, have pioneered in work with vitamin E for more than 20 years. *The Summary* condenses and abstracts for doctors and medical researchers some of the material on relevant subjects that has appeared in medical journals throughout the world.

For instance, a Hungarian doctor reports on the encouraging effects of 7 vitamin E in children born with certain defects. Of all vitamin deficiencies, she believes that vitamin E is the most important in preventing such occurrences. She has given the vitamin with good results in quite large doses to children who would otherwise be almost incapacitated. Mothers, too.

She tells the story of a woman who had three deficient children, two of 8 them with Down's Syndrome or mongolism. When she was pregnant for the fourth time, the physician sent her away for a rest—"tired, aging, torpid" as she was, with "a diet rich in proteins, liver, vegetables and fruit with large doses of vitamins, especially vitamin E, and thyroid hormone." She returned in six weeks to give birth to a perfectly healthy baby!

As for another insidious disorder—chronic phlebitis—Dr. Evan Shute 9 says that most doctors have no idea of how common this condition is. It should be looked for in everyone, he says, certainly every adult woman. After describing the symptoms—a warm swollen foot and an ache in the leg or foot which is relieved by raising the feet higher than the head—he tells his physician readers, "Look for chronic phlebitis and you will be astounded how common it is. Treat it with vitamin E and you will be deluged with grateful patients who never found help before."

Describing a symposium on the subject of vitamins E, A and K, Dr. 10 Shute tells us that speakers presented evidence that vitamin E is valuable in doses of 400 miligrams daily for treating claudication—a circulatory condition of the feet and legs—and that a similar dosage helps one kind of ulcer.

High dosage of vitamin E improves survival time of persons with 11 hardening of the arteries and should always be given to such patients, according to Dr. Shute. He adds that there are some 21 articles in medical literature, aside from the many he himself has written, showing that vitamin E dilates blood vessels and develops collateral vessels—thus permitting more blood to go through, even though the vessel is narrowed by deposits on its walls.

An article that appeared in *Postgraduate Medicine* in 1968 by Dr. Alton 12 Ochsner, a world-famous lung surgeon, states that he has used vitamin E on every surgical patient over the past 15 years and none has developed damaging or fatal blood clots.

Dr. Shute goes on to say that, at the Shute Clinic, all surgery patients 13 are routinely given vitamin E both as a preventive and as a curative measure.

He quotes an article in *Annals of Internal Medicine*, saying that throm- 14 bosis or clot formation "has become the prime health hazard of the adult population of the Western world." Dr. Shute adds these comments: "Here is a real tragedy. Twenty years after we introduced a simple and safe clotting agent, alpha tocopherol, to the medical world, everything else is tried, including dangerous drugs and the anti-coagulants, and with all these the results are extremely unsatisfactory. When will the medical profession use vitamin E as it should be used for this condition?"

He quotes a statement from the *Journal of the American Medical Associa-* 15 *tion* showing that the average teenage girl or housewife gets only about half the amount of iron she should have from her diet in the United States. Then Dr. Shute says, "Another nutritional defect in the best fed people on earth! In one issue the *JAMA* shows the average American is often deficient in iron and vitamin A. Now what about vitamin E?" He, of course, has pointed out many times that this vitamin is almost bound to be lacking in the average diet. As we mention elsewhere, up to 90% of the vitamin E content of various grains is lost during the flaking, shredding, puffing processess that are used to make breakfast cereals.

Dr. Shute then quotes a newsletter on the U.S. Department of Agricul- 16 ture survey revealing that only half of all American diets could be called "good." He comments thusly, "One continually reads claptrap by nutri- tionists contending that the wealthiest country in the world feeds every- body well. This obviously isn't true. It is no wonder that deficiency of vitamin E is so common when even the diet recommended by the Na- tional Research Council of the U.S.A. contains something like 6 milli- grams of vitamin E per day before it is cooked!"

In another issue of *The Summary*, we learn how two Brazilian re- 17 searchers are working on heart studies done on rats that were made deficient in vitamin E. Of 26 rats, only six normal ones were found. All the rest showed some heart damage when they were tested with elec- trocardiograms and other devices.

Two German researchers report on the action of an emulsified vitamin 18 E solution on the heart tissues of guinea pigs. They found that the vitamin protects the heart from damage by medication, and helps to prevent heart insufficiency. Dr. Shute adds that this paper indicates that vitamin E should be investigated further in hospital clinics.

Animals deficient in vitamin E produced young with gross and micro- 19 scopic defects of the skeleton, muscles and nervous system. They had harelips, abdominal hernias, badly curved backs and many more defects.

This was reported in *The Journal of Animal Science*, Volume 22, page 848, 1963.

Two American obstetricians report in the *American Journal of Obstetrics* 20 *and Gynecology* that they know of no way to prevent serious damage and death for many premature infants. Dr. Shute comments, "These authors apparently have not seen our reports on the use of vitamin E in the prevention of prematurity." He goes on to say, "No comparable results have been reported."

A report in the journal, *Fertility and Sterility*, indicates that in six 21 percent of patients studied, the cause of abortion and miscarriage lay in the father's deficient sperm, not in any deficit of the mother. The authors studied carefully the medical histories of many couples who had been married several times. Dr. Shute comments, "We have long advocated alpha tocopherol for poor sperm samples, especially in habitual abortion couples."

A Romanian farm journal reports that extremely large amounts of 22 vitamin E, plus vitamin A, were given to 77 sterile cows. Within one to one-and-a-half months, their sexual cycles were restored and 70 percent of them conceived.

A German veterinarian reports in a 1960 issue of *Tierarztliche Umschau* 23 that he uses vitamin E for treating animals with heart conditions. A one-year-old poodle with heart trouble regained complete health after 14 days on vitamin E. A three-year-old thoroughbred horse with acute heart failure was treated with vitamin E for two weeks, after which time its electrocardiogram showed only trivial changes even after exercise. The vet uses, he says, large doses of the vitamin.

And an Argentinian physician reports in *Semana Med.* that vitamin C is 24 helpful in administering vitamin E. It works with the vitamin to retain it in body tissues. Dr. A. Del Guidice uses the two vitamins together in cases of cataracts, strabismus and myopias. He also noted that patients with convulsive diseases are much helped by vitamin E—massive doses of it— so that their doses of tranquilizers and sedatives can be lessened.

A letter from Dr. Del Guidice to Dr. Shute tells of his success in treating 25 mongolism in children with vitamin E. For good results, he says, it must be given in large doses from the age of one month on. He continues his treatment for years sometimes, and claims that spectacular results can be achieved in this tragic disease.

Two Japanese scientists report in the *Journal of Vitaminology* that hair 26 grew back faster on the shaven backs of rabbits when they applied vitamin E locally for 10 to 13 weeks.

And again from Argentina comes word of vitamin E given to 20 27 mentally defective children in large doses. In 75 percent, the intelligence quota was raised from 12 to 25 points, "with improved conduct and scholarly ability. Less attention fatigue was noted in 80 percent, and 90 percent had improved memory." A short experience with neurotic adults showed that vitamin E brought a definite reduction in phobias, tic, obsessions and other neurotic symptoms.

In one issue of *The Summary*, Dr. Shute prints a letter of his to the editor 28 of the *British Medical Journal* (July 1966) urging this distinguished man to consider vitamin E as a treatment for pulmonary embolism. He says, "I have used nothing else for years and no longer even think of embolism (that is, blood clots) in my patients, even in those with records of previous phlebitis. Dosage is 800 International Units a day." He adds a PS to readers of *The Summary*: "The Editor could not find space for this letter unfortunately."

A *British Medical Journal* editorial comments on our present methods of 29 treatment for blood clots in leg veins. Raising the foot off the bed, bandaging the legs and getting the patient on his feet doesn't seem to be very helpful, says the editor. Using anticoagulants seems to help some, but we should speedily develop some new methods of treatment. Dr. Shute comments that one would think that vitamin E has a clear field, since nothing else is very effective. It is easy to use, he goes on, safe and effective.

Each issue of *The Summary* contains many articles that have appeared 30 in world medical literature on vitamin E and related subjects. In other countries, vitamin E is treated quite seriously in medical research, is routinely used in hospitals and clinics. In our country, such use is rare.

These are just a few of the case histories that Dr. Shute reports, at his 31 own expense, in *The Summary*. The book is not available for nonmedical people, since it is written in highly technical terms. However, we suggest that you recommend these publications to your doctor, if you or someone you know is suffering from a disorder that might be treated successfully with vitamin E. The address is: Dr. Evan Shute, Shute Foundation for Medical Research, London, Ontario, Canada.

In this article, the writers make use of a number of authorities ranging from articles in prestigious medical journals to such vague sources as "a Romanian farm journal." In some cases full documentation is given in the article.

Animals deficient in vitamin E produced young with gross and microscopic defects of the skeleton, muscles and nervous system. They had harelips, abdominal hernias, badly curved backs and many more defects. This was reported in *The Journal of Animal Science*, Volume 22, page 848, 1963.

In another case the authority is identified only as "a Hungarian doctor":

For instance, a Hungarian doctor reports on the encouraging effects of vitamin E in children born with certain defects. Of all vitamin deficiencies, she believes that vitamin E is the most important in preventing such occurrences.

Note, on the other hand, that Dr. Evan Shute and *The Summary*, which are quoted often in the article, are well identified.

From *The Summary*, a scientific journal published by the Shute Institute in Canada, a publication we will frequently refer to, we learn additional facts about vitamin E. Dr. Evan Shute, who heads the clinic, and Dr. Wilfrid E. Shute, his brother, have pioneered in work in vitamin E for more than 20 years. *The Summary* condenses and abstracts for doctors and medical researchers some of the material on relevant subjects that has appeared in medical journals thoughout the world.

Make a list of the authorities used in the essay and analyze each one as to its reliability.

CONDUCTING INTERVIEWS

Although you might ordinarily turn to journals and statistics for authoritative sources, you should not overlook the people around you who may have information on the subject about which you are writing. For example, if you are writing a paper on "College Athletics," your best sources of information may be one of the football coaches or the athletes themselves. Above all, it is important to remember that a university or college campus has on its faculty persons who are there because they are authorities in their fields. Interviewing such persons can be a rich source of information. However, to use your time and theirs to the best advantage, there are certain guidelines that might be followed.

Remember that these people are busy; you will probably need to contact them ahead of time to request an interview. Tell them why you wish to interview them and how much time you will need. You probably should not expect to take any more than thirty minutes. In order to use that time to full advantage, you need to prepare for your interview and know exactly what you are going to ask. These guidelines may help:

1. Prepare a list of questions in order of importance. You may not have time to ask all of them, so be sure to ask the most important ones first.

2. Ask if you may tape the interview. A tape will help you make sure that your information is accurate.

3. Take careful notes during the interview and be sure that you distinguish exact quotes—with quotation marks—from your own summary or interpretation of what was said.

4. Keep your own comments to a minimum. It will only take time away from the interview, and you will have ample opportunity to make your own observations in the paper that you are writing.

5. At the end of the interview, be sure that you have names spelled correctly—especially the name of the person that you are interviewing. Read direct quotations aloud to see if you have quoted correctly.

6. Be sure to get full information about the authority of the person you are interviewing. "How long have you coached football?" "Where have you played basketball?" "Where did you get your degree in Mechanical Engineering and have you written any books or articles on the subject?" Including this information in your paper will establish the authority of your source.

7. At the end of the interview, ask for bibliographical references or other persons who could give you information.

As a courtesy, it is well to give a copy of your completed paper to any person whom you have interviewed.

Today, you as a writer can draw on rich outside resources to support your opinions and clarify your ideas. You have in addition to your own observational powers vast amounts of information available to you in government documents, specialized journals, the people around you, and the authorities within your academic community. Such sources make up the inartistic proofs. Chapter 12 will treat in more detail the ways to draw information from the more sophisticated technological resources available to you.

Questions to Consider

1. Write a brief paragraph in which you provide a detailed physical description of yourself, but do not identify yourself by name. Be sure to select the most telling details to help your classmates distinguish you from anyone else. After your instructor collects all the paragraphs and redistributes them, try to determine the identity of the writer on the basis of the description.

2. Identify how the author has used his powers of observation in the following paragraphs. What do the details he has chosen contribute to his account? What impression of the event do they encourage? How?

The chair is bolted to the floor near the back of a 12-ft. by 18-ft. room. You sit on a seat of cracked rubber secured by rows of copper tacks. Your ankles are strapped into half-moon-shaped foot cuffs lined with canvas. A 2-in.-wide greasy leather belt with 28 buckle holes and worn grooves where it has been pulled very tight many times is secured around your waist just above the hips. A cool metal cone encircles your head. You are now only moments away from death.

But you still have a few seconds left. Time becomes stretched to the outermost limits. To your right you see the mahogany floor divider that separates four brown church-type pews from the rest of the room. They look odd in this beige Zen-like chamber. There is another door at the back through which the witnesses arrive. You stare up at two groups of flourescent lights on the ceiling. They are on. The paint on the ceiling is peeling.

You fit in neat and snug. Behind the chair's back leg on your right is a cable wrapped in gray tape. It will sluice the electrical current to three other wires: two going to each of your feet, and the third to the cone on top of your head. The room is very quiet. During your brief walk here, you looked over your shoulder and saw early morning light creeping over the Berkshire Hills. Then into this silent tomb.

The air vent above your head in the ceiling begins to hum. This means the executioner has turned on the fan to suck up the smell of burning flesh. There is little time left. On your right you can see the waist-high, one-way mirror in the wall. Behind the mirror is the executioner, standing before a gray marble control panel with gauges, switches and a foot-long lever of wood and metal at hip level.

The executioner will pull this lever four times. Each time 2,000 volts will course through your body, making your eyeballs first bulge, then burst, and then broiling your brains. . . .

Suggestions for Writing

1. Write a page in which you establish your own authority as an expert on a particular subject; be as convincing as you can. Remember that you are establishing your *ethos.*

2. Write a page or two in which you describe a scene or individual that elicited from you a strong emotional reaction. Choose your details carefully and try to evoke a similar emotional response in your reader.

3. Write a page or two in which you narrate an incident that became for you a genuine "learning experience." Be sure it is clear from your account exactly what you learned.

4. Exchange a photograph of your family for a photograph of the family of another member of your class. Then write a page or two in which you identify any inferences you can make about that family based purely on what you can observe in the photo. Be sure to support your inferences with details taken from the photograph. When you have finished, verify your inferences with the photograph's owner.

5. Using as an example Loren Eiseley's "The Brown Wasps" (reprinted in Chapter 6), write an essay explaining how some phenomenon you've observed in nature proves equally applicable to human beings.

Exercises in Revision

1. For those papers written by members of your workshop group in response to the first writing exercise suggested above, determine whether the writer has managed to convince you of his or her authority and explain why or why not.

2. Examine those papers written by members of your workshop group in response to the writing exercises suggested above to evaluate the authors' use of descriptive details. For what purpose does each author appear to have incorporated descriptive details? Do they enhance or detract from the writer's overall purpose in the paper? Are they sufficiently specific to recreate the experience for you as a reader? How might the description be improved?

For a Commonplace Book

All of us are authorities on something. Begin now to make a list in your commonplace book of all of those subjects on which you might be considered an authority and cite your credentials for claiming such expertise. For example, have you attended virtually every one of the local basketball team's games at home for the past five years? If nothing else, that experience could make you an expert on the fans that the team attracts. Have you recently purchased a used car that you are still satisfied with? You might be able to provide advice about how to avoid getting cheated. Did you spend part of the school year in a foreign country? In what areas might that experience qualify you as an expert? Remember to cite your credentials, and don't claim more "authority" than your experience and knowledge will allow.

Chapter 8

Avoiding Fallacies

MATERIAL FALLACIES

    Faulty Hidden Generalization
    Insufficient Sampling
    Unrepresentative Sampling

LOGICAL FALLACIES

    Faulty Cause
    Either/Or Fallacy
    The Rigged Question
    Equivocation

PSYCHOLOGICAL FALLACIES

    Appeal to Pity
    Ad Hominem
    Appeal to Force
    Bandwagon
    Appeal to Ceremony or Setting
    Appeal to Authority
    Appeal to Tradition
    Appeal to Ignorance
    Appeal to Humor
    Name-Calling

RICHARD M. NIXON, "THE CHECKERS SPEECH"

Rhetoric has always thrived in democracies and struggled for survival in totalitarian systems. In a society where every individual has a voice, the ability to persuade others represents power. But the health of that society depends, in turn, on every individual's taking on the responsibility of analyzing and evaluating the opinions of others. In a dictatorship or a monarchy, such matters are unimportant, since the ordinary citizen has no voice, but the democracy that has an ignorant or uncaring citizenry will fail to be a true democracy. Citizens who are unable or unwilling to listen and analyze the political speeches and the campaign rhetoric and who are unable or unwilling to express their opinions to their representatives will finally destroy that democracy by allowing other factions to take over their power through default.

The great period of rhetoric in the classical world was in the fifth century B.C. in Athens during the golden age of democracy. The survival and health of that democracy depended on a citizenry who could express their own views and could examine and question the views of others. In the twentieth century a defensive rhetoric—knowing how to analyze and judge the rhetoric of others—is as important as a persuasive rhetoric.

This chapter is dedicated to the idea that an informed and questioning citizenry is a necessity in a healthy democracy whether in the fifth century B.C. or in the twentieth century A.D. It is designed to demonstrate ways to test and question your own arguments as well as to refute those of others.

Today there is a technological language revolution that results in an unprecedented flow of words. In Aristotle's day, a person's words were largely limited by the reach of the human voice. In the twentieth century no such limitations exist. Through a myriad of electronic devices, voices can reach over time and space, deflected on satellites and bounced from towers. Persons long dead can speak through writing and recorded language; persons still alive can, in turn, speak to generations as yet unborn. The entertainer who made a record by harmonizing with his dead father's recorded voice is no longer science fiction. Singers who harmonize with themselves are commonplace. The bizarre reality is here. But a more significant result is that the twentieth century is bathed in a sea of words and drowned in palaver. Spoken language bombards the world from all directions—from musical lyrics to political speeches, transmitted through telephone, radio, tape, and television. Written language, as well, comes in a barrage of books, magazines, newspapers, reports, forms, directions, instructions, and letters. The flow of words is something that cannot be ignored.

In this sea of words, it is important to know not only how to produce information but also how to interpret it. So this chapter deals with understanding and interpreting that flow of words—with analyzing and evaluating the politician's statement, the advertising come-on, the newspaper report, or a friend's argument. This chapter demonstrates ways to test the arguments through an examination of fallacies—those errors in reasoning that have to do with the *truth* of premises, the material on which the conclusion is built, or the *validity* of the chain of reasoning, the logic on which the argument is based. This chapter will also look at rhetorical or psychological arguments that can lead to faulty reasoning—the emotional appeals that can cloud the facts and divert the audience from the matter at hand, but which can also be highly effective.

One of the historical criticisms leveled against rhetoric is that it can be used to convince an audience by appealing to their emotions or as Plato said, "it is from what seems to be true that persuasion comes, not from the real truth" (*Phaedrus* 260). The contemporary meaning of an "empty rhetoric" has a long history. Emotional appeals that are termed fallacies are those that can be used to make the seemingly true appear to be true. Hence the constant emphasis among the ancient philosophers on the rhetorician being a "good man" with a just cause. A knowledge of the fallacies we will discuss in this chapter may be used to refute the arguments of an opponent, but they can always be misused by the charlatan.

Some of these fallacies have been covered in previous sections when the ways to test definitions, or classifications, or generalizations were outlined. Some of the more important of those are reviewed here. We shall look then at three kinds of fallacies—*material, logical,* and *psychological.*

MATERIAL FALLACIES

Material fallacies have to do with the subject matter of the argument, the bedrock on which arguments are based. If the basic premises are untrue then the conclusion will be untrue. For example, the argument that Smith will be a good president because he is a lawyer is based on the premise, in this case an unstated premise, that all lawyers will be good presidents. The syllogism is:

All lawyers will be good presidents.

Smith is a lawyer.

Smith will be a good president.

The fallacy is in the unstated major premise—the basis of the whole argument, even though it was not stated. (See the discussion of the enthymeme in Chapter 6.)

The best argument derives from a knowledge of the subject. Nothing refutes false statements like truth. Therefore, the best arguments and the most effective refutations of an opponent's argument will come from proving the falsehood of a statement by demonstrating the truth.

Not all lawyers will necessarily be good presidents. Bill Smith is a lawyer and has been accused of embezzling his clients' money. John

Jones is a lawyer and has had difficulty running the elementary school PTA.

Note that a generalization that forms the basis of the original argument is refuted by instances that disprove it, which, in turn, refute the full argument.

One way of avoiding the fallacy of generalization characterized by *none, all,* or *every,* is to qualify or quantify the general statement. Thus *all* or *every* can become *many* or *most* while *none* can become *some* or a *a few.* When the premise of an argument is quantified, the conclusion then is qualified as in the following examples.

Most persons are capable of charity.
He is *probably* capable of charity.

A *few* people are geniuses.
She *may be* a genius.

It is well to question categorical generalizations like the following:

All people over six feet tall can play basketball.
Men don't know how to cook.
Never trust anyone over thirty.

Faulty Hidden Generalization

As we have discussed, in the *enthymeme* one of the premises is omitted. Because these premises are not stated, the generalizations they are based on often go unnoticed. What are the omitted premises in the following arguments?

She's a woman, so she can't do math.

He graduated from college, so he must be smart.

She's up on all the latest plays. She lives in New York.

The generalizations that underlie the conclusions, introduced by the word *so* are the following:

Women can't do math.

People who graduate from college are smart.

Everyone who lives in New York keeps up on the latest plays.

It is difficult to refute these arguments as they stand, until the unstated premise is brought into the open. Refutation becomes easier when the issues are clear.

But issues are not always clear in important political and moral decisions. What are the basic premises taken by the proponents of divestiture in South Africa? What are the premises taken by the opponents? How often are these basic premises stated in the discussions and in the news reports?

Can you analyze the basic premises behind the following issues?

1. Bilingual education

2. Legalization of marijuana

3. Nuclear disarmament

4. No smoking ordinances

Some of the basic premises behind the idea of bilingual education for those who support it might be the following:

1. The languages of different cultural and ethnic groups should be preserved.

2. Students who do not know English suffer educational and emotional damage when they enter a school where they are forced to speak English.

3. When people lose their native language, they lose an important part of their identity.

Some of the basic premises behind the arguments opposing bilingual education might be the following:

1. Students will do better economically and socially if they learn English.

2. Persons living in the United States should adopt the language of this country.

Insufficient Sampling

If a generalization is made about the members of a particular class, it will be faulty if too few members of the class have been sampled. For instance, if a person stated that the fishing in a particular lake was poor, that generalization may well be based on the experience of only one or two persons and, therefore, is not supported by a large enough sample.

Such generalizations are unreliable in the same way that a generalization about who will win an election based on a sampling of just a dozen people will not be reliable. This kind of generalization is usually called a "hasty generalization."

I'll never buy a banana at that store again; this one is rotten.

In this simple statement, the speaker is making the generalization that all bananas from a particular store are rotten on the basis of the experience with only one banana.

Unrepresentative Sampling

In the same way that generalizations can be based on too small a sample, they can also be false because they are based on samples that are not representative of the whole group, a fallacy called "converse accident." So, in making a generalization about what women think about a nominee for president, you may have heard only the opinions of those persons polled at a feminist meeting or only those persons who attended church on Sunday morning or only those persons who chose to respond to a mailing. All of these factors would make the generalization questionable since it is based on the opinions of an unrepresentative sample from within the larger group of women. For example,

> According to a poll of 2000 women taken at the national convention of the National Organization for Women, most women in the United States would support a woman president.

A poll taken at a NOW convention does not necessarily represent the opinion of all women in the United States.

LOGICAL FALLACIES

Logical fallacies have to do with the way the argument is structured, its validity. If the premises of an argument are true, the argument may be invalid because the chain of reasoning is flawed. Some of these fallacies were discussed in connection with the syllogism in Chapter 6.

Faulty Cause

This is called *post hoc ergo propter hoc* (post hok er-go PROP-ter hok), meaning "after this, therefore because of this." In this fallacy, the assumption is that because one event precedes another event, one is the cause of the other. It is a confusion of chronological sequence with cause and effect.

> It's raining because I washed my car.

> I forgot my umbrella, so it will probably rain.

> The phone only rings when I'm in the tub.

All of these quite common statements attribute false causes. Washing the car or carrying an umbrella cannot cause or prevent rain, anymore than getting in the tub will cause the phone to ring. Note that any of these examples might be stated in the form of a hypothetical syllogism. This fallacy would then fall into the class of material fallacies, since the major premise would be untrue, thereby producing an untrue conclusion, although the reasoning would be valid.

> If I wash my car, it will rain. (Untrue major premise)

> I washed my car.

> Therefore it will rain. (Conclusion valid but untrue)

Many superstitions such as the idea that breaking a mirror or walking under a ladder will cause bad luck are based on false cause as are many advertisements:

> Buy this new hairspray and you too will be handsome and desirable.

> The hairspray does not cause you to be handsome and desirable.

Either/Or Fallacy

In this fallacy, a complex issue is reduced to only two alternatives, neither of which is acceptable.

> You're either for me or against me.

> Either you believe me or you don't. It's that simple.

The fallacy, of course, is that few questions are so simple. Dividing a complex issue like being "for me or against me" into only two alternatives, forces the person to make a choice between two unacceptable possibilities, when there are other alternatives that are disallowed.

The child who asks her mother the following either/or question is presenting two unacceptable alternatives:

Would you rather be burned at the stake or eaten by a tiger?

Obviously there are other more attractive alternatives, but when the question is presented this way, it appears as though there are only two alternatives. Important political issues are often cast in the either/or mode.

Either vote for me, or admit you're a racist.

If you don't support aid to the Rebels, you're supporting Communism.

Either you're a Christian or an atheist.

This fallacy is very much present in ordinary conversation and finds its way into writing.

A writer in an article against nuclear disarmament presents the issue with only two alternatives.

We either disarm our huge nuclear arsenals now or we face
the extinction of the human race.

Other possibilities such as arms control, a limited nuclear war, effective treaties, or gradual disarmament are ignored.

The Rigged Question

This fallacy poses a question that requires an admission of guilt in any answer. It is often used in questioning court witnesses. The classic example is the lawyer who asks the witness if he has stopped beating his wife and says, "Just answer yes or no." Either answer—"Yes, I've stopped beating my wife," or "No, I haven't stopped beating my wife"—will incriminate him.

Equivocation

In equivocation, the same term is used with two different meanings.

Joe's religion is Catholicism, but Janet's religion is money.

In this statement, two different meanings of the word *religion* are used. In the case of Joe, religion is used in the sense of an organized system of beliefs, in this case Catholicism. For Janet, religion is used in the sense of an objective that is pursued. Using a stipulative definition, as described in Chapter 4, will help you avoid this fallacy.

PSYCHOLOGICAL FALLACIES

Many of the psychological fallacies mentioned below can be used effectively in rhetorical arguments. For example, the *Argumentum ad Populum* (ar-gu-MEN-tum ad PO-pu-lum) is a fallacy that plays on the feelings of the audience. Here is rhetoric's historical confusion. Rhetoric by its nature teaches that the writer must be aware of the feelings of the audience (see Chapter 2 on *pathos*), but the psychological fallacies discussed here may well divert the attention of the audience from the matter at hand; they may cloud the issues by introducing extraneous and irrelevant material.

The modern writer has difficulty coming to terms with this apparent contradiction. But historically the preacher who uses rhetoric to exhort nonbelievers has been considered to be justified while the charlatan who uses rhetoric to cheat his listeners is not.

Many of the following diversionary techniques are the politician's stock in trade and the advertiser's ploy and should be avoided in your writing.

Appeal to Pity

Students may argue for a higher grade on a paper or a report giving, for example, one of the following reasons:

My mother was sick, and I had to stay home last week.

My friend went to New York, and I had to drive her to the airport.

If you give me a D on this paper, I will flunk out of school.

An instructor may feel sympathetic to the student, but such matters cannot change the *grade*. The grade is based on the quality of the paper, not on extenuating circumstances. Another common remark:

But I worked *so* hard on this paper. It's not fair that I only got a C.

Again, the grade is based on the paper itself—not on the amount of work put into it. If instructors allowed for all of the extenuating circumstances, assigning grades would be an impossible and finally a meaningless task. Instructors can feel great sympathy for students; they can help them organize their time, they can give them extra help if they have been ill, but exam and paper grades must finally be awarded on the basis of the exam or paper itself. Appeals to pity can be very convincing, but it is necessary to separate the appeal and the response to the appeal from the issue at hand unless it actually has a proper place there.

The law courts have an equally difficult time separating the appeal from the issue. Should the woman who murders her husband because he abuses their children be treated the same as all other murderers? Is the act of murder then different? Lawyers in arguing their cases make broad appeals to pity, sometimes with justification.

Ad Hominem

The *ad hominem* (ad-HOM-mi-nem) fallacy shifts the argument away from the issue to a personal attack on the person involved—it means literally "against the man." Thus when national figures are attacked because of their religion, their haircuts, their clothes, or their accents, such criticisms can be damaging but have little to do with what the persons stand for.

I could never vote for a person who has been divorced.

Whether a person is divorced or not does not affect his or her ability to fill a public office. Nor does a person's religion, although sometimes it is falsely presented as an issue in a political campaign. Issues need to be clearly separated from attacks on the person and such personal attacks and their effect on the issue carefully weighed.

Another kind of *ad hominem* argument derives from guilt by association. Most of us are warned about this from childhood. Associating with criminals may lead someone to criminal activities, but association alone does not prove guilt.

Appeal to Force

This kind of appeal is undoubtedly persuasive in certain circumstances. The robber who threatens a person's life will probably win the argument. But there are more subtle appeals to force such as the veiled threat that one's job is on the line. This is the kind of appeal that would not be used by the just orator or writer.

Bandwagon

This is a common ploy used by children with their parents, "Everyone is doing it, so why can't I?" For example:

But everyone is going swimming. Why can't I go?

All my friends have swim goggles. Can I buy some too?

The rightness or wrongness of going swimming or buying goggles does not necessarily depend on what other people are doing. This is called the bandwagon technique because everyone is urged to get on the band-wagon, to join the crowd. Sometimes it is difficult for young persons to stand for their own opinions against the crowd, because the emotional need to be "one of the crowd" can be strong. But in the final analysis who or how many people are doing something has little to do with its right-ness or wrongness.

Appeal to Ceremony or Setting

The people on the television commercial sitting at a desk in white coats with stethoscopes around their necks present a picture of authority. There may be a diploma in a black frame on the wall behind them. It is never stated that they are doctors, but the setting lends credibility to their assertions by suggesting their medical association. When a pro-fessor lectures on the DNA chain from a podium his or her words carry more weight than if he or she had said the same thing while lounging over coffee at the local diner. The setting gives authority to what is said. In another way, the TV commercial that pictures an automobile parked in front of an expensive home suggests by the setting that owning such a car carries with it prestige and wealth.

In the same way, printed material carries credibility. The assumption is that once something is in print, it carries undisputed authority. Printed and published material need to be subjected to the same careful scrutiny that all other matters are. If facts are untrue and reasoning invalid, being in print cannot make it right.

Appeal to Authority

The appeal to authority can be a legitimate persuasive technique, when used correctly. You may wish to review the discussion of authority in

Chapter 7. In considering the use of authority in speech or writing, you should ask the following questions:

1. Is the authority speaking from a disinterested or unbiased viewpoint?

Obviously a person who owns stock in General Motors cannot make disinterested judgments about the company, nor can the captain of the football team make an unbiased forecast of the next game's score. And it goes without saying that anyone who is paid for advertising a product is influenced by the amount of money received.

2. Is the person an authority in the field in which he or she is being quoted?

We have a tendency to attribute wisdom in all things to popular or well-known figures. It should be carefully maintained that authority in one field does not automatically transfer to another. So the automobile mechanic may be an authority on repairing cars but not on servicing computers, and the good cook may not be the right person to ask about how to remove spots from the draperies. Similarly, the well-known athlete may know how to throw a pass but knows no more than the next person about cars.

3. Is the context clear?

Quotations by authorities taken out of context can be grossly distorted. One reviewer wrote that a book "was probably the best that he had read all summer, since he has spent the summer in an isolated cabin in the mountains with no access to libraries or bookstores." He was quoted as saying

the best book that he had read. . . .

Also, authoritative ideas can be quickly outdated, and dates should be made clear. Current statements invariably carry more weight.

4. Does the authority represent prevailing views in the field?

If an authority represents views which depart drastically from other authorities in the field, the authority cannot be used to represent the prevailing opinion in the field. Thus, the doctor working for a tobacco firm might not agree with most other doctors and the American Medical Association that smoking cigarettes causes cancer.

Authority properly used is a powerful persuasive tool, but for that very reason, it is doubly important that all use of authority be carefully scrutinized.

Appeal to Tradition

Closely allied to the appeal to authority is the appeal to tradition and precedent.

But we've always done it this way.

The legal system of the United States is based on precedent. Lawyers constantly search out past legal decisions on which to base their arguments. Tradition and precedent carry weight in an argument until they are proved no longer applicable. Just as precedent is constantly being tested in courts of law, so arguments based on tradition and precedent in writing need to be reexamined for validity.

Appeal to Ignorance

In this fallacy, the writer maintains that the proposition is true since it cannot be proved false. For example, it has traditionally been assumed that a psychosis had an emotional base. New research demonstrates that many psychoses have a physiological base, which affects arguments about appropriate sentences for the criminally insane. The existence of God cannot be disproved, but that fact does not prove the existence of God. Many fallacious arguments are built on this fallacy. If you can't prove it, it isn't so or if you can't disprove it, it must be so as in the following example:

Can you prove that nuclear power is unsafe? Well then, it's perfectly safe.

Appeal to Humor

Everyone loves a good laugh, and usually the person who uses humor at the right time and place will earn the goodwill of most audiences. But a joke can be used to divert attention or to make an opponent look foolish. By trivializing the speaker and the subject, the issue can be what one writer calls "lost in the laugh."

A well-known example is from a debate on evolution when one speaker asked the other:

Now, is it on your mother's side or your father's that your ancestors were apes?

When proponents fail to respond to the humor, they are accused of taking the matter too seriously. This can be a devastating technique for clouding and confusing the issue. In addition, jokes can undermine an argument. When an opponent of the Meramec Dam repeatedly referred to the construction site as the "damn dam site" it succeeded in diverting the attention of the audience from the real issues.

Name-Calling

Chapter 4 treated the way that categories or classes can be named for good effect. Name-calling can also be used to make a reader or hearer prejudge a case. When opponents of abortion call themselves "pro-life," the assumption is made that proponents are "anti-life"—thus assuming a conclusion that has not been proved. Terms such as *radicals, liberals, leftists, communists* can all, in certain contexts, have negative connotations; yet the precise meanings of these terms are almost impossible to determine. Notice how the speaker in the following address to the city council uses name-calling to advantage. How do the terms "smut-peddlers," "weepers and gnashers of teeth of the Civil Liberties Union," and "poor misguided souls" affect the argument? As you read, see what other fallacies you can recognize.

One of the fruits of your work (the drive against pornography) has been the recent ordinance passed by City Council giving a new and more precise, but broadened, definition of "obscenity," which has served to put the smut-peddlers on notice that we will root them out. "Obscenity," according to this carefully worded definition, "is when a piece of writing exploits, is largely devoted to, is made up of, stresses, emphasizes, or otherwise places prominently on view, descriptions of illicit sex or sexual immorality." One of the clarifying features of this definition is that it makes obscenity a species of description along with descriptions of other aspects of human life, such as Western stories and science fiction; obscene fiction then becomes a special category, containing those books filled with sex, and any bookseller who places such books on sale, whether knowingly or unknowingly, can be severely fined.

The weepers and gnashers of teeth of the Civil Liberties Union, who are always more concerned to protect so-called "rights" than to protect the public against harm, have argued that the law could be applied against many works of genuine literary merit, even classics, like *Anna Karenina* and *Nana*. But these literary works can easily be distinguished from hard-core pornography, which is what the law prohibits. Hard-core pornography has a tendency to corrupt and deprave: look, for example, at the memoirs of Casanova and Fanny

Hill, the books of the Marquis de Sade, the *Life and Loves* of Frank Harris, and so forth. All these are definitely harmful. Now I realize that some highbrow psychologists disagree here—I don't know what their secret motives are, but I do know that scientists are always eager to experiment on poor human beings. I suppose that the psychologists would be happy to see what happens if you expose innocent people to filth; and so I wouldn't put much stock in what they say. Anyway . . . they argue that these books are not necessarily harmful, and may even be beneficial to some poor misguided souls. But take any one of the books I mentioned—or rather, don't take it, of course, but just consider it. It is easy enough to see that reading the Marquis de Sade is not good for you, when it is so obviously pornographic.

You need to be able to recognize such fallacies and then learn how to avoid them in your own writing and not be persuaded by them in other people's writing. Recognizing them helps you examine the validity of your own arguments and refute the arguments of others.

Refutation is an important part of persuasion. Your argument will carry more weight if you recognize the possible opposing positions and in part refute them when you present your argument. In rhetorical argument, where conclusions are only probable, the writer who demonstrates that a part of an opponent's argument is false casts doubt on all of the opponent's argument. Often by successfully demonstrating the falsity of another person's position, the *ethos* of that person becomes doubtful.

The following speech was delivered on national television by Richard M. Nixon in 1952 when he was running for vice president with Dwight D. Eisenhower. He had been accused of accepting illegal campaign funds, and he defends himself against the charge. How valid is his defense? What fallacies can you detect? How many invalid arguments can you find?

THE CHECKERS SPEECH

RICHARD M. NIXON

My Fellow Americans:

I come before you tonight as a candidate for the Vice Presidency and as 1 a man whose honesty and integrity have been questioned.

The usual political thing to do when charges are made against you is to either ignore them or to deny them without giving details. 2

I believe we've had enough of that in the United States, particularly with the present Administration in Washington, D.C. To me the office of the Vice Presidency of the United States is a great office, and I feel that the people have got to have confidence in the integrity of the men who run for that office and who might obtain it. 3

I have a theory, too, that the best and only answer to a smear or to an honest misunderstanding of the facts is to tell the truth. And that's why I'm here tonight. I want to tell you my side of the case. 4

I am sure that you have read the charge and you've heard it that I, Senator Nixon, took $18,000 from a group of my supporters. 5

Now, was that wrong? And let me say that it was wrong—I'm saying, incidentally, that it was wrong and not just illegal. Because it isn't a question whether it was legal or illegal, that isn't enough. The question is, was it morally wrong? 6

I say that it was morally wrong if any of that $18,000 went to Senator Nixon for my personal use. I say that it was morally wrong if it was secretly given and secretly handled. And I say that it was morally wrong if any of the contributors got special favors for the contributions that they made. 7

And now to answer those questions let me say this: 8

Not one cent of the $18,000 or any other money of that type ever went to me for my personal use. Every penny of it was used to pay for political expenses that I did not think should be charged to the taxpayers of the United States. 9

It was not a secret fund. As a matter of fact, when I was on "Meet the Press," some of you may have seen it last Sunday—Peter Edson came up to me after the program and said, "Dick, what about this fund we hear about?" And I said, "Well, there's no secret about it. Go out and see Dana Smith, who was the administrator of the fund. And I gave him his address, and I said that you will find that the purpose of the fund simply was to defray political expenses that I did not feel should be charged to the Government." 10

And third, let me point out, and I want to make this particularly clear, that no contributor to this fund, no contributor to any of my campaigns, has ever received any consideration that he would not have received as an ordinary constituent. 11

I just don't believe in that and I can say that never, while I have been in the Senate of the United States, as far as the people that contributed to this fund are concerned, have I made a telephone call for them to an agency, or have I gone down to an agency in their behalf. And the record will show that, the records which are in the hands of the Administration. . . . 12

But then I realize that there are still some who may say, and rightly so,   13
and let me say that I recognize that some will continue to smear regardless of what the truth may be, but that there has been understandably
some honest misunderstanding on this matter, and there's some that will
say: "Well, maybe you were able, Senator, to fake this thing. How can we
believe what you say? After all, is there a possibility that maybe you got
some sums in cash? Is there a possibility that you may have feathered
your own nest?"

And so now what I am going to do—and incidentally this is unprece-   14
dented in the history of American politics—I am going at this time to
give to this television and radio audience a complete financial history;
everything I've earned; everything I've spent; everything I owe. And I
want you to know the facts. I'll have to start early.

I was born in 1913. Our family was one of modest circumstances and   15
most of my early life was spent in a store out in East Whittier. It was a
grocery store—one of those family enterprises. The only reason we were
able to make it go was because my mother and dad had five boys and we
all worked in the store.

I worked my way through college and to a great extent through law   16
school. And then, in 1940, probably the best thing that ever happened to
me happened. I married Pat—sitting over here. We had a rather difficult
time after we were married, like so many of the young couples who may
be listening to us. I practiced law; she continued to teach school. I went
into the service.

Let me say that my service record was not a particularly unusual one. I   17
went to the South Pacific. I guess I'm entitled to a couple of battle stars. I
got a couple of letters of commendation but I was just there when the
bombs were falling and then I returned. I returned to the United States
and in 1946 I ran for the Congress.

When we came out of the war, Pat and I—Pat during the war had   18
worked as a stenographer and in a bank and as an economist for a
Government agency—and when we came out the total of our savings
from both my law practice, her teaching and all the time that I was in the
war—the total for that entire period was just a little less than $10,000.
Every cent of that, incidentally, was in Government bonds.

Well that's where we start when I go into politics. Now what have I   19
earned since I went into politics? Well here it is—I jotted it down, let me
read the notes. First of all I've had my salary as a Congressman and as a
Senator. Second, I have received a total in this past six years of $1,600
from estates which were in my law firm at the time that I severed my
connection with it.

And, incidentally, as I said before, I have not engaged in any legal   20
practice and have not accepted any fees from business that came into the
firm after I went into politics. I have made an average of approximately

$1,500 a year from non-political speaking engagements and lectures. And then, fortunately, we've inherited a little money. Pat sold her interest in her father's estate for $3,000 and I inherited $1,500 from my grandfather.

We live rather modestly. For four years we lived in an apartment in 21
Park Fairfax, in Alexandria, Va. The rent was $80 a month. And we saved for the time that we could buy a house.

Now, that was what we took in. What did we do with this money? What 22
do we have today to show for it? This will surprise you, because it is so little, I suppose, as standards generally go, of people in public life. First of all, we've got a house in Washington which cost $41,000 and on which we owe $20,000.

We have a house in Whittier, Calif., which cost $13,000 and on which 23
we owe $3,000. My folks are living there at the present time.

I have just $4,000 in life insurance, plus my G.I. policy which I've never 24
been able to convert and which will run out in two years. I have no life insurance whatever on Pat. I have no life insurance on our two young-sters, Patricia and Julie. I own a 1950 Oldsmobile car. We have our furniture. We have no stocks and bonds of any type. We have no interest of any kind, direct or indirect, in any business.

Now, that's what we have. What do we owe? Well, in addition to the 25
mortgage, the $20,000 mortgage on the house in Washington, the $10,000 one on the house in Whittier, I owe $4,500 to the Riggs Bank in Wash-ington, D.C., with interest 4½ per cent.

I owe $3,500 to my parents and the interest on that loan which I pay 26
regularly, because it's part of the savings they made through the years they were working so hard. I pay regularly 4 per cent interest. And then I have a $500 loan which I have on my life insurance.

Well, that's about it. That's what we have and that's what we owe. It isn't 27
very much but Pat and I have the satisfaction that every dime that we've got is honestly ours. I should say this—that Pat doesn't have a mink coat. But she does have a respectable Republican cloth coat. And I always tell her that she'd look good in anything.

One other thing I probably should tell you, because if I don't they'll 28
probably be saying this about me too, we did get something—a gift—after the election. A man down in Texas heard Pat on the radio mention the fact that our two youngsters would like to have a dog. And, believe it or not, the day before we left on this campaign trip we got a message from Union Station in Baltimore saying they had a package for us. We went down to get it. You know what it was?

It was a little cocker spaniel dog in a crate that he sent all the way from 29
Texas. Black and white spotted. And our little girl—Trisha, the 6-year-old—named it Checkers. And you know the kids love the dog and I just want to say this right now, that regardless of what they say about it, we're gonna keep it.

It isn't easy to come before a nation-wide audience and air your life as 30
I've done. But I want to say some things before I conclude that I think
most of you will agree on. Mr. Mitchell, the chairman of the Democratic
National Committee, made the statement that if a man couldn't afford to
be in the United States Senate he shouldn't run for the Senate.

And I just want to make my position clear. I don't agree with Mr. 31
Mitchell when he says that only a rich man should serve his Government
in the United States Senate or in the Congress.

I don't believe that represents the thinking of the Democratic party, 32
and I know that it doesn't represent the thinking of the Republican party.

I believe that it's fine that a man like Governor Stevenson who inher- 33
ited a fortune from his father can run for President. But I also feel that it's
essential in this country of ours that a man of modest means can also run
for President. Because, you know, remember Abraham Lincoln, you remember what he said: "God must have loved the common people—he
made so many of them." . . .

Now, let me say this: I know that this is not the last of the smears. In 34
spite of my explanation tonight other smears will be made; others have
been made in the past. And the purpose of the smears, I know, is this—to
silence me, to make me let up. . . .

. . . [But] I intend to continue the fight. Why do I feel so deeply? Why 35
do I feel that in spite of the smears, the misunderstandings, the neces-
sities for a man to come up here and bare his soul as I have? Why it is
necessary for me to continue this fight?

And I want to tell you why. Because, you see, I love my country. And I 36
think my country is in danger. And I think that the only man that can save
America at this time is the man that's running for President on my
ticket—Dwight Eisenhower.

. . . I say that the only man who can lead us in the fight to rid the 37
government of both those who are Communists and those who have
corrupted this government is Eisenhower, because Eisenhower, you can
be sure, recognizes the problem and he knows how to deal with it.

Now let me say that, finally, this evening I want to read to you just 38
briefly excerpts from a letter which I received, a letter which, after all this
is over, no one can take away from me. It reads as follows:

Dear Senator Nixon,

Since I'm only 19 years of age I can't vote in this Presidential election 39
but believe me if I could you and General Eisenhower would certainly get
my vote. My husband is in the Fleet Marines in Korea. He's a corpsman on
the front lines and we have a two-month-old son he's never seen. And I
feel confident that with great Americans like you and General
Eisenhower in the White House, lonely Americans like myself will be
united with their loved ones now in Korea.

I only pray to God that you won't be too late. Enclosed is a small check 40
to help you in your campaign. Living on $85 a month it is all I can afford
at present. But let me know what else I can do.

Folks, it's a check for $10, and it's one that I will never cash. 41

And just let me say this. We hear a lot about prosperity these days but I 42
say, why can't we have prosperity built on peace rather than prosperity
built on war? Why can't we have prosperity and an honest government in
Washington, D.C., at the same time? Believe me, we can. And Eisenhower
is the man that can lead this crusade to bring us that kind of prosperity.

And, now, finally, I know that you wonder whether or not I am going to 43
stay on the Republican ticket or resign.

Let me say this: I don't believe that I ought to quit because I'm not a 44
quitter. And, incidentally, Pat's not a quitter. After all, her name was
Patricia Ryan and she was born on St. Patrick's Day, and you know the
Irish never quit.

But the decision, my friends, is not mine. I would do nothing that 45
would harm the possibilities of Dwight Eisenhower to become President
of the United States. And for that reason I am submitting to the Republican National Committee tonight through this television broadcast the
decision which it is theirs to make.

Let them decide whether my position on the ticket will help or hurt. 46
And I am going to ask you to help them decide. Wire and write the
Republican National Committee whether you think I should stay on or
whether I should get off. And whatever their decision is, I will abide by it.

But just let me say this last word. Regardless of what happens I'm going 47
to continue this fight. I'm going to campaign up and down America until
we drive the crooks and Communists and those that defend them out of
Washington. And remember, folks, Eisenhower is a great man. Believe
me. He's a great man. And a vote for Eisenhower is a vote for what's good
for America.

The Nixon speech is an outstanding example of a rhetoric that is filled
with fallacies. He uses an appeal to pity as he describes his youth—"the
only way we were able to make it" was because we all "worked in the
family grocery store." The early years of his marriage—"the rather difficult time" with Pat working as "a stenographer,"—and his savings during
his years of military service amounting to "a little less than $10,000" are
also appeals to pity. His use of the word, "smear," throughout is a type of
name-calling that assumes a purpose behind the allegations that he never
proves. His final paragraph, which refers to the "crooks and Communists" is a more blatant example of name-calling. His attack on Eisenhower's Democratic opponent, Adlai Stevenson, "who inherited a for-

tune from his father," is an example of an *ad hominem* argument. His story of the "little cocker spaniel dog" is another blatant appeal to pity. Finally, he climbs on the bandwagon of those who support Eisenhower, an immensely popular public figure at the time. Although many people were offended by this speech, Nixon was allowed to retain his spot on the Republican ticket in 1952 and was subsequently elected vice president.

Questions to Consider

1. Analyze the following statements and explain what is wrong with each of them. If possible, identify the fallacies they represent by name, but remember that it is more important to be able to explain the errors than merely to name them.

A. Either I turn in this assignment or I flunk the course. I will turn in the assignment, so I will not flunk the course.

B. If most doctors are opposed to socialized medicine, then it must be a bad policy. But it must be a bad policy; therefore, most doctors are opposed to it.

C. On this essay exam, you told us we were supposed to think for ourselves. Well, when I didn't know the answer, I thought for myself and wrote down what I thought. How could you then give my answer an F?

D. If he didn't actually steal the money, why are there all of these rumors floating around? Where there's smoke, there's fire. He's got to be guilty.

E. Given the three lousy students I've had in my class who came from Ridgemont High School, I'd say the students there are all losers.

F. Look at that car weaving in and out of traffic and exceeding the speed limit! That driver's got to be a man.

G. If there's one thing the disaster at Three Mile Island teaches us, it is this: Nuclear power reactors endanger the lives of every American every day they are in operation.

H. If today weren't Friday the 13th, I wouldn't be in this mess.

I. I don't see how you can give me a B– on this essay. I *always* made A's in high school.

J. Your sister never failed chemistry, nor did your brother. Why are you having so much trouble with the class?

K. Either you failed because you didn't study, or you failed because you didn't care. Now, which is it?

L. But, Mom, everybody's wearing green tennis shoes this year at school, and I won't be popular unless I get some, too.

M. What's all this talk today about a need for sex education in our public schools? We had no such classes in my day, and we turned out all right.

2. The ancient orators stressed the necessity of the orator being a "good" person. You might want to review that discussion in Chapter 2. How do such ethical concerns affect the twentieth-century writer? How do they affect you? How do they affect the use of fallacies?

Suggestions for Writing

For this assignment, you are to write a short paper in which you analyze either an advertisement (be sure to choose one that lends itself to this assignment; you might want to discuss your choice with your instructor before you begin) or Nixon's "Checkers Speech," identifying and explaining the kinds of fallacies they promote. To prepare for writing your paper, begin by reading the ad or the speech closely. Then make a list of any fallacies you detect and classify them according to the three kinds described in this chapter: material, logical, and psychological. Based on what you find, you may then choose to organize your discussion according to these three kinds and consider each in turn. Or, should you find one category of fallacies to be prominent (e.g., the psychological ones), you may focus solely on that category and organize your discussion according to the particular types (e.g., appeal to pity, ad hominem).

Moreover, you will need to do more than simply identify and locate the fallacies; you will need to *explain how* the statements are fallacious to support your claim. Thus, your discussion of each fallacy you select to focus on should probably proceed according to four steps: (1) identify the fallacy; (2) define it; (3) cite an example of it in the ad or speech; and (4) explain how the example illustrates or conforms to your definition. Be selective in the fallacies you focus on; choose the best examples to support your assertions.

Exercises in Revision

While the paper you wrote in response to the exercise above is primarily expository, in another sense it can also be considered an example of persuasion insofar as you are arguing that the fallacies you cite actually exist in the ad you've chosen or in Nixon's "Checkers Speech." Therefore, exchange your paper with another member of your workshop group (or focus in turn on each member's essay as a group), read the paper carefully, and examine it in light of the following questions:

1. Are all statements well supported and documented? Which need more development? By what means might they be developed more fully? Suggest some possibilities.

2. Does the writer identify and describe each fallacy accurately and clearly? If not, where do problems occur? What suggestions can you make for improvement?

3. Does the writer commit any of the fallacies described in this chapter in the course of his or her own discussion? (Pay particular attention to his or her generalizations.) If so, where? What fallacies do you detect? How are the statements fallacious? Based on his or her reasoning, are the conclusions valid?

4. On the basis of the paper alone, what overall impression does the writer convey of himself or herself? Does he or she manage to convince you to accept the conclusions presented? Why, or why not? Take into account here your responses to questions 1-3 above, as well as any grammatical and mechanical errors, and write a paragraph summarizing your evaluation. Now in light of the response you received from the above, revise your paper.

For a Commonplace Book

The skill needed to detect fallacies is not readily acquired. It requires careful attention, thoughtful consideration, and, above all, practice. Keep an "ear" out for statements you encounter in conversation, on television, in your own reading that somehow don't seem quite "right" to you and copy them in your commonplace book. Then, when you have a moment, sit down, consider them carefully, and try to identify exactly what's wrong. You may be surprised to find how much of what we hear and say every day is really, ultimately, fallacious.

PART II

ARRANGEMENT

> "—however abundant the matter may be, it will merely form a confused heap unless arrangement be employed to reduce it to order and to give it connection and firmness of structure"
>
> (QUINTILIAN *INSTITUTIO ORATORIA* 7 PREFACE.2).

The Roman rhetorician Cicero called arrangement *dispositio*, the arranging or ordering of material, the moving from a jumble of ideas to a well-developed, well-organized, coherent whole. There can be a moment of panic in this process of bringing order out of chaos. It is like facing the room that has to be put in order, the car motor that has to be reassembled, the suitcase that has to be packed.

Quintilian emphasizes that arrangement of the parts of a discourse is never static or fixed and that since there is no single case exactly like any other, the speaker or writer "must rely upon his sagacity, keep his eyes open, exercise his powers of invention and judgment and look to himself for advice" (*Institutio Oratoria* 7 Preface 4). So as you arrange and order your ideas, take into account matters of occasion and audience, asking yourself if an introductory example is appropriate for a particular occasion and one that the audience will relate to and understand. In addition, present your arguments so clearly that your sagacity and common sense are apparent, and select your premises so that your goodwill and credibility are apparent. Cicero emphasizes that, although the introduction and the conclusion are the most appropriate places for the inventional arguments based on the credibility of the speaker (*ethos*) and the appeal to the audience (*pathos*), the use of these inventional strategies should "like blood in the body be diffused throughout the speech" (*De Oratore* 2.77.310). Although arrangement follows invention in the classical canon, they are not separate steps but work together in a circular or recursive manner. As you think of new ideas they may begin to fall into a logical order, or as you find an order in the material, new ideas or connections may appear. Questioning issues and developing arguments may well suggest ways of organizing a subject, and organizing and writing may well generate new ideas or suggest gaps that need to be filled.

The classical rhetoricians treated arrangement as dependent on occasion and audience, dividing oratory into three branches, representing the kind of public activities that they commonly pursued. In *deliberative* rhetoric, the political oratory of the day, they argued civil questions of taxation, of treaties, or of elections. *Forensic* (fo-REN-zik) rhetoric was the rhetoric of the law courts, and *epideictic* (epi-DIK-tik) was the rhetoric of ceremony—funeral orations and tributes. However, persuasion, the art of rhetoric, was considered fundamental to all of these. Although modern forms of communication may differ to meet the demands and needs of a technological society, persuasion is still basic to them all. Reports, grant applications, essays, examination answers, research papers all attempt to persuade to a viewpoint or a perspective and sometimes to promote action. Even a document such as a resumé must be persuasive when you are applying for a job or entrance into professional school. Socrates called rhetoric a universal art of persuasion having to do with all matters, great as well as small. Aristotle defines rhetoric as the "faculty of observing *in any given case* the available means of persuasion." So persuasion is basic to all human communication. Consequently, the processes of exploring the issues and developing strategies and arguments can never be entirely separated from the strategies used in arranging material and structuring the essay.

The parts of a discourse outlined in the following chapters can serve as points of departure for your writing and thinking, and as you arrange your material the inventional procedures outlined in the last section should never be far from your mind and can never, in fact, be considered as separate from the parts of a discourse.

Chapter 9

Structuring the Essay

Classical rhetoricians observed that persuasive orators arranged their material in fairly regular ways. At the outset, the orator gained the audience's attention and interest in what they called the *exordium* (ek-ZOR-de-um). Today we might call it the opening. The orator then furnished background information in a *narratio* (na-RA-tee-o), defined terms and outlined the issues through an *explicatio* (eks-plee-KA-tee-o), and announced the particular issue in question in a *partitio* (par-TI-tee-o) or thesis. In a *confirmatio* (con-fir-MA-tee-o) or proof, orators proved or supported their stand, then answered the arguments of the opposition in a *refutatio* (re-fyoo-TA-tee-o), and concluded in a *peroratio* (per-er-RA-tee-o). These parts were the strategies associated with structuring the oration.

All of the classical rhetoricians agreed that the order could be rearranged and one or the other of the parts omitted depending on the audience and the occasion.

Aristotle taught his students that the most important parts of the oration are the opening, the thesis, the proof, and the conclusion. He added that the only necessary parts for all occasions and all audiences are the thesis and the development or proof of that thesis. The writer must state the case and prove it.

Modern writing often follows the classical arrangement with appropriate modifications. For example, in writing a highly technical article on word processing software for a computer journal, the author can safely assume the reader's interest and knowledge about computers in general. In such a case the opening and background might well be omitted. In all situations the writer needs to be aware of the audience's general level of interest and knowledge on a subject and on that basis judge the appropriate strategy of including or omitting certain parts.

As you begin to draft an essay for a particular audience and occasion, you might wish to keep these parts in mind and consider when and how you might use them to convince and persuade. In a paper written in an English literature class you can probably assume that your instructor has read the work in question, but in an analysis of a journal article that most of your readers have not read, you will have to summarize or quote to give them the necessary background information. In answering a question on an essay exam you will probably not have to gain the reader's attention or interest and your answer might well include only the thesis and support of that thesis. The classical rhetoricians recognized that there were infinite variations to this pattern, but they recognized all of these parts as persuasive strategies in the speeches of successful orators and included them in their treatises on rhetoric.

The English words associated with the parts of the oration are:

1. Opening (*Exordium*): Gains the reader's attention and interest.

2. Background (*Narratio*): Provides the facts or history of the situation.

3. Definition of Issues (*Explicatio*): Defines terms and explains issues.

4. Thesis (*Partitio*): States the proposition or particular issue that is to be proved.

5. Proof (*Confirmatio*): Supports and develops the thesis.

6. Refutation: (*Refutatio*): Answers the opposing arguments.

7. Conclusion (*Peroratio*): Summarizes the arguments and sometimes urges the audience to action.

OPENING

The purpose of the opening is to secure the interest and attention of your reader and to establish your credibility as the writer. The opening is closely connected with the ethical appeal and the appeal to the audience discussed in Chapter 3. You should establish how you know what you know on a subject. If you are writing about the results of air pollution from carbon monoxide, you may wish to point out your own experience with air pollution and your subsequent study of the subject. You may want to gain the readers' interest by telling them why the subject is important to them and how air pollution may affect them directly in the next twenty years. You might gain the goodwill of the readers by acknowledging their sense of community responsibility and their continuing involvement in environmental matters.Try to establish your own credibility by emphasizing your knowledge on the subject, demonstrate your intelligence by cogent and reasonable arguments, and establish your goodwill by acknowledging the interests and concerns of the readers.

In the following excerpt from William Faulkner's Nobel Prize acceptance speech, the author minimizes his role in earning the coveted prize and emphasizes his spirit of humility while stressing the importance of the young writers to whom he is speaking.

> I feel that this award was not made to me as a man but to my work—a life's work in the agony and sweat of the human spirit, not for glory and least of all for profit, but to create out of the materials of the human spirit, something which did not exist before. So this award is only mine in trust. It will not be difficult to find a dedication for the money part of it commensurate with the purpose and significance of its origin. But I would like to do the same with the acclaim too, by using this moment as a pinnacle from which I might be listened to by the young men and women already dedicated to the same anguish and travail, among whom is already that one who will some day stand here where I am standing.

How does Faulkner minimize his role in accepting the award? What words and phrases signal his humility? By minimizing his own role, notice how he actually lifts himself and his work out of the individual and personal. Which sentences accomplish this? What words and phrases does Faulkner use to make his audience feel good about themselves, to gain their interest and attention? How does he include them in the award? Imagine a situation where you might receive an award from your department at a dinner made up of faculty and students. How might you signal your humility? How might you gain the interest of your audience? How might you praise them? Picture your readers and speak directly to them. Consider who they are, what they value, what they hope for, and what they fear; then address those concerns.

Gaining the attention of the reader is especially important in writing, since readers will quickly turn the page or move on to something else if the author has not caught their interest in the first or second paragraph. Notice how the opening of George Orwell's essay "Marrakech" immediately attracts the attention of the reader.

> As the corpse went past the flies left the restaurant table in a cloud and rushed after it, but they came back a few minutes later.
>
> The little crowd of mourners—all men and boys, no women— threaded their way across the market-place between the piles of pomegranates and the taxis and the camels, wailing a short chant over and over again. What really appeals to the flies is that the corpses here are never put into coffins, they are merely wrapped in a piece of rag and carried on a rough wooden bier on the shoulders of four friends. When the friends get to the burying-ground they hack an oblong hole a foot or two deep, dump the body in it and fling over it a little of the dried-up, lumpy earth, which is like broken brick. No gravestone, no name, no identifying mark of any kind. The burying-ground is merely a huge waste of hummocky earth, like a derelict building-lot. After a month or two no one can even be certain where his own relatives are buried.

By immediately immersing the readers in a situation, Orwell arouses their curiosity with the first sentence and catches their attention by the unusual choice of details. The readers ask "What corpse?" "Why do the flies come back?" And readers go on to find that the author is watching the funeral procession of a Marrakech native which is of so little concern to the general populace that even the flies abandon the corpse. Why is this opening particularly effective in an essay that develops the thesis that the cares and trials of the natives are ignored and actually invisible to the general population?

There are a number of ways that you can gain the reader's interest. You may choose an apt quotation, pose a question or series of questions, or open with an appropriate anecdote. Finally, you may choose to start with a direct statement of the thesis. What follows are ways of beginning a paper, of opening a subject, of introducing an essay.

With a Quotation

A carefully chosen quotation can serve as an opener by setting the tone, often by either reinforcing or opposing what you are going to argue. You may choose a quotation that opposes your general stand and then go on in your essay to disprove the quotation. You may choose a quotation that reinforces your thesis, and use the reputation of the speaker to support your ideas. You may want to use a quotation familiar to your audience as a starting point for the essay. For example, an essay on teenage suicide started with the quotation from Hamlet's soliloquy— "To be or not to be, that is the question." The author then continued by exploring the worries and concerns that are most common in teenage suicides, moving to some of the causes and possible preventive measures, demonstrating that the quotation is a real question for some teenagers at certain points in their lives.

Well-known sayings, proverbs, even quotations from friends or relatives—such as "My grandmother always told me . . ."—may be appropriate for an essay that builds on personal experience. A dictionary of familiar quotations is available in the reference section of the library and furnishes quotations on a number of subjects. But quotations must be used with care and should relate to the essay in some significant way that will lead the reader to start thinking about the subject.

In the following opening paragraph of an essay criticizing sexual polarization, Carolyn Heilbrun, an English scholar who writes on feminist issues, begins with a quotation from Virginia Woolf who asserts that in any question of sex, one can only show "how one came to hold whatever opinion one does hold." This quotation leads naturally into the author's expression of her own opinion—"the ideal toward which I believe we should move is best described by the term 'androgyny.'"

> "When a subject is highly controversial," Virginia Woolf observed to an audience forty-five years ago, "and any question about sex is that—one cannot hope to tell the truth. One can only show how one came to hold whatever opinion one does hold." My opinion is easily enough expressed. I believe that our future salvation lies in a movement away from sexual polarization and the prison of gender toward a world in which individual roles and the modes of personal behavior can be freely chosen. The ideal toward which I believe we should move is best described by the term "androgyny." This ancient Greek word—from *andro* (male) and *gyn* (female)—defines a condition under which the characteristics of the sexes, and the human impulses expressed by men and women, are not rigidly assigned. Androgyny seeks to liberate the individual from the confines of the appropriate.

What would be the effect of the paragraph if Heilbrun had started with the third sentence: "I believe that our future salvation . . ."? In what way does the quotation add to the effectiveness of this opening?

With a Question

Notice how in the following paragraph the student uses questions in an opening to a process paper on how to bathe a dog.

> Has your curly black poodle ever knocked over the flour canister? Does your Old English Sheepdog ever wander into the woods and come out disguised as a thorn bush? Or has your snow-white Samoyed ever gone swimming in your neighbor's algae-covered pond? If so, you probably know what trouble it is to get your dog clean again.

Questions immediately involve the reader. If you think of your reader as sitting across the table from you, start writing as though you were beginning a conversation. Think of your writing as a continuing dialogue in which the reader is an active participant.

Often opening questions are not necessarily meant to have actual answers, as in the preceding example, but to engage your reader's interest. On the other hand, writers often pose questions in their opening sentence which they then answer in presenting their thesis and giving proof for their position. In the following paragraph, Brand Blanchard opens his essay "The Purpose of College " with this type of question:

> What should we get from college? Some students will tell you very definitely what they want. One wants to take all those subjects, and only those, that will help her get into medical school; another, knowing that a job awaits him in his father's firm, wants to become an engineer as quickly and painlessly as he can. On the other hand is the person, who I suspect is in the majority, whose only definite aim is to discover some definite aim.

In the above case the author answers the initial question in the rest of the essay. It is a question designed to focus and direct the reader's attention to the subject of the essay. Cicero termed the thesis the *questio*, recognizing that it can often be cast in the form of a question and answer rather than a statement. You might try examining some of your own papers and see if posing the thesis in the form of a question can provide a smoother opening. Here are a few examples of theses recast in question form.

Thesis: Nuclear power is not economically feasible.

Question: Will nuclear power really save money?

Thesis: There are too many cultural differences for Iran and the United States to ever come to an understanding on certain issues.

Question: Are there too many cultural differences for Iran and the United States to ever arrive at an understanding on certain issues?

In both of these cases, you might suggest alternative answers before you state the answer that you intend to argue in your essay.

Will nuclear power really save money for the consuming public? That was the hope held out to us by the power companies. That was the original incentive provided by the government agencies. But the fact is that for the individual consumer, energy costs have risen over 100 percent in the last ten years.

Papers on controversial subjects lend themselves to the use of questions since a question rather than a statement may acknowledge an understanding of other viewpoints and an awareness of opposing opinions that need to be refuted. Why are such questions more effective than statements? You might try to recast as questions some of the theses that you formulated in the exercises in Chapter 2. Ask yourself when questions are more effective and examine the reasons.

With an Anecdote

Readers are often attracted to real situations involving real people. Well-chosen anecdotes arouse interest and curiosity. For example, few readers will fail to be drawn in by the following anecdote opening Joseph Blank's essay "They've Killed My Daughter Twice":

Gail Tietjin was eighteen when the accident happened. Her nineteen-year-old boyfriend was driving her home from a dinner party. He was drunk. About 1:30 A.M. that July morning in 1972, he drove the car around a curve and into a tree. It was two hours before the crash was discovered. Police thought Gail was dead until they heard a gurgle in her throat. Gail regained consciousness after two weeks, but she had suffered brain damage. This young woman who had earned two university scholarships now began learning how to use eating utensils, a comb, and the toilet. She did not know her family and was unable to remember her home when she finally returned there. For fourteen long months after the accident, she worked to relearn everything she could. When she had finally progressed enough to enter Stanford University, she had to forego the science courses she had always excelled in and settle instead for a less demanding major. In her first year she failed almost every course, but university officials allowed her to remain when they learned of the accident. She worked hard and graduated in June 1978. She got a job as an office secretary, though she had to struggle to keep it. Six years after Gail had suffered her injuries, it was still doubtful whether she could live independently.

Gail's boyfriend, meanwhile, had fully recovered from his accident injuries and had paid his court-ordered punishment for a misdemeanor—a $500 fine.

The author leaves some questions unanswered: Why did Gail's boyfriend only get a $500 fine, "court-ordered punishment for a misdemeanor"? He follows this first incident with another account of an accident caused by drunk driving to support his contention that drunk driving should be considered a felony rather than a misdemeanor.

Anecdotes should have a direct connection to your subject and should be chosen carefully to support or illustrate the thesis. Often a single incident such as the one above can be more convincing than many cogent and well-selected arguments because they appeal directly to the emotions of the audience, arousing pity or compassion. Also anecdotes may establish how you feel about your subject. Is your treatment going to be serious or humorous? Readers of the anecdote about Gail Tietjin can hardly fail to realize that the reader is approaching a serious subject from a strongly personal viewpoint. The opening anecdote suggests what your subject is and often indicates whether your treatment will be humorous or serious, personal or objective. Anecdotes should be written with specific details, and dialogue can be included to make them more immediate. You might try to think of illustrative anecdotes that could be used as openings in papers that you have written. What kind of writing have you done this semester where the anecdotal opening would be inappropriate? Why would it be inappropriate? You might wish to review the strategies of narration and description suggested in Chapter 7.

The anecdote or illustration may follow the statement of the thesis or the thesis may come at the end of the illustration or at the beginning of the second paragraph. In the first case you state the main point of your essay and follow that with an illustrative anecdote; in the latter case you begin with the anecdote and state the general truth that it illustrates in the thesis that immediately follows. If you feel that your readers will accept the general statement you may safely open with it, but a vivid anecdote may well prepare your reader for your thesis.

With a Thesis Statement

There are readers who will read what you have to say because they need the information, because the subject matter is inherently interesting to them, or simply because they must. It would be inappropriate to start the answer to an essay exam, or a lab report, or a report for a busy executive with an anecdote, a quotation, or a question. For those readers, a more direct opening is usually preferable. Such readers may well want to know what you have to say without the distraction of an anecdote or quotation. In this case, you may choose to start with a statement of the thesis at the beginning of the first paragraph, as in this example from Albert H. Marckwardt's "Brief History of the English Language":

> Language, like any other aspect of life and human behavior, changes from one generation to the next. As children we learn our first or native language from our parents. It is then modified through association with playmates, who learned their language from their elders. This learning process is heightened and extended in school. In adulthood our language attains relative stability. It reflects our education, our occupation, our personal interests and contacts—in short, our total environment. By this time, however, we are already conveying the language to our children, and the process begins a new cycle. The history of a language is an account of what has happened to it in the course of its continuous transmission from one generation to another.

When you open with your thesis statement you must be able to assume that your reader is already interested and attentive to your subject. In some cases, such as a report of an event or action that you have witnessed or performed, you may not have to establish your credibility. An awareness of what your readers know about you and a knowledge of their interests and purpose in reading what you have to say will help you to know when a plain and direct statement of the thesis is most appropriate.

PROVIDING BACKGROUND INFORMATION

In this part of the paper the writer furnishes the necessary background information that the reader needs to understand the issues at hand. It is closely allied to the conjectural question of "what happened?" At this point you might review some of the questions of conjecture, essence, and quality that you posed in connection with your subject in Chapter 2. Since these questions may well be ones that your readers will ask, you might want to share some of these questions and answers with your readers.

This part of your paper can be expanded or shortened depending largely on the knowledge that your readers have on your subject. However, even if you consider them knowledgeable on the subject you may wish to present the history of the case as you see it. This part of your paper comes directly after the opening if you plan to include it.

Note how the student in the following essay immediately follows the opening quotation with the background information as he writes about the effects of the 55 mile an hour speed limit that recent legislation has negated.

> "Slow down, you move too fast," a line from a Simon and Garfunkel song, used to be applicable to American drivers. However, on January 2, 1974, Congress passed the Emergency Highway Energy Conservation Act which stated that no state would receive federal highway funds if they did not reduce speed limits to 55 MPH (miles per hour). By March 3, 1974 all states had complied. The main idea of this law was to conserve fuel, which it has. By August, 1975, the Safety Administration attributed a savings of about 104,000 barrels of oil per day to the 55 speed limit. However, the Safety Administration soon observed an extra bonus to the law—lives were being saved. Between 1973 and 1974 there was a reduction from 55,096 traffic fatalities to 49,049, a decrease of 16%, due mainly to the 55 speed limit.

In this essay the student is arguing for the continuation of the 55 mile-per-hour speed limit, not only because it would save fuel but would also save lives. Although the bulk of his essay is based on proving the second unexpected bonus—lives saved—the background information of the original intent of the law—that fuel would be saved—also supports his argument.

In providing background information for your readers, you may be giving them facts that they do not already have or reminding them of what they already know in order to support your argument.

DEFINING THE TERMS AND EXPLAINING THE ISSUES

In the *explicatio* you define the terms involved and explain the issues. It is a continuation of the kind of background material that the reader may need as preparation for the particular issue that you plan to take up in the thesis. Chapter 2 provides guidance for addressing the issues connected with the question of essence "what is it?" In effect you will take the reader through some of the exploratory definition questions that you posed in forming your thesis. In connection with euthanasia, for example, you might want to explore and try to define the difference between murder and mercy killing. Your thesis may be that euthansia is murder or that it is mercy killing. Either definition will involve a series of questions that must be examined in your essay. Can it be considered murder if the so-called victim has agreed ahead of time? Is it always merciful to release a person from suffering? What if that person has a chance for recovery? Often the development of the thesis will depend heavily on the way that you define the issues involved and the terms that you use.

In the following passage from *We're Not Really Equal*, Thomas Sowell, an economist, argues for a careful definition of equality. He defines the mathematical concept of equality and then explains that this definition cannot be applied to people because mathematics and people are not alike. He uses a number of examples to support this point. What does he define as the real issue? How then does he alter the definition of equality so that it can be applied to political reasoning?

"Equality" is one of the great undefined terms underlying much current controversy and antagonism. This one confused word might even become the rock on which our civilization is wrecked. It should be worth defining. Equality is such an easily understood concept in mathematics that we may not realize it is a bottomless pit of complexities anywhere else. That is because in mathematics we have eliminated the concreteness and complexities of real things. When we say that two plus two equals four, we either don't say two *what* or we say the same what after each number. But if we said that two apples plus two apples equals four oranges, we would be in trouble.

Yet that is what we are saying in our political reasoning. And we are in trouble. Nothing is more concrete or complex than a human being. Beethoven could not play center field like Willie Mays, and Willie never tried to write a symphony. In what sense are they equal—or unequal? The common mathematical symbol for inequality points to the smaller quantity. But which is the smaller quantity—and in whose eyes—when such completely different things are involved?

When women have children and men don't, how can they be either equal or unequal? Our passionate desire to reduce things to the simplicity of abstract concepts does not mean that it can be done. Those who want to cheer their team and boo the visitors may like to think that the issue is equality versus inequality. But the real issue is whether or not we are going to talk sense. Those who believe in inequality have the same confusion as those who believe in equality. The French make better champagne than the Japanese, but the Japanese make better cameras than the French. What sense does it make to add champagne to cameras to a thousand other things and come up with a grand total showing who is "superior"?

When we speak of "equal justice under law," we simply mean applying the same rules to everybody. That has nothing whatsoever to do with whether everyone performs equally. A good umpire calls balls and strikes by the same rules for everyone, but one batter may get twice as many hits as another.

Often these three parts of the essay—the opening, the background, and the definition of the issues—form what writers customarily call an introduction. In effect you are leading your reader through the kind of thinking and questioning process that you went through in examining your subject and demonstrating to your reader the nature of the issues involved. An introduction should do three things:

1. Gain the reader's goodwill and attention.

2. Give background information.

3. Define the issues involved.

Aristotle told his students that the introduction to a speech was like the prologue in poetry and the prelude in flute-music; "they are all beginnings, paving the way, as it were for what is to follow" (3.14.1414b.20). Note how the student in the following paper builds an introduction that includes the opening, the background, and the definition of the issues which then leads into the thesis.

The social institution of marriage in recent years has been criticized and reexamined. Prospective marriage couples today question whether legal marriage is worthwhile in view of the increasing divorce rate. Historically, many societies have prescribed marriage as the usual and accepted way of expressing adult love and establishing a family and they have supported it through their legal and religious systems. Today people very often criticize marriage, without realizing that it is not the institution of marriage that is to blame, but the partners' attitudes and expectations

Opening: Catches reader's interest by saying that it is a timely subject.

Background: Tells about the institution of marriage.

Definition of Issues: Defines terms and explains issues.

of each other. Before we condemn an institution that has endured so long we should look
at the reasons for its importance. Marriage has
been an important factor in the development
of our culture; it satisfies the human need for
emotional security and serves as the foundation of the family.

*Thesis: States the issue that is
to be proved.*

PRESENTING THE THESIS

After the introduction, the writer may move to present the thesis.
Often the thesis arises out of the questions of quality—"Is it right or
wrong?" "Good or bad?" As we noted in Chapter 2, these questions were
of vital importance in classical rhetoric. After you provide any necessary
background and define the issues, you may then state your thesis, the
particular issue that you will take up in the rest of your essay.

The thesis must grow out of the thinking and questioning process
suggested in Chapter 2, and as you structure your essay you will wish to
review part of that process for your reader.

What are the questions that you posed in connection with your subject?
You can assume that your reader will be asking the same questions. In the
case of rehabilitation for criminals, the reader might ask such questions
as the following: What is the nature of rehabilitation? Is it always possible
in the case of a criminal with repeated offences or in the case of sexual
offenders? What does it involve? How does it affect the criminal? How
might it affect society? If your thesis is "rehabilitation is possible especially for sexual offenders," you may wish to pose some of those
questions before stating the thesis, or you may wish to state the thesis at
the outset and then develop your essay by answering those questions.

The thesis follows that questioning procedure, but it does not necessarily follow that order in the finished essay. You may wish to state your
thesis at the beginning so that your reader has no doubt about what you
are going to argue and then fill in the introductory material. However, in
subjects that deal with emotional and controversial issues, it is probably
preferable to lead into your thesis through a discussion of the history and
background issues—preparing your reader for what you are going to
discuss as the classical rhetoricians suggest.

The thesis is the statement for which you argue acceptance, the stand
that you support, the idea that requires development in your proof and
refutation. You may wish to review the section in Chapter 2 that discusses
the thesis in more detail.

GIVING PROOF

The proof of the thesis is the most important part of the essay. Other parts may be omitted or treated only briefly, but, as Aristotle points out, the thesis and the proof of the thesis are essential. The proof makes up the body of the paper.

In rhetoric, proof is never absolute, since rhetoric is concerned with probable truth and its communication. Today, we are inclined to think of the sciences such as chemistry and physics as the realm of truth and we may feel that we know with certainty how water is formed from hydrogen and oxygen, but it is another matter to be sure of the causes of the Vietnam War. But the more we discover about the causes of the Vietnam War, the more we can learn about the prevention of wars in the future. The fact is that we live much of our lives in the realm of probabilities. Our important decisions, both at the national level and at the professional and personal level, are, in fact based on probabilities. Such decisions are within the realm of rhetoric.

In presenting your rhetorical proofs, or arguments, as the classical rhetoricians called them, you will employ those strategies for development that are derived from *logos*, the classical *topics*—definition, classification, comparison, and causal analysis—as well as deduction and induction. At this point in your essay you present the material you gathered during the invention process discussed at length in Chapters 4, 5, and 6. You need to evaluate that material, selecting information that follows logically from your introduction and statement of thesis. You may find, as you select material, that you need to do some more research, or discover that the jumble of material falls neatly into place. Arrangement and invention are part of a recursive process.

In addition to presenting these arguments you should include those arguments of *ethos*, establishing your credibility and *pathos*, appealing to the audience, that are described in Chapter 3. Although these appeals dominate the introduction and conclusion of your essay, they are also an important part of the proof. As Cicero reminds us, these appeals permeate the whole work. You establish your credibility by good reasoning from propositions that your reader can accept. You can prove your good sense by avoiding overly emotional words and sweeping generalizations.

In rhetorical proof, you support ideas that are doubtful by reference to things which are believed to be true by your readers. Ancient rhetoricians advise that you may regard three things as certainties. First you may build your proof on those things that you perceive through your senses, things that you see and hear. Secondly, you can base your proof on things for which there is general agreement. In these cases you must assess the beliefs and convictions of your readers. You may assume certain shared political beliefs when writing for a group of Republicans, that you cannot assume with a general audience. Third, you may assume as certain those things that have passed into law or are part of current usage. You may safely rest your proof on the traditional separation of the church and state in the United States but such a belief cannot be assumed in a world community. Proof often rests on such shared beliefs and an awareness of audience will shape your reasoning.

Although Aristotle thought that it was essential that orators understand logic, particularly induction and deduction that was described briefly in Chapter 6, he felt that the kind of reasoning appropriate for rhetoric was in the enthymeme and the example. The enthymeme consists of a simple proposition and reason and omits the premise that you can assume the reader will accept.

In the following enthymeme only the proposition and reason are stated.

John will be a good politician because he has a way with people.

The unstated premise that is widely accepted and therefore not stated is that good politicians must have "a way with people." The premise that will have to be proved is not the unstated one, which most readers will accept, but the stated one that John has a "way with people." It is well to omit the obvious and readily accepted premises since they will only make your writing wordy and introduce unnecessary material. In the enthymeme, you state only the premise that must be proved to the reader.

The example proves through parallel cases as in the following example. John Lempesis supports his position in favor of stricter penalties for drunk driving by arguing that enforcement of the law and strict penalties will cause people to change their habits. He uses as one proof the parallel example of Sweden.

When the law is enforced and penalties are certain, people change their habits. In Sweden, where people can be arrested for drunken driving if they have a BAC of .05 or more, police set up roadblocks to test drivers for drunkenness. A driver who is over the limit receives a mandatory jail sentence. Even a member of Sweden's royal family, sentenced for drunken driving several years ago, could not escape the required penalty. And the result of such rigid enforcement? The Swedes, who drink as much as Americans do, determine at the start of their parties who may drink freely and who must stay sober. Then they form carpools or take taxis so nobody has to drive drunk.

In this passage, the author, using the parallel example of the Swedes "who drink as much as Americans," argues for stricter enforcement of drunk driving laws in the United States. He proves by his example that such laws, strictly enforced, can prevent drunk driving by forcing the use of those measures commonly employed by Swedes.

You can use this method of proving a point when you can think of a similar case where the point you are advocating has been tried and proven successful. In arguing for a rehabilitation program, if you know of a similar country or state or institution where rehabilitation has been successful, citing such examples can be powerful arguments.

It is best to arrange arguments so that the strongest ones come either at the beginning or the end of the proof section of the paper and the weaker ones [or those which are not essential to the proof] fall in the middle. Readers need a strong argument immediately after the facts have been stated and also at the end, so that their initial interest is captured at the beginning and sustained until they finish.

So rhetorical proof operates in the area of probabilities and is concerned with judgments and decisions primarily in the area of human affairs where absolute truth is difficult to determine. Rhetoric can help us arrive at better decisions not only in our personal daily lives, but as we participate as citizens in the larger community. It also helps us to report information and to communicate what we know and what we believe to people around us.

ANSWERING OPPOSING ARGUMENTS

Refutation is the part of an essay that disproves the opposing arguments. It is always necessary in a persuasive paper to refute or answer those arguments. A good method for formulating your refutation is to put yourself in the place of your readers, imagining what their objections might be. In the exploration of the issues connected with your subject you may have encountered possible opposing viewpoints in discussions with classmates or friends. In the refutation you refute those arguments by proving the opposing basic propositions untrue or showing the reasons to be invalid. You might review the fallacies discussed in Chapter 8, to see if you can find any in your opponents' arguments.

You will always want to include a refutation when subjects are highly controversial and when there are many well-known opposing viewpoints. Abortion is a prime example of such a subject. No one can argue effectively and hope to persuade readers unless they acknowledge and attempt to refute the opponents' arguments. In addition, if you are arguing for a viewpoint that goes against commonly held beliefs, you must, as the following author does, prove those beliefs to be misguided or erroneous.

In the following paper, the student argues for the hiring of handicapped persons. She uses the results of a survey to disprove many of the commonly held beliefs about handicapped employees.

Most handicapped individuals are well aware that on the job their handicaps do not cause any real problems. The real problems for the handicapped are not in holding a job, but in obtaining the job in the first place. An otherwise qualified job-seeker who has a visible handicap is working against a number of myths and misunderstandings that cause prospective employers to be reluctant to hire them. These myths include the following:

1. Insurance rates will skyrocket.
2. Adjustments will have to be made in the work area.
3. Safety records will be jeopardized.
4. Handicapped persons will expect special privileges.
5. Job performance and attendance will decline.

A recent survey on handicapped workers' performance was conducted by E.I. du Pont de Nemours and Company. Du Pont is one of America's largest employers and their eight-month study gathered information on over a thousand workers with physical handicaps, including persons with orthopedic problems, blindness, heart disease, vision impairment, amputations, paralysis, epilepsy, hearing impairments, and total deafness. The findings were as follows:

1. Insurance: No increases in compensation costs or time lost due to injuries.
2. Physical Adjustments: No special work arrangements required in most cases.
3. Safety: Rating of average or better both on and off the job. Rating of above average by 96 percent.
4. Special Privileges: Desire of handicapped workers to be treated as regular employees.
5. Job Performance: Rating by 91 percent of average or better.
6. Attendance: Rating by 79 percent of average or better.

The du Pont study proves further that there is very little difference between handicapped and non-handicapped workers as far as ability to perform in the workplace is concerned.

In this essay the author placed her refutation right after her proposition or thesis and the refutation of the myths became her main proof. What strategy does she use to refute the arguments? You may wish to review the inartistic proofs described in Chapter 7.

In general, there is a question about whether the refutation should come before or after the proof. The arrangement will differ according to the particular subject and the number and strength of the opposing arguments. If the opposing arguments are strong and widely held, they should be answered at the beginning. In this case, the refutation becomes a large part of the proof, as the preceding passage demonstrates. At other times when the opposing arguments are weak, the refutation will play only a minor part in the overall proof.

CONCLUDING

The conclusion is the last part of the paper and is as important as the opening. If the opening is the reader's first impression, the ending is the final impression—the taste left in the mouth. Aristotle believes that the conclusion should do four things:

1. Make the audience well-disposed toward the speaker.

2. Summarize the leading facts.

3. Excite the required state of emotion in the audience.

4. Refresh the audience's memory.

Not all of these points are required in every conclusion, but they can serve as a checklist as you work toward the end of your essay. Most writers review the highlights of the argument in order to refresh their readers' memories. The following paragraph concludes a student paper on the depiction of women on television.

> Such misrepresentation and underrepresentation are indicative of the inaccurate portrayal of women on TV. If people could see these women for what they are, as unreal fantasies, not much harm would be done. But all too often, as in the case of my three friends, TV women are taken at face value as what every woman is or should be. And that's why watching a "harmless" TV show becomes a lesson in frustration for many real women today.

In this conclusion the writer refreshes the readers' memory by reminding them of the cases of her three friends who were unable to see the women on TV as unreal fantasies and summarizes her conclusion by moving to the larger issue that TV is not only not "harmless" but can be truly frustrating for many women. Often the concluding paragraph summarizes what has been said and then moves to the larger consequences of the issues involved. The following paragraph concludes "The Reciprocity of Numbers," an essay by Joan Baum that argues that the two apparently disparate fields of math and writing require similar skills and thus could well reinforce each other—particularly in teaching. The conclusion suggests wider consequences for such a collaboration.

> If the basics of reading, writing, and math have a common foundation that English teachers with no special training in math can be helped to see and to use, there may be reason to hope not only that students will fare better in all the basic skills, but that the sciences and the humanities, though different in subject matters, forms, and styles, may be perceived as part of the same culture.

How many of the points that Aristotle suggests does Baum use in this conclusion before she moves to the larger cultural issue? Does the addition of the last clause "that the sciences and the humanities though different . . . may be perceived as part of the same culture" improve the conclusion? Why, or why not?

Although often the conclusion to a persuasive paper moves to larger issues—in the following paper from battered women to the issue of the survival of the whole family—it can also suggest what should be done—urging action or a change in attitude. What action does Miller urge in this conclusion from *Batter or Worse*?

> As a society, we have a commitment to these people: to keep them safe and to keep them alive. And not until we begin to listen to and believe them will we be able to break the vows of secrecy and make sure the family has a future.

Both of the preceding conclusions urge a change in attitude on the part of the reader, as essays on public issues often do. Joan Baum urges that we perceive the sciences and humanities "as part of the same culture," and Miller urges us to listen and believe the stories of battered women. An essay on drunk driving laws might urge better enforcement of such laws. You may wish to conclude your essays that argue questions of public policy with a call to some action or by urging a change in attitude.

The following essay, written in 1981 by Stephen Jay Gould, a geologist who teaches at Harvard, is a well-developed essay arguing in favor of evolution and opposing creationism. He opens the essay with the description of his friendship with Kirtley Mather who testified at the Scopes trial in 1925. In this trial John Scopes was accused of teaching evolution in high school and was defended by Clarence Darrow, who won the day for the evolutionists. Gould maintains that nothing has changed since that time and that creationism is a political issue raised by the "resurgent evangelical right."

EVOLUTION AS FACT AND THEORY

STEPHEN JAY GOULD

Kirtley Mather, who died last year at age eighty-nine, was a pillar of both science and the Christian religion in America and one of my dearest friends. The difference of half a century in our ages evaporated before our common interests. The most curious thing we shared was a battle we each fought at the same age. For Kirtley had gone to Tennessee with Clarence Darrow to testify for evolution at the Scopes trial of 1925. When I think that we are enmeshed again in the same struggle for one of the best documented, most compelling and exciting concepts in all of science, I don't know whether to laugh or cry. 1

According to idealized principles of scientific discourse, the arousal of dormant issues should reflect fresh data that give renewed life to abandoned notions. Those outside the current debate may therefore be excused for suspecting that creationists have come up with something new, or that evolutionists have generated some serious internal trouble. But nothing has changed; the creationists have not a single new fact or argument. Darrow and Bryan were at least more entertaining than we lesser antagonists today. The rise of creationism is politics, pure and simple; it represents one issue (and by no means the major concern) of the resurgent evangelical right. Arguments that seemed kooky just a decade ago have reentered the mainstream. 2

Creationism Is Not Science

The basic attack of the creationists falls apart on two general counts before we even reach the supposed factual details of their complaints against evolution. First, they play upon a vernacular misunderstanding of the word "theory" to convey the false impression that we evolutionists are covering up the rotten core of our edifice. Second, they misuse a popular philosophy of science to argue that they are behaving scientifically in attacking evolution. Yet the same philosophy demonstrates that their own belief is not science, and that "scientific creationism" is therefore meaningless and self-contradictory, a superb example of what Orwell called "newspeak." 3

In the American vernacular, "theory" often means "imperfect fact"— part of a hierarchy of confidence running downhill from fact to theory to 4 hypothesis to guess. Thus the power of the creationist argument: Evolution is "only" a theory, and intense debate now rages about many aspects of the theory. If evolution is less than a fact, and scientists can't even make up their minds about the theory, then what confidence can we have in it? Indeed, President Reagan echoed this argument before an evangelical group in Dallas when he said (in what I devoutly hope was campaign rhetoric): "Well, it is a theory. It is a scientific theory only, and it has in recent years been challenged in the world of science—that is, not believed in the scientific community to be as infallible as it once was."

Well, evolution *is* a theory. It is also a fact. And facts and theories are   5
different things, not rungs in a hierarchy of increasing certainty. Facts are the world's data. Theories are structures of ideas that explain and interpret facts. Facts do not go away when scientists debate rival theories to explain them. Einstein's theory of gravitation replaced Newton's, but apples did not suspend themselves in mid-air pending the outcome. And human beings evolved from apelike ancestors whether they did so by Darwin's proposed mechanism or by some other, yet to be discovered.

Moreover, "fact" does not mean "absolute certainty." The final proofs   6
of logic and mathematics flow deductively from stated premises and achieve certainty only because they are *not* about the empirical world. Evolutionists make no claim for perpetual truth, though creationists often do (and then attack us for a style of argument that they themselves favor). In science, "fact" can only mean "confirmed to such a degree that it would be perverse to withhold provisional assent." I suppose that apples might start to rise tomorrow, but the possibility does not merit equal time in physics classrooms.

Evolutionists have been clear about this distinction between fact and   7
theory from the very beginning, if only because we have always acknowledged how far we are from completely understanding the mechanisms (theory) by which evolution (fact) occurred. Darwin continually emphasized the difference between his two great and separate accomplishments: establishing the fact of evolution, and proposing a theory—natural selection—to explain the mechanism of evolution. He wrote in *The Descent of Man*: "I had two distinct objects in view; firstly, to show that species had not been separately created, and secondly, that natural selection had been the chief agent of change. . . . Hence if I have erred in. . . having exaggerated its natural selection's power. . . . I have at least, as I hope, done good service in aiding to overthrow the dogma of separate creations."

Thus Darwin acknowledged the provisional nature of natural selection   8
while affirming the fact of evolution. The fruitful theoretical debate that Darwin initiated has never ceased. From the 1940s through the 1960s, Darwin's own theory of natural selection did achieve a temporary hegemony that it never enjoyed in his lifetime. But renewed debate

characterizes our decade, and, while no biologist questions the importance of natural selection, many now doubt its ubiquity. In particular, many evolutionists argue that substantial amounts of genetic change may not be subject to natural selection and may spread through populations at random. Others are challenging Darwin's linking of natural selection with gradual, imperceptible change through all intermediary degrees; they are arguing that most evolutionary events may occur far more rapidly than Darwin envisioned.

Scientists regard debates on fundamental issues of theory as a sign of intellectual health and a source of excitement. Science is—and how else can I say it?—most fun when it plays with interesting ideas, examines their implications, and recognizes that old information may be explained in surprisingly new ways. Evolutionary theory is now enjoying this uncommon vigor. Yet amidst all this turmoil no biologist has been led to doubt the fact that evolution occurred; we are debating *how* it happened. We are all trying to explain the same thing: the tree of evolutionary descent linking all organisms by ties of genealogy. Creationists pervert and caricature this debate by conveniently neglecting the common conviction that underlies it, and by falsely suggesting that we now doubt the very phenomenon we are struggling to understand. 9

Using another invalid argument, creationists claim that "the dogma of separate creations," as Darwin characterized it a century ago, is a scientific theory meriting equal time with evolution in high school biology curricula. But a prevailing viewpoint among philosophers of science belies this creationist argument. Philosopher Karl Popper has argued for decades that the primary criterion of science is the falsifiability of its theories. We can never prove absolutely, but we can falsify. A set of ideas that cannot, in principle, be falsified is not science. 10

The entire creationist argument involves little more than a rhetorical attempt to falsify evolution by presenting supposed contradictions among its supporters. Their brand of creationism, they claim, is "scientific" because it follows the Popperian model in trying to demolish evolution. Yet Popper's argument must apply in both directions. One does not become a scientist by the simple act of trying to falsify another scientific system; one has to present an alternative system that also meets Popper's criterion—it too must be falsifiable in principle. 11

"Scientific creationism" is a self-contradictory, nonsense phrase precisely because it cannot be falsified. I can envision observations and experiments that would disprove any evolutionary theory I know, but I cannot imagine what potential data could lead creationists to abandon their beliefs. Unbeatable systems are dogma, not science. Lest I seem harsh or rhetorical, I quote creationism's leading intellectual, Duane Gish, Ph.D., from his recent (1978) book *Evolution? The Fossils Say No!* "By creation we mean the bringing into being by a supernatural Creator of 12 the basic kinds of plants and animals by the process of sudden, or fiat, creation. We do not know how the Creator created, what processes He used, *for He used processes which are not now operating anywhere in the natural universe* [Gish's italics]. This is why we refer to creation as special creation. We cannot discover by scientific investigations anything about the creative processes used by the Creator." Pray tell, Dr. Gish, in the light of your last sentence, what then is "scientific" creationism?

The Fact of Evolution

Our confidence that evolution occurred centers upon three general 13 arguments. First, we have abundant, direct, observational evidence of evolution in action, from both the field and the laboratory. It ranges from countless experiments on change in nearly everything about fruit flies subjected to artificial selection in the laboratory to the famous British moths that turned black when industrial soot darkened the trees upon which they rest. (The moths gain protection from sharp-sighted bird predators by blending into the background.) Creationists do not deny these observations; how could they? Creationists have tightened their act. They now argue that God only created "basic kinds," and allowed for limited evolutionary meandering within them. Thus toy poodles and Great Danes come from the dog kind and moths can change color, but nature cannot convert a dog to a cat or a monkey to a man.

The second and third arguments for evolution—the case for major 14 changes—do not involve direct observation of evolution in action. They rest upon inference, but are no less secure for that reason. Major evolutionary change requires too much time for direct observation on the scale of recorded human history. All historical sciences rest upon inference, and evolution is no different from geology, cosmology, or human history in this respect. In principle, we cannot observe processes that operated in the past. We must infer them from results that still survive: living and fossil organisms for evolution, documents and artifacts for human history, strata and topography for geology.

The second argument—that the imperfection of nature reveals evolu- 15 tion—strikes many people as ironic, for they feel that evolution should be most elegantly displayed in the nearly perfect adaptation expressed by some organisms—the chamber of a gull's wing, or butterflies that cannot be seen in ground litter because they mimic leaves so precisely. But perfection could be imposed by a wise creator or evolved by natural selection. Perfection covers the tracks of past history. And past history— the evidence of descent—is our mark of evolution.

Evolution lies exposed in the *imperfections* that record a history of 16 descent. Why should a rat run, a bat fly, a porpoise swim, and I type this essay with structures built of the same bones unless we all inherited them from a common ancestor? An engineer, starting from scratch, could design better limbs in each case. Why should all the large native mammals of Australia be marsupials, unless they descended from a common ancestor isolated on this island continent? Marsupials are not "better," or ideally suited for Australia; many have been wiped out by placental mammals imported by man from other continents. This principle of imperfection extends to all historical sciences. When we recognize the etymology of September, October, November, and December (seventh, eighth, ninth, and tenth, from the Latin), we know that two additional items (January and February) must have been added to an original calendar of ten months.

The third argument is more direct: Transitions are often found in the fossil record. Preserved transitions are not common—and should not be, according to our understanding of evolution (see next section)—but they are not entirely wanting, as creationists often claim. The lower jaw of reptiles contains several bones, that of mammals only one. The non-mammalian jawbones are reduced, step by step, in mammalian ancestors until they become tiny nubbins located at the back of the jaw. The "hammer" and "anvil" bones of the mammalian ear are descendants of these nubbins. How could such a transition be accomplished? the creationists ask. Surely a bone is either entirely in the jaw or in the ear. Yet paleontologists have discovered two transitional lineages or therapsids (the so-called mammal-like reptiles) with a double jaw joint—one composed of the old quadrate and articular bones (soon to become the hammer and anvil), the other of the squamosal and dentary bones (as in modern mammals). For that matter, what better transitional form could we desire than the oldest human, *Australopithecus afarensis*, with its apelike palate, its human upright stance, and a cranial capacity larger than any ape's of the same body size but a full 1,000 cubic centimeters below ours? If God made each of the half dozen human species discovered in ancient rocks, why did he create in an unbroken temporal sequence of progressively more modern features—increasing cranial capacity, reduced face and teeth, larger body size? Did he create to mimic evolution and test our faith thereby?

An Example of Creationist Argument

Faced with these facts of evolution and the philosophical bankruptcy of their own position, creationists rely upon distortion and innuendo to buttress their rhetorical claim. If I sound sharp or bitter, indeed I am—for I have become a major target of these practices.

I count myself among the evolutionists who argue for a jerky, or episodic, rather than a smoothly gradual, pace of change. In 1972 my colleague Niles Eldredge and I developed the theory of punctuated equilibrium [*Discover*, October]. We argued that two outstanding facts of the fossil record—geologically "sudden" origin of new species and failure to change thereafter (stasis)—reflect the predictions of evolutionary theory, not the imperfections of the fossil record. In most theories, small isolated populations are the source of new species, and the process of speciation takes thousands or tens of thousands of years. This amount of time, so long when measured against our lives, is a geological microsecond. It represents much less than 1 percent of the average life span for a fossil invertebrate species—more than 10 million years. Large, widespread, and well-established species, on the other hand, are not expected to change very much. We believe that the inertia of large populations explains the stasis of most fossil species over millions of years.

We proposed the theory of punctuated equilibrium largely to provide a   20
different explanation for pervasive trends in the fossil record. Trends, we argued, cannot be attributed to gradual transformation within lineages, but must arise from the differential success of certain kinds of species. A trend, we argued, is more like climbing a flight of stairs (punctuations and stasis) than rolling up an inclined plane.

Since we proposed punctuated equilibria to explain trends, it is infu-   21
riating to be quoted again and again by creationists—whether through design or stupidity, I do not know—as admitting that the fossil record includes no transitional forms. Transitional forms are generally lacking at the species level, but are abundant between larger groups. The evolution from reptiles to mammals, as mentioned earlier, is well documented. Yet a pamphlet entitled "Harvard Scientists Agree Evolution Is a Hoax" states: "The facts of punctuated equilibrium which Gould and Eldredge ... are forcing Darwinists to swallow fit the picture that Bryan insisted on, and which God has revealed to us in the Bible."

Continuing the distortion, several creationists have equated the theory   22
of punctuated equilibrium with a caricature of the beliefs of Richard Goldschmidt, a great early geneticist. Goldschmidt argued, in a famous book published in 1940, that new groups can arise all at once through major mutations. He referred to these suddenly transformed creatures as "hopeful monsters." (I am attracted to some aspects of the non-caricatured version, but Goldschmidt's theory still has nothing to do with punctuated equilibrium.) Creationist Luther Sunderland talks of the "punctuated equilibrium hopeful monster theory" and tells his hopeful readers that "it amounts to tacit admission that anti-evolutionists are correct in asserting there is no fossil evidence supporting the theory that all life is connected to a common ancestor." Duane Gish writes, "According to Goldschmidt, and now apparently according to Gould, a reptile laid an egg from which the first bird, feathers and all, was produced." Any evolutionist who believed such nonsense would rightly be laughed off the intellectual stage; yet the only theory that could ever envision such a scenario for the evolution of birds is creationism—God acts in the egg.

Conclusion

I am both angry at and amused by the creationists; but mostly I am 23 deeply sad. Sad for many reasons. Sad because so many people who respond to creationist appeals are troubled for the right reason, but venting their anger at the wrong target. It is true that scientists have often been dogmatic and elitist. It is true that we have often allowed the white-coated, advertising image to represent us—"Scientists say that Brand X cures bunions ten times faster than. . . ." We have not fought it adequately because we derive benefits from appearing as a new priesthood. It is also true that faceless bureaucratic state power intrudes more and more into our lives and removes choices that should belong to individuals and communities. I can understand that requiring that evolution be taught in the schools might be seen as one more insult on all these grounds. But the culprit is not, and cannot be, evolution or any other fact of the natural world. Identify and fight your legitimate enemies by all means, but we are not among them.

I am sad because the practical result of this brouhaha will not be 24 expanded coverage to include creationism (that would also make me sad), but the reduction or excision of evolution from high school curricula. Evolution is one of the half dozen "great ideas" developed by science. It speaks to the profound issues of genealogy that fascinate all of us—the "roots" phenomenon writ large. Where did we come from? Where did life arise? How did it develop? How are organisms related? It forces us to think, ponder, and wonder. Shall we deprive millions of this knowledge and once again teach biology as a set of dull and unconnected facts, without the thread that weaves diverse material into a supple unity?

But most of all I am saddened by a trend I am just beginning to discern 25 among my colleagues. I sense that some now wish to mute the healthy debate about theory that has brought new life to evolutionary biology. It provides grist for creationist mills, they say, even if only by distortion. Perhaps we should lie low and rally round the flag of strict Darwinism, at least for the moment—a kind of old-time religion on our part.

But we should borrow another metaphor and recognize that we too 26 have to tread a straight and narrow path, surrounded by roads to perdition. For if we ever begin to suppress our search to understand nature, to quench our own intellectual excitement in a misguided effort to present a united front where it does not and should not exist, then we are truly lost.

This essay follows the classical order fairly regularly. Can you identify the parts? After the opening incident of the Scopes trial and the background information, Gould presents his argument in the form of a syllogism.

Major Premise: Raising dormant issues should reflect the discovery of fresh data.

Minor Premise: Creationisn does not reflect fresh data.

Conclusion: Therefore creationism should not be raised as an issue.

His thesis is in the conclusion of the syllogism and he supports it by arguing for the minor premise since the major premise is accepted as "an idealized principle of scientific discourse." First he points out the distinctions between fact and theory, affirming the fact of evolution and the provisional nature of natural selection. After carefully defining fact, he refutes the claim that creationism is a scientific theory since the primary criteria of science is the assertion that its theories can be falsified. Scientific creationism is a contradiction in terms since it cannot be falsified by any potential data. Gould then continues by giving three proofs for evolution and then refutes the creationists' arguments by proving that they rely upon distortion and inuendo. In his conclusion Gould moves to a larger issue than the creation/evolution debate. What is that issue and how does it relate to this debate? This arrangement that closely follows the classical model is effective. Can you explain why?

Questions to Consider

1. Examine the following introductory paragraphs and see if you can recognize the opening, the background, the definition of issues, and the thesis in each. Determine which among them would prompt you to continue reading the entire essay and why. Based on your conclusions, consider what suggestions you would make as a reader to writers desiring to create effective introductions. How do your suggestions compare with those offered in this chapter?

A.

"When I was a child, I spake as a child, I understood as a child, I thought as a child. But when I became a man, I put away childish things."—Corinthians I.

What about the years in between childhood and adulthood? How do we speak then? How do we think? How do we become men and women?

For most of history there was no in-between, no adolescence as we know it. There was no such lengthy period of semi-autonomy, economic "uselessness," when the only occupation of a son or daughter was learning. (Ellen Goodman, "The Long Transition to Adulthood")

B.

Good evening, ladies and gentlemen.
Welcome to *The Seven o'Clock News.*
Nothing happened today.
Goodnight.

That's the way television *should* handle the four out of seven days every week when current events go into suspended animation. But don't hang by your rabbit ears waiting for it to happen. Because the television news, contrary to FCC disclaimers, is not really the news at all. It's just another way for the networks to sell Efferdent, and for corporate America to unwind after its collective tough day at the office. (Brendan Boyd, "Packaged News")

C.

Warts are wonderful structures. They can appear overnight on any part of the skin, like mushrooms on a damp lawn, full grown and splendid in the complexity of their architecture. Viewed in stained sections under a microscope, they are the most specialized of cellular arrangements, constructed as though for a purpose. They sit there like turreted mounds of dense, impenetrable horn, impregnable, designed for defense against the world outside.

In a certain sense, warts are both useful and essential, but not for us. As it turns out, the exuberant cells of a wart are the elaborate reproductive apparatus of a virus. (Lewis Thomas, "On Warts")

D.

Some time ago, I received a call from a colleague who asked if I would be the referee on the grading of an examination question. He was about to give a student a zero for his answer to a physics question, while the student claimed he should receive a perfect score and would if the system were not set up against the student. The instructor and the student agreed to submit this to an impartial arbiter, and I was selected.

I went to my colleague's office and read the examination question: "Show how it is possible to determine the height of a tall building with the aid of a barometer."

The student had answered: "Take the barometer to the top of the building, attach a long rope to it, lower the barometer to the street, and then bring it up, measuring the length of the rope. The length of the rope is the height of the building." (Alexander Calandra, "Angels on a Pin")

Suggestions for Writing

1. Many of the suggestions this chapter provides for writing effective introductions for essays apply to other kinds of literature as well. Analyze the opening sentences or paragraphs of a short story you have read recently and determine whether you think the author has provided an effective introduction. Then write a paragraph in which you explain and justify your conclusion.

2. Scan your local newspaper for a report about a situation involving real people attempting to resolve some moral or ethical problem. Then write an essay arguing for a way to resolve it.

3. Write an essay addressed to the Textbook Committee of your department in which you argue that a textbook you are currently using in one of your classes should either be retained or dropped next semester.

Exercises in Revision

1. Rewrite the introduction or conclusion from one of your previous essays twice, using two different methods described in this chapter.

2. Rewrite the introduction or conclusion for an essay written by one of your classmates using a different method from that of the original. Discuss your revision with the author.

3. Exchange one of the essays written in response to exercises 1 or 2 with another student and determine how closely his or her essay conforms to the traditional six-part structure described in this chapter. Mark the parts you can identify in the margin.

A. Now determine the writer's main point and isolate the reasons he or she provides for support. If you have difficulty picking them out, alert the writer to the problem.

B. Now examine carefully the argument you've isolated. Which of the writer's supporting evidence or reasons seem weak? Why? Suggest ways he or she could strengthen his or her case in a well-developed paragraph. Include in that paragraph as well any additional arguments in favor of that case that occur to you but that the writer has neglected to mention.

C. Now make a list of all the reasons or arguments you can think of that refute the writer's position and that he or she does not respond to in the essay.

D. Return the essay, the paragraph you wrote for exercise 3B, and the list you made for exercise 3C to the writer so that he or she may revise his or her essay accordingly.

For a Commonplace Book

1. At least once a week, pick out an editorial from your local newspaper, cut it out, and secure it in your commonplace book. Then try to identify the writer's main point, isolate the arguments he or she offers in support, and evaluate them. Does the writer manage to convince you to accept his or her position? Why, or why not?

2. Begin keeping track of introductions in your reading that strike you as particularly effective; copy them into your commonplace book with notations explaining why they seem effective to you.

PART III

STYLE

Style, the third part of rhetoric, was known by the Greeks as *lexis* and by the Romans as *elocutio* The modern English words *lexical*, relating to words, and *eloquence*, meaning "persuasive or fluent discourse," are derived from those terms. Style is *how* you say *what* you mean. Quintilian advises that it is to style that the orator or writer "devotes the energies of a lifetime."

Most of the classical rhetoricians warned against thinking of style as something laid on and separate from subject matter, like jewelry added to the basic black dress. In addition, they stress the natural style, maintaining that the worst fault is a style inconsistent with ordinary speech. Quintilian compares an inadequate subject matter and an unnatural style to cosmetics covering the unhealthy body.

> Healthy bodies, enjoying a good circulation and strengthened by exercise, acquire grace from the same source that gives them strength, for they have a healthy complexion, firm flesh and shapely thews. But, on the other hand, persons who attempt to enhance these physical graces by the use of cosmetics, succeed merely in defacing them by the very care which they bestow on them. . . . Similarly, a translucent and iridescent style merely serves to emasculate the subject which it arrays with such pomp of words (*Institutio Oratoria* 8.Preface 19–20).

In the classical tradition, the stylistic choices of the orator depend on the speaker, the subject, and the audience. Effective orators alter their style according to the feelings of the audience, the subject matter, and the view of themselves that they wish to present. Most classical rhetoricians suggest four qualities of good style to consider for all situations:

1. Correctness

2. Clarity

3. Appropriateness

4. Embellishment

Correctness then as now was governed by the current usage of the educated class and then as now is an important rhetorical consideration since incorrect grammer—"they was," and "he don't"—negates the *ethos* of the writer in a very real way. Clarity in the classical tradition, depends for the most part on good word choice and coherence, and appropriateness refers to the stylistic choices to suit the subject and the occasion. Embellishment is the use of figures of speech, those unusual patterns of language that enhance or enrich meaning.

In the classical world students practiced and developed style in three ways. Their masters required them to know the rules, to practice writing, and to imitate models of good writers and speakers. These methods are still effective ways of improving writing, and you will have an opportunity to try them yourself.

Chapter 10 presents the general rules for achieving clarity and appropriateness. Some of the more common figures of speech are described in Chapter 11, followed by exercises for imitating model sentences.

Chapter 10

Achieving Clarity
and Appropriateness

CLARITY

    Increasing Your Vocabulary
    Using Words for Good Effect
    Coherence

APPROPRIATENESS

    Level of Style
    Stylistic Choices
    Sexist Language

NAN DESUKA, "WHY HANDGUNS MUST BE
    OUTLAWED"

Clarity, according to Quintilian, is the first virtue of style and he criticizes those who "would wrap up everything in a multitude of words simply and solely because they are unwilling to make a direct and simple statement. . . ." On the other hand, he criticizes those who are so consumed with a passion for brevity that they "omit words which are actually necessary to the sense, regarding it as a matter of complete indifference whether their meaning is intelligible to others, so long as they know what they mean themselves" (8.2.18–19).

The first hallmark of clarity for the classical rhetoricians is "propriety in the use of words." Selecting the proper word for the subject and the occasion is a constant challenge for the writer, and the wider range of vocabulary choices that are available to you, the more precise and selective you can be. Consequently, the first part of this chapter will suggest ways of increasing your vocabulary in order to broaden your options as a writer. The second part will suggest ways to make word choices for good effect, and then, following the example of the classical rhetoricians, the last section under clarity will discuss coherence—ways of putting those words together.

Appropriateness is the subject of the second part of this chapter—the way to make stylistic choices appropriate for the audience and the occasion. Aristotle tells his students that their language is appropriate if it expresses emotion and character and corresponds to its subject. Thus appropriateness suggests the ways that stylistic choices can establish the credibility and goodwill of the speaker, can appeal to the audience, and can develop the subject—all matters closely connected with the invention process.

CLARITY

The first qualification for clarity is a vocabulary that is adequate for your subject and your audience. Reading about your subject helps you to achieve this breadth. Secondly, knowing enough words is not enough, because you will need to develop the ability to choose the right word in order to say best what you want to say. Finally, words cannot be just strung into sentences. Words, sentences, and paragraphs have to cohere, to be joined together so that your reader can move from one idea to another with ease. All of these elements go together to make your writing clear and coherent. Aristotle reminds us that if our meaning is not clear, our communication serves no purpose at all.

Increasing Your Vocabulary

Anyone who has taken a college entrance exam knows how important vocabulary is. Vocabulary recognition is a big part of examinations for entrance and placement, primarily because a large vocabulary usually represents a wide reading background. There is absolutely no substitute for reading, but there are other things that can enrich and enlarge vocabulary.

Passive to Active   All of us have two kinds of vocabularies. On the one hand, there are words that we understand because we have heard and read them, but that we do not use ourselves. These words make up a "passive vocabulary." Our "active vocabulary," on the other hand, is composed of words that we use in our own speech and writing. It is important not only to increase that passive vocabulary, but also to keep words moving from passive vocabulary into active vocabulary. Try out words, use them, experiment with them. Keeping vocabulary alive and growing involves misusing words occasionally, but if you don't use them, they will finally disappear. So to keep your vocabulary alive and growing, move those words out of your head onto the piece of paper. Try them out on your friends, experiment with them, play with them, but make a point to use them.

Prefixes and Suffixes An important way to increase vocabulary is to gain a knowledge of prefixes and suffixes, those letters or syllables, usually derived from Latin or Greek, added to the beginning or end of words which change the meaning of the base words. Look at the following example:

> Possible
> *Im*possible
> Possib*ility*

In this example, possible is the base word. Its meaning is changed by adding the prefix *im*, or it can be changed from an adjective to a noun by adding the suffix *ility*. So we have *in*credible, credible, and credib*ility;* and *un*able, able, and ab*ility*. Notice that the prefixes and suffixes may have slightly different forms depending on the first letter of the word to which they are attached. For example, the common prefix *con*, which means "with," can take either of two forms: *con* as in *consult* or *com* as in *compare*. Following is a list of the most common prefixes in English, their possible variations, their meanings, and word examples.

PREFIX	MEANING	EXAMPLES
ab-, a-, abs-	from, away	apathetic, absent
ad-, ac-,	to, near, at	addict, access
ambi-	both, around	ambivalent, ambidexterous
anti-	against	antinuclear
circum-	around	circumnavigate
co-, con-, com-	with, together	coworker, companion
contra-, contro-	against	contradict, controversy
de-	down	descend
dif-, di-, dis-	apart, not	disable, divert, diffuse
ex-, e-, ef-	out, from, completely	expel, evade, efficient
extra-, extro-	outside, beyond	extraordinary, extrovert
hyper-	over, excessive	hypercritical, hypertension
hypo-	below, less than normal	hypodermic, hypotension
in-, im-	in, into, against	inject, impose
in-, im-	not	ineffective, impartial
meta-	after, changed	metacarpal, metamorphosis
para-	beside, disordered	parasite, paranoia

peri-	around, near	perimeter, periscope
post-	after, behind	posthumous, posterior
pre-	before, in front of	preschool, precede
pro-	forward, in front of, for	progress, project, profess
pros-	toward, in addition to	proselyte, prosthetic
re-, red-	back, again	reject, redress
retro-	backward, behind	retroactive, retrogress
se-, sed-	aside, away	secrete, seduce
syn-	with, together	synthetic, sympathy

Suffixes, like prefixes, add meaning to words, but they can also do something else: they change nouns to adjectives (*beauty* to *beautiful*), adjectives to adverbs (*beautiful* to *beautifully*), or adjectives to nouns (*real* to *reality*). In other words, they enrich the vocabulary by allowing one meaning to be extended to a number of parts of speech. Being familiar with some of the more common suffixes will greatly increase your vocabulary.

-able, -ible	able to be	applicable
-arch	one who rules	monarch
-arion, -arium	little	aquarium
-ary	pertaining to	dietary
-graph	writing	paragraph
-ician	specialist in	physician
-(i)fy, -(e)fy	to make	rectify
-ile	able to be	tactile
-itude	quality of	magnitude
-logy	science of	pathology
-mania	madness about	kleptomania
-or	one who does	actor
-ory	tending to	transitory
-phobe	one who fears or hates	claustrophobe

A knowledge of prefixes and suffixes will help you to decipher new words as you encounter them in a context. It follows that if you know what *pathetic* means, then with a knowledge of the meaning of prefixes *a-*, *sym-*, and *em-*, you can make an educated guess at what *apathetic, sympathetic,* and *empathetic* mean. If you understand that the suffix *-phobe* means fear, you can take a stab at the meaning of *hydrophobe*.

Word Families Another way to increase vocabulary is to see new words as related to other words—not just through related prefixes and suffixes, but through word "roots." It is unusual to find a word that has no connection with any other word in the language. New words usually come with numerous cousins, aunts, and uncles, and an acquaintance with one member of the family makes it easier to know the others. For example, a knowledge of the one root *carn* can add at least five words to your vocabulary.

carn = "flesh"

carnage: massacre (killing of flesh)
carnal: pertaining to appetites of the flesh
carnivore: flesh eating mammal
carnivorous: flesh eating
carnival: festival before Lent (farewell to the flesh)

Language is alive and growing, and words are seldom plucked out of nowhere. They usually come from roots that are already in the language. New words are coming into the language all of the time, but they are usually born out of a family of prefixes, suffixes, and roots that are already in use.

Using the Dictionary Finally, learning to use a dictionary—not for meaning or spelling alone—but to discover the history of a word and its roots can enrich your understanding of a word's meaning and give more depth of meaning to the words you use. It is often revealing to explore those root relationships and speculate how they came about. *Carrels*, those small studies in the stacks of the library, come from the same root as *carol* and *chant*, because in the Middle Ages, students used to go to their studies and read their lessons aloud. Understanding the derivation of words will also help you to remember meanings of new words after you look them up.

Using Words for Good Effect

You may often find yourself working over a single word trying to find the right one that says just what you want to say—no more and no less. Or you may sense that a word doesn't quite fit or a sentence is awkward but not know what to do about it. This section may guide you in making alternative choices. It will help you find specific words and examine their denotations and connotations. It will aid you in an awareness of the way you use verbs. It will also help you avoid unnecessary and awkward repetition and achieve that cardinal virtue of classical rhetoric—brevity.

Being Specific In naming persons, places, or things, effective writers are as specific as possible. Instead of talking about cereal, they talk about "Grapenuts." The general words in the following sentence add little to its effectiveness.

As I sit here in my apartment with wet hair wearing dirty old clothes, I can honestly say I would hate to be photographed.

Notice how the addition of specific words improves the sentence.

As I sit here in my apartment with wet hair, wearing dirty Adidas, grubby sweats, and a tattered T-shirt, I can honestly say I would want to give bodily harm to any photographer who tried to "freeze this moment."

"Old clothes" have become "Adidas, grubby sweats, and a tattered T-shirt," and "I would hate" has become "I would want to give bodily harm," and "photograph" has become "freeze this moment," all moving from generalized words and phrases to specific ones, which make the scene described more vivid. In your own writing you may wish to examine your nouns to see if making them more specific will make your writing more effective.

Denotation and Connotation Denotation is the ordinary meaning that a word has for most people. It is the meaning listed in the dictionary, but words often mean much more than the dictionary definition indicates. *Pudgy, chubby*, and *portly* all mean "overweight" but carry hidden meanings far beyond the denotative meanings found in a dictionary: How old is a person who is portly compared to one who is chubby or pudgy? What is the age and sex of a person who is portly? These suggested meanings are called *connotations*. Some words are more connotative than others. For instance, *overweight* is a somewhat neutral term while *chubby* carries unpleasant connotations.

Connotations can be used to advantage by giving an added meaning to a word, but highly connotative words must be used with care. Reading such words in context is the best way to become familiar with connotative meanings, but often such connotations may be suggested by dictionary word histories or by obsolete usages. *Pudgy* comes from a Scottish word that meant a "plump, healthy child," thus *pudgy* is used to describe an overweight child more frequently than to describe an overweight adult. Such historic meanings often suggest and account for modern connotations.

Choosing Strong Verbs Try not to rely on the use of the verb *be*. If your writing has too many words like *is, are,* or *was*—variant forms of the verb *be*—it may be wordy. They often act as unnecessary links between two ideas or words.

It is my intention. (weak)
I intend. (better)

It is eating that I can't resist. (weak)
I can't resist eating. (better)

Make your verbs as specific as possible. Consider the subject of the verb and the ideas you wish to convey. Instead of the verb *walk,* consider whether *hurried, dragged,* or *limped* may be more accurate. Instead of using the verb *cried,* ask yourself if *sobbed, blubbered,* or *sniffed* better describes the action, better fits the situation.

Passive Voice In revising an essay, examine your "be" verbs to see if you really need them, and look carefully at other verbs to see if describing the action with a more specific verb improves your writing.

Often some variant of the verb *be (is, are, was)* indicates the passive voice. In the active voice, the subject performs the action; in the passive voice, the subject is acted on.

Active: Joan Evans instigated the miners' strike.

Passive: The miners' strike was instigated by Joan Evans.

This example demonstrates that the passive voice carries the same meaning but uses more words, with the addition of *was* and *by,* and distances the actor, in this case Joan Evans, from the action that she is performing. Consequently, excessive use of the passive voice adds wordiness and a certain impersonality or deadness to your writing and should, in most cases, be avoided.

The passive voice can be changed to active by transposing the agent, introduced by *by,* to the subject position at the beginning of the sentence and eliminating the form of the verb, *be.*

Passive: Five hundred Caucasian males between the ages of thirty and forty were interviewed by Dr. Smith.

Active: Dr. Smith interviewed five hundred Caucasian males between the ages of thirty and forty.

The experiment becomes personal as excessive wordiness is avoided in the second example. Scientific writers may use the passive voice in order to preserve the objectivity of the experiment and the distance of the experimenter, but you should avoid the passive voice unless there is good reason to omit or distance the actor or subject.

Verb Tenses Usually you will wish to use the past tense to describe action that takes place in the past, although under the special circumstances described in the following discussion, you may substitute the present tense. An important guideline to remember is not to shift from present to past or past to present within a single paragraph.

Verb tenses should be consistent within a paragraph. Notice the confusion caused by the shifting tense in the following:

> We were sitting in the library studying one afternoon, and all of a sudden we see a large man dressed like a clown come walking toward our table. He had bright orange-colored hair, and wears yellow baggy overalls. He pulls up a chair beside me and asked, "Do you happen to have any mustard?"

The present tense can add vividness when telling about a past event.

> I can never forget that night. It is dark and stormy, and I can hear the wind whistling around the walls of the tent. It begins to rain and all I can do is hope that the canvas of my tent will keep me dry. I snuggle down in my sleeping bag trying to get a little sleep. Suddenly, I feel water around my ankles and know that the tent must be leaking. I reach for the flashlight and the light shows a pool of water creeping up over my feet. Then I realize to my horror that the water is not coming from above. It is coming from the river. I open the flap on the tent to find the river lapping at my feet. The gentle stream of the afternoon has become an ugly, brown, swirling, angry torrent.

The present tense is often used in a historical sense, especially to refer to an author who wrote in the past and who may be dead, as in the following sentence: "George Orwell uses the example of shooting an elephant as an effective example of what imperialism can do to people as they themselves conform to the masks they are forced to assume."

The present tense used in connection with authors is preferred and appropriate since authors continue to speak with every reading of their works.

Brevity The classical rhetoricians warned against "useless words" and recognized brevity as a great virtue. The first drafts of experienced writers are often just as wordy as those of new writers. The only difference is that most professional writers know how to revise in order to eliminate wordiness that bogs down an idea and wearies the reader.

Most wordiness is characterized by an unnecessary use of the passive voice, overuse of the verb *be*, and an excessive use of prepositional phrases. The passive voice and how to avoid it have been discussed. Other uses of the verb *be* can also add unnecessary words. Here are a few common examples of wordy constructions:

> This is a subject that interests me. (wordy)
> This subject interests me.

She is a person who works hard. (wordy)
She works hard.

There is no doubt that she works hard. (wordy)
No doubt she works hard.

Phrases such as "who is" and "which is" are often not necessary.

His sister, who is a member of the same firm, stayed away.
His sister, a member of the same firm, stayed away.

Hamlet, which was his finest work, will be our subject.
Hamlet, his finest work, will be our study.

In the following examples, we may eliminate each use of the phrase "the fact that" to reduce wordiness.

The fact that he had not succeeded discouraged her.
That he had not succeeded discouraged her.

I was unaware of the fact that they had arrived.
I was unaware that they had arrived.

Simple conjunctions also may be substituted for certain expressions with "fact."

Owing to the fact that she was drunk on the job, she was fired.
Because she was drunk on the job, she was fired.

Look for places where a single word could replace a phrase or where a short phrase could replace a longer one.

He spoke in a hasty manner.
He spoke hastily.

Those were acts of a hostile character.
Those were hostile acts.

I read all the works of Jane Austen.
I read all of Jane Austen's works.

Also try to avoid using qualifiers such as *very, little,* or *rather*. Although appropriate to spoken language, they are usually unnecessary in writing and add little to meaning.

Wordiness always puts an unnecessary burden on the reader and obscures the message that you are trying to get across. Make your writing direct, spare, and to the point.

Coherence

Quintilian often compares the organic nature of rhetoric to the human body. So with coherence he tells us that "we must struggle not merely to place thoughts in their proper order, but to link them together and give them such cohesion that there will be no trace of limbs." He advises against making facts appear like "perfect strangers thrust into uncongenial company from distant places" (*Institutio Oratoria* 7.10.16–17).

Coherence—the logical linking of ideas—starts in your mind early in the inventional process as focus develops and one idea leads to another. But this logical linking of ideas must be communicated to the reader. It is important to provide signals that will lead the reader through the paper. The following coherence devices—repetition through key words and synonyms, and other transitional devices such as transitional phrases, signposts, and transitional paragraphs—help your reader move from one idea to another. These devices will not work unless they represent a logical progression inherent in your thinking and writing. You cannot attach a paragraph to a paper with a word or phrase unless it belongs to the organic whole anymore than you can tack a limb to the body with a Band-Aid. The devices described in the following pages are outward signs of an inherent logical progression.

Coherence through Repetition A common coherence device is the repetition of key words that tie ideas together. In the following paragraph from "Master of Babble: Turning Language into Stone," James P. Degman repeats the key word, *illiterate*, finally pairing it with an apparently contradictory term, "the straight-A illiterate."

> Despite all the current fuss and bother about the extraordinary number of ordinary illiterates who overpopulate our schools, small attention has been given to another kind of illiterate, an illiterate whose plight is, in many ways, more important, because he is more influential. This illiterate may, as often as not, be a university president, but he is typically a Ph.D., a successful professor and textbook author. The person to whom I refer is the straight-A illiterate, and the following is written in an attempt to give him equal time with his widely publicized counterpart.

In the following paragraph from the same essay, the ideas are connected through the repetition of a phrase, *to recognize the truth that.*

To recognize the truth that writing well tends to mean writing simply, clearly, vividly, and forcefully, whether such writing is done by a philosopher or an engineer; *to recognize the truth that*, having nothing to say, one should refrain from using thousands of words to say it; *to recognize the truth that* pretentious nonsense is not profundity, is painful for many, and, as I have suggested, perhaps economically disastrous.

Repeating a phrase such as this one at the beginning of a series of clauses is a good rhetorical device while merely repeating the same word throughout a paragraph can be monotonous.

Instead of repeating the same word or phrase, you can also carry an idea through a paragraph by using synonyms. In the following paragraph the author repeats the key idea of vocabulary and words, altering the form by using synonyms

In many ways the changes in the *vocabulary* of English over the past centuries have been more pervasive than those in sound and structure. Alteration of the *stock of words* in a language may take different forms. New words may be taken from other languages with which speakers of English for one reason or another have come into contact. Words may become old-fashioned or archaic and ultimately drop out of use altogether. Words or *word elements* may be combined in various ways to form new words. They may be clipped or shortened; they may be used in new grammatical functions. They may change in meaning. The English *lexicon* gives ample illustration of all of these.

This author avoids the monotony of unnecessary repetition by using synonyms such as vocabulary, stock of words, and lexicon. The key idea of words or vocabulary runs, however, through the full paragraph and holds it together.

Distinguishing effective repetition in the form of key words and phrases from unnecessary repetition is often difficult but can best be done by reading a paper aloud. Your ear is often the best judge, for as the author of the *Ad Herennium* advises, there inheres in effective repetition "an elegance which the ear can distinguish more easily than words can explain." Unnecessary repetition, on the other hand, involves "frequent recourse to the same word . . . dictated by verbal poverty" (4.14.21).

When such poverty strikes, you may wish to resort to a dictionary of synonyms or a *thesaurus*, Latin for "treasure." Here you may look up a word and find a listing of synonyms and cross references to other related words. Thus, for the word *controversy*, a thesaurus will provide the following alternatives: *argument, contention, dispute, quarrel, altercation, wrangle, debate, disagreement,* and *embroilment.* These words are not all synonymous and differ widely in connotations, but they may serve as suggestions to vary the monotony of the repetition of one word over and over again. It is important that you not use a synonym unless you are familiar with its connotations. Never choose a synonym unless your ear tells you that your writing is too repetitious, and always use the simpler word over the polysyllabic one if both words serve your purpose equally well.

Often key words or phrases are repeated in the introduction, title, and conclusion of a paper. These elements are often logically connected to one another, because they all usually refer to the main idea of the paper in some way. The introduction presents the main idea; the conclusion often repeats it. This inherent logical connection may be represented in repeated or synonymous words or phraseology. Experienced writers often pick up a phrase, word, or idea from the introduction, reintroduce it in the conclusion, and use it in the title.

A title should at least tell the reader what the essay is about, but in doing that it can also help unify the author's ideas. Thus titles like "Resistance to New Ideas," "The Moral Unneutrality of Science," and "The Black Psyche" all furnish the reader with some idea of the subject of the essay. But notice how the title in the following essay, drawn from the first paragraph and the conclusion, helps to give a cohesiveness to the paper.

Getting Out of the Way:
A Man's Role in the Feminist Movement

The speaker that night was a fiery, middle-aged black woman with a liquid baritone voice that held the whole audience enthralled. Her speech was intelligent and sensitive, but spiced with flashes of emotion that spoke straight to the heart. At the conclusion of the talk I joined in the applause, then fired by the zeal known only to recent converts, I approached the corner to which the speaker had retreated. Feeling I should convey my enthusiasm, but not knowing quite how, I managed to mumble, "What can I do?" With narrowing eyes and the slightest trace of a smile, she paused, then calmly replied, *"Get out of the way."*

This student picked up this remark for his title and comes back to it, developing it further, in his conclusion.

At this point, with masculinity discarded, and an increased understanding of what it is like to be a woman in today's world, we have reached a turning point. If men can obtain this level of understanding, we will not only be *out of the way,* but it will be time for us to walk side by side with women through the doorway to a new future. I wish I could say it will be easy to reach this point, but I know from experience that it isn't. I am still struggling with my own masculinism—I've come a long way, but I know in my heart that I'm still blocking the door.

When the author starts an essay with an anecdote, it can be effective to refer to the anecdote in the conclusion, thus giving the reader a sense of logical cohesion. In a paper on anorexia, the student started with a description of a patient named Amanda.

Amanda walks in the house with a ghostly look on her face. She can barely push the heavy front door far enough to let her boney figure enter. As I grab the door to help her, my hand brushes across her cold, clammy arms. She trips over her jeans that are too long and two sizes too large, and as I walk away I hear the thud of Amanda's anorexic figure fall to the floor in a faint. Before I turn around, I pray that I know how to help her.

Amanda is not mentioned throughout the paper as the subject of anorexia is explored, but in the conclusion, the writer picks up the thread of Amanda again.

Even though some anorexics appear to be in control of their lives, they may relapse and lose a drastic amount of weight every time they change environments. The potential for anorexia remains long after recovery. In fact, 20 percent of the victims have recurrent bouts with the disease. Amanda is on the road to a self-help recovery, and she feels better about herself, "I'm glad I went for help, but I won't promise I'll never go back, because I'd rather be skinny and have this problem than be fat and not have it."

The title of this paper, "How to Handle Amanda," reinforces the sense of logical unity.

Coherence through Transitions Writers use copious transitional phrases to make their writing smooth, to demonstrate the logical connections between their ideas. The sentences in the following paragraph appear disconnected; the thinking seems illogical.

You must water your plants adequately. You must be careful as to how much water you give them. So many people feel that plants are always thirsty. This is not true. If you water your plants too much you will give them rootrot. The leaves will turn yellow, begin to droop, and eventually die.

The author revised the passage by adding only four transitional phrases and thus improved the paragraph by helping the reader move from one idea to another.

You must water your plants adequately, *but* you must be careful as to how much water you give them. So many people feel that plants are always thirsty, *but* this is not true. *In fact*, if you water your plants too much, you will give them rootrot, *and* the leaves will turn yellow, begin to droop, and eventually die.

Following is a list of transitional devices that can be helpful.

Addition:	moreover, further, furthermore, again, in addition, first, second (etc.), finally, last.
Contrast:	but, yet, nevertheless, still, however, on the other hand, on the one hand . . . on the other hand, it is true, on the contrary, after all.
Comparison:	likewise, similarly.
Coincidence:	equally important, meanwhile, in the meantime, at the same time, at the same place.
Purpose:	for this purpose, to this end, with this object.
Result:	hence, accordingly, consequently, thus.
Emphasis:	indeed, in fact, in any event.
Exemplification:	for example, for instance, thus.
Summary:	in sum, to sum up, on the whole, in brief.
Time:	at length, meanwhile, in the meantime, immediately.
Place:	nearby, beyond, adjacent to, opposite to.

If the underlying thinking is logical and coherent, these words can demonstrate those logical connections to the reader. It is a mistake, however, to think that such words and phrases can be added like pink rosebuds on a birthday cake. They must be indications of an order and progression that comes out of your inventional and arrangement choices. If such transitions do not come easily, you may wish to review the way that you arrived at those choices. Such difficulties may indicate logical gaps that need to be filled out.

Two ideas can be connected in a number of different ways.

John jumped.
Mary laughed.

John jumped while Mary laughed.
John jumped but Mary laughed.
John jumped; hence, Mary laughed.
John jumped, and at the same time Mary laughed.
John jumped and, nevertheless, Mary laughed.
John jumped, and, in addition, Mary laughed.
John jumped, and, finally, Mary laughed.

In some of the above sentences, Mary laughed because John jumped, in some she laughed while he jumped, and in some Mary laughed in spite of John's jumping. The transitional phrases can show very different connections between two ideas, but they indicate to the reader what that connection is. Such phrases grace good writing and lead to easy reading.

Notice how Daniel J. Boorstin, the writer in the following paragraph, uses both key ideas and transitional phrases to achieve cohesion.

The radical is distinguished from the man who simply has a bad digestion by the fact that the radical's belief has some solid subject matter, while the other man is merely dyspeptic. A stomachache or sheer anger or irritability cannot be the substance of radicalism. Thus, while a man can be ill-natured or irritable in general, he cannot be a radical in general. Every radicalism is a way of asserting what are the roots. Radicalism, therefore, involves affirmation. It is distinguished from conservatism precisely in that the conservative can be loose and vague about his affirmation. The conservative is in fact always tempted to let his affirmation become mere complacency. But the true radical cannot refuse to affirm, and to be specific, although of course he may be utopian. The radical must affirm that this is more fundamental than that. One great service of the radical, then is that by his experimental definitions he puts the conservative on the defensive and makes him discover, decide, and define what is really worth preserving. The radical does this by the specificity (sometimes also by the rashness) of his affirmation—of the dictatorship of the proletariat, of the Kingdom of God on earth, or of whatever else. ("The New Barbarians")

Often writers find it useful to give very explicit directions to the reader about what they have said or are going to say in signposts that number sections of an essay. In the following paragraph the author divides autobiography into three kinds.

Apparently there are *three* kinds of autobiography: *three* different ways of telling the story of one's life. We can leave out journals like Pepys' Diary, which was not meant to be published, and collections of letters, and disguised autobiographies, which so many modern novels are. (Gilbert Highet, "The Face in the Mirror")

The following paragraph starts:

> The *first* group could all be issued under the same title. They could all be called "What I Did."

Four paragraphs later, another signpost indicates the end of the discussion of the first type of autobiography and the beginning of discussion of the second type.

> So much for the *first* type of autobiography: "What I Did." The *second* type might be called "What I Saw."

One page later, the reader finds the following paragraph:

> Then there is the *third* kind of autobiography. It does not describe "What I Did," or "What I Saw," but "What I Felt."

In this essay, the author is giving the reader clear indications, *first, second, third* of his organization. Each of these signposts tells readers what they have just read and what they are about to read. They point backwards and forwards. You may wish to use such devices in a long and complex paper or to indicate connections that are not obvious to the reader.

Although using a numbering system is the clearest kind of transitional device, it may, in some situations, appear too mechanical. There are other ways of effecting transitions between paragraphs.

Often the first sentence in a paragraph serves as a transition, referring in some way to the idea treated in the last paragraph while introducing a new idea. There are several ways that writers accomplish this transition.

One way is to pick up a word or phrase from the former paragraph and use it in the first sentence of the new paragraph. Notice how the following writer does this:

> Some are simply *"fortified* with vitamins," while others are specifically *"fortified* with vitamin D," or some other letter. But what does it all *mean?*
> *"Fortified"* means "added on to."

In this example the writer picks up two words used in the last two sentences of the preceding paragraph. The repetition of the word here indicates a logical connection that already exists between the two paragraphs.

Another way is to pick up an idea from the former paragraph and use it in the first sentence of the new paragraph. Rather than use the exact words from the previous paragraph, you can use synonyms or phrases that refer to an idea in the preceding paragraph to carry the idea to the new one. Here is an example:

There is a direct, *inverse proportion* between the number of adjectives and the number of facts. To put it succinctly, the *more* adjectives we use, the *less* we have to say.
   You can almost make a scale, based on *that simple mathematical premise.*

You can also use transitional words or phrases to link your ideas and at the same time to move onto new ones. Words such as *this, that, also, in addition, another* are effective transitional devices and often appear in the first sentence of a new paragraph. Even pronouns can serve this function. While a new thought is being introduced, they point to the thought that preceded. Here are a few examples of first sentences in paragraphs that use these transitional devices.

There is *another* subdivision of the cheap case that the editor generally describes as "too gruesome."

Perhaps *one more* incident would illustrate this strange concept further.

It's a copywriter's dream, because we don't have to establish anything.

Be careful that pronouns used as transitions have a clear referent.
   In longer papers you may use a transitional paragraph to move your reader from one idea to another. These are customarily short paragraphs that introduce large segments and spell out transitions that are not immediately apparent. In an essay on "Television and Children: Not Always a Good Mix," the writer discusses, in the first 1,000 words of the paper, the bad effects of television. She then moves to the second half of her paper through a well-formed and smooth transitional paragraph.

It would be unfair to look at only the negative side of this issue when many positive changes are occurring every year. Though prime time shows (7 P.M.–11 P.M.) are still guilty of showing violence and an unreal picture of life, at least one network has taken great strides toward creating programming for children that is entertaining, educational, and inspiring.

This paragraph sums up what the author has discussed so far and points forward to what she plans to take up in the remainder of the paper.

APPROPRIATENESS

"We must neither speak casually about weighty matters, nor solemnly about trivial ones," warns Aristotle. A tuxedo is inappropriate for a picnic just as "ain't" or "cute" is inappropriate for an essay on nuclear diarmament. Words and phrases must come out of and be appropriate for the subject, the occasion, and the audience.

Level of Style

The classical rhetoricians delineated three kinds of style—the grand style, the middle style, and the plain style. Aristotle told his students that every kind of rhetorical style is capable of being used "in season or out of season." They warned against the too grand style calling it "swollen," or the too plain style which when misused they called "meagre," and "dry and bloodless." The middle style used inappropriately they called "slack, without sinews and joints . . . drifting."

A contemporary example of "swollen" language is found in the responses received by a plumber who wrote to the National Bureau of Standards. He said he found that hydrochloric acid opens plugged pipes quickly and asked whether it was a good thing for a plumber to use. A scientist at the Bureau replied as follows:

> The uncertain reactive processes of hydrochloric acid place pipe in jeopardy when alkalinity is involved. The efficiency of the solution is indisputable, but the corrosive residue is incompatible with metallic permanence.

The plumber wrote back, thanking the Bureau for telling him that his method was all right. The scientist was disturbed about the misunderstanding and showed the correspondence to his boss—another scientist—who immediately wrote the plumber.

> Hydrochloric acid generates a toxic and noxious residue which will produce submuriate invalidating reactions. Consequently, some alternative procedure is preferable.

The plumber wrote back and said he agreed with the Bureau—hydrochloric acid works just fine. Greatly disturbed, the two scientists took their problem to the top boss. The next day the plumber received this telegram:

> Don't use hydrochloric acid. It eats the hell out of the pipes.

Today rhetoricians speak of formal and informal styles. The former is characterized by more advanced vocabulary, longer, more complex sentences, use of *one* instead of *you*, and is appropriate for more formal occasions such as lectures, scholarly papers, or ceremonial addresses. The informal style has features such as contractions, the use of the first and second person pronouns *I* and *you*, simpler vocabulary, and shorter sentences. It is appropriate for informal essays and certain kinds of letters. The choice of style is ultimately determined by the relationship between you and the reader, the nature of the occasion, and equally important, the way you wish to present yourself on that occasion to that reader. A letter applying for a position would be formal while a letter to a friend would be informal.

The following letter by Professor Robert Frye, an accomplished stylist, was written for his students. It falls somewhere between the formal and informal style while maintaining the professor-student relationship and the teaching-learning situation. What words and phrases establish that relationship? How would you characterize this particular relationship and teaching situation?

> Dear Daphne and all:
>
> You may recall that in my last letter to you we were visiting, you and I, about my partiality for letters. They provide, among other pleasures (I almost wrote things), a means for me to go fishing in my sea of memory, for, having captured out of time a special experience in a letter, I can, whenever I please, call that experience back and make it as real as it ever was. I am a different person now than I was when first I used loops and curves and squiggles on a page to hold that event, that incident, and I find it fun and educational to mingle my present self with my earlier self speaking in a letter. There is a kind of community in this experience of selves, and there is joy in it. Perhps this communion is what John Donne had in mind when he wrote that "letters mingle souls."

Contrast this personal letter dotted with the first person *I* with the formal style in the following excerpt.

> It is evident that education, from the lowest to the highest levels, was conceived as preparing the youngster for participation in a society in which he or she now had a greater and more personal

stake. One was to be "developed" as an individual—though this meant just about everything *but* preparation for a livelihood. In fact, this development as an individual was, in the general education sense, precisely to help make one a better citizen, one who understood his or her rights and obligations but who could also live up to the demands of these privileges and duties.

In this excerpt there is no *I*. The writer's voice is not obviously present as in Frye's letter, nor is the reader directly addressed through the pronoun *you*. The formal, impersonal *one* is substituted. How would you characterize the writer, the audience, and the occasion based on the style of this article?

Choosing styles to suit the audience and the occasion is one of the spoken language abilities characteristic of all human beings in all societies. You do not use the same words and phrases in talking with your grandmother that you would use to a friend. We unconsciously alter our language to fit the particular situation. In writing we need to adjust to different styles more consciously since the audience may be remote. You need to write with the audience and the occasion firmly in mind and the appropriate words and sentences will fall more easily into place. The following are a few conscious stylistic choices you should consider as you choose your words.

Stylistic Choices

All writers have a number of stylistic choices that are made on the basis of three considerations: the ethical stance of the writer, the subject matter, and the audience and occasion for which they are writing. What follows is a description of some of those choices.

Colloquialisms Colloquialisms are words and phrases that are commonly found in spoken language and very informal written language. They include such devices as contractions (*I'd* rather, *I'd* do it), slang expressions such as *hang out*, and exaggerated adjectives such as *tremendous* or *great*. Colloquialisms are more appropriate for informal than formal writing.

Localisms Localisms are words characteristic of a certain geographical area. A person who writes about *tonic* as meaning any kind of soft drink may well be misunderstood in the Midwest, while a Midwesterner who uses *pop* in the same context may be equally obscure to residents of other parts of the country. Such expressions, while adding color, may not be understood by an audience outside of the region where they are used. How many people outside of Texas know that a *tank* is a pond?

Often, speakers and writers are unaware of the local features in their own speech, but as they travel and read in ever-widening circles awareness develops. In writing you need to use localisms with discrimination. Generally, localisms are appropriate when you are establishing regional character or local color, or when writing for a local audience; in most other cases they should be avoided.

Slang Slang expressions are colorful words and phrases often used by speakers to identify them as part of a group. Thus teenagers, or students at a certain high school, or members of an occupational group such as waiters or academics will develop their own slang expressions. Such expressions not only identify them as members of a group, they also serve to exclude outsiders. Slang expressions are sometimes short-lived and thus understandable to a limited geographical, occupational, or age group. For example, *jellying* was the 1930 counterpart of the contemporary *hanging out*. Today *jellying* is not only quaint and comic but, more important, incomprehensible to most people. Consequently, the use of slang in writing is best limited to informal letters to friends.

Jargon Jargon is the highly technical language of a specialized group. Technical language is appropriate in writing for these specialized audiences but would likely confuse a general audience. Linguists, for example, make careful distinctions between an "illocutionary act" and a "perlocutionary act." In an article directed to that group, such words carry distinctive meanings. The fault is when such terminology is picked up and used by writers who do not understand the specialized meanings and who use them simply to impress an audience rather than to convey meaning. Such usage is jargon and should be avoided.

Clichés Clichés are words and expressions that were once vivid and full of meaning, but like many good expressions are so overused that they have lost their meaning altogether. They go in one ear and out the other (a cliché in itself). Often metaphors or comparisons that were once effective become clichés. Some of the more common clichés include:

> busy as a bee
> all's well that ends well
> as honest as the day is long
> stiff as a poker

Other clichés include such phrases as "at this point in time," and the overused "in this modern world." Such phrases can unnecessarily aggravate your readers. They are acceptable in informal written or spoken language, but when the meaning of your words is important, clichés are not usually effective because they distract your readers.

Sexist Language

Sexist language is not appropriate in contemporary writing. The sensitive reader may have noticed that many of the quotations from classical rhetoric use the generic *he*—the singular masculine pronoun—for both men and women. Such practice was common in the classical period because women were usually confined to the roles of wife and mother and were denied an education. So orators, rhetoricians, and students were in fact mostly male. Because this is no longer the case, such usage, as exemplified in the following sentences, is neither correct nor appropriate in modern English.

Every student should turn in *his* exam promptly.

A doctor has a great deal invested in *his* education.

Each lawyer signed *his* name in the register.

Every elementary teacher found *her* classroom.

The average nurse is concerned about *her* patients.

Through such use, students, doctors, and lawyers are stereotyped as male, and nurses and elementary school teachers as female. Because in today's world there are many female students, doctors, and lawyers and many male elementary school teachers and nurses, you should avoid such usage.

Sometimes writers use *his or her* for the generic *his*:

Every student should turn in *his or her* exam promptly.

This solution is sometimes stylistically awkward and may detract from your primary message. Therefore, you should use it sparingly.

You can best avoid the sexist language in the above examples by recasting the subject in the plural.

Students should turn in *their* exams promptly.

Doctors have a great deal invested in *their* education.

All the *lawyers* signed *their* names in the register.

The elementary *teachers* all found *their* classrooms.

Average *nurses* are concerned about *their* patients.

It is also important that roles and personal characteristics not be characterized by sex.

No one under the influence of alcohol should drive a car. *He* should ask a friend to take *him* home.

When a person goes to the grocery store, *she* should shop from a prepared list.

Such sentences are unfair to both sexes. You can avoid the problem by recasting these sentences in the plural.

People who drink should never drive. *They* should ask a friend to drive them home.

Shoppers should take carefully prepared lists to the grocery store.

Finally you should make an effort to avoid such terms as *chairman* and *salesman* and substitute *person*.

The chair*person* called the meeting to order.

Many readers expect writers to use nonsexist language. The most important consideration is finally an ethical concern. The use of sexist language marks the writer as either sexist or ignorant of contemporary writing conventions and may, in effect, destroy credibility at the outset.

The following essay by Nan Desuka is clearly and carefully organized. Can you pick out the methods that she uses to make her writing clear and coherent? Signposts, key words, transitions? Can you identify her audience by her stylistic choices? How does her language add to her credibility? How does she avoid sexist language?

WHY HANDGUNS MUST BE OUTLAWED

NAN DESUKA

"Guns don't kill people—criminals do." That's a powerful slogan, much   1
more powerful than its alternate version, "Guns don't kill people—people kill people." But this second version, though less effective, is much nearer to the whole truth. Although accurate statistics are hard to come by, and even harder to interpret, it seems indisputable that large

numbers of people—not just criminals—kill, with a handgun, other people. Scarcely a day goes by without a newspaper in any large city reporting that a child has found a gun—kept by the child's parents for self-protection—and has, in playing with this new-found toy, killed himself or a playmate. Or we read of a storekeeper, trying to protect himself during a robbery, who inadvertently shoots an innocent customer. These killers are not, in any reasonable sense of the word, criminals. They are just people who happen to kill people. No wonder the gun lobby prefers the first version of the slogan, "Guns don't kill people—criminals do." This version suggests that the only problem is criminals, not you or me, or our children, and certainly not the members of the National Rifle Association.

Those of us who want strict control of handguns—for me that means 2 the outlawing of handguns, except to the police and related service units—have not been able to come up with a slogan equal in power to "Guns don't kill people—criminals do." The best we have been able to come up with is a mildly amusing bumper sticker showing a teddy bear, with the words "Defend your right to arm bears." Humor can be a powerful weapon (even in writing *on behalf of* gun control, one slips into using the imagery of force), and our playful bumper sticker somehow deflates the self-righteousness of the gun lobby, but doesn't equal the power (again the imagery of force) of "Guns don't kill people—criminals do." For one thing, the effective alliteration of *"c*riminals" and *"k*ill" binds the two words, making everything so terribly simple. Criminals kill; when there are no criminals, there will be no deaths from guns.

But this notion won't do. Despite the uncertainty of some statistical 3 evidence, everyone knows, or should know, that only about 30 percent of murders are committed by robbers or rapists (Kates, 1978). For the most part the victims of handguns know their assailants well. These victims are women killed by jealous husbands, or they are the women's lovers; or they are drinking buddies who get into a violent argument; or they are innocent people who get shot by disgruntled (and probably demented) employees or fellow workers who have (or imagine) a grudge. Or they are, as I've already said, bystanders at a robbery, killed by a storekeeper. Or they are children playing with their father's gun.

Of course this is not the whole story. Hardened criminals also have 4 guns, and they use them. The murders committed by robbers and rapists are what give credence to Barry Goldwater's quip, "We have a crime problem in this country, not a gun problem" (1975, p. 186). But here again the half-truth of a slogan is used to mislead, used to direct attention away from a national tragedy. Different sources issue different statistics, but a conservative estimate is that handguns annually murder at least 15,000 Americans, accidentally kill at least another 3,000, and wound at least another 100,000. Handguns are easily available, both to criminals and to decent people who believe they need a gun in order to protect themselves from criminals. The decent people, unfortunately, have good cause to believe they need protection. Many parts of many cities are utterly unsafe, and even the tiniest village may harbor a murderer. Senator Goldwater is right in saying there is a crime problem (that's the truth of his half-truth), but he is wrong in saying there is not also a gun problem.

Surely the homicide rate would markedly decrease if handguns were   5
outlawed. The FBI reports (*Uniform Crime Reports*, 1985) that more than 60 percent of all murders are caused by guns, and handguns are involved in more than 70 percent of these. Surely many, even most, of these handgun killings would not occur if the killer had to use a rifle, club, or knife. Of course violent lovers, angry drunks, and deranged employees would still flail out with knives or baseball bats, but some of their victims would be able to run away, with few or no injuries, and most of those who could not run away would nevertheless survive, badly injured but at least alive. But if handguns are outlawed, we are told, responsible citizens will have no way to protect themselves from criminals. First, one should remember that at least 90 percent of America's burglaries are committed when no one is at home. The householder's gun, if he or she has one, is in a drawer of the bedside table, and the gun gets lifted along with the jewelry, adding one more gun to the estimated 100,000 handguns annually stolen from law-abiding citizens (Shield, 1981). Second, if the householder is at home, and attempts to use the gun, he or she is more likely to get killed or wounded than to kill or deter the intruder. Another way of looking at this last point is to recall that for every burglar who is halted by the sight of a handgun, four innocent people are killed by handgun accidents.

Because handguns are not accurate beyond ten or fifteen feet, they are   6
not the weapons of sportsmen. Their sole purpose is to kill or at least to disable a person at close range. But only a minority of persons killed with these weapons are criminals. Since handguns chiefly destroy the inno-cent, they must be outlawed—not simply controlled more strictly, but outlawed—to all except to law-enforcement officials. Attempts to control handguns are costly and ineffective, but even if they were cheap and effective stricter controls would not take handguns out of circulation among criminals, because licensed guns are stolen from homeowners and shopkeepers, and thus fall into criminal hands. According to Wright, Rossi, and Daly (1983, p. 181), about 40 percent of the handguns used in crimes are stolen, chiefly from homes that the guns were supposed to protect.

The National Rifle Association is fond of quoting a University of   7
Wisconsin study that says, "gun control laws have no individual or collec-tive effect in reducing the rate of violent crime" (cited in Smith, 1981, p. 17). Agreed—but what if handguns were not available? What if the

manufacturer of handguns is severely regulated, and if the guns may be sold only to police officers? True, even if handguns are outlawed, some criminals will manage to get them, but surely fewer petty criminals will have guns. It is simply untrue for the gun lobby to assert that all criminals—since they are by definition lawbreakers—will find ways to get handguns. For the most part, if the sale of handguns is outlawed, guns won't be available, and fewer criminals will have guns. And if fewer criminals have guns, there is every reason to believe that violent crime will decline. A youth armed only with a knife is less likely to try to rob a store than if he is armed with a gun. This commonsense reasoning does not imply that if handguns are outlawed crime will suddenly disappear, or even that an especially repulsive crime such as rape will decrease markedly. A rapist armed with a knife probably has a sufficient weapon. But *some* violent crime will almost surely decrease. And the decrease will probably be significant if in addition to outlawing handguns, severe mandatory punishments are imposed on a person who is found to possess one, and even severer mandatory punishments are imposed on a person who used one while committing a crime. Again, none of this activity will solve "the crime problem," but neither will anything else, including the "get tough with criminals" attitude of Senator Goldwater. And of course any attempt to reduce crime (one cannot realistically talk of "solving" the crime problem) will have to pay attention to our systems of bail, plea bargaining, and parole—but outlawing handguns will help.

What will the cost be? First, to take "cost" in its most literal sense, there 8 will be the cost of reimbursing gun owners for the weapons they surrender. Every owner of a handgun ought to be paid the fair market value of the weapon. Since the number of handguns is estimated to be between fifty million and ninety million, the cost will be considerable, but it will be far less than the costs—both in money and in sorrow—that result from deaths due to handguns.

Second, one may well ask if there is another sort of cost, a cost to our 9 liberty, to our constitutional rights. The issue is important, and persons who advocate abolition of handguns are blind or thoughtless if they simply brush it off. On the other hand, opponents of gun control do all of us a disservice by insisting over and over that the Constitution guarantees "the right to bear arms." The Second Amendment in the Bill of Rights says this: "A well-regulated militia being necessary to the security of a free State, the right of the people to keep and bear arms shall not be infringed." It is true that the Founding Fathers, mindful of the British attempt to disarm the colonists, viewed the presence of "a well-regulated militia" as a safeguard of democracy. Their intention is quite clear, even to one who has not read Stephen P. Halbrook's *That Every Man Be Armed*, an exhaustive argument in favor of the right to bear arms. There can be no doubt that the framers of the Constitution and the Bill of Rights believed that armed insurrection was a justifiable means of countering oppression and tyranny. The Second Amendment may be fairly para-phrased thus: "*Because* an organized militia is necessary to the security of the State, the people have the right to possess weapons." But the owners of handguns are not members of a well-regulated militia. Furthermore, nothing in the proposal to ban handguns would deprive citizens of their rifles or other long-arm guns. All handguns, however, even large ones, should be banned. "Let's face it," Guenther W. Bachmann (a vice presi-dent of Smith and Wesson) admits, "they are all concealable" (Kennedy, 1981, p. 6). In any case, it is a fact that when gun-control laws have been tested in the courts, they have been found to be constitutional. The constitutional argument was worth making, but the question must now be regarded as settled, not only by the courts but by anyone who reads the Second Amendment.

Still, is it not true that "If guns are outlawed, only outlaws will have   10 guns"? This is yet another powerful slogan, but it is simply not true. First, we are talking not about "guns" but about handguns. Second, the police will have guns—handguns and others—and these trained professionals are the ones on whom we must rely for protection against criminals. Of course the police have not eradicated crime; and of course we must hope that in the future they will be more successful in protecting all citizens. But we must also recognize that the efforts of private citizens to protect themselves with handguns has chiefly taken the lives not of criminals but of innocent people.

In this essay, the author develops the thesis that handguns "should be outlawed—not simply controlled more strictly, but outlawed, to all ex-cept to law-enforcement officers," largely through refuting the argu-ments of her opponents. She begins with a slogan used by the National Rifle Association in their effort to retain citizen control of handguns and refutes it by pointing out the fallacy in the slogan. What is this fallacy?

She makes use of statistics and leads the reader through the essay by using the words *first* and *second* in three different places. Can you point these out? How do they help to organize the essay? Can you analyze the way in which she moves from paragraph to paragraph? Are the transi-tions smooth?

What are the key words in the essay? How does she handle the repeti-tion of these key words?

How does Desuka handle nonsexist language? She is not consistent in such usage. Can you find any instances where the language demonstrates a sexist attitude?

Questions to Consider

1. To increase your vocabulary, you may wish to try a game called "The Dictionary Game" or "Fictionary." You should bring a dictionary to class and begin by assembling into groups of no more than four players each, designating one player of the four to be "it" for the first round. That player should then choose a word from the dictionary that no one else in the group will know the meaning of, announce the word to the group, spell it, and indicate its part of speech. The other members of the group should then make up what they think will be a believable definition for the word, write the "definition" anonymously on a slip of paper (make sure the slips of paper are of uniform size for all the contributors), and pass them to the player designated as "it," who mixes up the slips (together with a slip on which is secretly written the actual definition of the word) and reads all four definitions to the other players. The other three players then vote on which definition they think is the genuine one.

Each vote in favor of an incorrect definition results in two points for the player providing the incorrect definition and one point for the player responsible for the original word; each vote in favor of the correct definition results in one vote for the player who so voted for it. Because the object of the game is to accrue more points than any other member of the group, that player having the most points after each has had a turn to be "it" wins.

(Hint: In part, winning this game depends upon bluffing the other players into believing that a false definition is the real one, and in part it depends on disguising the real one so that it is not immediately recognized. As a result, players whose turn it is to make up a definition should try to word it to sound as much like a dictionary definition as they can. Those designated as "it," on the other hand, should try to express the actual dictionary definition (accurately, of course) in their own words while retaining as much of the dictionary "style" as possible. A definition that appears too casually written will be as much a dead giveaway as one that appears suspiciously as though it were the product of editors formally trained in writing dictionaries.)

2. Examine the action verbs in one of your essays. Try to substitute more specific verbs when possible. Then discuss how your impression of the agent and the action described changes accordingly.

3. In any essay, if your paragraphs are coherent, you should be able to reconstruct them even when the sentences are jumbled. Try reconstructing the following paragraph by indicating the order in which the sentences are to appear.

_____1.   In any case, the child who has made the mistake knows it, and feels foolish, stupid, and ashamed, just as any of us would in the same situation.

_____2.   This means that when they don't know a word, they are going to make a mistake, right in front of everyone.

_____3.   From the very beginning of school we make books and reading a constant source of possible failure and public humiliation.

_____4.   Perhaps the teacher will say, "Are you sure?" or ask someone else.

_____5.   When children are little, we make them read aloud, before the teacher and other children, so that we can be sure they "know" all the words they are reading.

_____6.   Perhaps some of the other children will begin to wave their hands and say, "Ooooh! O-o-o-oh!"

_____7.   Or perhaps, if the teacher is kindly, she will just smile a sweet, sad smile—often one of the most painful punishments a child can suffer in school.

_____8.   Instantly they are made to realize that they have done something wrong.

_____9.   Perhaps they will just giggle, or nudge each other, or make a face.

4. As an exercise to remind yourself of the importance of titles for your own writing and for the material you read, examine the following titles of actual essays and try to anticipate from them what the essay will be about, what questions it will answer, or what tone the writer will adopt. Then consider whether you think the titles are provocative enough to encourage you to read the essay.

A.   "High School and Other Forms of Madness," Pauline Kael

B.   "Four-Letter Words Can Hurt You," Barbara Lawrence

C.   "The Black and White Truth About Basketball," Jeff Greenfield

D.   "Sinners in the Hands of an Angry God," Jonathan Edwards

E.   "A Proposal to Abolish Grading," Paul Goodman

F.   "The Rewards of Living a Solitary Life," May Sarton

Now examine the titles of a few of your own essays and ask the same questions about them.

5. Compare the styles of the following paragraphs. What clues do these styles provide as to the authors' subject, context, audience, and purpose?

A. You've all heard the advertising jingle "everybody doesn't like something but nobody doesn't like Sara Lee"—right?

Well, forget it. There is somebody who doesn't like Sara Lee and his name is Sen. James Abourezk.

Now, it isn't just Sara Lee who bugs Sen. Abourezk, he's also down on the folks at Pepperidge Farm, Wonder Bread, Dad's Root Beer, Mama Celeste's Pizza, Minute Maid, and Madria-Madria Sangria, among others.

The reason? Well, the South Dakota Democrat thinks that consumers are being tricked because these businesses "deceptively advertise themselves as small business or family-owned business" when they are not.

B. It is probably fair to say that most present-day Americans show rather more respect for the dictionary than they do for the Bible. It is significant that we speak of "the dictionary" rather than "a dictionary" as if there were only one. When we say, "The dictionary says so," we feel that we have settled the matter once and for all, that we have carried the appeal to the final authority. The popular feeling seems to be that the dictionary editor visits heaven every few years to receive the material for the next edition.

C. There are two kinds of propaganda—rational propaganda in favor of action that is consonant with the enlightened self-interest of those who make it and those to whom it is addressed, and non-rational propaganda that is not consonant with anybody's enlightened self-interest, but is dictated by, and appeals to, passion. . . . Propaganda in favor of action that is consonant with enlightened self-interest appeals to reason by means of logical arguments based upon the best available evidence fully and honestly set forth. Propaganda in favor of action dictated by the impulses that are below self-interest offers false, garbled or incomplete evidence, avoids logical argument and seeks to influence its victims by the mere repetition of catchwords, by the furious denunciation of foreign or domestic scapegoats, and by cunningly associating the lowest passions with the highest ideals, so that atrocities come to be perpetrated in the name of God and the most cynical kind of *Realpolitik* is treated as a matter of religious principle and patriotic duty.

6. Make a list on the board of all the slang terms you can think of that describe women. Try the same exercise for slang terms used to refer to men. On the basis of these lists, can you conclude anything about the way slang words function and, perhaps, why some consider them offensive?

7. Make a list on the board of all of the clichés you can think of. You may be surprised by how many you are able to identify and by how readily they come to mind. This list may come in handy for one of the writing exercises described below.

Suggestions for Writing

1. Those of you who have seen the program "Not Necessarily the News" on cable television are no doubt familiar with a segment of that program devoted to "sniglets." A "sniglet" is a word made up and submitted by a member of the viewing audience to denote something that no word currently in our language adequately expresses such as ambipathetic or jazzology.

For this assignment, make up your own "sniglet" (you may find the list of prefixes and suffixes provided in this chapter useful), and using the entries in your dictionary as models, provide a typical dictionary entry for it, including the word's syllabification, pronunciation, etymology, part of speech label, definition, and examples of the word used in context. Then, you might write a paragraph arguing for the inclusion of your new word in the dictionary. (This part of the assignment could be expanded to an essay if you include in your argument a convincing demonstration that other words denoting similar meanings are ultimately incapable of expressing exactly the same meaning as your new word.)

2. Try to write a short essay demonstrating that no two synonyms mean exactly the same thing, supporting your conclusion by using words from one of the following groups:

A. beautiful, lovely, pretty, fair, gorgeous

B. fat, stout, obese, chubby, stocky

C. considerate, kind, philanthropic, good-natured, well-meaning

D. child, kid, youngster, young person, juvenile

E. student, pupil, scholar, classmate, trainee

    F. teacher, educator, instructor, professor, mentor

    G. associate, colleague, coworker, partner, accomplice

You might begin your essay by indicating the meaning shared by the words in its group, and then devote the body paragraphs to distinguishing the meaning of each word from the other words of that group. In addition to providing the denotation and connotation distinguishing each word, try using the words in some example sentences to clarify your points.

    3. Choose an essay from a magazine or book and write a paragraph in which you identify and illustrate the different methods by which the writer makes the essay coherent.

    4. Write a paragraph addressed to a future employer in which you identify and explain your greatest fault; then write a second paragraph describing that fault to your closest friend. How do the two versions differ? To what extent do the different audiences account for those differences?

    5. Write a paragraph in which you explain the meaning of some particular localism or word that has special meaning for you (or you and your family alone). In addition to a definition, provide examples of the word's use in context and, perhaps, its etymology (or an explanation of the word's history that accounts for its particular meaning) if you know it; if not, you might make up an etymology for the word that seems plausible. Again, this assignment could be expanded into an essay in which you explain several localisms or words having special meaning for you and your family.

    6. Choose a technical term used by the experts in your major and write a paragraph defining it for an audience made up of people outside the discipline.

    7. Write a page-long narrative of some personal experience using as many clichés as you can. Then read it to the class or to your workshop group and see whether they can identify them all.

Exercises in Revision

    1. Exchange one of your essays with another student in the class. Read your classmate's essay carefully, circling any unnecessary wordiness or any need for more specific word choice. Return the essays and rewrite your own essay to eliminate the problems that are circled if you think such changes are appropriate. Defend your reasons for not making certain changes.

2. Find an advertisment for a product you are familiar with that relies primarily upon written copy rather than a picture to sell the product. Identify all of the abstract words you can find, and substitute for them words that you believe are more specific (and perhaps, more accurate.) Attach a paragraph to your revision in which you speculate about why the abstract language you detected was initially used in the original advertisement.

3. Exchange one of your essays with another student. Then examine that essay, noting all of the methods the author has used to ensure coherence. Suggest other methods the author could use to improve the coherence of his or her essay.

4. Choose a previous essay you've written and annotate it in the margins to indicate the methods you used to make it coherent. As you deem necessary, write sentences to improve the coherence of the essay.

For a Commonplace Book

1. Begin to pay attention to titles and copy down in your commonplace book any that you find particularly memorable and effective. In a brief note appended to each, explain why you've included it.

2. Find and copy three examples of transition paragraphs from your own reading. Try to determine and indicate what functions they serve.

Chapter 11

Using Figures of Speech

Embellishment, the fourth quality of good style, is, in classical rhetoric, the study of the figures of speech—the ways in which we give language a conformation different from the obvious or ordinary. Quintilian divided figures of speech into two kinds: *tropes* in which *meaning* is altered from the usual or expected, and *schemes* in which *word order* is altered from the usual or expected.

In the following excerpt Rachel Carson uses figurative language to describe an evergreen forest that she often walked through.

> One of my own favorite approaches to a rocky seacoast is by a rough path through an evergreen forest that has its own peculiar enchant-ment. It is usually an early morning tide that takes me along that forest path, so that the light is still pale and fog drifts in from the sea beyond. It is almost a ghost forest, for among the living spruce and balsam are many dead trees—some still erect, some sagging earthward, some lying on the floor of the forest. All the trees, the living and the dead, are clothed with green and silver crusts of lichens. Tufts of the bearded lichen or old man's beard hang from the branches like bits of sea mist tangled there. Green woodland mosses and a yielding carpet of reindeer moss cover the ground. In the quiet of that place even the voice of the surf is reduced to a whispered echo and the sounds of the forest are but the ghosts of sound—the faint sighing of evergreen needles in the moving air; the creaks and heavier groans of half-fallen trees resting against their neighbors and rubbing bark against bark; the light rattling fall of a dead branch broken under the feet of a squirrel and sent bounding and ricocheting earthward.
>
> But finally the path emerges from the dimness of the deeper forest and comes to a place where the sound of surf rises above the forest sounds—the hollow boom of the sea, rhythmic and insistent, striking against the rocks, falling away, rising again.

As Carson describes the trees, they become like people—a trope that we call personification. They are "living and dead," "clothed with green and silver crusts of lichens." They "sigh"; they "groan." The voice of the surf is a "whispered echo"; the evergreen needles "sigh." She compares the forest to a ghost forest with the "living spruce and balsam" among the "many dead trees" in a metaphor that pervades the passage. She uses onomatopoeia—words that sound like what they mean—and alliteration and assonance—the repetition of similar sounds—in the hush of the repeated *s* sounds. The "voice of the surf" is a "whispered echo and the sounds of the forest are but the ghosts of sound." The *s* sounds are carried through the paragraph until the last few lines when the quiet is shattered by the abrupt noise of the *d, b,* and *t* sounds in the "rattling fall" of a "dead broken branch" that is sent "bounding and ricocheting earth-ward." In this short excerpt, Carson uses at least five of the tropes that will be described in this chapter.

In addition, she uses a number of schemes—unusual word orders. She uses anastrophe in a reversal of subject and verb in "among the living spruces are many dead trees—some erect, some sagging earthward, some lying on the floor of the forest." In this single sentence she uses five figures of speech characteristic of unusual word order in reversing the subject verb order, in placing the adjectives describing the dead trees after the noun and in apposition to them, and in the repetition of the word "some" that introduces the series of parallel phrases that move the dead trees in climactic order from those that are "erect" to those that are "sagging" to those "lying on the floor of the forest."

The classical rhetoricians recognized the power and effectiveness of figurative language that builds on the disruption of the expected meaning and the disordering of the usual sentence construction. They felt that figurative language not only relieved monotony but also helped an argument "steal its way into the minds of the audience." Quintilian argues that just as in sword play, sidestrokes and feints are more effective than direct blows and straightforward thrusts, so in rhetoric figures of speech commend what we say to those who hear us whether we seek approval for our characters or favor for our cause (*Institutio Oratoria* 9.1.20-21).

Figures are closely connected to the *ethos*, *logos*, and *pathos* of argument. The skillful use of figures wins approval for us as writers and favor for our arguments. Certain figures stir the interest and excitement of our readers while others are related to the strategies of the *topics*. Metaphor and simile, comparing one thing to another, are related to comparison, while irony, saying one thing and meaning the opposite, involves contrast. So in many ways the figures demonstrate the close relation between thought and expression inherent in classical rhetoric.

TROPES

Tropes involve alterations in the usual meanings of words or phrases. For example, the trees in Carson's writing became people who sighed, whispered, and died. Perhaps the most familiar trope is the pun, a play on the meaning of words. The classical rhetoricians, in their fascination with language and words distinguished three different kinds of pun. They recognized the repetition of a single word in two different senses as one kind of pun.

"But if we don't hang together, we will hang separately"—Benjamin Franklin.

They also recognized a kind of pun that plays on words that sound alike but are different in meaning.

He couldn't get his bearings straight in the Bering Straits.

Finally, they recognized the kind of pun that uses a single word with two different meanings within the context of the sentence.

> The photograph that appeared in the *London Times* caused a royal flush.

> The ink, like our pig, keeps running out of the pen.

> Our investment in cattle was our steak in the future.

Puns may be used effectively in writing, especially in titles. A student used "The Grim Fairy Tale" as a title for a theme about battered women that played on the words Grimm and grim. "Reading, Writing, and Athletics" is another title that plays on the familiar phrase "reading, writing, and arithmetic."

You can use this kind of play on words from familiar quotations to evoke images that reinforce what you are saying, as in the following sentence from Martin Luther King, Jr.'s "I Have a Dream" speech.

> Five score years ago, a great American, in whose symbolic shadow we stand today, signed the Emancipation Proclamation.

As King reminds his audience of Abraham Lincoln by *what* he says, he reinforces that reminder by *how* he says it—playing on the familiar opening words of the *Gettysburg Address*: "Four score and seven years ago. . . ."

Tropes include those usages that are most familiar in the study of poetry: metaphor, simile, metonymy, and synecdoche. But the classical rhetoricians recognized that these devices were also common in good prose and effective speaking. They are widely used, perhaps unconsciously, in conversation to make a meaning clear or to color or enliven spoken language. Often the short-lived slang expressions discussed in the last chapter rely on metaphor. Calling a person by the uncomplimentary name of "turtle" attributes to that person the slow, plodding, stupid-looking demeanor of that animal.

The tropes are closely related to the topic of comparison and contrast discussed in Chapter 5 and in comparing one thing to another present to the reader a double image. Thus you reinforce or enlighten one meaning by bringing in additional images. What follows are examples of the most familiar tropes.

Metaphor

The most important and widely used trope, in both prose and poetry is metaphor. A metaphor is an implied comparison between two unlike things. Thus in the sentence, "John is a lamb," the writer attributes to

John all the qualities of a lamb—gentleness, docility, and innocent sweetness. Many common words are metaphors. When a writer says that a person "growled" or "barked a reply" that person is being identified with an animal. Ordinarily, only animate things can be killed, so in the terms, "killing time" or "killing an exam" there is an implied comparison or metaphor. As such words become more commonly used, however, they lose their metaphoric sense and become an established part of the vocabulary.

Metaphor adds to the copiousness of language by providing meanings where there is no literal term or where the transferred term makes the meaning clearer than the literal term, according to Quintilian (*Institutio Oratoria* 8.6.6). In the following metaphor John McPhee describes running the rapids in a raft. In calling "ridgelines of water" "cordilleras," he implies a comparison between the rapids and chains of mountains.

> The raft shudders across the ridgelines of water cordilleras to crash softly into the valleys beyond. Space and time in there are something other than they are out here. Tents of water form overhead, to break apart in rags.

In the second metaphor he compares the water to a tent that breaks apart "in rags." Often metaphors are carried beyond single words and sentences. In the Carson example, the metaphor of comparing the forest to a ghost forest is carried through the paragraph. In the following excerpt, Martin Luther King compares a 1963 civil rights demonstration to a financial transaction.

> In a sense we have come to our nation's capital to cash a check. When the architects of our republic wrote the magnificent words of the Constitution and the Declaration of Independence, they were signing a promissory note to which every American was to fall heir. This note was a promise that all men would be guaranteed the unalienable rights of life, liberty, and the pursuit of happiness.
>
> It is obvious today that America has defaulted on this promissory note insofar as her citizens of color are concerned. Instead of honoring this sacred obligation, America has given the Negro people a bad check; a check which has come back marked "insufficient funds." But we refuse to believe that the bank of justice is bankrupt. We refuse to believe that there are insufficient funds in the great vaults of opportunity of this nation. So we have come to cash this check—a check that will give us upon demand the riches of freedom and the security of justice. . . .

Which words and phrases reinforce the extended metaphor? If you reworded these two paragraphs without the metaphor would they be as effective?

Simile

A simile is an explicit comparison between two unlike things signaled by the use of *like* or *as*. Thus "John is a lamb" is a metaphor while "John is like a lamb" is a simile. In the following example, the author describes driving on a snow-covered highway with large trucks, which he compares to giants.

> One minute the road feels firm, and the next the driver is sliding over it, light as a feather, in a panic, wondering what the heavy trailer trucks coming up from the rear are going to do. The trucks are like giants when you have to pass them, not at sixty or seventy as you do when the road is dry, but at twenty-five and thirty.

In comparing the trucks to giants, the writer brings in the idea not only of size, but also of strength, inexorable movement, and malevolence. Comparing the trucks to trees would convey the sense of size, but not of movement. Effective metaphors enrich meaning by bringing in all the meanings and connotations clustered around a word or image that the writer hopes to convey.

To practice thinking in terms of metaphor, you might try comparing some familiar objects or scenes to other things. For instance, when you wake up, what does the morning light look like? What does the laundry basket of dirty clothes smell like, or what does that morning cereal taste like? or look like?

Synecdoche

While metaphor and simile are related to comparison, synecdoche is related to classification and division, discussed in Chapter 4. Translated from Greek, synecdoche means "understanding one thing for another"; thus a part is substituted for the whole, or the species for the genus. Quintilian tells us that one word makes us think of all the things in the class, so "bread" stands for food, "hands" refer to helpers, and the slang expression "wheels" means a car.

In the following passage from his well-known speech, "I Have a Dream," Martin Luther King, Jr., quotes from the Bible and uses a synecdoche in his final sentence: "all flesh shall see it together." He builds to that trope through emphasizing the difference in the first paragraph where he distinguishes between "little black boys and black girls" and "little white boys and white girls." In the synecdoche he goes to the flesh that stands for all human beings, thus bonding black and white together in their shared humanity. While the color of their skin divides them, their flesh binds them together.

I have a dream today.

I have a dream that one day . . . little black boys and black girls will be able to join hands with little white boys and white girls and walk together as sisters and brothers.

I have a dream today.

I have a dream that one day every valley shall be exalted, and every hill and mountain shall be made low, the rough places will be made plain, and the crooked places will be made straight, and the glory of the Lord shall be revealed, and all flesh shall see it together.

In this excerpt, King leads us "to realize many things from one," as he encourages us to think of all humanity by mentioning the flesh that is common to all people and that lies just below the color of the skin.

Metonymy

In metonymy, a figure closely allied to synecdoche, we designate one thing by something closely associated with it. Thus we call the head of the committee the *chair*, the king the *crown*, and the newspaper the *press*.

"He is a man of the cloth." In this common expression, "man of the cloth" is used to designate a priest, because of the customary cloth collar associated with the position.

Personification

In personification, the writer or speaker attributes human qualities to an inanimate object. In the Carson example, the trees became people who are clothed, the surf has a voice, and the evergreen needles sigh. Notice how two students use personification in the following sentences:

The grass is green and neatly cut, and the buildings cast a watchful eye over the clean, quiet campus.

High blood pressure is very real and dangerous, snatching the lives of many people.

In the first example the buildings are depicted as guards casting "a watchful eye" on the campus. In the second example high blood pressure "snatches" lives. You can use personification to give life and motion to an otherwise static scene.

Hyperbole

The literal meaning of hyperbole is exaggeration. As a figure of speech, hyperbole is deliberate exaggeration for emphasis. Richard Selzer, a writer and surgeon, often uses hyperbole in his writing. In the following passage, he describes extracting the larva of a tiny warble fly that is lodged under the skin of a patient.

> Now—thrust—and clamp—and yes. Got him!
> Transmitted to the fingers comes the wild thrashing of the creature. Pinned and wriggling, he is mine. I hear the dry brittle scream of the dragon, and a hatred seizes me, but such a detestation as would make of Iago a drooling sucktit. It is the demented hatred of the victor for the vanquished, the warden for his prisoner. It is the hatred of fear. Within the jaws of my hemostat is the whole of the evil of the world, the dark concentrate itself, and I shall kill it. For mankind. And, in so doing, will open the way into a thousand years of perfect peace. Here is Surgeon as Savior indeed.

Notice that Selzer uses a number of other figures to form the hyperbole. In what way are these a part of the exaggeration? Hyperbole adds drama to an event and excitement to a narrative

In ordinary speech, you may say that you "died laughing" or assert your disgust by remarking that you think you "are going to vomit." These expressions are hyperboles that have found their way into ordinary conversation.

Litotes

The opposite of hyperbole, *litotes* (LIT·o·tes) intensifies an idea by understatement.

> It wasn't my best moment.

> Jim is not the best student in the Western world.

In the following example a politician running for office effectively uses litotes to point out that his opponent has great inherited wealth.

> My opponent is not exactly a rags to riches Horatio Alger type.

Both litotes and hyperbole draw the reader's attention to what you are saying.

Irony

The Greek word from which irony is derived meant "liar" or "dissembler," and in using irony, the writer takes on another voice or role that states the opposite of what is expressed. Quintilian tells us that if the character of the speaker or the nature of the subject is out of keeping with the words, it becomes clear that the speaker means something other than what is said. Thus something that is ironical in one context may be quite true in another (*Institutio Oratoria* 8.6.55). So for two students trudging to class through the pouring rain calling the weather "beautiful" would be irony, but for two farmers after an extended drought, the rain could be truly "beautiful." Consequently, your decision to use irony depends on your understanding of the audience and the subject and the role that you are playing as writer.

One of the most famous examples of irony in the English language is Jonathan Swift's "A Modest Proposal." To understand the irony in this essay, the reader must know that Swift was deeply involved in Irish politics and a great philanthropist and supporter of the Irish people. He was known for his criticism of the unsympathetic and callous attitude that the English Parliament evidenced against the Irish people during a famine.

The excerpt that follows is the first section of that essay. At what point do you realize that Swift is being ironical?

It is a melancholy object to those who walk through this great town, or travel in the country, when they see the streets, the roads and cabin-doors crowded with beggars of the female sex, followed by three, four, or six children, all in rags, and importuning every passenger for an alms. These mothers, instead of being able to work for their honest livelihood, are forced to employ all their time in strolling, to beg sustenance for their helpless infants, who, as they grow up, either turn thieves for want of work, or leave their dear native country to fight for the Pretender in Spain, or sell themselves to the Barbadoes.

I think it is agreed by all parties that this prodigious number of children, in the arms, or on the backs, or at the heels of their mothers, and frequently of their fathers, is in the present deplorable state of the kingdom a very great additional grievance; and therefore whoever could find out a fair, cheap, and easy method of making these children sound and useful members of the commonwealth would deserve so well of the public as to have his statue set up for a preserver of the nation.

But my intention is very far from being confined to provide only for the children of professed beggars; it is of a much greater extent, and shall take in the whole number of infants at a certain age who are born of parents in effect as little able to support them as those who demand our charity in the streets.

As to my own part, having turned my thoughts for many years upon this important subject, and maturely weighed the several schemes of other projectors, I have always found them grossly mistaken in their computation. It is true a child just dropped from its dam may be supported by her milk for a solar year with little other nourishment, at most not above the value of two shillings, which the mother may certainly get, or the value in scraps, by her lawful occupation of begging, and it is exactly at one year old that I propose to provide for them, in such a manner as, instead of being a charge upon their parents, or the parish, or wanting food and raiment for the rest of their lives, they shall, on the contrary, contribute to the feeding and partly to the clothing of many thousands.

There is likewise another great advantage in my scheme, that it will prevent those voluntary abortions, and that horrid practice of women murdering their bastard children, alas, too frequent among us, sacrificing the poor innocent babes, I doubt, more to avoid the expense than the shame, which would move tears and pity in the most savage and inhuman breast.

Would you have known that Swift was being ironical if you had not known him by reputation? What indications do you have that he is playing a role? What values can you assume that he shares with his readers within the context that he was writing? What values does he share with you as a reader? What is Swift's real message? Why is it more meaningful when stated as irony?

For irony to work, you must establish the role that you are playing and write within a known context and value system you share with your reader. In the following passage from an essay on army basic training from the viewpoint of a woman private, this student describes her experiences.

Firing with a chemical suit, usually referred to as MOPP gear, is one of the most enjoyable days—it's well over 100 degrees, and you get to spend your day in a one-inch thick, carbon-lined outfit complete with rubber boots and gloves. After all of this fun stuff comes qualification day.

Both the writer and the reader understand that there is nothing "enjoyable" or "fun" about spending your day in a one-inch thick, carbon-lined outfit in 100 degree weather. How does this student build the sense of irony? Note her use of the words "one of the most enjoyable days," "you get to spend your day," and "all of this fun stuff." At what point do you realize that this writer means something other than what she is saying?

Oxymoron and Paradox

Both oxymoron and paradox involve contradiction. In oxymoron, two contradictory terms or ideas are used together.

Parting is such sweet sorrow.

Extremes meet, and there is no better example than the haughtiness of humility.

Paradox is a statement that appears to be contradictory but, in fact, has some truth.

He worked hard at being lazy.

Frank and explicit—this is the right line to take when you wish to conceal your own mind and to confuse the minds of others.

Rhetorical Questions

Questions are an effective way of engaging the reader in what you are saying and urging that reader into a dialogue. In Chapter 9, we saw how questions can be used to introduce a paper or a section of a paper and how the thesis itself can be stated in a question. The classical rhetoricians were aware of a number of different kinds of questions that could be used to engage the reader in different ways.

Rhetorical questions are commonly defined as those questions that do not really require an answer. Thus when you turn to a friend at a party and ask, "What am I doing here?" you would be very surprised if the answer were, "You are eating potato chips and listening to a band." Actually no answer is expected. But classical rhetoricians went further and recognized that there are different kinds of rhetorical questions, and that each serves quite a different function. They identified and named at least four kinds.

Asking the Reader The Greeks saw this kind of question as a way of taking counsel with the reader. You address the question to your reader expecting that reader to consider the answer.

What would you have done under the same circumstances?

Have you ever felt so much like crying that you actually felt a real lump in your throat?

In this way you directly involve the reader in the subject and guide that reader's attention to what you are going to talk about.

Asking the Writer   In this figure, the question is addressed to the writer, thus suggesting the writer's thinking process.

Was this really what I wanted? I knew it was not what I expected when I enrolled in the program.

With this kind of rhetorical question, you review with the reader the questions that you raised in thinking about your subject. It is a way of talking through an idea with your reader.

Criticizing   In this kind of question, the writer is making a criticism in the form of a question.

How can you be so intolerant?

Why can't you behave?

How can citizens fail to vote?

You can often make a statement or a request by putting it in the form of a question. Such a device varies the monotony of a series of statements or requests and gives them added emphasis.

Asking and Answering   In this kind of rhetorical question, the writer asks a question and then proceeds to answer it. This is a common device in prose, and may serve as a way of organizing a paper or making the writer's method of development clear to the reader.

Why has the incidence of rape increased in our society? Studies show that rape has increased as violence and sex on television has increased.

Sometimes whole papers can be organized by this kind of question. The writer poses questions and then answers them in the course of the paper. Note the following paragraph.

AIDS is a far more pervasive problem than many people are aware of. If we want to become informed we must ask ourselves certain questions. First what is the nature of this illness? Second, how is it contracted and spread? Third, what kind of research into this disease is now being conducted?

This opening paragraph is followed, as you might suspect, by three sections addressing these questions in turn. The first section discusses the nature of AIDS, the second the ways that it can and cannot be contracted, and the third addresses the research that is being done, who is conducting such research, and how it is financed.

Rhetorical questions are a way of involving your reader in what you are saying, a way of stimulating that reader to engage in a dialogue with you. In addition, you may use a question as an alternative way to introduce new ideas or to state a thesis or a topic idea. You might wish to recast statements as questions in order to add variety to your writing and to draw your reader into your subject.

Onomatopoeia

Even though writing and reading are, for the most part, silent activities, sound still plays an important part. There appears to be a reader inner ear that hears and responds to sound patterns in language. Onomatopoeia refers to the use of words whose sound reinforces their meaning, such as *drip, cackle, bang,* and *snarl.* In the following excerpt from "In the Jungle" by Annie Dillard notice how the sounds of the verbs *plodded, clattered, fussed, slid,* and *slapped* reinforce their meaning.

> This lake was wonderful. Herons, egrets, and ibises *plodded* the sawgrass shores, kingfishers and cuckoos *clattered* from sunlight to shade, great turkeylike birds *fussed* in dead branches, and hawks lolled overhead. There was all the time in the world. A turtle *slid* into the water. The boy in the bow of my canoe *slapped* stones at birds with a simple sling, a rubber thong and leather pad.

SCHEMES

Schemes are arrangements of ideas, words, or phrases that are stylistically effective. Often, as in parallelism, the pattern of the words effectively serves to reinforce the meaning.

Patterns that depart from the ordinary or expected pattern are also effective since they relieve monotony and catch the reader's attention. Writers are aware of the reader's expectations and the importance, in most cases, of fulfilling those expectations. Certain schemes, however, gain the reader's attention by not doing the expected, by changing the pattern. It is like going down a familiar flight of steps and finding the bottom step missing. You do not ordinarily think of how to move your feet, how to place them on the tread, how to measure the distance of the risers every time you go down the steps—until the bottom step is missing. Then you are forced to stop, to think, and to notice. In the same way, an arrangement of words, a sentence pattern, a sound pattern, or a meaning that is unusual will force the reader to stop, to think, and to notice what you are saying.

Cicero defined the schemes as the "gestures of language"—the poetic or rhetorical alteration from the simple and obvious expression—and suggested their use primarily to avoid monotony. The patterns described in the following pages are often used unconsciously by good writers and speakers, and you have undoubtedly used them in your spoken and written language without being aware of them. Becoming aware of them will give you more mastery over them so you can use them consciously and effectively.

Balance

In the following three schemes of balance, the syntactic structure of each sentence supports its meaning. Similar ideas are expressed in similar grammatical structure, contrasting ideas in contrasting grammatical structure, or a series of ideas in climactic order. In these schemes the argument from comparison and contrast discussed in Chapter 5 is stylistically supported.

Parallelism Parallelism expresses similar or related ideas in similar grammatical construction. Not only is this considered an effective measure in prose, but its absence is distracting. Consider the following versions. Which is the more effective?

> There were several reasons that I joined the Guard, the greatest of which being money, but also for a sense of order and regimentation, not to mention the fact that I was curious about the whole affair.

> There were several reasons that I joined the Guard. I had a desire for money, a sense of order and regimentation. And of course, I was curious about the whole affair.

The second version not only eliminates much of the wordiness, but also arranges the ideas in parallel structure.

The following concluding passage from Lincoln's Gettysburg Address makes use of parallelism in the series of clauses introduced by *that*.

It is rather for us to be here dedicated to the great task remaining before us—that from these honored dead we take increased devotion to the cause for which they here gave the last full measure of devotion—that we here highly resolve that the dead shall not have died in vain; that the nation shall, under God, have a new birth of freedom, and that the government of the people, by the people, and for the people, shall not perish from the earth.

Here Lincoln concludes his address by outlining the four tasks that are before the people. He delineates each of these in a clause introduced by "that." The similar syntactic structure emphasizes the equal importance of these tasks that lie before the people.

Chiasmus In *chiasmus*, derived from the Greek letter *chi* (X), the grammatical structure of the first clause or phrase is reversed in the second, sometimes repeating the same words. John Kennedy used this scheme in the long remembered phrases from his first inaugural address.

And so, my fellow Americans, ask not what your country can do for you; ask what you can do for your country.

In this passage, Kennedy asks two questions, reversing the subjects and objects.

What can your country do for you?

What can you do for your country?

In reversing the syntactic order he emphasizes the reversal in meaning. Such a device is useful in your writing to emphasize differences in meaning.

Climax In the figure of climax, the writer arranges ideas in order of importance from the least to the most important.

I spent the day cleaning the house, reading poetry, and putting my life in order.

For me it was his humility, his gentleness, wisdom, wit, and a great compassionate friendliness.

Word Order

In English, standard word order usually follows the subject-verb-object pattern. Adjectives ordinarily precede nouns. Deviation from normal word order, as in anastrophe, attracts the reader's attention. In this scheme, word order is reversed or rearranged. Anastrophe in Greek means a "turning back," and in this figure the usual word order is reversed. Note how Annie Dillard in the following passage from *Teaching a Stone to Talk* reverses the order of the sentences, thus emphasizing the predicate adjectives which, instead of their usual place after the verb *are*, come at the beginning of the sentence.

Unseen in the jungle, but present are tapirs, jaguars, many species of snake and lizard, ocelots, armadillos, marmosets, howler monkeys, toucans and macaws and a hundred other birds, deer bats, peccaries, capybaras, agoutis, and sloths. Also present in this jungle, but variously distant, are Texaco derricks and pipelines, and some of the wildest Indians in the world, blowgun-using Indians, who killed missionaries in 1956 and ate them.

Addition

Information can be added to sentences in certain stylistically effective ways, as in the following two schemes, apposition and parenthesis.

Apposition Apposition is the placing next to a noun another noun or phrase that explains it.

Pollution, the city's primary problem, is an issue.

John, my brother, is coming home.

Nouns and phrases that add information and are in apposition to another noun are separated by commas.

Parenthesis Parenthesis is the insertion of words, phrases, or a sentence that is not syntactically related to the rest of the sentence. Such material is set off from the rest of the sentence in one of two ways. Either is acceptable.

By dashes: He said that it was going to rain—I could hardly disagree—before the game was over.

By parentheses: He said that it was going to rain (I could hardly disagree) before the game was over.

The following excerpt from Thomas Wolfe's *Death to Morning* describes his and his brother's experience in going to meet the circus that has just come to town. Wolfe makes use of many of the schemes described above: parallelism, chiasmus, climax, anastrophe, apposition, and parenthesis. Can you identify them? Why are they effective?

At the sculptural still square where at one corner, just emerging into light, my father's shabby little marble shop stood with a ghostly strangeness and familiarity, my brother and I would "catch" the first street car of the day bound for the "depot" where the circus was—or sometimes we would meet some one we knew, who would give us a lift in his automobile.

Then, having reached the dingy, grimy, and rickety depot section, we would get out, and walk rapidly across the tracks of the station yard, where we could see great flares and steamings from the engines, and hear the crash and bump of shifting freight cars, the swift sporadic thunders of a shifting engine, the tolling of bells, the sounds of great trains on the rails.

And to all these familiar sounds, filled with their exultant prophecies of flight, the voyage, morning, and the shining cities—to all the sharp and thrilling odors of the trains—the smell of cinders, acrid smoke, of musty, rusty freight cars, the clean pine-board of crated produce, and the smells of fresh stored food—oranges, coffee, tangerines and bacon, ham and flour and beef—there would be added now, with an unforgettable magic and familiarity, all the strange sounds and smells of the coming circus.

The gay yellow sumptuous-looking cars in which the star performers lived and slept, still dark and silent, heavily and powerfully still, would be drawn up in long strings upon the tracks. And all around them the sounds of the unloading circus would go on furiously in the darkness. The receding gulf of lilac and departing night would be filled with the savage roar of the lions, the murderously sudden snarling of great jungle cats, the trumpeting of the elephants, the stamp of the horses, and with the musty, pungent, unfamiliar odor of the jungle animals: the tawny camel smells, and the smells of panthers, zebras, tigers, elephants, and bears.

Note the piling up of details added through parentheses. You might try to rewrite the third paragraph without parentheses or apposition, putting the sentences in normal word order. What is lost?

Omission

Not only can words and ideas be added in stylistically effective ways, they can also be omitted for emphasis.

Zeugma In *zeugma*, the writer uses one word to govern several successive words or clauses.

She discovered New York and her world.

In this example the verb *discovered* governs both "New York" and "her world."

Asyndeton In *asyndeton*, conjunctions are omitted, producing a fast-paced and rapid prose.

I came, I saw, I conquered.

But in a larger sense we cannot dedicate, we cannot consecrate, we cannot hallow this ground (Gettysburg Address).

Polysyndeton In *polysyndeton*, on the other hand, the use of many conjunctions has the opposite effect—it slows the pace of the writing.

I kept remembering everything, lying in bed in the mornings—the small steamboat that had a long rounded stern like the lip of a Ubangi, and how quietly she ran on the moonlight sails, when the older boys played their mandolins and the girls sang and we ate doughnuts dipped in sugar, and how sweet the music was on the water in the shining night, and what it had felt like to think about girls then.

The feeling of lassitude is heightened by the long sentence with the series of clauses joined by the conjunction *and*, describing the "everything" that he remembered. You can use asyndeton and polysyndeton to slow or quicken the pace of your writing to match the action or progression of the idea you are working with.

Repetition

Repetition of words or patterns of words can be used for good stylistic effect, for reinforcement of meaning, and for emphasis. Following are three common schemes of repetition.

Anadiplosis In anadiplosis, which in Greek means "doubling back," the last word of one clause or phrase is used as the beginning word in the following clause or phrase.

People are trapped in history, and history is trapped in them.

He was enriched, and enriched others.

Polyptoton In polyptoton, the same root word is used in different parts of speech, such as *final* and *finalize* or *sense* and *sensible* used in the same sentence.

I agree if agreement is required.

Variety is the spice of living life.

You can use these kinds of repetition to good effect when you wish to emphasize an idea or drive home a point. Note how in the following passage from his inaugural address John F. Kennedy makes effective use of both of these figures.

Now the trumpet summons us again—not as a call to bear arms, though arms we need; not as a call to battle, though embattled we are; but a call to bear the burden of a long twilight struggle, year in and year out, "rejoicing in hope, patient in tribulation," a struggle against the common enemies of man: tyranny, poverty, disease and war itself.

The classical rhetoricians would have called the repetition of *arms* an anadiplosis and *battled* and *embattled* a polyptoton.

Anaphora One of the most common and effective kinds of repetition is anaphora, which means "carrying back" in Greek, and which refers to the regular repetition of the same word or phrase at the beginning of successive phrases or clauses. This kind of repetition helps to emphasize a point, to make it stick in the minds of your readers. In one of the most highly rhetorical and memorable passages in the English language, Martin Luther King, Jr., repeats over and over again the "I have a dream" refrain.

I say to you today, my friends, that in spite of the difficulties and frustrations of the moment I still have a dream. It is a dream deeply rooted in the American dream.

I have a dream that one day this nation will rise up and live out the true meaning of its creed: "We hold these truths to be self-evident; that all men are created equal."

I have a dream that one day on the red hills of Georgia the sons of former slaves and the sons of former slaveowners will be able to sit down together at the table of brotherhood.

I have a dream that one day even the state of Mississippi, a desert state sweltering with the heat of injustice and oppression, will be transformed into an oasis of freedom and justice.

I have a dream that my four little children will one day live in a nation where they will not be judged by the color of their skin but by the content of their character.

I have a dream today.

I have a dream that one day the state of Alabama, whose governor's lips are presently dripping with the words of interposition and nullification, will be transformed into a situation where little black boys and black girls will be able to join hands with little white boys and white girls and walk together as sisters and brothers.

I have a dream today.

I have a dream that one day every valley shall be exalted, every hill and mountain shall be made low, the rough places will be made plain, and the crooked places will be made straight, and the glory of the Lord shall be revealed, and all flesh shall see it together.

What effect does this repetition have on you, the reader? Why is it effective? Is it possible that this repetition accounts to some extent for the familiarity of this phrase today?

Sound

Another kind of repetition that is particularly effective in oratory is the repetition of certain sounds within a paragraph or a sentence. Such use of sounds reinforces meaning not only in orations, but in written prose as well. However, sounds must serve a purpose. Meaningless repetition of sounds would be monotonous, and to be effective sounds must reinforce the meaning in some way. In the Dillard example, the *s* sounds reinforced the sound of the movement of the stone from a sling shot; the *d*, *b*, and *t* sounds in the Carson example supported the idea of the branch falling.

Alliteration   One of the most commonly used figures, alliteration is the repetition of the same sound at the beginning of successive words.

Even though large tracts of Europe have *f*allen or may *f*all into the *g*rip of the *G*estapo, we shall not *f*lag or *f*ail.

Assonance Closely allied to alliteration, assonance is another repetitive sound pattern, but it involves the repetition of sounds within words.

From nose to toes, the body is beginning to sag.

No pain, no gain.

Sometimes writers may use assonance to reinforce meaning, but often the mere repetition is effective, because repetition makes a phrase memorable. Repetition and rhyme were used in oral societies to pass down information that had to be remembered from generation to generation. The use of repetition made such information easier to retain. Advertising slogans make ample use of repetition and rhyme for just such reasons.

The following inaugural address by John F. Kennedy is a rhetorical masterpiece, employing many stylistic devices described here. It was delivered immediately after he was sworn into the office of President of the United States on January 21, 1961.

INAUGURAL ADDRESS

JOHN F. KENNEDY

We observe today not a victory of party but a celebration of freedom,   1
symbolizing an end as well as a beginning, signifying renewal as well as
change. For I have sworn before you and Almighty God the same solemn
oath our forebears prescribed nearly a century and three-quarters ago.

    The world is very different now. For man holds in his mortal hands the   2
power to abolish all forms of human poverty and all forms of human life.
And yet the same revolutionary belief for which our forebears fought is
still at issue around the globe, the belief that the rights of man come not
from the generosity of the state but from the hand of God.

    We dare not forget today that we are the heirs of that first revolution.   3
Let the word go forth from this time and place, to friend and foe alike,
that the torch has been passed to a new generation of Americans, born in
this century, tempered by war, disciplined by a hard and bitter peace,
proud of our ancient heritage, and unwilling to witness or permit the
slow undoing of those human rights to which this nation has always been

committed, and to which we are committed today at home and around the world.

Let every nation know, whether it wishes us well or ill, that we shall pay 4 any price, bear any burden, meet any hardship, support any friend, oppose any foe to assure the survival and the success of liberty.

This much we pledge—and more.   5

To those old allies whose cultural and spiritual origins we share, we 6 pledge the loyalty of faithful friends. United, there is little we cannot do in a host of co-operative ventures. Divided, there is little we can do, for we dare not meet a powerful challenge at odds and split asunder.

To those new states whom we welcome to the ranks of the free, we 7 pledge our word that one form of colonial control shall not have passed away merely to be replaced by a far more iron tyranny. We shall not always expect to find them supporting our view. But we shall always hope to find them strongly supporting their own freedom, and to remember that, in the past, those who foolishly sought power by riding the back of the tiger ended up inside.

To those peoples in the huts and villages of half the globe struggling to 8 break the bonds of mass misery, we pledge our best efforts to help them help themselves, for whatever period is required, not because the Communists may be doing it, not because we seek their votes, but because it is right. If a free society cannot help the many who are poor, it cannot save the few who are rich.

To our sister republics south of our border, we offer a special pledge: 9 to convert our good words into good deeds, in a new alliance for progress, to assist free men and free governments in casting off the chains of poverty. But this peaceful revolution of hope cannot become the prey of hostile powers. Let all our neighbors know that we shall join with them to oppose aggression or subversion anywhere in the Americas. And let every other power know that this hemisphere intends to remain the master of its own house.

To that world assembly of sovereign states, the United Nations, our last 10 best hope in an age where the instruments of war have far outpaced the instruments of peace, we renew our pledge of support: to prevent it from becoming merely a forum for invective, to strengthen its shield of the new and the weak, and to enlarge the area in which its writ may run.

Finally, to those nations who would make themselves our adversary, we 11 offer not a pledge but a request: that both sides begin anew the quest for peace, before the dark powers of destruction unleashed by science engulf all humanity in planned or accidental self-destruction.

We dare not tempt them with weakness. For only when our arms are 12 sufficient beyond doubt can we be certain beyond doubt that they will never be employed.

But neither can two great and powerful groups of nations take comfort 13 from our present course—both sides over-burdened by the cost of modern weapons, both rightly alarmed by the steady spread of the deadly atom, yet both racing to alter that uncertain balance of terror that stays the hand of mankind's final war.

So let us begin anew, remembering on both sides that civility is not a 14 sign of weakness, and sincerity is always subject to proof. Let us never negotiate out of fear, but let us never fear to negotiate.

Let both sides explore what problems unite us instead of belaboring 15 those problems which divide us.

Let both sides, for the first time, formulate serious and precise pro- 16 posals for the inspection and control of arms, and bring the absolute power to destroy other nations under the absolute control of all nations.

Let both sides seek to invoke the wonders of science instead of its 17 terrors. Together let us explore the stars, conquer the deserts, eradicate disease, tap the ocean depths and encourage the arts and commerce.

Let both sides unite to heed in all corners of the earth the command of 18 Isaiah to "undo the heavy burdens . . . [and] let the oppressed go free."

And if a beachhead of co-operation may push back the jungle of 19 suspicion, let both sides join in creating a new endeavor, not a new balance of power, but a new world of law, where the strong are just and the weak secure and the peace preserved.

All this will not be finished in the first one hundred days. Nor will it be 20 finished in the first one thousand days, nor in the life of this Administration, nor even perhaps in our lifetime on this planet. But let us begin.

In your hands, my fellow citizens, more than mine, will rest the final 21 success or failure of our course. Since this country was founded, each generation of Americans has been summoned to give testimony to its national loyalty. The graves of young Americans who answered the call to service surround the globe.

Now the trumpet summons us again—not as a call to bear arms, though 22 arms we need; not as a call to battle, though embattled we are; but a call to bear the burden of a long twilight struggle, year in and year out, "rejoicing in hope, patient in tribulation," a struggle against the common enemies of man: tyranny, poverty, disease and war itself.

Can we forge against these enemies a grand and global alliance, North 23 and South, East and West, that can assure a more fruitful life for all mankind? Will you join in that historic effort?

In the long history of the world, only a few generations have been 24 granted the role of defending freedom in its hour of maximum danger. I do not shrink from this responsibility; I welcome it. I do not believe that any of us would exchange places with any other people or any other generation. The energy, the faith, the devotion which we bring to this endeavor will light our country and all who serve it, and the glow from that fire can truly light the world.

And so, my fellow Americans, ask not what your country can do for 25 you; ask what you can do for your country.

My fellow citizens of the world, ask not what America will do for you, 26 but what together we can do for the freedom of man.

Finally, whether you are citizens of America or citizens of the world, 27 ask of us here the same high standards of strength and sacrifice which we ask of you. With a good conscience our only sure reward, with history the final judge or our deeds, let us go forth to lead the land we love, asking His blessing and His help, but knowing that here on earth God's work must truly be our own.

This address was appropriate for a highly ceremonial occasion such as an inauguration and is oratory in the best classical tradition. As such it makes ample use of figurative language and especially of repetition. The repeated phrases are still remembered and widely quoted years after the speech was delivered. President Kennedy was addressing the citizens of his country, but he was also speaking to the citizens of the world, asking them to join in a "long twilight struggle . . . against the common enemies of man: tyranny, poverty, disease and war itself." This speech makes use of almost all the figures of speech covered in this chapter. How many can you identify?

LEARNING FROM MODELS

In the classical world and for hundreds of years afterwards, students learned style by copying and imitating models of good writing. Quintilian asserted that it is "a universal rule of life that we should wish to copy what we approve in others." Thus musicians take the voices of their teachers, painters the works of great artists, and farmers the principles of successful farmers as models for imitation (*Institutio Oratoria* 10.2.2–8). So successful writers have always taken as models the works of writers whom they admire.

Students in the classical world customarily used models of good writing in three ways: they translated passages from other languages, they imitated sentences, and they paraphrased. In translation exercises, students learned a great deal about their own language by translating passages from other languages. Such translation exercises were common in Rome where most educated people spoke their own Latin and were also familiar with the language and literature of Greece. As late as the nineteenth century, translating a selection from Latin into English was a requirement of the English entrance exam at Harvard. Although translation exercises are not possible here, it might be well to remember that learning the vocabulary and grammar of a second language enriches your knowledge of the vocabulary and grammar of your own language.

The second kind of exercise—sentence imitation—was a three-part procedure in the classical curriculum. The model sentence was first analyzed to ascertain its structural and syntactic pattern, so that the students understood what they were trying to imitate and could consider why it was good. The students then copied the model sentence in order to establish the patterns and words more firmly in their mind. They then wrote an imitation, following the syntactic pattern but altering the words and meaning. For instance, the first sentence from Kennedy's Inaugural Address might furnish a model.

> We observe today not a victory of party but a celebration of freedom, symbolizing an end as well as a beginning, signifying renewal as well as change.

After discussing the two participial phrases modifying the object of the verb, the students would copy the sentence in order to establish the pattern in their minds and then write their own imitation. It was in this way that they learned the grammar of their language within a written context. An imitation of this sentence might read as follows:

> We see today not the dull side of a brick building, but a vibrant painting, demonstrating this man's devotion to his city, manifesting his support of the arts.

The third kind of exercise using models was paraphrase. Unlike sentence imitation, paraphrase dealt with the content rather than the structure of the model. In these exercises, the student was asked to rephrase the idea in the original using different words, or to transfer a poem into prose, or to express a simple idea in a number of different ways.

It is important to make the distinction between imitation and paraphrasing exercises and plagiarism. The word *plagiarius* meant "a kidnapper" and denoted a literary thief—one who kidnapped another writer's words. Cicero makes the distinction clear by saying that if you acknowledge it, you have borrowed it, but if you deny it or fail to acknowledge it, you have stolen it (*Brutus* 19.76). A paraphrased passage must always be acknowledged. Plagiarism and ways to avoid it will be discussed more fully in Chapter 13.

Exercises in Sentence Imitation

What follows are imitation exercises of model sentences based on the classical procedure. For each sentence, you are to do three things:

1. Analyze the grammatical structure of the sentence and try to understand the parts. Identify the main subject and verb; then identify the modifiers. Modifiers may be single words, phrases or clauses. Verify your analysis with your instructor or with your classmates.

2. To establish the pattern of the original sentence in your mind copy the sentence slowly.

3. Now write your own imitation, changing the original words and imitating the grammatical structure as closely as possible. An example of an imitation sentence is given for each model.

1. He heard the sound of grown-up voices, casual in the silence, welling up almost to spilling over, then subsiding.

This sentence catches the special sound of overheard conversations through the use of a series of modifiers. "The sound of grown-up voices" is the object of the verb "heard" and is modified by three phrases: "casual in the silence," "welling up almost to spilling over," "then subsiding." The last two are participles, verbal modifiers that suggest movement—an ebb and flow—reinforcing the meaning with the sound and rhythm of the words. Note that participles are modifiers derived from verbs. Here is the sentence done in imitation:

He heard the sound of little children gentle on the breeze, sputtering with giggles, then bursting into laughter.

Copy the model in order to get the pattern more firmly in your mind and then write your own imitation.

2. It was an ordinary farm, a calf-raising, haymaking farm, and very beautiful.

In this sentence, the word farm is modified by a phrase that stands in apposition to it, "a calf-raising, haymaking farm," and an adjective with an intensifier, "and very beautiful" (see discussion of apposition).

Imitation example: He was a mongrel puppy, a dirt-digging, trouble-making puppy, and very lovable.

Copy the model and write your own imitation sentence.

> 3. But also we can read such books with another aim, not to throw light on literature, not to become familiar with famous people, but to refresh and exercise our own creative powers.

In this sentence a series of verbs called infinitives complement the verb, "read."

> *Imitation example*: But also we can take such courses for another purpose, not to stack up A's on our record, not to fill out our graduation requirements, but to stimulate and exercise our own minds.

Copy the model and write your own imitation sentence.

> 4. As I wandered along, the toc toc of ping-pong balls drifted from an attic window.

This sentence starts with a clause that modifies the verb "drifted" telling "when" the "toc toc . . . drifted from an attic window." Note that the introductory clause is followed by a comma.

> *Imitation example*: As I drowzed lazily, the click-click of high heels came through the living room window.

Copy the model and write an imitation sentence of your own.

> 5. In front of the Reuben Brown house, a Buick was drawn up.

This sentence is introduced by a prepositional phrase of place, indicating where the Buick is.

> *Imitation example*: Behind the living room sofa, a small ball was gathering dust.

Copy the model and write your own imitation sentence.

> 6. A camp dog, seeing me in the road, barked petulantly.

In this sentence model the subject, "a camp dog," is followed by a participial phrase, "seeing me in the road," which modifies it. The verb, "barked," is modified by a single adverb.

Imitation example: An old man, reading a book in the library, laughed loudly.

Copy the model and write your own imitation sentence.

7. Before my eyes the sloop began to expand.

Ordinarily this sentence would read "the sloop began to expand before my eyes," but the unusual order emphasizes the introductory phrase. Since the adverbial phrase of place, "before my eyes" is so short, it is not followed by a comma.

Imitation example: In the backyard the children shouted.

Copy the model and write your own imitation sentence.

8. We load the boats, secure the hatches, lash down all baggage, strap on life jackets, face the river and the sun, the growing roar of the rapids.

Although this sentence has only one subject "we," it has a number of verbs—"load," "secure," "lash down," "strap on," and "face." The last verb, "face," has three objects: the river, the sun, and the growing roar of the rapids.

Imitation example: We creamed the butter, added sugar, cut out wonderfully shaped cookies, and put the cookie stars, wreaths, and angels into the oven.

Copy the model and write your own imitation sentence.

Exercises in Paraphrasing

In this section, we will explore three kinds of paraphrase. Whereas sentence imitation required you to preserve the grammatical structure while changing the meaning, paraphrase asks you to preserve the meaning while changing the structure. The main purpose of the paraphrase exercise described here is to help you delineate meaning and analyze different ways of saying things. Often a paraphrase may lack the stylistic grace of the original, but analyzing such differences will help you understand stylistic choices and appreciate what they add to a passage. Paraphrasing model passages will also help you understand the stylistic choices that are available to you.

In the first kind of paraphrase, there are three steps. First you analyze the meaning of the original, paying special attention to the figures of speech and the strategies that the author uses to support the argument. Then you analyze how the author establishes credibility and goodwill and appeals to the audience. Second, you copy the model slowly and carefully to establish the vocabulary, spellings, and sentence patterns in your mind. Finally, write your own paraphrase. An example of a paraphrase is given.

In the following selection from Virginia Woolf's "How Should One Read a Book?" the critic in the press is compared to a person in a shooting gallery who takes pot shots and often misses the mark. How does Woolf establish her own credibility? How does she appeal to the reader?

If this is so, if to read a book as it should be read calls for the rarest qualities of imagination, insight, and judgment, you may perhaps conclude that literature is a very complex art and that it is unlikely that we shall be able, even after a lifetime of reading, to make any valuable contribution to its criticism. We must remain readers; we shall not put on the further glory that belongs to those rare beings who are also critics. But still we have our responsibilities as readers and even our importance. The standards we raise and the judgments we pass steal into the air and become a part of the atmosphere which writers breathe as they work. An influence is created which tells upon them even if it never finds its way into print. And that influence, if it were well instructed, vigorous and individual and sincere, might be of great value now when criticism is necessarily in abeyance; when books pass in review like the procession in a shooting-gallery, and the critic has only one second in which to load and aim and shoot and may well be pardoned if he mistakes rabbits for tigers, eagles for barndoor fowls, or misses altogether and wastes his shot upon some peaceful cow grazing in a further field. If behind the erratic gunfire of the press the author felt that there was another kind of criticism, the opinion of people reading for the love of reading, slowly and unprofessionally, and judging with great sympathy and yet with great severity, might this not improve the quality of his work? And if by our means books were to become stronger, richer, and more varied, that would be an end worth reaching.

In the following paraphrase, the metaphor is omitted, although the basic meaning is preserved.

Reading a book is a complicated activity that calls for imagination and judgment and good readers can exert a powerful influence over authors and the kinds of books that are produced in a society. The critic judges just once and is often wrong. The judgment of a careful and sympathetic body of readers, on the other hand, can exert more lasting influence than the single judgment of the professional critic. Ordinary, thoughtful readers by exerting such judgment can improve the quality of literature and that alone would make reading worthwhile.

Notice that the paraphrase is shorter, although all of the major ideas are included. The paraphrase, while sacrificing the metaphor, is briefer and more direct.

In a second kind of paraphrase you express the main ideas of a poem in prose. This is often a difficult task since at the outset you must have a clear idea of the meaning of the poem. This kind of paraphrase requires you to pay special attention to figurative language, to the persona (or speaker) in the poem, and to the poetic context. First, analyze Andrew Marvell's poem "To His Coy Mistress," searching out the meaning; second, copy the poem; and third, write a paraphrase.

Had we but world enough, and time,
This coyness, lady, were no crime.
We would sit down, and think which way
To walk, and pass our long love's day.
Thou by the Indian Ganges' side
Should'st rubies find: I by the tide
Of Humber would complain. I would
Love you ten years before the Flood,
And you should, if you please, refuse
Till the conversion of the Jews.
My vegetable love should grow
Vaster than empires, and more slow.
An hundred years should go to praise
Thine eyes, and on thy forehead gaze;
Two hundred to adore each breast,
But thirty thousand to the rest;
An age at least to every part,
And the last age should show your heart.
For, lady, you deserve this state,
Nor would I love at lower rate.
   But at my back I always hear
Time's winged chariot hurrying near:
And younder all before us lie

Deserts of vast eternity.
Thy beauty shall no more be found;
Nor, in thy marble vault, shall sound
My echoing song: then worms shall try
That long-preserved virginity.
And your quaint honor turn to dust,
And into ashes all my lust.
The grave's a fine and private place,
But none, I think, do there embrace.
   Now, therefore, while the youthful hue
Sits on thy skin like morning dew,
And while thy willing soul transpires
At every pore with instant fires,
Now let us sport us while we may;
And now, like amorous birds of prey,
Rather at once our Time devour,
Than languish in his slow-chapt power.
Let us roll all our strength and all
Our sweetness up into one ball,
And tear our pleasures with rough strife
Thorough the iron gates of life.
Thus, though we cannot make our sun
Stand still, yet we will make him run.

In a third kind of paraphrase, you are asked to express one idea in a number of different ways. Cicero suggests that students use a sentence from their own writing. This kind of exercise, using sentences from your own writing or from models, suggests the number of stylistic choices available to you. For example:

1. It was a beautiful day and I didn't want to be inside.

2. It was a sunny day and I wanted to be outside.

3. A beautiful day it was and I longed to be in it.

4. I didn't want to be inside because it was a beautiful day.

5. The weather was great and I hated not to be outside.

Some of these variations are more effective than others and some are more appropriate for certain kinds of situations. For example, sentences 1, 2, and 4 could be used in most ordinary situations. Why is sentence 2 different? What effect does the word *sunny* have? Would you use sentence 3 in ordinary conversation? When might you use it? Would you use sentence 5 in formal written language?

You might wish to practice such imitation and paraphrase exercises on your own to heighten your awareness of figurative language and its use in good writing.

What follows are several sentences that might serve as models:

He was a very good neighbor, always present in times of mirth and happiness and need.

And in the dreamers' talk that comes on a beach on such a sun-filled day, we mused about whether we had been someone else in another life.

She was a young woman in her thirties, who kept us all laughing at the vagaries of her life as a student while admiring her courage.

Select writers whose work you admire to use as models. A close study of models reinforced by imitation and paraphrase will help in making you aware of the tremendous variety of available stylistic choices and help you in making the appropriate choices depending finally on the subject, the audience, and the occasion.

Questions to Consider

1. Read the following commentary on the Kennedy address that appeared in the *New Yorker* magazine, February 4, 1961.

Answer the following questions in connection with the Kennedy speech. You may have to use the library.

> A. What was the state of the country at the time of Kennedy's address? Of the world? What appears to be Kennedy's subject and purpose in this address?

> B. Discuss how Kennedy's speech is appropriate, given the state of the country and the world, the occasion, his purpose, the subject, and the audience.

As rhetoric has become an increasingly dispensable member of the liberal arts, people have abandoned the idea, held so firmly by the ancient Greeks and Romans, that eloquence is indispensable to politics. Perhaps President Kennedy's achievements in both spheres will revive a taste for good oratory—a taste that has been alternately frustrated by inarticulateness and dulled by bombast. There have been a few notable orators in our day—most recently Adlai Stevenson—but they have been the exceptions, and it has taken Mr. Kennedy's success as a politician to suggest that the power to "enchant souls through words" (Socrates) may soon be at a premium once more. Whatever the impact of the Inaugural Address on contemporary New Frontiersmen, we find it hard to believe that an Athenian or Roman citizen could have listened to it unmoved, or that Cicero, however jealous of his own reputation, would have found reason to object to it.

We are all familiar by now with the generally high praise the President received for his first speech, but before the responsibility for a final judgment is yielded to Time it would be a shame not to seek the opinion of a couple of true professionals. Both Aristotle and Cicero, the one a theorist and the other a theorizing orator, believed that rhetoric could be an art to the extent that the orator was, first, a logician and, second, a psychologist with an appreciation and understanding of words. Cicero felt further, that the ideal orator was the thoroughly educated man. (He would be pleased by Mr. Kennedy's background, with its strong emphasis on affairs of state: the philosopher-orator-statesman.) Of the three types of oratory defined by the ancients—political, forensic, and display (in which audience participation was limited to a judgment of style)—

the political was esteemed most highly, because it dealt with the loftiest of issues; namely, the fate of peoples, rather than of individuals. ("Now the trumpet summons us again . . . against the common enemies or man. . . .") The ideal speech was thought to be one in which three kinds of persuasion were used by the speaker: logical, to present the facts of the case and construct an argument based on them; emotional, to reach the audience psychologically; and "ethical," to appeal to the audience by establishing one's own integrity and sincerity. The Inaugural Address, being a variation on the single theme of man's rights and obligations, is not primarily logical, although it contains no illogic; it is an appeal to men's souls rather than to their minds. During the Presidential campaign, Mr. Kennedy tested and patented an exercise in American psychology that proved to be all the emotional appeal he required for the inaugural speech: "And so, my fellow-Americans, ask not what your country can do for you, ask what you can do for your country." His ethical persuasion, or indication of his personal probity, consisted of an extension of that appeal: ". . . ask of us here the same high standards of strength and sacrifice which we ask of you."

Aristotle recognized only one (good) style, while Cicero thought that there were three styles—the plain, the middle, and the grand. To Aristotle, who considered it sufficient for a style to be clear and appropriate, avoiding undue elevation (whence bombast) and excessive lowliness, it would have seemed that Mr. Kennedy had achieved the Golden Mean. The formality of the Inaugural Address ("To that world assembly of sovereign states, the United Nations . . .") is appropriate to the subject; the language ("In your hands, my fellow-citizens, more than mine, will rest the final success or failure of our course") is clear and direct. Cicero's ideal orator was able to speak in all three styles, in accordance with the demands of his subject, and in that respect Mr. Kennedy filled the role by speaking plainly on the practical ("All this will not be finished in the first one hundred days"), by speaking formally but directly on the purpose of national defense ("For only when our arms are sufficient beyond doubt can we be certain beyond doubt that they will never be employed"), and by speaking grandly on the potential accomplishments of the movement toward the New Frontier ("The energy, the faith, the devotion which we bring to this endeavor will light our country and all who serve it—and the glow from that fire can truly light the world").

The address, however, is largely in the grand style, which is characterized by Cicero as the ultimate source of emotional persuasion, through figures of speech and a certain degree of dignified periodic rhythm, not iambic ("The world is very different now. For man holds in his mortal hands the power to abolish all forms of human poverty, and all forms of human life"). The oration is so rich in figures of speech—the many metaphors include a torch, a beachhead, jungles, a trumpet, a tiger—that we can imagine students of the future studying it for examples of antithesis ("If a free society cannot help the many who are poor, it cannot save the few who are rich"), personification (". . . the hand of mankind's final war"), and anaphora ("Not as a call to bear arms, though arms we need; not as a call to battle, though embattled we are . . ."). "Battle" and "embattled"—an excellent example of paronomasia.

And so we leave the speech to the students of rhetoric, having invoked for Mr. Kennedy the blessings of Aristotle and Cicero, and for ourself the hope that he has re-established the tradition of political eloquence.

2. In this article the editors of the *New Yorker* suggest that political oratory has lost its eloquence. Do you believe that this is true? Can you support your belief with examples?

3. Recast the following sentences in as many different ways as you can, primarily by altering word order, or by recasting in the passive voice. Then consider which version is most appropriate for a class essay, for a letter to a friend, or for an oral presentation.

Two flags and two young men attended this structure and the scatter of camping equipment around and within it.

In the first place, he approached hesitantly, haltingly, hanging his head as though he were ashamed.

All eyes were on Gloria in her blue aviator glasses and miniskirt, dramatic and cool with her soft voice and waist-long blond hair.

The climbers set out that morning, well equipped, well supplied, and firm in purpose.

My intent was to be kind, gentle, understanding, and patient.

In the world in which I lived, honesty was no virtue.

I ran home, firmly convinced that I had made a life-long enemy.

I wanted to be intelligent in all things, wise in the important things, and kind to the people that I would have to deal with.

Examine your sentence variations and discuss how certain word choices or arrangements have altered the effectiveness of what is being said, or its appropriateness, or its meaning. Are some arrangements more effective than others? Why?

4. Return to Adlai Stevenson's essay "The Hard Kind of Patriotism" reprinted in Chapter 2. Locate as many of the figures described in this chapter as you can in his essay and then discuss how Stevenson's use of figures conveys an *ethos* appropriate for his subject, his purpose, and his audience.

Suggestions for Writing

1. Write a short paper describing how individuals express who they are by the language that they use. You might choose a well-known personality or a friend. Be sure to support your viewpoint with specific details. Focus on such things as their use of the schemes and tropes, stylistic choices, and arrangement of ideas.

2. Using the three steps suggested by the classical rhetoricians, paraphrase the following excerpts. Analyze the selection, paying special attention to the figurative language and the ethical and emotional arguments. Copy the passage slowly and carefully, noting words and sentence patterns. Write a paraphrase.

> A. Second, for every disease there is a single key mechanism that dominates all others. If one can find it, and then think one's way around it, one can control the disorder. This generalization is harder to prove, and arguable—it is more like a strong hunch than a scientific assertion—but I believe that the record thus far tends to support it. The most complicated, multicell, multitissue, and multiorgan diseases I know of are tertiary syphilis, chronic tuberculosis, and pernicious anemia. In each, there are at least five major organs and tissues involved, and each appears to be affected by a variety of environmental influences. Before they came under scientific appraisal each was thought to be what we now call a "multifactorial" disease, far too complex to allow for any single causative mechanism. And yet, when all the necessary facts were in, it was clear that by simply switching off one thing—the spirochete, the tubercle bacillus, or a single vitamin deficieny—the whole array of disordered and seemingly unrelated pathologic mechanisms could be switched off, at once.

> B. No, I distrust Great Men. They produce a desert of uniformity around them and often a pool of blood too, and I always

feel a little man's pleasure when they come a cropper. Every now and then one reads in the newspapers some such statment as: "The coup d'état appears to have failed, and Admiral Toma's whereabouts is at present unknown." Admiral Toma had probably every qualification for being a Great Man—an iron will, personal magnetism, dash, flair, sexlessness—but fate was against him, so he retires to unknown whereabouts instead of parading history with his peers. He fails with a completeness which no artist and no lover can experience, because with them the process of creation is itself an achievement, whereas with him the only possible achievement is success.

Exercises in Revision

1. Examine one of your recent essays. Are there places where a metaphor or simile might make what you are saying clearer or more effective? If so rewrite to incorporate the figure of speech. Can you find places where other figures might be used?

2. Discuss your revision with your workshop group. Are the figures you have incorporated effective? Why, or why not?

3. Select a sentence from one of your recent essays and try to rewrite it in as many different ways as you can. Which way is most effective for your essay? Why?

For a Commonplace Book

1. Find examples from your reading of as many of the figures of speech identified in this chapter as you can. Copy the examples and label them.

2. Make a note of figures of speech that you hear in conversations around you.

3. Often song lyrics use figures of speech. Listen to some popular song lyrics and make a note of the figures of speech that you hear.

4. Try to compose your own examples for each of the figures of speech identified in this chapter.

PART IV

MEMORY

Quintilian advised his students that it was important "to learn much by heart and to think much, and if possible, to do this daily, since there is nothing that is more increased by practice or impaired by neglect than memory. . . . For our whole education depends on memory" and "it is the power of memory alone that brings before us all the store of precedents, laws, rulings, sayings and facts which the orator must possess in abundance" (Quintilian *Institutio Oratoria* 11.2.2). Quintilian urged his students to increase that store of resources so that they would have "a copious supply of words and matter . . . to suit all and every case."

For the classical rhetoricians, memory meant the natural memory—the store of experiences and knowledge within the individual mind. Invention, the first part of the art of rhetoric, taught the orator how to draw on those resources to define, to compare, to explain, and to persuade on any subject. It is important today for you as a writer to broaden your knowledge on all subjects and to enrich your experience by reading and learning. The last part of Chapter 12 demonstrates how writers can draw on their own personal experiences in their writing. So enlarging and enriching what you store in your own memory is important.

Modern rhetoric, however, must add another dimension to the concept of memory. In addition to the individual memory, there are a number of sophisticated ways of storing cultural knowledge in books, libraries, computers, and databases. No longer does one need to rely on one's own memory for "the store of precedents, laws, . . . and facts." Today, through technology, more and more information is being stored in computers. The large bulk of the culture's information, however, is still preserved in writing in libraries. Written materials are usually bound in book form, but as the amount of these materials has increased, new and more efficient ways of storing them have developed. Many newspapers, magazines, and journals are in microforms, greatly reduced photographic reproductions of written materials. These microforms must be read through special machines located in most libraries. Today, writers need to know how to explore not only their own memories but also how to gain access to this cultural store of information.

Students in the ancient world had no such wealth of books and libraries. The physical act of writing was difficult, and books were rare. Most important government documents were carved on stone. Books were made of rolls of papyrus or wax tablets and were heavy, awkward and fragile. In the later classical world, students used wax tablets and parchment. Persons of any importance dictated their letters to scribes who performed the hard physical task of writing. There were a few private libraries in ancient Greece and Rome such as the one of Aristotle, but libraries open to the public were limited in number and contained only a tiny fraction of the volumes in the smallest of public libraries today.

Books in the early Middle Ages were laboriously copied by hand and were very valuable. Only the Church or the very wealthy owned such treasures. A single book might cost the equivalent of $10,000, and a rich patron might trade a piece of land for a single manuscript. Books were carefully stored in cabinets or chained to desks and only monastaries or members of the nobility had anything that could even be called a library. With books and libraries so rare and inaccessible, students and orators had to memorize facts and rely heavily on their own individual memories to supply them with ideas to support their arguments.

Today, the millions of books and great public libraries are treasure houses of information embodying the memory of whole cultures. Any person who learns how to read and use books and how to find information in a library or a computer can have access to this treasure. Not only can you find material for your term paper, but you can get information on the stock market or look up the address of a friend in Minneapolis.

In addition, technology has made all kinds of information available to the researcher. Through computer searches information on almost any subject is readily available. Books and article citations, statistics, and government documents can be printed out at command. Search facilities are proliferating as technology improves. The modern student needs to know how to use these search systems and computer terminals to access this body of knowledge.

Where classical rhetoric limited the study of memory to cultivating the natural memory, modern rhetoric must consider memory in terms of the resources available through books and databases. Therefore the following chapter will consider two kinds of memory: the cultural memory and the individual memory. As the classical rhetoricians devised ways to store and retrieve information from the human memory, the modern rhetorician must also consider ways to retrieve information from books, libraries, and computers.

Chapter 12

Tapping Available Resources

BOOKS

The Dust Jacket
The Title Page
The Table of Contents
Prefaces and Introductions
References, Bibliographies, and Notes
The Index
Skimming a Book

THE LIBRARY

The Card Catalog
Other Catalogs
Catalog Cards
Locating Books
Finding Journal and Magazine Articles
Finding Newspaper Articles
Databases
Reference Books
Other Library Resources

PERSONAL EXPERIENCE
MAXINE HONG KINGSTON, "NO NAME
WOMAN"

W hen books and libraries are so readily accessible, it is important to know how to use them. Information is organized in fairly ordered and regular ways so that persons who learn the system can more easily find their way through any library and extract necessary information from books and databases. The first two sections will help you in searching through books and libraries just as ancient rhetoric helped students search through the pages of their memory and the hallways of their minds. The last section demonstrates how to use experiences drawn from personal memory.

BOOKS

You are probably familiar with the common parts of a book—dust jacket, title page, table of contents, index, and body of the text. This section discusses each of these parts in turn to discover what information each part contains that will help you find your way through a book to the material you need and help you decide whether the book can be useful to you. Modern books are organized to make this information readily available.

Just as you write for different purposes, you also read for different purposes. You might read a biography of a favorite sports figure or writer from cover to cover, but if you were writing a term paper on anorexia you would probably search through a number of books on nutrition and eating disorders looking only for information on anorexia and skipping material on unrelated subjects. Particularly when you are faced with the heavy reading load of a semester, you will benefit by learning how to read selectively and how to use the different parts of a book as aids to doing so.

Most of the books examined here are nonfiction, whose primary function is to supply information. In general there are two kinds of nonfiction books—the first is a book written by a single author; the second is a collection of articles written by a number of different authors that have been collected by one person, whose name appears as the author or editor. The author or the editor's last name usually appears on the spine of the book along with the title and the library call number so that it can be identified easily among the shelved books.

There are several parts of a book that will help in your search for useful material.

The Dust Jacket

The dust jacket of a book, the detachable, heavy paper cover, is customarily discarded when a book is added to a library collection, but more and more they are being preserved not only because they are attractive and help to protect the book, but also because of the useful information that they provide. The front flap will usually tell what the book is about and may include quotations from the book and information about special introductions or afterwords by noted authorities. Often on the back flap there will be a short biographical sketch of the author, sometimes accompanied by a picture. For example, the information given below, from the front flap of *Pioneer Women* by Joanna L. Stratton, includes information on where the idea for and contents of the book originated, what the book is about, and states that there is an introduction by the historian Arthur M. Schlesinger, Jr., which gives the book credibility.

> In the winter of 1975, Joanna Stratton made a remarkable discovery. In the attic of her grandmother's home in Kansas, buried among old toys, trunks, and fading antiques, was a set of priceless autobiographical manuscripts written by hundreds of pioneer women. The memoirs had been commissioned and collected by Ms. Stratton's great-grandmother, Lilla Day Monroe, a prominent nineteenth-century suffragist, lawyer, and publisher, who intended to edit them into a book. Now, three generations later, Ms. Stratton has rescued these extraordinary accounts from obscurity to finish her great-grandmother's project.
>
> Never has there been such a detailed record of women's courage or such a living portrait of the women who civilized the frontier. Replete with drama, here are stories of wilderness mothers, schoolmarms, Indian squaws, immigrants, homesteaders, and circuit riders. Their personal recollections of prairie fires, locust plagues, cowboy shoot-outs, Indian raids, and blizzards on the plains portray vividly the dangers and excitement of pioneering. And their intimate remembrances of day-to-day life reveal the special heroism and industriousness of the pioneer woman as never before.
>
> They were women of relentless determination, whose tenacity helped them conquer loneliness and withstand privations. Their work was the work of survival, and it demanded as much from them as from their men—whether it found them fashioning clothes out of raw wool or homes out of sod, coaxing vegetables out of the sun-parched earth or defending their cabins against raids by wolves. Husband and wife were equal partners on the frontier, and at last that partnership has been recognized
>
> In the words of Lilla Day Monroe: "History chronicles the large and glorious deeds of the standard beavers but tells little of the men on whose shoulders they are borne to victory, and tells nothing at all of the courageous women who keep the business of the house going. The world has never seen such hardihood, such perseverance, such devotion, nor such ingenuity in making the best of everything as was displayed by America's pioneer women. Their like has never been known."
>
> Illustrated with photographs from the period and introduced by historian Arthur M. Schlesinger, Jr., commenting on its uniqueness

and significance, *Pioneer Women* is a beautiful, important, and fas-
cinating book, as well as a priceless contribution to American
history.

About the Author
Joanna L. Stratton was born and raised in Washington D.C. but
considers Kansas and her family there as her second home. She
began her work on *Pioneer Women* while attending Harvard College,
from which she graduated with honors in 1976. She is currently
pursuing graduate studies at Stanford University.

The Title Page

The title page, contains important bibliographical information. First
of all, it lists the complete title together with the subtitles, which are not
included in the short title or on the spine of the book. For example, the
title page of the preceding book lists the full title of the book as *Pioneer
Women: Voices from the Kansas Frontier*. The subtitle provides additional
information about the book. Underneath the full title is the author's *full*
name—an important fact if you are trying to find a common name in a
large card catalog. This title page also contains the name of the author of
the introduction since, in this case, it is different from the author of the
rest of the book. Finally, at the bottom of the title page is the full name of
the publisher with the city or cities where the publisher is located. See
Figure 1.

This sample title page lists the standard information found in most
books. Additional information that may appear on the title page includes
the full name of a coauthor, editor, translator, or contributor; the author's
academic or organizational affiliation; volume number if the book is
part of a multivolume series; and the date of publication.

On the back of the title page is the copyright page, which includes the
date of publication, the owner of the copyright (usually the publisher or
author), the dates of subsequent printings or editions, and the Library of
Congress catalog card number.

If you plan to use the book as a reference for a paper it is important
when you take your first notes that you record the following information.

1. Full name of author (and any coauthors)

2. Full title and subtitle

3. Publication information
   a. Place of publication
   b. Publisher
   c. Date of publication

PIONEER WOMEN

Voices from the Kansas Frontier

———◆———

JOANNA L. STRATTON

Introduction by
ARTHUR M. SCHLESINGER, JR.

SIMON AND SCHUSTER   NEW YORK

Figure 1.

344

You may also wish to record the call number in case you need to refer to the book later. You will need all of this information when you list the book in your bibliography. The bibliographic entry for *Pioneer Women* would look like this.

Stratton, Joanna L. *Pioneer Women: Voices from the Kansas Frontier.* New York: Simon and Schuster, 1981.

The Table of Contents

The table of contents is probably the most valuable key to the book. It can vary considerably in format, but, by and large, it indicates what information is contained in the book and how this information is organized. Figure 2, which presents a partial table of contents for a book on nutrition, divides the book into six parts: "What to Eat," "The Non-caloric Nutrients," "What to Drink," "What to Do about Your Weight," "Food for Special Lives," and "What's in Your Food." Each of these parts is further divided into subheads. As a result page numbers are provided for almost seventy different subjects. If you are writing a paper on menu planning or proteins or cholesterol, a quick glance through the table of contents will tell you exactly where to find the information without having to read through material that is unnecessary for your subject. This table of contents also provides page numbers for features such as recipes, tables, and charts.

Prefaces and Introductions

Prefaces state the overall purpose of the book and contain the acknowledgments. Introductions can be extremely helpful since the editor or author may explain the rationale behind the book, the particular approach, and possibly a guide to the order and content. If the book is a new edition of an already published work, the introduction will elaborate on changes made in that edition. All of this prefatory material is a guide to the overall purpose of the book, the content and arrangement, the author's special approach and other information possibly useful to the reader.

References, Bibliographies, and Notes

A list of references includes books and articles that are referred to within the text of the book and may appear at the end of each section or at the end of the book. Bibliographies may also appear at the end of the book or of each section, however, they contain not only books and articles referred to in the text, but also other materials on the subject. An

CONTENTS

PART ONE

What to Eat

Figure 2.

entry in a bibliography or reference list for a book or article contains all of the information (author, title, publication facts) that you need to look it up in the library. Both bibliographies and lists of references provide a door through which you can move beyond the particular book that you are reading to find more information on the subject. See Figure 3 for an example of a bibliography.

The Index

Another extremely important part of a book that should not be overlooked is the index, a detailed alphabetical list of subjects or titles, or works, or persons covered in the book. You may be referring to a book on computer software, but the subject of your paper is word processing. If you turn to the index and look under *word processing*, you will find the page numbers where word processing is discussed. The main entry, word processing, will also refer to sections in the text where word processing is discussed in conjunction with other subjects. These secondary locations are indicated by *see also* and the entry name in parentheses following the main entry. On occasion, a subject you look for in an index may be listed under another entry because it is referred to in the particular book by a different name or because it is included as part of a discussion of a related subject. In this case, you will find *see* and the name of the correct entry in parentheses after the entry you consulted. By consulting the index first you need not read through the entire book since the index will easily point you to the sections that you need. The following excerpt from the index to Karl Worner's book on Karlheinz Stockhausen includes examples of main entries and cross-references indicated by *see* and *see also*. See Figure 4.

Skimming a Book

Books are written and organized in much the same manner that writers organize their ideas. Topic sentences and thesis statements introduce main segments of discourse and contain main ideas that are developed through examples and details. By skimming such sentences, you can usually ascertain the writer's basic arguments. Often an introduction will state the proposition or main idea just as the conclusion will present a summary of the author's arguments. Scanning such elements can help you to eliminate material not germane to your subject. So, it helps to read first and last paragraphs and to search out theses and topic sentences that introduce main ideas and sections, as they were described in Chapter 2, in order to find information without having to wade through material that is unnecessary for a current writing or reading project. Also, visual signals such as indentation for paragraphs, headings in

Bibliography

This Bibliography contains, first, general works with which the student of the history of rhetoric should be familiar, many of which are also cited in the Notes; second, all books cited in the Notes except a small number cited in passing, for which full bibliographical information is supplied in the note itself; third, a small number of important works published as articles.

Abrams, M. H. *The Mirror and the Lamp*. New York: Oxford Univ. Pr., 1953.

Adams, John Quincy. *Lectures on Rhetoric and Oratory*. Edited with a New Introduction by J. Jeffrey Auer and Jerald L. Banninga. 2 vols. New York: Russell and Russell, 1962.

Arts libéraux et philosophie au Moyen Age: actes du Congrès international de philosophie médiévale, Montreal, 1967. Paris: J. Vrin, 1969.

Baldwin, Charles Sears. *Ancient Rhetoric and Poetic*. New York: Macmillan, 1924.

————. *Medieval Rhetoric and Poetic (to 1400) Interpreted from Representative Works*. New York: Macmillan, 1928.

————. *Renaissance Literary Theory and Practice*. Edited by Donald L. Clark. New York: Macmillan, 1939.

Baldwin, T. W. *William Shakespere's Small Latine and Lesse Greeke*. 2 vols. Urbana: Univ. of Illinois Pr., 1944.

Barnes, Timothy David. *Tertullian: A Historical and Literary Study*. Oxford: Clarendon Pr., 1971.

Baron, Hans. *The Crisis of the Early Italian Renaissance: Civic Humanism and Republican Liberty in an Age of Classicism and Tyranny*. Princeton: Princeton Univ. Pr., 1966.

Baynes, Norman H., and Moss, H. St. L. B. *Byzantium: An Introduction to East Roman Civilization*. Oxford: Clarendon Pr., 1948.

Beck, Hans-Georg. *Kirche und theologische Literatur im byzantinischen Reich*. Handbuch der Altertumswissenschaft 12, no. 2, part 1. Munich: Beck, 1959.

Blair, Hugh. *Lectures on Rhetoric and Belles Lettres*. Edited with a Critical

Figure 3.

duration: impulse (*see* frequency)
duration: unending, 108–11, 112,
   183–4
dynamic/static (*see also* state), 37, 42,
   45, 84, 91, 129, 168, 177, 192, 194,
   195, 198, 203
dynamics (*see* intensities)

echo, 35, 37, 70, 102, 156, 157, 161
education: musical, 134, 172–3, 175,
   176, 243–9, 250
effects (*see* sound effects)
electronic music (*see also* instrumental; modulation; transformation),
   32–4, 40, 46, 57–60, 67, 68, 87, 90,
   99, 119–54, 167, 209, 219, 235,
   239, 253, 254
entropy, 94
equal participation (*see also* serial-
   ism), 84, 87, 92, 128–30, 167, 168,
   199, 245
eternity (*see also* moment; religion),
   47, 66, 68

Figure 4.

different type size or color, numeral and letter headings all indicate the introduction of a new idea. Topic and thesis sentences are often found at these junctures.

THE LIBRARY

The library is the academic heart of a university. Often it is the physical center as well, the largest and most imposing building on the campus. As a student you should learn how to use the library and be able to take advantage of its great resources. Find out if there are tours available, or if there is a printed library guide. Reading such material and the material that follows in this chapter will be more helpful, however, if you start working through the card catalog and prowling the stacks yourself. Learning your way around the library is a voyage of discovery; with any perseverance on your part, the campus library can yield a treasure.

Luckily, there are people there whose main job is to help you. Librarians can be a rich source of information and they are always willing to answer reasonable and courteous questions and to help search out bits of information. When you don't know where to turn, a polite question to the person behind the information/reference desk will get you back on the right track. Get to know your librarians, and, above all, appreciate them.

The Card Catalog

The usual place to start in the library is with the card catalog, a listing of the library's books, periodicals, and other materials. Periodicals are journals and magazines that publish issues at regular intervals, or "periodically." In some large libraries there is a separate "Serials Catalog," which lists each periodical title received by the library and past issues in the library holdings.

The card catalog usually lists books alphabetically by subject, title, and author. Thus the book *The Dewey Experiment in China* by Barry Keenan would have at least three cards in the card catalog, one under the subject, *China—History—Republic, 1912–1949*, one under the title, and one under the author's last name. See Figure 5 for examples of each kind of catalog card.

A card catalog, because of its size, can present difficulties when you want to find a book by Richard Young and you discover that there are many authors with the last name of Young, or when you can't find St. Augustine because he is filed under *Saint* Augustine.

Here are a few rules. Authors' names are always filed alphabetically by last name. If two or more authors have the same last names, they are filed alphabetically by their first names. Thus *George* Young would come ahead of *Richard* Young in the catalog. When people and places have the same names, people will precede places. The author John Buckingham will come before Buckingham Palace in the catalog. Also, a person as author will come ahead of a person as subject. So, under the heading William Shakespeare, *Hamlet* will precede a biography of Shakespeare.

There are a few rules for alphabetizing any material, and knowing these will help you search through not only the card catalog but also other large and involved alphabetical listings such as indexes or a telephone book.

1. Articles (*the, a, an*) at the beginning of titles are ignored. Thus *The Philosophy of Rhetoric* is filed under *P* for *Philosophy*.

2. Numbers are filed as if they are spelled out. So, 263 is filed under *T* for two hundred and sixty-three.

3. Names beginning with *Mc* are usually grouped together under *Mac*.

4. Abbreviations such as St. Augustine or Mt. St. Helen are filed as if they were spelled out: Saint Augustine or Mount Saint Helen.

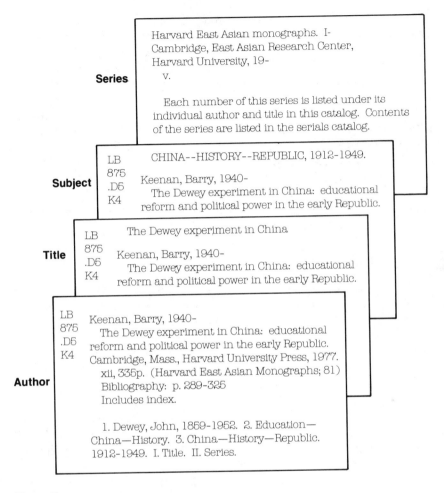

Figure 5.

Other Catalogs

Each year more and more libraries are acquiring computerized catalogs. The library's holdings are put in a computer database, which is then accessible through terminals in the library. Since this is an expensive undertaking libraries may be slow in putting all their holdings in the database, thus most online catalogs are incomplete and reflect only the most recent acquisitions of the library. Online catalogs are more powerful than card catalogs. The online catalog provides the traditional information of author, title, and subject search but can also provide call number, series and boolean searches. Most such searches operate by keywords, so it is not necessary to do an alphabetical search through the catalog. For example, you can enter the keywords in a title in any order and the computer will search all titles in the database with those keywords and then display the relevant titles on the terminal screen. Printed directions are usually available, or you can get help from a librarian or a friend. The online catalog record will provide exactly the same information as that on the catalog card. Besides the card catalog and the online catalog, some libraries are using microfiche or microfilm to list their holdings. The microfiche catalog is a sheet of negatives—actual pictures of the cards in the catalog—that can be viewed through a microfiche reader. Microfilm is the same except the negatives are on a roll instead of a card. Most microfilm and microfiche readers have simple directions for use. Microfiche and microfilm catalogs arrange their entries alphabetically as described earlier.

Catalog Cards

Catalog cards carry a great deal of information. For instance, if you are looking for the birth and death dates of Adam Smith, you can find that information on the catalog card under his name as author. You can also find where and when a book was published, the number of pages, and whether it is illustrated or has a bibliography and an index. The information at the bottom of the card is called the "tracings." These are subject headings that reflect the contents of the book. The tracings can also give you ideas of other subject headings in the card catalog under which you can find additional information on your subject, another door to discovering material for your paper. In the upper left-hand corner of the card is the call number, the key to the location of the book. A detailed illustration of a catalog card is given in Figure 6.

Taking the time to read the whole card can save you unnecessary steps and at the same time suggest new avenues of information. For example, the publication date may tell you that the book was published too early to contain certain aspects of information on a timely subject, and a notation that the book is part of a series may lead you to books on a related subject.

Locating Books

Every library has a directory of book locations similar to the one in Figure 7. They are usually posted at key locations around the library, and you can usually get printed maps to carry with you.

As you can see from Figure 7, there are two cataloging systems in general use in American libraries. Once you become familiar with these systems, all library directories will be easier to follow. The most com-

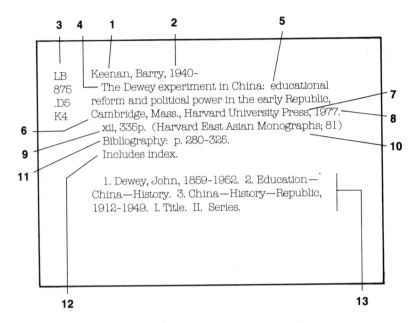

Figure 6: Catalog Card

1. *Author*—the author's name, last name first

2. *Author's Birth and Death Dates*

3. *Call Number*

4. *Title*—title of the book

5. *Subtitle*

6. *Place of Publication*

7. *Publisher*

8. *Date of Publication*

9. *Collation*—number of pages, presence of illustrations, maps, etc., and the height of the book in centimeters

10. *Series Note*—the name of the series, if the book is a part of a series

11. *Bibliography Note*

12. *Index Note*

13. *Tracings*—exact headings for the subject cards which reflect the subject content of the book, title tracing and series tracing

To locate a book listed in the card catalog, use the letters, numbers or special location symbol on the top line of the call number to determine the area in which the book is shelved (unless the call number is followed by a special location stamp).

LIBRARY OF CONGRESS CLASSIFICATION	LOCATION	DEWEY DECIMAL CLASSIFICATION	LOCATION
A–BX (except AM & BF)	3 East		
AM	4 East	000–049	1 West Stacks
BF	2 Central Stacks	050–299 (except 130–9, 150–9)	3 East
C (except CC, CJ, CN)	3 East	130–9	2A Central Stacks
CC, CJ, CN	4 East	150–9	2A Central Stacks
D, E, F	3 East	300–399 (except 370-9)	2 East
G–GF	3 East	370–9	2A Central Stacks
GN–GT	4 East	400–499	3 West Stacks
GV	2 Central Stacks	500–699 (except 571–2)	Library Annex
H, J, K	2 East	571–2	4 East
L–LT	2 Central Stacks	700–789	4 East
M–N	4 East	790–799	2A Central Stacks
P–PM	1A West Stacks	800–899	3 West & Central Stacks
PN–PQ	2 West Stacks	900–999 (except 913)	3 East
PR–PZ	2A West Stacks	913	4 East
Q, R, S, T, U, V	1 East		
Z	1 West Stacks		

CALL NUMBERS begin with 1 to 3 letters (e.g. H or HF) or 3 numbers sometimes followed by decimals (e.g. 780.1).

LOCATION SYMBOLS are composed of 3 or more letters on the top line of the call number. These indicate that a book will be found in a place other than that in which the call number below is located. (See the reverse side of this sheet for a list of location symbols.) Letters with a dash after the location symbol also indicate special locations:

-C = Closed Shelf material available from the AAM Library Office (4 East)
-L = Large volumes shelved in the oversize section of the area library
-R = Reference book

Special symbols preceding Dewey call numbers are:

Q = Quarto or large book, may be shelved with regular-sized books or in the oversize section of the area library
M = Music located with other books in the 780's
T = Textbook, shelved according to call number

Figure 7: Book Location Guide (from Library at University of Missouri-Columbia)

354

monly used is the Library of Congress system, which categorizes subjects under twenty major headings indicated by letters of the alphabet and which is largely supplanting the older Dewey Decimal system.

In a large university that has special libraries located either in the main building or at locations around the campus, a special location symbol immediately above the call number will indicate the location of the book in a special room or library immediately above the call number. Special locations for large size books, reference books, and other special holdings are also designated on the catalog card.

Virtually all libraries have an interlibrary loan service that arranges for short-term loans of books from other libraries. Check if your college library has this service and if it is available to undergraduates. Allow ample time—3 to 6 weeks—for the library to get the material.

Finding Journal and Magazine Articles

The card catalog does not list individual articles in magazines or periodicals so another source is necessary to find periodical articles on a subject. The best general index to start with is the *Readers' Guide to Periodical Literature*. This general index began publication in 1905 and is updated frequently. It is available in virtually all libraries. It is the place to find the most recent and readily available articles on all but very specialized subjects. Articles are listed under subject, author, and title. Another general periodical index is INFOTRAC, which is a laser disk periodical index that indexes approximately nine hundred magazines and two newspapers.

In addition, there are a number of indexes to professional journals in specialized fields, such as the *Humanities Index* or the *Engineering Index*. Any librarian can guide you to these. When you have located articles in one of these indexes and are ready to find a particular article in your library, return to the serials card catalog to find the location of the periodical that contains the article. Most libraries have a periodical reading room which houses the most recent issues, where you may look up your article or choose to spend a few hours reading the latest newspapers or journals. Older issues are usually bound in book form and shelved in the stacks or are reproduced in some microform.

Finding Newspaper Articles

Newspaper articles are another source of information, particularly for material on recent events or contemporary coverage of earlier events. If you are writing about a particular event, such as the 1984 World Series, or attempting to compare the treatment of a subject, such as the contemporary coverage of the presidential election of 1920 in two different newspapers, you may be able to locate newspaper articles, even if you are unable to remember the exact dates. Since 1913, the *New York Times* has maintained an index on news events covered in that newspaper. The prior series of the *New York Times* goes back to 1851. It is useful in itself, but it can also be used as an index to other newspapers and magazines. For example, if you look up the Lindbergh kidnapping and find the date it was covered in the *New York Times* you can look up the news coverage in other newspapers or magazines for the same date. Other newspapers have their own indexes, including the *Chicago Tribune, Los Angeles Times, Christian Science Monitor*, and *Washington Post*.

Databases

More and more, information is being stored in large computerized databases. In this form information can be accessed through computers stationed all over the country by means of specialized computer searches. More and more libraries now offer such services, usually for a fee. Many libraries have after-dark search services that have discount rates in the evening, but most universities underwrite the cost to some degree.

One such database in the field of education is the ERIC database. There are two parts to the ERIC index. The first, CIJE, indexes journals in the field; the second, RIE, indexes non-journal documents such as speeches and conference papers. The interactive mode of the computer helps in the search by providing citations on the topic. One of the most widely used laser disk computerized periodical indexes is INFOTRAC, which indexes popular magazines and topics, much like the *Readers' Guide*. Such computerized indexes furnish bibliographic citations such as authors, titles, and names of periodicals for a particular subject.

Databases are still in the developmental stages and are expensive additions to libraries. During your tour of your campus library, find out whether it has access to these systems. Although many libraries do not have such sophisticated facilities, it is important for you to know about them since they will become more common means of storing and retrieving information in the future.

Reference Books

The library is indeed a treasure house of information. You can look up the meaning of the word *insoucient*, or look up the derivation of the word *charm*. You can find out who wrote *Pride and Prejudice*, get information on nuclear power plants, or discover who said "Give me liberty or give me death." You can read about a subject that interests you, settle an argument with a friend, or find more than enough material for a term paper. Within the library in the stacks of books is the accumulated knowledge of centuries, the memory of your culture.

One of the best places to start a search for information is the reference room, where general sources of information are gathered conveniently in one location and include two general kinds of refernce books: those that contain the immediate information you desire and those that will direct you to more information about a subject. Use of these books is restricted to the library so that they are readily available to everyone.

Encyclopedias A good place to start the information search on an unfamiliar subject is a general encyclopedia which covers all branches of knowledge. Usually it will give a brief overview of a subject with a definition, a short history, and a list of books that can give you more detailed information. Articles in encyclopedias are always written by well-known authorities, and looking up their other works can offer even more information on a subject. Listed below are three important encyclopedias available in most libraries:

> *Collier's Encyclopedia.* 24 vols. New York: Crowell Collier Educational Corporation, 1978.
>
> Volume 24 includes an index, a bibliography, and a study guide to twenty three different subjects.
>
> *The Encyclopedia Americana.* 30 vols. New York: America Corporation, 1978.
>
> A full encyclopedia with good coverage of almost every topic that you can think of with excellent coverage of science and technology.
>
> *Encyclopedia Britannica.* 15th ed. 30 vols. Chicago: Encyclopedia Brittanica, Inc., 1986.
>
> Probably the most comprehensive of the encyclopedias. The place to start is in the *Micropedia*, a ready reference source with more than 100,000 articles, which refer you to longer, more comprehensive articles in the *Macropedia*.

Encyclopedias are not always current, as the dates on these volumes indicate. For example, AIDS, the disease so much in the current press, is not included in any of the above encyclopedias. Some encyclopedias have been computerized so that current information can be added without the necessity of an expensive new printing. Until more are available however, printed encyclopedias serve as a source of general information while timely subjects must be searched in journal and newspaper indexes.

Dictionaries The word *dictionary*, related to the words *diction* and *dictate*, means a collection of words. The ordinary dictionary used to check spellings or find meanings is only one of the many different kinds of available dictionaries, and this ordinary dictionary does more than provide definitions and spellings. General dictionaries carry an introduction that contains information about the English language, its history, and usage. The introductory material also explains the symbols and abbreviations used in that particular dictionary since these may vary among dictionaries. Dictionaries do not include every word in the English language; that would be an impossible task. The large unabridged dictionaries usually include only about 400,000 words. These unabridged dictionaries are in most libraries and are useful for finding the complete history of most words and definitions of unusual words. Desk or abridged dictionaries are smaller and contain definitions and a brief history of most words you encounter in your reading and writing. This is the kind that you will want to keep handy on your desk.

The English language has one of the most complete historical dictionaries in the world, the *Oxford English Dictionary*, abbreviated O.E.D. The *Oxford English Dictionary* gives the historical development of each word introduced into the language since 1150. The original dictionary was completed in 1900; there are supplements for words and meanings that have entered the language since 1900. Through a series of quotations, painstakingly gathered by hundreds of volunteers, the *Oxford English Dictionary* indicates the first time a word appeared in the language and the meanings that it has had over the years. It also gives pronunciations, the languages that the word came from, and synonyms. It is a wealth of information on words and the ideas that words represent.

In addition to general dictionaries, there are dictionaries that deal with certain aspects of language, dictionaries that deal with a specific subject area such as philosophy or linguistics, and finally dictionaries for foreign languages. Most of these are readily available in the library. The most useful of these specialized dictionaries are those that deal with different aspects of the English language. Listed below are a few of the more common ones. Knowing where to find them in your library and how to use them will open up a world of information to you and allow you to be the authority in all of those disputes that arise about language, for example, "Where does the expression *ok* come from?"

> *Webster's New Dictionary of Synonyms; a Dictionary of Discriminated Synonyms and Antonyms and Analogous and Contrasted Words.* 2d ed. Springfield, Mass.: Merriam, 1968.
>
> As this long title indicates, this dictionary contains words that mean the same or the opposite of the word that you are looking up, or are similar or different. It is an invaluable aid when you are trying to avoid repetition or are looking for a more precise word to express your idea.

Roget's International Thesaurus. 3d ed. New York: Crowell, 1962.

Similar to the above. Thesaurus means a treasure, which these dictionaries can be in helping you in your writing. There are inexpensive versions of both of these dictionaries.

Partridge, Eric. *A Short Etymological Dictionary of Modern English.* 4th ed. London: Routledge, 1966.

This dictionary tells you the origins of a word.

Ehrlich, Eugene et al. *Oxford American Dictionary.* New York: Oxford University Press, 1980.

This is a compact up-to-date guide to American English. It includes common words used in writing as well as slang and informal and technical words.

Partridge, Eric. *Slang Today and Yesterday.* 4th ed. rev. London: Routledge; New York: Barnes and Noble, 1970.

This dictionary lists slang expressions, modern and old, that are seldom listed in general dictionaries, since many of them are so temporary. A slang expression in common usage today may be outdated in two or three years. These dictionaries can be disappointing through no fault of their own, but simply because it is an almost impossible task to keep up with the slang of any period.

Wood, Clement. *Wood's Unabridged Rhyming Dictionary.* Cleveland and New York: World Publishing Co., 1943.

A useful aid for the aspiring poet. A list of words grouped according to similar sounds.

Bartlett, John. *Familiar Quotations: A Collection of Passages, Phrases and Proverbs Traced to Their Sources in Ancient and Modern Literature.* E. M. Beck. 14th ed. Boston: Little, Brown, 1968.

For many years, *Bartlett's Quotations*, as it is familiarly called, has been the place to go to find who said what, when, and where. You can find the source of a quotation by looking up the key word in the index. For example, "My heart leaps up when I behold" can be found in the index under the key word, *heart*, which then lists familiar quotations that include that word, and refers you to the page that gives the full quotation, the author, date, and source—a speech, a poem, a play, and so on.

Dictionary of American Biography. New York: Scribner, 1928–37.
Dictionary of National Biography. 63 vols. London: Smith, Elder, 1885–1901. Reprinted in 1938 by Oxford University Press in 21 vols.

Who's Who in America. Chicago: Marquis, 1899—Biennial.
Who's Who. London: Black, 1949—Annual.

These four dictionaries will furnish you with biographies of most
well-known figures in the United States and Great Britain. If you do
not find the biographical information that you need in these dictionaries, your librarian can refer you to a number of specialized biographical dictionaries.

These reference books are only a brief listing of the sources that are
available to you for finding information. For example, there is a *Dictionary of Costume* that describes and pictures worldwide costumes of the past
and present, and *The Official Museum Directory* that lists 6,700 museums in
the United States and Canada together with their contents. Most librarians are familiar with all of these publications. They can show you
how to locate almost any information that you may need, for example,
the population of Cincinnati or the date of the Chernobyl incident.
Librarians have the real key to the treasure house of information stored
in our libraries and are there to unlock the door for you.

Other Library Resources

Your library may have other resources listed in their informational
pamphlets or tours. They may include

A Reserve Desk: When a particular book is being heavily used in a
course, the instructor may put the book "on reserve." This simply
means that no one student can take the book out of the library for
an extended period, but that it will be loaned out only for a limited period of time or only for use inside the library. This procedure allows many students to have access to the book.

Government Documents: These documents, produced at government expense, are a fertile source of statistics and information of
all kinds. You may wish to ask your librarian if these documents
are available.

Microforms: Libraries could not possibly hold all of the materials
that have accumulated over time, so in the late 1930s microforms
were produced to help store this mass of information. Microforms
are reprints of materials photographically reduced in size to make
storage easier. Since they cannot be read by the naked eye, libraries have special machines for viewing microforms. Microfiches reduce the print so that an entire issue of a periodical can be put on
a three-by-five sheet. Microfilms can contain many editions of a
newspaper on a single reel. Your librarian can show you how to
use the microform readers or how print-outs can be made.

Many libraries also include map rooms, rare book rooms, and other regional and special collections. You would do well to find out what your own library has to offer.

Book Location Information. Most libraries have a microfiche, a computer print-out, or a library handout that will indicate a book's location. At the circulation desk they can tell you if the book is loaned out and the date it is due back. If the book is not on the proper shelf and is not loaned out, you can ask the librarian to initiate a search for the book. Some libraries make such information available to everyone, and, in other cases, it is available only to librarians. But, in either case, when you are unable to find a book, such information is available.

Knowing how to find information, being able to access the cultural memory, does not replace the habit of listening and reading as a way to increase your own knowledge. Quintilian advises that the orator "must accumulate a certain store of resources to be employed whenever they may be required" (*Institutio Oratoria* 10.1.5). Books and libraries supply a rich reference source, but reading and listening increases the resources of your own personal memory.

PERSONAL EXPERIENCE

All writers have resources within themselves from which they can draw: books they have read, scenes they remember, people who influenced them, childhood hopes and disappointments, unforgettable events, and a host of family stories. Writers also learn to draw on the memories and knowledge of other persons: experts, friends, teachers, elderly relatives who often have much to tell the ready and receptive listener who will take the time. You might wish to review the section on interviewing in Chapter 7 to guide your talks with other people.

There is, in addition to the kind of interviewing described in Chapter 7, a kind of informal unstructured way of listening to other people. Listening to an elderly person may give you insights into another era or understanding of a different way of living and thinking. Listening to casual conversation between business or political associates may give you new perspectives on how people arrive at their views. Such listening cannot be ordered or structured like the formal interview but it can add to your personal memory and be used as a resource.

In the following passage from "The Girl's Room," Laura Cunningham describes what she learned from sharing her room with her aged and sometimes fractious grandmother. She describes what her grandmother said to her and what it meant in light of her own experience.

Yet, in these times of age segregation, with grandmothers sent off to impersonal places, I wonder if the love and the comedy weren't worth the intermittent difficulties? Certainly I learned what it might be to become old. And I took as much comfort as my grand-mother did in a nightly exchange of Russian endearments—"Ya tebya lyublyu," "Ya tebya tozhe lyublyu"—"I love you," "I love you, too."

If I sold my grandmother blouses and baubles, maybe she gave me the truth in exchange. Once, when we were alone in the girls' room, she turned to me, suddenly lucid, her good eye as bright as it would ever be—a look I somehow recognized as her "real" gaze—and said, "My life passes like a dream."

In this excerpt Cunningham moves from her own personal experience with her grandmother, from their simple conversations, to a general thesis. How would you state that thesis?

As the classical rhetoricians remind us, writing often starts with per-sonal experience, but rhetoric is the art of structuring and ordering that experience. James Baldwin, a modern American writer, echoes that idea in *Notes of a Native Son.*

One writes out of one thing only—one's own experience. Everything depends on how relentlessly one forces from this experience the last drop, sweet or bitter, it can possibly give. This is the only real concern of the artist, to recreate out of the disorder of life that order which is art.

You may be asked at some point to write an essay drawing from your personal experience and developing a general conclusion from that experience. In *Memory and Imagination*, Patricia Hampl explains how using a personal memory is a way to structure experience, to generalize it, to make sense out of it.

There may be no more pressing intellectual need in our culture than for people to become sophisticated about the function of memory. The political implications of the loss of memory are ob-vious. The authority of memory is a personal confirmation of self-hood. To write one's life is to live it twice, and the second living is both spiritual and historical, for a memoir reaches deep within the personality as it seeks its narrative form and also grasps the life-of-the-times as no political treatise can.

Many writers who rely heavily on their own experience speak of creat-ing a shape or an order out of that experience. It is not enough merely to recount an incident just as it happened. Rhetoric advises you to pose the first questions of conjecture, definition, and quality asked in Chapter 2. Did it happen? How did it happen? What happened? and What was its quality? Was it good or bad? Out of these questions arises the thesis that orders and shapes the experience. In recounting the experience of serving a week in jail for protesting nuclear war, one writer formed the following thesis: "Protestors have to be prepared to take the legal consequences arising from the nature of their protests. In my case I trespassed on private property and I was sentenced to a week in jail."

You then need to explore ways to develop the thesis for a particular audience in a particular situation. How do you establish your credibility? How do you appeal to the reader? And finally, what strategies can you use to develop your thesis? Definition? Comparison? Classification? Causal analysis? All of these strategies are ways of ordering that experience, of drawing on your memory to relate that experience and its meaning to other people. All of these strategies belong to the art of rhetoric that is covered in this book.

Maxine Hong Kingston in the following passage from the book *The Woman Warrior* draws from a story told to her by her mother. She relates that story to memories of her own upbringing and adds to those recollections her imaginings of how that upbringing might have been. She explores the question of what happened and considers its moral implications. She compares her imagined version of the story of her aunt and what may have happened with what little information she actually knew, searching her memory and her mind for possible causes and effects. In weaving it all together she tries to come to terms with the story of her aunt, the "No Name Woman."

NO NAME WOMAN

MAXINE HONG KINGSTON

"You must not tell anyone," my mother said, "what I am about to tell you. In China your father had a sister who killed herself. She jumped into the family well. We say that your father has all brothers because it is as if she had never been born.   1

"In 1924 just a few days after our village celebrated seventeen hurry-up weddings—to make sure that every young man who went 'out on the road' would responsibly come home—your father and his brothers and your grandfather and his brothers and your aunt's new husband sailed for America, the Gold Mountain. It was your grandfather's last trip.   2

Those lucky enough to get contracts waved good-bye from the decks. They fed and guarded the stowaways and helped them off in Cuba, New York, Bali, Hawaii. 'We'll meet in California next year,' they said. All of them sent money home.

"I remember looking at your aunt one day when she and I were 3 dressing; I had not noticed before that she had such a protruding melon of a stomach. But I did not think, 'She's pregnant,' until she began to look like other pregnant women, her shirt pulling and the white tops of her black pants showing. She could not have been pregnant, you see, because her husband had been gone for years. No one said anything. We did not discuss it. In early summer she was ready to have the child, long after the time when it could have been possible.

"The village had also been counting. On the night the baby was to be 4 born the villagers raided our house. Some were crying. Like a great saw, teeth strung with lights, files of people walked zigzag across our land, tearing the rice. Their lanterns doubled in the disturbed black water, which drained away through the broken bunds. As the villagers closed in, we could see that some of them, probably men and women we knew well, wore white masks. The people with long hair hung it over their faces. Women with short hair made it stand up on end. Some had tied white bands around their foreheads, arms, and legs.

"At first they threw mud and rocks at the house. Then they threw eggs 5 and began slaughtering our stock. We could hear the animals scream their deaths—the roosters, the pigs, a last great roar from the ox. Familiar wild heads flared in our night windows; the villagers encircled us. Some of the faces stopped to peer at us, their eyes rushing like searchlights. The hands flattened against the panes, framed heads, and left red prints.

"The villagers broke in the front and the back doors at the same time, 6 even though we had not locked the doors against them. Their knives dripped with the blood of our animals. They smeared blood on the doors and walls. One woman swung a chicken, whose throat she had slit, splattering blood in red arcs about her. We stood together in the middle of our house, in the family hall with the pictures and tables of the ancestors around us, and looked straight ahead.

"At that time the house had only two wings. When the men came back, 7 we would build two more to enclose our courtyard and a third one to begin a second courtyard. The villagers pushed through both wings, even your grandparents' rooms, to find your aunt's, which was also mine until the men returned. From this room a new wing for one of the younger families would grow. They ripped up her clothes and shoes and broke her combs, grinding them underfoot. They tore her work from the loom. They scattered the cooking fire and rolled the new weaving in it. We could hear them in the kitchen breaking our bowls and banging the pots. They overturned the great waist-high earthenware jugs; duck eggs, pickled fruits, vegetables burst out and mixed in acrid torrents. The old woman from the next field swept a broom through the air and loosed the spirits-of-the-broom over our heads. 'Pig.' 'Ghost.' 'Pig,' they sobbed and scolded while they ruined our house.

"When they left, they took sugar and oranges to bless themselves. They 8 cut pieces from the dead animals. Some of them took bowls that were not broken and clothes that were not torn. Afterward we swept up the rice and sewed it back up into sacks. But the smells from the spilled preserves lasted. Your aunt gave birth in the pigsty that night. The next morning when I went up for the water, I found her and the baby plugging up the family well.

"Don't let your father know that I told you. He denies her. Now that you 9 have started to menstruate, what happened to her could happen to you. Don't humiliate us. You wouldn't like to be forgotten as if you had never been born. The villagers are watchful."

Whenever she had to warn us about life, my mother told stories that 10 ran like this one, a story to grow on. She tested our strength to establish realities. Those in the emigrant generations who could not reassert brute survival died young and far from home. Those of us in the first American generations have had to figure out how the invisible world the emigrants build around our childhoods fit in solid America.

The emigrants confused the gods by diverting their curses, misleading 11 them with crooked streets and false names. They must try to confuse their offspring as well, who, I suppose, threaten them in similar ways—always trying to get things straight, always trying to name the unspeakable. The Chinese I know hide their names; sojourners take new names when their lives change and guard their real names with silence.

Chinese-Americans, when you try to understand what things in you are 12 Chinese, how do you separate what is peculiar to childhood, to poverty, insanities, one family, your mother who marked your growing with stories, from what is Chinese? What is Chinese tradition and what is the movies?

If I want to learn what clothes my aunt wore, whether flashy or 13 ordinary, I would have to begin, "Remember Father's drowned-in-the-well sister?" I cannot ask that. My mother has told me once and for all the useful parts. She will add nothing unless powered by Necessity, a riverbank that guides her life. She plants vegetable gardens rather than lawns; she carries the odd-shaped tomatoes home from the fields and eats food left for the gods.

Whenever we did frivolous things, we used up energy; we flew high 14 kites. We children came up off the ground over the melting cones our parents brought home from work and the American movie on New Year's Day—*Oh, You Beautiful Doll* with Betty Grable one year, and *She Wore a Yellow Ribbon* with John Wayne another year. After the one carnival ride each, we paid in guilt; our tired father counted his change on the dark walk home.

Adultery is extravagance. Could people who hatch their own chicks 15 and eat the embryos and the heads for delicacies and boil the feet in vinegar for party food, leaving only the gravel, eating even the gizzard lining—could such people engender a prodigal aunt? To be a woman, to have a daughter in starvation time was a waste enough. My aunt could not have been the lone romantic who gave up everything for sex. Women in the old China did not choose. Some man had commanded her to lie with him and be his secret evil. I wonder whether he masked himself when he joined the raid on her family.

Perhaps she encountered him in the fields or on the mountain where 16 the daughters-in-law collected fuel. Or perhaps he first noticed her in the marketplace. He was not a stranger because the village housed no strangers. She had to have dealings with him other than sex. Perhaps he worked an adjoining field, or he sold her the cloth for the dress she sewed and wore. His demand must have surprised, then terrified her. She obeyed him; she always did as she was told.

When the family found a young man in the next village to be her 17 husband, she stood tractably beside the best rooster, his proxy, and promised before they met that she would be his forever. She was lucky that he was her age and she would be the first wife, an advantage secure now. The night she first saw him, he had sex with her. Then he left for America. She had almost forgotten what he looked like. When she tried to envision him, she only saw the black and white face in the group photograph the men had had taken before leaving.

The other man was not, after all, much different from her husband. 18 They both gave orders: she followed. "If you tell your family, I'll beat you. I'll kill you. Be here again next week." No one talked sex, ever. And she might have separated the rapes from the rest of living if only she did not have to buy her oil from him or gather wood in the same forest. I want her fear to have lasted just as long as rape lasted so that the fear could have been contained. No drawn-out fear. But women at sex hazarded birth and hence lifetimes. The fear did not stop but permeated everywhere. She told the man, "I think I'm pregnant." He organized the raid against her.

On nights when my mother and father talked about their life back 19 home, sometimes they mentioned an "outcast table" whose business they still seemed to be settling, their voices tight. In a commensal tradition, where food is precious, the powerful older people made wrongdoers eat alone. Instead of letting them start separate new lives like the Japanese, who could become samurais and geishas, the Chinese family, faces averted but eyes glowering sideways, hung on to the offenders and fed them leftovers. My aunt must have lived in the same house as my parents and eaten at an outcast table. My mother spoke about the raid as if she had

seen it, when she and my aunt, a daughter-in-law to a different household, should not have been living together at all. Daughters-in-law lived
with their husbands' parents, not their own; a synonym for marriage in
Chinese is "taking a daughter-in-law." Her husband's parents could have
sold her, mortgaged her, stoned her. But they had sent her back to her
own mother and father, a mysterious act hinting at disgraces not told me.
Perhaps they had thrown her out to deflect the avengers.

She was the only daughter; her four brothers went with her father, 20
husband, and uncles "out on the road" and for some years became
western men. When the goods were divided among the family, three of
the brothers took land, and the youngest, my father, chose an education.
After my grandparents gave their daughter away to her husband's family,
they had dispensed all the adventure and all the property. They expected
her alone to keep the traditional ways, which her brothers, now among
the barbarians, could fumble without detection. The heavy, deep-rooted
women were to maintain the past against the flood, safe for returning.
But the rare urge west had fixed upon our family, and so my aunt crossed
boundaries not delineated in space.

The work of preservation demands that the feelings playing about in 21
one's guts not be turned into action. Just watch their passing like cherry
blossoms. But perhaps my aunt, my forerunner, caught in a slow life, let
dreams grow and fade and after some months or years went toward what
persisted. Fear at the enormities of the forbidden kept her desires delicate, wire and bone. She looked at a man because she liked the way the
hair was tucked behind his ears, or she liked the question-mark line of a
long torso curving at the shoulder and straight at the hip. For warm eyes
or a soft voice or a slow walk—that's all—a few hairs, a line, a brightness,
a sound, a pace, she gave up family. She offered us up for a charm that
vanished with tiredness, a pigtail that didn't toss when the wind died.
Why, the wrong lighting could erase the dearest thing about him.

It could very well have been, however, that my aunt did not take subtle 22
enjoyment of her friend, but, a wild woman, kept rollicking company.
Imagining her free with sex doesn't fit, though. I don't know any women
like that, or men either. Unless I see her life branching into mine, she
gives me no ancestral help.

To sustain her being in love, she often worked at herself in the mirror, 23
guessing at the colors and shapes that would interest him, changing them
frequently in order to hit on the right combination. She wanted him to
look back.

On a farm near the sea, a woman who tended her appearance reaped a 24
reputation for eccentricity. All the married women blunt-cut their hair in
flaps about their ears or pulled it back in tight buns. No nonsense.
Neither style blew easily into heart-catching tangles. And at their weddings they displayed themselves in their long hair for the last time. "It

brushed the backs of my knees," my mother tells me. "It was braided, and even so, it brushed the backs of my knees."

At the mirror my aunt combed individuality into her bob. A bun could 25 have been contrived to escape into black streamers blowing in the wind or in quiet wisps about her face, but only the older women in our picture album wear buns. She brushed her hair back from her forehead, tucking the flaps behind her ears. She looped a piece of thread, knotted into a circle between her index fingers and thumbs, and ran the double strand across her forehead. When she closed her fingers as if she were making a pair of shadow geese bite, the string twisted together catching the little hairs. Then she pulled the thread away from her skin, ripping the hairs out neatly, her eyes watering from the needles of pain. Opening her fingers, she cleaned the thread, then rolled it along her hairline and the tops of her eyebrows. My mother did the same to me and my sisters and herself. I used to believe that the expression "caught by the short hairs" meant a captive held with a depilatory string. It especially hurt at the temples, but my mother said we were lucky we didn't have to have our feet bound when we were seven. Sisters used to sit on their beds and cry together, she said, as their mothers or their slave removed the bandages for a few minutes each night and let the blood gush back into their veins. I hope that the man my aunt loved appreciated a smooth brow, that he wasn't just a tits-and-ass man.

Once my aunt found a freckle on her chin, at a spot that the almanac 26 said predestined her for unhappiness. She dug it out with a hot needle and washed the wound with peroxide.

More attention to her looks than these pullings of hairs and pickings at 27 spots would have caused gossip among the villagers. They owned work clothes and good clothes, and they wore good clothes for feasting the new seasons. But since a woman combing her hair hexes beginnings, my aunt rarely found an occasion to look her best. Women looked like great sea snails—the corded wood, babies, and laundry they carried were the whorls on their backs. The Chinese did not admire a bent back; goddesses and warriors stood straight. Still there must have been a marvelous freeing of beauty when a worker laid down her burden and stretched and arched.

Such commonplace loveliness, however, was not enough for my aunt. 28 She dreamed of a lover for the fifteen days of New Year's, the time for families to exchange visits, money, and food. She plied her secret comb. And sure enough she cursed the year, the family, the village, and herself.

Even as her hair lured her imminent lover, many other men looked at 29 her. Uncles, cousins, nephews, brothers would have looked, too, had they been home between journeys. Perhaps they had already been restraining their curiosity, and they left, fearful that their glances, like a field of nesting birds, might be startled and caught. Poverty hurt, and that was their first reason for leaving. But another, final reason for leaving the crowded house was the never-said.

She may have been unusually beloved, the precious only daughter, 30 spoiled and mirror gazing because of the affection the family lavished on her. When her husband left, they welcomed the chance to take her back from the in-laws; she could live like the little daughter for just a while longer. There are stories that my grandfather was different from other people, "crazy ever since the little Jap bayoneted him in the head." He used to put his naked penis on the dinner table, laughing. And one day he brought home a baby girl, wrapped up inside his brown western-style greatcoat. He had traded one of his sons, probably my father, the youngest, for her. My grandmother made him trade back. When he finally got a daughter of his own, he doted on her. They must have all loved her, except perhaps my father, the only brother who never went back to China, having once been traded for a girl.

Brothers and sisters, newly men and women, had to efface their sexual 31 color and present plain miens. Disturbing hair and eyes, a smile like no other, threatened the ideal of five generations living under one roof. To focus blurs, people shouted face to face and yelled from room to room. The immigrants I know have loud voices, unmodulated to American tones even after years away from the village where they called their friendships out across the fields. I have not been able to stop my mother's screams in public libraries or over telephones. Walking erect (knees straight, toes pointed forward, not pigeon-toed, which is Chinese-feminine) and speaking in an inaudible voice, I have tried to turn myself American-feminine. Chinese communication was loud, public. Only sick people had to whisper. But at the dinner table, where the family members came nearest one another, no one could talk, not the outcasts nor any eaters. Every word that falls from the mouth is a coin lost. Silently they gave and accepted food with both hands. A preoccupied child who took his bowl with one hand got a sideways glare. A complete moment of total attention is due everyone alike. Children and lovers have no singularity here, but my aunt used a secret voice, a separate attentiveness.

She kept the man's name to herself throughout her labor and dying; 32 she did not accuse him that he be punished with her. To save her inseminator's name she gave silent birth.

He may have been somebody in her own household, but intercourse 33 with a man outside the family would have been no less abhorrent. All the village were kinsmen, and the titles shouted in loud country voices never let kinship be forgotten. Any man within visiting distance would have been neutralized as a lover—"brother," "younger brother," "older brother"—one hundred and fifteen relationship titles. Parents researched birth charts probably not so much to assure good fortune as to circumvent incest in a population that has but one hundred surnames.

Everybody has eight million relatives. How useless then sexual mannerisms, how dangerous.

As if it came from an atavism deeper than fear, I used to add "brother"   34 silently to boys' names. It hexed the boys, who would or would not ask me to dance, and made them less scary and as familiar and deserving of benevolence as girls.

But, of course, I hexed myself also—no dates. I should have stood up,   35 both arms waving, and shouted out across libraries, "Hey, you! Love me back." I had no idea, though, how to make attraction selective, how to control its direction and magnitude. If I made myself American-pretty so that the five or six Chinese boys in the class fell in love with me, everyone else—the Caucasian, Negro, and Japanese boys—would too. Sisterliness, dignified and honorable, made much more sense.

Attraction eludes control so stubbornly that whole societies designed   36 to organize relationships among people cannot keep order, not even when they bind people to one another from childhood and raise them together. Among the very poor and the wealthy, brothers married their adopted sisters, like doves. Our family allowed some romance, paying adult brides' prices and providing dowries so that their sons and daughters could marry strangers. Marriage promises to turn strangers into friendly relatives—a nation of siblings.

In the village structure, spirits shimmered among the live creatures,   37 balanced and held in equilibrium by time and land. But one human being flaring up into violence could open up a black hole, a maelstrom that pulled in the sky. The frightened villagers, who depended on one another to maintain the real, went to my aunt to show her a personal, physical representation of the break she made in the "roundness." Misallying couples snapped off the future, which was to be embodied in true offspring. The villagers punished her for acting as if she could have a private life, secret and apart from them.

If my aunt had betrayed the family at a time of large grain yields and   38 peace, when many boys were born, and wings were being built on many houses, perhaps she might have escaped such severe punishment. But the men—hungry, greedy, tired of planting in dry soil, cuckolded—had had to leave the village in order to send food-money home. There were ghost plagues, bandit plagues, wars with the Japanese, floods. My Chinese brother and sister had died of an unknown sickness. Adultery, perhaps only a mistake during good times, became a crime when the village needed food.

The round moon cakes and round doorways, the round tables of   39 graduated size that fit one roundness inside another, round windows and rice bowls—these talismans had lost their power to warn this family of the law: a family must be whole, faithfully keeping the descent line by having sons to feed the old and the dead, who in turn look after the family. The villagers came to show my aunt and lover-in-hiding a broken house. The villagers were speeding up the circling of events because she was too shortsighted to see that her infidelity had already harmed the village, that waves of consequences would return unpredictably, sometimes in disguise, as now, to hurt her. This roundness had to be made coin-sized so that she would see its circumference: punish her at the birth of her baby. Awaken her to the inexorable. People who refused fatalism because they could invent small resources insisted on culpability. Deny accidents, and wrest fault from the stars.

After the villagers left, their lanterns now scattering in various directions toward home, the family broke their silence and cursed her. "Aiaa, we're going to die. Death is coming. Death is coming. Look what you've done. You've killed us. Ghost! Dead Ghost! Ghost! You've never been born." She ran out into the fields, far enough from the house so that she could no longer hear their voices, and pressed herself against the earth, her own land no more. When she left the birth coming, she thought that she had been hurt. Her body seized together. "They've hurt me too much," she thought. "This is gall, and it will kill me." With forehead and knees against the earth, her body convulsed and then relaxed. She turned on her back, lay on the ground. The black well of sky and stars went out and out and out forever; her body and her complexity seemed to disappear. She was one of the stars, a bright dot in blackness, without home, without a companion, in eternal and cold and silence. An agoraphobia rose in her, speeding higher and higher, bigger and bigger; she would not be able to contain it; there would be no end to fear.

Flayed, unprotected against space, she felt pain return, focusing her body. This pain chilled her—a cold, steady kind of surface pain. Inside, spasmodically, the other pain, the pain of the child, heated her. For hours she lay on the ground, alternately body and space. Sometimes a vision of normal comfort obliterated reality: she saw the family in the evening gambling at the dinner table, the young people massaging their elders' backs. She saw them congratulating one another, high joy on the mornings the rice shoots came up. When these pictures burst, the stars drew yet further apart. Black space opened.

She got to her feet to fight better and remembered that old-fashioned women gave birth in their pigsties to fool the jealous, pain-dealing gods, who do not snatch piglets. Before the next spasms could stop her, she ran to the pigsty, each step a rushing out into emptiness. She climbed over the fence and knelt in the dirt. It was good to have a fence enclosing her, a tribal person alone.

Laboring, this woman who had carried her child as a foreign growth that sickened her every day, expelled it at last. She reached down to touch the hot, wet, moving mass, surely smaller than anything human, and could feel that it was human after all—fingers, toes, nails, nose. She pulled it up on to her belly, and it lay curled there, butt in the air, feet precisely tucked one under the other. She opened her loose shirt and buttoned the child inside. After resting, it squirmed and thrashed and she pushed it up to her breast. It turned its head this way and that until it found her nipple. There, it made little snuffling noises. She clenched her teeth at its preciousness, lovely as a young calf, a piglet, a little dog.

She may have gone to the pigsty as a last act of responsibility: she would 44 protect this child as she had protected its father. It would look after her soul, leaving supplies on her grave. But how would this tiny child without family find her grave when there would be no marker for her anywhere, neither in the earth nor the family hall? No one would give her a family hall name. She had taken the child with her into the wastes. At its birth the two of them had felt the same raw pain of separation, a wound that only the family pressing tight could close. A child with no descent line would not soften her life but only trail after her, ghost-like, begging her to give it purpose. At dawn the villagers on their way to the fields would stand around the fence and look.

Full of milk, the little ghost slept. When it awoke, she hardened her 45 breasts against the milk that crying loosens. Toward morning she picked up the baby and walked to the well.

Carrying the baby to the well shows loving. Otherwise abandon it. Turn 46 its face into the mud. Mothers who love their children take them along. It was probably a girl; there is some hope of forgiveness for boys.

"Don't tell anyone you had an aunt. Your father does not want to hear 47 her name. She has never been born." I have believed that sex was unspeakable and words so strong and fathers so frail that "aunt" would do my father mysterious harm. I have thought that my family, having settled among immigrants who had also been their neighbors in the ancestral land, needed to clean their name, and a wrong word would incite the kinspeople even here. But there is more to this silence: they want me to participate in her punishment. And I have.

In the twenty years since I heard this story I have not asked for details 48 nor said my aunt's name; I do not know it. People who comfort the dead can also chase after them to hurt them further—a reverse ancestor worship. The real punishment was not the raid swiftly inflicted by the villagers, but the family's deliberately forgetting her. Her betrayal so maddened them, they saw to it that she would suffer forever, even after death. Always hungry, always needing, she would have to beg food from other ghosts, snatch and steal it from those whose living descendants give them gifts. She would have to fight the ghosts massed at crossroads for the buns a few thoughtful citizens leave to decoy her away from village and home so that the ancestral spirits could feast unharassed. At peace, they could act like gods, not ghosts, their descent lines providing them with paper suits and dresses, spirit money, paper houses, paper automobiles, chicken, meat, and rice into eternity—essences delivered up in smoke and flames, steam and incense rising from each rice bowl. In an attempt to make the Chinese care for people outside the family, Chairman Mao encourages us now to give our paper replicas to the spirits of outstanding soldiers and workers, no matter whose ancestors they may be. My aunt remains forever hungry. Goods are not distributed evenly among the dead.

My aunt haunts me—her ghost drawn to me because now, after fifty 49 years of neglect, I alone devote pages of paper to her, though not origamied into houses and clothes. I do not think she always means me well. I am telling on her, and she was a spite suicide, drowning herself in the drinking water. The Chinese are always very frightened of the drowned one, whose weeping ghost, wet hair hanging and skin bloated, waits silently by the water to pull down a substitute.

In this excerpt Kingston seeks to order and structure what her mother has told her about her aunt, together with her own upbringing and her Chinese heritage. She compares two different scenarios and two different versions of the character and personality of her aunt. Throughout the narrative she explores possible causes for the event, drawing on her own knowledge of Chinese and American cultural mores. What is the significance of the last line and how does "the drowned one" relate to her aunt and to her? What larger issues is Kingston concerned with? Kingston uses her mother's stories together with her own imaginings to structure her feelings about her cultural heritage in an attempt to make sense of those feelings.

The classical rhetoricians tell us that memory is the treasure house of the ideas supplied by invention, the guardian of all parts of rhetoric. Memory helps us to relate a subject to what we already know. We look for causes, for comparisons, for effects, for associations as we search our memory for knowledge and experience already acquired. As the classical rhetoricians remind us and as modern writers like Baldwin and Hampl tell us, it is through our own experience that we order the world around us. We explore a subject by relating it in some structured way to knowledge we already have.

As you search through the resources of a library you are drawing from the knowledge and experience of others; as you read and listen you are increasing your own store of information. But finally you search through your own life to draw on your own knowledge and experience. Understanding and using both kinds of memory is important. Drawing on both the cultural and the individual memory helps us to make sense of our worlds.

Questions to Consider

1. Consult the *Oxford English Dictionary* to discover the history of the following English words: *cute, charm, woman, corn.* How have the meanings changed? Discuss how and why such changes might have occurred.

2. Look at the table of contents of this book. Where would you find information on metaphor? On topic sentences? On cause and effect? Where else might you look to find where such information might be located in this book?

3. Have you used any computerized indexes? Discuss your experience with them. Are they easy to use? How did you learn how to use them?

4. What kind of a catalog does your library have? Discuss your experiences in using it.

Suggestions for Writing

1. Visit your college library and locate the edition of the newspaper published in the city you were born in for the date of your birth. (If your library does not have it, locate the newspaper published in the city closest to your birthplace.) Then write an essay summarizing the news reported for that day on page one. To organize and develop your essay, you might classify the reports into three groups (international, national, and city/local) and devote a paragraph to each. Be sure to identify the exact source of your summary in your introduction.

2. Choose an occupation, preferably one that you might wish to pursue, and find out all you can about it. What education or training is required? What is the average salary? You might consult the *Readers' Guide* for articles about it, and you might consider interviewing someone currently practicing that occupation (see Chapter 7). You might consider asking the person, for example, why he or she chose that occupation, what he or she has found to be most fulfilling about it, and what he or she thinks are its greatest drawbacks, among other questions. Then write an essay reporting what you have found out. Be sure to unify your essay with a clear thesis.

3. Interview your oldest living relative. You might ask about a memorable event or person. You might ask them to tell you about their school. Can you compare this experience with one of your own? Develop a thesis on the basis of this comparison.

Exercises in Revision

1. Choose from among your previous essays one that you think would benefit from the inclusion of some additional pieces of information taken from outside sources. Consider your intended audience. Are all your arguments fully developed? Take note of the information you need, retrieve it from the appropriate sources in your library, and then rewrite the essay to incorporate it, citing your sources.

2. Provide a classmate with a copy of one of your previously written essays and have him or her read it carefully to determine where it could benefit from added information. Discuss with that classmate where you might best find that information.

For a Commonplace Book

1. Obtain from a professor a copy of the preferred bibliographical form used by those writing in your proposed major. Keep it with your commonplace book for future reference.

2. Obtain from a professor the names of three reputable journals in your area of interest. Locate them in your library and jot down titles and authors that you find interesting. Consult these journals periodically to keep up with current advancements.

PART V

───────

PRESENTATION

───────

> *"But a presentation which is rendered unbecoming*
> *. . . almost entirely destroys the effect of what is said."*
> (QUINTILIAN *INSTITUTIO ORATORIA.* 3.3.3.)

For students in the classical period, the fifth part of rhetoric was the study of the presentation or delivery of the oration. Called *actio* in Latin, it involved voice and gesture and is often translated as presentation. Although Aristotle admitted that the style of presentation affected a speech greatly, he also considered it an unworthy matter for study and therefore gave it little attention. Cicero, however, declared presentation to be the "dominant power in oratory" and Quintilian devoted almost an entire book of his twelve volume *Institutio Oratoria* to the subject. He uses Demosthenes, a highly respected Greek orator, as an example of what training might accomplish. Demosthenes, according to Quintilian, used to practice his orations while climbing hills and rolling pebbles under his tongue in order to increase his fluency.

Presentation for the orator and the writer involves the same principle: in the final analysis, it is the presentation of your ideas in the best and most appropriate way. Orators who slur their speech or slouch before the audience are ineffective—so also writers who do not understand the conventions of the essay exam or the research paper and turn in papers without appropriate citations, or with misspelled words and many erasures. In writing no proof is so secure as not to lose its force if the writer fails to drive it home by a good presentation.

Effective presentation of a written work has two aspects. First there are the customary written forms that academic writing takes—and you will want to be familiar with the rules and conventions of those forms. A research paper requires you to search out information on a subject by going beyond your own knowledge to materials in the library, or interviews, or investigation. There are rules and conventions about how such papers are put together and presented. Essay exams involve short essays whose purpose is to demonstrate your knowledge of a subject. The organization and conventions of essay exams are dictated by the instructor's question. Another common form is the essay about literature—not a critical paper—but one that takes its subject matter from a poem, a novel, a play, or a short story. Each of these has its own rules and conventions although each also depends heavily on invention, arrangement, style, and memory the other parts of rhetoric as outlined in the earlier chapters.

Presentation always depends on the effectiveness of the examples that you use, the appropriateness of the comparisons, the precision of your definitions, the subtlety of the style, and a selective and sensitive use of personal experience. A presentation that fails to establish the writer's *ethos* or fails in its appeal to the reader or builds its arguments on poor reasoning and false premises will in the end fail in its persuasive appeal. As you prepare the final draft, you will want to review all of these elements.

Thus your ideas, whether cast as a research paper, essay exam, literary essay depend on the first four parts of rhetoric—invention, arrangement, style, and memory—but you can enhance all of your ideas, increase the good and effective, by good presentation.

The second aspect of presentation is the physical appearance of the paper. Like the speaker who cannot be heard, the paper that is marred by misspellings, poor typing, erasures, and coffee rings will hurt the credibility of the author. Such a paper gives the impression that the writer does not care either about the subject or the reader. Such papers do irreparable damage to the *ethos* of the writer. A neat paper with good margins, typed with a dark ribbon, does a great deal toward gaining the initial goodwill of the reader.

Chapters 13 and 14 will cover the conventions of the research paper, the short paper about literature, and the essay exam. These chapters build heavily on the earlier chapters, for whatever final form your message takes, it must be rooted in the inventional, organizational, and stylistic choices that you have made and will continue to make until the final draft is turned in.

Chapter 13

The Research Paper

In the research paper, you are expected to go beyond your own knowledge and experience and seek out the knowledge and experience of others. In doing so you may do outside reading, interview authorities, and do other kinds of investigation. The most important aspect of the research paper, like all writing tasks, is clear and coherent presentation of a subject, because presentation always necessarily depends on the strategies you have drawn on to present that subject. At this point you might wish to review such things as the development of yourself as the writer, the appeal to the reader, the validity of the arguments, the organization of your ideas, and the appropriateness of the style for the reader and the occasion. All of these aspects are part of an effective presentation of your message, and the mechanics—footnotes, bibliography, title page—are only the icing on the cake.

The important thing in a research paper is knowing how to find and use outside authorities and how to incorporate their ideas into your own thinking and writing about a subject. In that way, it depends heavily on the other parts of rhetoric and the preceding chapters in this book. Chapter 12 reviewed the resources available in the library and in books. This chapter will describe the process of gathering outside information and the preparation of the final draft in conventional form. The subject you select will focus your reading, but your reading in turn will alter and focus your subject and the development of that subject.

SELECTING A SUBJECT

Whether your instructor gives you guidance in selecting a subject or you are on your own, pick a subject that interests you. Start your initial reading on a broad idea and as you read, explore possible ways of narrowing your subject by asking yourself the three questions of conjecture, definition, and quality suggested in Chapter 2.

To begin with, it is good sense to select a subject that has available materials. A quick check of the card catalog and the *Readers' Guide to Periodical Literature* in your library will help. Don't overlook the possibility of finding information from authorities on the campus or in the community as suggested in Chapter 7. Also don't overlook the possibility of finding facts and figures on your own. Your library is a good source. But surveys and garnering information on your own can also help. One student wrote a research paper comparing the amount and arrangement of cosmetic items and sporting goods in two large department stores serving very different clienteles in her city.

As you think about narrowing your subject, consider the amount of time given to complete the paper, the required length, and the degree of research required. For example, a subject like "Federal Parks" is unwieldy in a five-to-ten-page paper. It might be narrowed to "Federal Parks in California," and then to "Yosemite National Park." It helps to direct your reading if you make your limitation early in your exploration of general background information. Finding a focus as early as possible narrows and directs the rest of your reading and research. Chapter 2 suggests ways of narrowing or limiting a subject.

Finally choose a subject that interests and challenges you. Working on a research paper allows you the opportunity of reading and writing on a subject of special interest to you.

FINDING MATERIAL

Before you begin work on your paper, be sure to ask your instructor which form for the bibliography she or he prefers. All forms include the necessary author, title, and publication information but they vary in the order and manner of presentation. If you know from the beginning which style to use, you can simplify final typing, because it becomes a matter of copying the bibliography cards.

Most English instructors require the Modern Language Association form (abbreviated MLA), which is demonstrated here and explained more fully in the *MLA Handbook for Writers of Research Papers* (Joseph Gibaldi and Walter S. Achtert, eds. 2nd ed. New York: MLA, 1984). All works referred to in the paper are listed with full publication information at the end in a section entitled "Works Cited." Specific page numbers and authors not mentioned in the text itself are inserted in parentheses at the place where reference to them is made.

The last chapter covered in some detail ways of finding information on a subject. In particular you might wish to review the section in that chapter on selective reading. A good place to start is with one of the general encyclopedias. From there the following sources, also described in Chapter 12, are helpful.

1. The card catalog in your library

2. *The Readers' Guide to Periodical Literature*

3. The *New York Times Index*

4. Specialized journal indexes

All of these can open new doors on a subject. The tracings on the catalog card will lead to other subject headings in the catalog that may have materials. In addition, every book and article that you look at may have references or bibliographies that will lead to more information. Learn to watch for those doorways and follow them through when they look promising.

As you look for useful information, start to compile a working bibliography, a list of sources that you will want to consult. A good system for organizing this working bibliography is to create a bibliography card for each possible source. You may later choose to follow up some of these sources; others you may abandon as your ideas become more focused and your thesis develops. This broad list of sources will also help you re-define, revise, and refocus your ideas.

Bibliography Cards

When you find an article or book that is helpful and that you may want to use as a source for your research paper, make a *bibliography card*. Many people find that three-by-five-inch cards work well for this purpose. The bibliography card should contain the following information.

1. The author, with last name first.

2. The title of the book (underlined) or the title of the article (in quotes).

3. Publication Information
   For a book: Place of publication, Publisher, Date of publication.
   For an article: Name of periodical or magazine (underlined), Volume No., Date of publication, Page numbers.

4. The call number of the book or journal.

Recording this information now will be a great help when you evolve your working bibliography into the final list of works cited in your paper.

For most college research papers, at least five or six library sources are necessary to treat a subject with breadth and these sources should in-clude a mix of books, general news magazines, and specialized journals. One or two short articles are just not enough because your paper will reflect a limited view on the subject and, more important, will lean too heavily on those limited sources. You want to consult enough sources to allow you to draw your own conclusions. Your paper should demonstrate your knowledge of your subject and your effort in researching it from different perspectives.

TAKING NOTES

Once you have your working bibliography compiled, begin reading and evaluating the material. When you come across information relevant to your subject, take notes on specific points that you will want to remember or incorporate in your paper. It is wise to read an article through first and then go back and make notes of the material that you might wish to retain. Learning to use a system of taking notes, such as note cards, will help you not only in your composition course, but also in other courses, and often in your professional career.

Note Cards

When you consult the sources you have found, record ideas that might be used in your final paper. One common method is to use note cards. The card should list the name of the author, complete title, and the page number, followed by the jotted note. The note may be a summary of an author's general idea, a paraphrase of an author's specific points, or a direct quotation. We will discuss incorporating these three kinds of notes in your paper later in this chapter. Try to be as precise as possible in taking notes. Be sure to include the exact page number the material appears on and *always enclose quoted material in quotation marks* when quoting an author's exact words.

Sometimes the note card may include both your words and the author's words. It is important to differentiate your words from the authority's words by the use of quotation marks. Exercising care at this point will help you avoid uncertainty later.

OUTLINING YOUR MATERIAL

At some point in your reading you will have narrowed your subject and focused on a thesis (see discussion of thesis in Chapter 2), and after examining a number of sources, you will have some idea of the main points that you wish to make to support that thesis. Even though a rough outline may have been forming in your head as you have been reading, at some point you need to begin to write out an outline of your ideas. Outlines are useful in a number of ways. They can help you plan your paper and check your organization.

As you gather material through interviews or reading, you may find yourself faced with a great many of what appear to be only loosely related ideas. The question is how to put it all together. At this point a preliminary outline can be helpful. Jot down your thesis statement, as you see it at this stage, main points you want to make, and ideas that would fall under each main point. Many writers then gather their note cards before they start to write, sort the cards, and group them together under subjects. Eventually they wind up with five or six stacks that fall under five or six main headings. When they revise their outlines, each pile of cards becomes an item on the outline. Such a system can also be an indication of areas where they need to do more reading or interviewing. For shorter papers an outline can be helpful; for the longer research paper it is essential for most writers in sorting through a large number of ideas and putting them in orderly relationships.

An outline arranges material under headings and subheadings to demonstrate the organization of your material. Thus you start with a statement of your proposed thesis and a series of sentences or subjects that you will use to develop the thesis. Under each sentence or subject heading you jot down the strategy that you will use to develop that idea. As you read and write, your outline will become more detailed. The more detailed your outline the easier your writing will be.

As you work toward a fuller outline, you may run into a few possible problems. First, you will find notes that do not fit into any category and those you may have to discard, much as you may hate to do so. Count them as byways on your main road, and even though you don't use them, they contribute to your overall mastery of the subject, which will show in the final paper. Second, you will find places in your outline where you don't have enough material, points that need more support. You may need to review your own knowledge or return to your working bibliography and the library to do more reading. Finally, you may have to recognize that some ideas you gathered cannot be supported and, therefore, must be abandoned.

Another important use of the outline is to communicate ideas not yet in final written form or to summarize the main ideas in a long paper for another person. More and more writing is being done by collaboration, and sometimes it is necessary to consult with a coauthor about ideas. Often an instructor will ask that at some point in your writing process, you outline your ideas to help you in the development of your paper or to check your organization. Making such an outline can also reveal to you problems or gaps in the paper.

In contrast to the planning outline, the outline that communicates ideas to other people will have a traditional form, which in itself aids in communication. The indentation and headings assigned to items will indicate their importance in relation to each other and to the main idea. Usually the parts of the outline are labelled in a descending order of importance from Roman numerals to capital letters to arabic numerals to small letters:

I.
  A.
  B.
    1.
    2.
      a.
      b.

Sometimes the outline uses the decimal system:

1.
   1.1
   1.2
      1.2.1
      1.2.2
         1.2.2.1
         1.2.2.2

Either system helps your instructor understand the important parts of your paper and their relationship to each other. The headings in this kind of an outline should be complete sentences. Its purpose is to communicate your plan to someone else—a different purpose from the planning outline which is for your use alone. An awareness of audience is necessary in making the outline that communicates to someone else.

WRITING THE FIRST DRAFT AND INCORPORATING SOURCE MATERIAL

Writers differ in their uses of outlines and the point at which they begin drafting a paper. You may have already written an introduction or sketched out parts of your paper or you may not begin the first draft until you have developed a careful and detailed outline. Approaches to the writing process differ, and it is important that you find your own best approach. At some point, however, you will begin to put together a first draft.

In your first draft, you need not and should not worry about formal documentation style. If your note cards are complete, in your first draft you can assign a quotation or an idea or opinion from an outside source with a reference number (1), then enter that number on the note card from which you have taken it. Put that card aside and also put aside the bibliography card that goes with it. As you continue writing, you will begin to accumulate a stack of note cards and a stack of bibliography cards. This procedure will make the preparation of formal citations in the final draft easier.

As you write, remember that a research paper is a blending of your ideas with the ideas of other people. Incorporate the material from outside sources into your paper to support *your* ideas. Keep yourself always present as author and organizer in your paper. When you do incorporate outside material you can choose to summarize and paraphrase an author's ideas or quote an author directly. What follows are some suggestions about how to use outside authorities effectively.

Summarizing and Paraphrasing

Instead of using an author's exact words, you may choose to summarize or paraphrase in cases where the quotation is too long or too involved for your purposes. If the quotation is too long, you will probably choose to summarize—that is, include only the author's main points without the supporting examples or details. If the language of the original is inappropriate for your paper you may choose to paraphrase—that is, recast the author's idea in your own words. In summarizing and paraphrasing you must be careful not to use another writer's ideas as the basis for your whole paper and you must acknowledge such ideas from other sources with a parenthetical reference. It is also important when using paraphrase and summary that you make a careful distinction between your own ideas and those of another writer by signaling the beginning of such borrowed material with an introduction and the conclusion with a reference.

> John White points out that dialectic is not different from dialogue but rather a kind of dialogue (86).

Quoting

In some cases, you may want to include direct quotations in your research paper because an author uses vivid, unique, or noteworthy words, phrases, or sentences. When you do use direct quotations, be brief. Quote only as much as necessary to make your point. As a general rule, do not use anyone else's words to say something that you yourself can say as well. Avoid picking up well-turned phrases by well-known authors and using them in place of your own words because you think they sound better. Notice the use of direct quotation in the following example.

> The sport of fishing is a way of relaxing for many people. "A day of fishing can be better therapy than a weekend at the Ritz" (Shipley 34). Fishing allows the mind to wander and the body to relax.

The quotation does not add to the effectiveness of the writer's idea; the writer might just as well have made the same point in her own words, as in this revision:

> The sport of fishing is a way of relaxing for many people. Just sitting by a lake with my fishing pole can refresh my mind and rest my body. Fishing allows the mind to wander and the body to relax.

Mention within the text the authority of the person that you are quoting or whose ideas you are using if he or she may be unfamiliar to your readers. Otherwise your reader will not know whom you are quoting or why. If the person you are quoting is well known to your readers you need not identify her or him. For example:

Mary Smith, a noted marine biologist, says. . . .

Bill Jones, who has lived in a dorm for two years, maintains. . . .

but

Ralph Waldo Emerson declared . . . .

Note that Bill Jones's having lived in a dorm for two years makes him an authority on dorm food, but not necessarily on football, or the student newspaper. In other words, make clear the source of the person's authority in the field in which you are using him or her as an authority.

When you incorporate a quotation in a sentence of your own, be sure the quotation fits the context and grammatical structure of the sentence.

He accepts his error as a result of his being ". . . one that loved not wisely but too well" (line 344).

instead of

He knows that he is wrong ". . . that loved not wisely but too well" (line 344).

If a quotation is longer than four typed lines, set it off from the text by indentation and do not enclose it in quotation marks. You should introduce it with a sentence in the text, for example,

In his introduction to Allan Bloom's recent book, *The Closing of the American Mind*, Saul Bellow comments on the goals of education.

Every educational system has a moral goal that it tries to attain and that informs its curriculum. It wants to produce a certain kind of human being. This intention is more or less explicit, more or less a result of reflection; but even the neutral subjects, like reading and writing and arithmetic, take their place in a vision of the educated person (26).

Avoiding Plagiarism

Plagiarism is defined as knowingly using another person's words or ideas without giving credit to that person. The penalties can be severe. In many colleges or universities, a student may fail the paper or the course or, in some cases, be expelled from school. The penalties, however, may be far more severe after graduation since it then becomes a legal process involving copyright laws. With the advent of printing and the widespread use of books the written word became an important piece of property, and copyright laws came into being. In the same way, laws are being formed today to protect composers' and musicians' rights to songs, as they are being reproduced on tapes and records.

It is important to know how to use outside materials while avoiding plagiarism and staying within copyright laws for college papers and for professional work as well. In general, sources must be acknowledged for the following kinds of material:

1. Another person's idea or opinion:

   Mary Darwin, a noted film critic, maintains that it is one of the best movies of this century (76).

2. Quotations of any length over two or three words:

   Mary Darwin, a noted film critic, states that it "comes close to being the finest movie in the twentieth century" (76).

3. Any statistics or factual information:

   In 1982, inflation dropped to a low of 7 percent (Jana 22).

General knowledge on a subject does not have to be acknowledged, but the problem is that you have to do a lot of reading on a subject to know what is general knowledge and what is one person's opinion. If you are in doubt, always cite the source. You want to avoid giving the impression that someone else's work or ideas are your own. As you become more knowledgeable about a subject, when you become a professional in your field, you will be able to make these distinctions with more ease.

EXPLANATORY REFERENCES

Occasionally you may wish to make some comment on your subject that does not explicitly belong within the text of the paper. Your comment may explain or enlarge a point; it may make clear a procedure that you are using. If you have only one explanatory reference you may use an asterisk at the appropriate place in the paper and make the note either at the bottom of the page or at the end of the paper. If you have more than one, you may wish to number them; using superscript numbers.

*All further quotations from the novel will include only page numbers.

[1]Even though John called Mary his sister, they were in fact not related at all. Mary's mother married his father when they were both two years old.

At this point you may feel that you are bogged down in mechanical details and it might be a good time to stand back from your paper and look at it again in terms of what you wish it to do. Have you established your credibility and goodwill as the writer and have you written with an awareness of your reader? Is your introduction interesting to that reader and have you provided the necessary background information including definitions of key terms? You may wish to examine your arguments to make sure that they are based on premises that your reader will accept and that they follow a valid chain of reasoning. Finally, does your conclusion sum up the ideas in your paper and possibly connect those ideas to larger issues? At this point try to put yourself in the place of the reader and read your paper for overall effectiveness of style and argument.

PREPARING THE FINAL DRAFT

If you have followed all of the steps in preparing your first draft and revised for content, organization, audience, and style, you can focus on mechanics in polishing your final draft. The most difficult part of your work is behind you. As you recheck the mechanics of your paper, remember that what you are doing from here on is like the paint job on a car that you are trying to sell. If the motor is bad the good paint job won't help much but, on the other hand, if the paint is scratched and marred, buyers may not bother to try the motor. Just as the ancient orator saw tone of voice and gesture as important in getting the message across, so final editing and the appearance of your paper establishes your credibility and seriousness. In preparing the final draft you will need your revised draft and the two stacks of cards: note and bibliography.

Check with your instructor for any special directions about the format of the paper and the materials used. What follows are common guidelines suggested by the Modern Language Association.

All research papers should be typed, if at all possible. If it is handwritten the handwriting must be clear and legible. Use only one side of the paper and use a good quality paper. If you use erasable paper, make a copy and turn in the copy. Use only 8 1/2-by-11-inch paper and allow one-inch margins at the top, bottom, and sides.

Most instructors prefer that your paper not be in a folder or binder. Some instructors do not want papers secured with staples or pins. Paper clips are often the best means of keeping the pages of your paper together. On these matters, you should check with your instructor.

Always keep a copy of your paper. Instructors are only human and they have been known to lose or misplace a paper.

Heading and Title

For most research papers, you do not need a separate title page. Instead use the top of the first page for your heading and title. For the heading, type your name, the instuctor's name, the name of the course, and the date double-spaced, flush with the left margin. Double-space again and center the title of the paper on the page. Quadruple-space, then start typing the body of your paper.

Pagination

Number all pages in the upper right-hand corner one-half inch from the top. Include your last name directly before the number, for easy identification in case the pages get separated.

Listing References

If you prepared the bibliography cards with some care this part of the paper will not be difficult. Arrange the cards for sources you have used in your paper alphabetically with the one closest to the beginning of the alphabet on top. The list of these sources should appear alphabetically on a separate page at the end of your paper under the title Works Cited. This list may also be titled Bibliography or Literature Cited. Works Cited is the title suggested by the MLA because it accounts for sources other than books or articles, such as interviews, recordings, or films.

The entry for each source that you cite should give the reader the complete source information you recorded on your bibliography cards: the name of the author or editor or person interviewed; the name of the book, article, film, or an indication of the source such as "personal interview," "editorial," or "computer software"; publication information, including the city of publication, name of publisher, and for an article, the name of the journal where it was published, volume number, and inclusive page numbers; and date of publication.

The Works Cited entries for other sources such as lectures, tapes, or television shows should also contain this information and any additional information necessary to make it possible for your readers to locate the source.

There are many different forms for references, although all of the forms will include the basic information listed above.

For example, papers written for the social sciences such as psychology should follow the format suggested by the American Psychological Association (APA). There are other accepted styles that your instructor may require. Once you learn what information must be included, you can readily adapt to other forms.

Below are some sample entries that follow the form suggested by the Modern Language Association. You do not have to memorize the following forms. For now, familiarize yourself with the conventions of capitalization and punctuation of entries for a few common sources. For more detailed information, you may wish to refer to the *MLA Handbook for Writers of Research Papers*, 2nd edition. It is readily available in every college or university bookstore.

A book with a single author

Give the author's name (last name first), title (underlined), and publication information. Note that the second line is indented five spaces.

Eby, Frederick. *The Development of Modern Education*. Englewood Cliffs, N.J.: Prentice-Hall, Inc., 1934.

An anthology or collection

Record the name of the editor or compiler, followed by a comma, a space, and the abbreviation "ed." (The abbreviation UP means University Press.)

Graff, Harvey, ed. *Literacy and Social Development in the West: A Reader.* Cambridge and New York: Cambridge UP, 1981.

A book by two or more persons

The authors' names are listed in the order in which they appear on the title page. Reverse only the name of the first author, add a comma, and give the other name(s) in normal order. If there are more than three authors, name only the first and add "et al." ("and others"). If other persons are listed on the title page as editors, translators, or compilers, place a comma (not a period) after the last name and add the appropriate abbreviation (eds., trans., or comps.).

Young, Richard E., Alton L. Becker, and Kenneth L. Pike. *Rhetoric: Discovery and Change*. New York: Harcourt, 1970.

Babb, Howard S. ed. *Essays in Stylistic Analysis*. New York: Harcourt, 1946.

A work in an anthology or collection

State the author and title of the piece you are citing, enclosing the title in quotation marks and underlining the title of the collection. Cite the inclusive pages for the piece at the end of the citation after the year of publication.

Jolly, Peggy. "The Bottom Line: Financial Responsibility." *Writing Centers: Theory and Administration*. Ed. Gary A. Olson. Urbana: NCTE, 1984.

An article in a periodical

An entry for an article in a periodical, like an entry for a book, has three main divisions: author, title of the article, and publication information. For scholarly journals, publication information generally includes the journal title, volume number, the year of publication, and inclusive page numbers.

Bruffee, Kenneth. "Collaborative Learning and 'The Conversation of Mankind.'" College English 46 (1984): 635–52.

An article from a monthly or bimonthly periodical

In citing a periodical published every month or every two months, give the month(s) and year instead of the volume number and issue.

Trilling, Lionel. "Why We Read Jane Austin." *Times Literary Supplement* (March 1976): 50–52.

Citing Sources

The information about the source that your reader will need within the text will include the author's last name and the specific page number in the book or article. This information is included within parentheses immediately after the reference. From this, your reader can refer to the Works Cited for further publication information. The citation in the text is enclosed in parentheses and should follow immediately after the quotation or idea cited:

"It is evident that no theory concerned with literary texts can make much headway without bringing in the reader" (Iser 34).

Notice that the parenthetical reference appears after the closing quotation marks but before the period.

If you cite the author's name within the text, only the page reference needs to go in the parentheses:

> Iser maintains that "no theory concerned with literary texts can make much headway without bringing in the reader" (34).

or

> Wolfgang Iser maintains that the reader must be considered in literary critisism (34).
> Work Cited: Iser, Wolfgang. *The Implied Reader*. Baltimore and London: The Johns Hopkins UP, 1974.

Journal articles are cited in the same manner.

> Arthur Applebee for one cites research that reveals that the textbooks are in charge of training writing teachers before they teach the students (127).
> Work Cited: Applebee, Arthur N. *Tradition and Reform in the Teaching of English*. Urbana: NCTE, 1974.

When referring to an entire book, no page numbers are necessary.

> Willard Espy's *The Garden of Eloquence* is a light but informative description of the figures of speech.
> Work Cited: Espy, Willard. *The Garden of Eloquence: A Rhetorical Bestiary*. New York: Harper & Row, 1983.

SOME MATTERS OF PUNCTUATION AND MECHANICS

There are some mechanics to putting your term paper together. Of course these matters apply to all writing, but they are of particular importance in a research paper. Most of them are there for a purpose and tell your readers something that they would not otherwise know. For example, you indicate that you are using another person's words by indentation or by placing them within quotation marks. Titles are indicated by underlining or quotations marks, and omitted material is conventionally indicated by an ellipsis. In all of these cases, the punctuation marks carry meanings that will help your reader follow your ideas. What follows is a review of some of these rules or conventions.

Titles

All books, plays, long poems, periodicals, films, television programs, operas, ships, and paintings should be underlined or italicized.

> *Revising Prose* (book)
> *Hamlet* (play)
> *Dallas* (television program)
> *Paradise Lost* (long poem)
> *Don Giovanni* (opera)

Articles, stories, essays, chapter titles—all pieces that appear within a larger published work—should be enclosed in quotation marks.

> "The Bear" (a short story)
> "Willa Cather and History" (article in a journal)

Names

The first time that you use a person's name, give the full name. In subsequent references, use only the last name. In general, do not use titles such as Professor, Mr., Mrs., Ms., or Dr.

> John R. Mackey (first reference)   Margaret Mead (first reference)
> Mackey (subsequent references)   Mead (subsequent references)

Numbers

Except for a few established exceptions, use arabic instead of Roman numerals (4 instead of IV). You should write out numbers one to nine (six for 6) and use numerals for numbers over 10 (650), except where a number begins a sentence.

> Two hundred and thirty men made the long trip.

instead of

> 230 men made the long trip.

but

> There were 230 men who made the 10 mile trip.

Quotations

Prose quotations can be indicated in one of two ways. If the quotation is less than four typed lines, it should be placed in the text and enclosed in quotation marks.

> Edward M. White maintains, "Most of those who teach writing in America dislike and distrust testing" (1).

If the quotation is more than four lines, it should begin on a new line and each line should be indented ten spaces and double spaced. Do not use quotation marks.

> Most of those who teach writing in America dislike and distrust testing. While this negative attitude stems in part from a general distrust of the use of numbers to measure people, a more important factor is the great gulf that now exists between the measurement and the teaching of writing (1).

When citing only one or two lines of poetry, they may be run in the text with a slash (/) to indicate line breaks, and enclosed in quotation marks.

> The "plums" that he ate, referred to in the lines "Forgive me/ they were delicious/ so sweet/and so cold," can be thought of in a number of ways.

Or the lines may be set off as they were in the poem.

> The "plums," referred to in the following lines can be thought of in a number of ways:

> > Forgive me
> > they were delicious
> > so sweet
> > and so cold

Never alter a quotation in any way without indicating that you have done so. If a word is misspelled and you want to make it clear that it is not your misspelling, you may indicate that by *sic* enclosed in parentheses. Sic is a Latin word meaning "thus" or "so" and indicates that the error or odd spelling was indeed that way in the original quotation.

> The woman wrote that "she knew nothing about grammer (sic) and didn't need it" (4).

You may add information to make the quotation clear in the context of the sentence, but you must put any such added information within brackets.

"They [the warriors] fought bravely and well."

She felt strongly that "he [her father] was unkind to her."

You may wish to underline part of a quotation in order to emphasize certain points, but any such added emphasis should be made clear to the reader.

She felt strongly that "he was *unkind* to her" (emphasis added).

You may not wish or need to quote a sentence or a paragraph in its entirety, but you need to indicate where you have omitted material. Omitted phrases or words in the middle of a sentence are indicated with three periods with a space before and after each (. . .). If the omission occurs at the end of a sentence, use a period followed by the ellipsis (. . . .) with no space before the first period.
Consider material omitted from the following quotation.

"Shakespeare was a young playwright, caught up in the cares of the world, with a family to support, and he needed and wanted money for himself and that family."

"Shakespeare was a young playwright . . . with a family to support, and he needed and wanted money for himself and that family."

"Shakespeare was a young playwright, caught up in the cares of the world, with a family to support. . . ."

When there is a parenthetical reference at the end of the quotation the period that ends the sentence goes after the final parenthesis.

"Shakespeare was a young playwright with a family to support caught up in the cares of the world . . ." (4).

Quotations are often set off by such words as *says, maintains, states, agrees, disagrees, argues, concludes* followed by a comma; or in a formal introduction by a colon.

"*Hamlet*" Johnson agrees, "is his finest play."
Johnson agrees thus: "*Hamlet* is his finest play."

Use single quotation marks for quotes within quotes.

"The line 'singled out for only one' is difficult to understand in the context," according to Johnson.

Commas and periods go inside the closing quotation marks. All other punctuation marks—colons, questions marks, semicolons—go outside the quotation marks except when they are part of the quotation.

He believed in "the revolution."
He believed in "the revolution," without qualification.
Did he believe in "the revolution"? (the question mark belongs to the full sentence)
He asked: "Do you believe in the revolution?" (the question mark belongs to the quotation)

Final editing of your research paper is an important step in your work for it establishes your credibility in a way nothing else can. Establishing this important first impression, although important, will not, however, rescue a poorly organized, poorly argued paper from final failure. The following research paper, written by a student, is a good example of one that combines careful final editing with an effective argument.

ANOREXIA NERVOSA: DIETING AND DYING

Figure of Speech: Paradox assonance and alliteration.

STUDENT RESEARCH PAPER

Imagine if you can a young boy around the age of fourteen. Jerry is a normal adolescent—happy, energetic, and smart. He enjoys the fruitful life of a vigorous teenager. But something begins to go wrong. Suddenly, this boy becomes very distressed. He feels as if the world is closing in on him, with pressures coming at him from all sides. He feels tension from his parents, his peers, and his teachers. Almost immediately, he becomes very conscious of and obsessed with his self-image and how other people feel about him. He decides that he will gain respect and avoid added tension by becoming physically strong and fit,

Use of example (illustration) in introduction. Leads into thesis statement.

Present tense makes illustration more vivid.

so he begins an extensive exercise program. Then he begins to act compulsively. As he increases his physical activity, he decreases his daily intake of food until he finds it "normal" to consume, as his only meal, unsweetened tea and bouillon, even after a 70-mile bike hike. And slowly, his body deteriorates.

Now, imagine if you can this same young boy in a hospital bed. You can see all the bones and veins through his skin, and his total body weight is a mere 70 pounds. He has just undergone surgery to remove part of his stomach that has died and decayed from lack of use, for practically no food has been absorbed through its walls. Although he will be lucky enough to be cured, he will remain in the hospital for several weeks undergoing physical and psychological therapy that will continue for months or possibly even years.

Contrast to picture of normal boy.

This young boy is a victim of anorexia nervosa, a disease involving a tragic process of self-starvation that was relatively rare until a few years ago and that is far from being fully understood today. According to a recent interview with Robert Hyatt, M.D., a doctor of internal medicine in Columbia, Missouri, this case of the young boy described above is unusual only in that 95 percent of those suffering from anorexia are females.* In fact, the typical anorexic is a young woman who has all her life been thought of as a perfect young lady. As a child, she is likely to have been the pride and joy of her parents, displaying such commendable behavior as obedience in school, helpfulness at home, eagerness to please, cleanliness in habits, and a willingness to be seen and not heard (Conger and Petersen 666). As an adolescent, she is usually the model, straight-A student, well-behaved, bright, artistic, and pretty (*U.S. News and*

Definition of term, "anorexia nervosa."

Use of interview as source, giving authority of source.

Description of anorexic.

*Because of this statistics, the anorexic will be referred to in this paper by the feminine pronouns "she" and "her."

Explanatory reference.

World Report 47). She comes from a white, middle- to upper-class, affluent, and well-educated family (Conger and Petersen 666). In short, she seems to have everything going for her. What, then, makes such adolescents literally starve themselves almost to death? While modern science does not yet have all the answers, recent research indicates that anorexia nervosa is mainly the product of certain psychological disorders that bring about severe physical side effects, with the result that it must be treated as a psychophysiological disease requiring nutritional therapy, psychotherapy, and family counseling for its cure.

Might well be general knowledge but when in doubt, give reference.

Use of question for rhetorical effect.

Thesis statement as last sentence of introduction indicates cause and effect organization of paper.

Undoubtedly one important psychological factor contributing to the rising number of reported cases of anorexia is the social pressure exerted on women today to be thin. In our Western society, thin is "in," a fact that becomes apparent by looking at today's models, who are thinner than ever before. For example, Craig Johnson, director of an eating disorder project at Michael Reese Hospital in Chicago, recently showed that *Playboy* centerfold models have become thinner every year since the magazine's inception. He also found that recent winners of the Miss America contest have been an average of 10 percent thinner than other winners in the last several years (*U.S. News and World Report* 48). It is tragic indeed that the ideal contemporary beauty has not even a natural, healthy look; models are committed to excessive dieting and exercise, and many have been treated for anorexia. Given the ideal these models have come to represent, it is no wonder that more than 70 percent of women in Western cultures feel they are overweight (*U.S. News and World Report* 48). Nor is it surprising to learn that, according to recent surveys, 80 percent of adolescent American girls have been on a diet by the time they reach the age of eighteen (Seligmann 59). Paradoxically, in Third World nations where food is scarce, there are no

Topic sentence brings up first point mentioned in thesis statement: psychological factors.

Identifies authority's credentials.

Statistic requires source.

known cases of the disease (*U.S. News and World Report* 47).

In addition to the pressures exerted on the adolescent by our culture, there is also evidence to suggest that pressures exerted by the more immediate, home environment can contribute to the development of the disease. It is thought that women are especially likely to develop the disorder when their parents set excessively high standards for them or try to exert too much control over their lives (Seligmann 59). In fact, the parents of an anorexic can be characterized in very predictable and general terms. The mother is usually described as dominant and excessively intrusive, while the father is thought of as an "emotional absentee" (Coleman and Butcher 259). Marybeth Bigelow, a counselor in Englewood, Colorado, reports that "The father is more or less an absent figure. If he is home, he's unobtrusive. . . . The mother is the major disciplinarian" (*U.S. News and World Report* 47). These parents, particularly the mothers, typically exert firm control and regulation over their children, causing difficulty in the child's development of a self-identity. They are generally overprotective and do not encourage autonomy. They do, however, encourage perfectionism and often try to control their child's pleasures. As a result, the child becomes so dependent on external clues as determinants of behavior that she fails to recognize and respond to internal emotions and motivations (Conger and Petersen 666).

At the same time, while family members are typically involved excessively in each other's lives, they are often unable to deal effectively with any small conflict that may arise. They may even deny that any conflict exists. As a result, they are usually unable to recognize any real problems within the family (Dove 85). Yet, as Dr. Eugene Piazza, the director of the anorexia clinic at Children's Hospital Medical Center in Boston, declares, "Eating disorders

Good transition to relate paragraphs. Use of "In addition" and "also."

Note four dots indicating ellipsis plus period.

Use of transition "At the same time."

Credentials of authority.

almost invariably disturb family relationships. Siblings get locked because the whole family is disrupted and controlled by this eating problem" (Seligmann 59). Leslie Gershman, a recovering anorexic, agrees with Dr. Piazza and admits, "It's such a manipulative disease. You get people wrapped around your little finger. Any time I wanted my father to visit me in the hospital, I knew he'd be there in a second" (Seligmann 59).

Another kind of credential supplied here.

Good integration of quoted material.

Still, there are countless other psychological reasons why an adolescent may become anorexic. Emotional traumas, for example, have been known to initiate the disease, such as unpleasant or upsetting experiences, depression, fear of change and development, or a poor self-image (APA 68). As a result, anorexia often begins when an individual experiences changes in her life, including entering puberty, enrolling in college, or getting married, that make her feel inadequate. She feels confused and insecure and is afraid that she may not be able to live up to the expectations of others (Coleman and Butcher 259). Dieting usually begins because the anorexic feels that everything will be okay as long as she is thin. As Julie Dadone of Greeley, Colorado, admits, "I thought I could be more popular with my friends and like myself better if [I were] thin" (*U.S. News and World Report* 48).

Topic sentence locates paragraph in context of paper. Points both backward and forward.

Brackets to indicate inserted material.

On closer investigation, it appears that almost all anorexics share some distinctive personality characteristics that made them psychologically susceptible to the disease. The typical anorexic lacks individual initiative and self-identity and feels unable to accomplish her own goals. Often she is childish in her thinking and does not, like most teenagers, exhibit feelings of youthful rebellion (Dove 97). She tends to feel that she is enslaved, that no one will allow her to lead her own life. The patient usually feels a need to be in control of every aspect of her life, yet is certain that she has no such control (Conger

Repetitions of key word, "psychologically."

and Petersen 667). Consequently, the anorexic uses her diet as the sole weapon to control her *body* and her life.

To do so, the anorexic views her *body* as something separate, not as a part of herself. It is something external over which she exercises rigid discipline, and she gains a sense of great power from manipulating it (Coleman and Butcher 259). As she views her emaciated body in the mirror, the anorexic sees herself as the winner of a battle and desires continual victory. She will remain in a state of elevation as long as her weight loss continues, until she wastes away to nothing. Unlike the average dieter, who does not enjoy dieting and looks forward to eating, the anorexic loves her diet and will never allow herself to "cheat." To her, failing to lose weight amounts to destroying the instrument she uses to control her life. If she regains weight, the anorexic tends to experience feelings of deep depression and self-hatred (Coleman and Butcher 259).

Note transition using "body."

Accompanying these motions in an anorexic are distorted perceptions of herself and the way others see her. As the anorexic loses weight, she becomes obsessed with her goal. She sees fat where there is none and continually denies the growing seriousness of her problem. According to a 1983 *Newsweek* article by Jean Seligmann, one reason anorexics do not realize the risks they face is that most victims vastly overestimate their body size. In this article, psychologist Craig Johnson is quoted to observe, "Anorexics rarely see the dangers. . . . They often insist they have never felt better in their lives" (60). Psychiatrist Dr. Arnold Anderson, who is also quoted by Seligmann, maintains, "A sixty-five pound person who tells you, 'Gee, I still feel a little heavy, I'd better take off some more weight' is backing off a cliff without knowing it" (60). Hilde Bruch, an expert in the treatment of eating disorders, confirms these views by reiterating

Having already identified the source, she need only give page number here.

Note introducing terms "maintains," "confirms."

three common symptoms of psychological malfunctioning in anorexics: (1) a disturbance in the perception of the individual's body image; (2) a failure to recognize cues of hunger; and (3) a paralyzing feeling of ineffectiveness (Conger and Petersen 667).

A case in point is that of Karen Tipple of Indiana. She is a thirty-two-year-old woman who, at 5'9", weighs a mere 105 pounds. She says that anorexia makes her feel like two different people—one who sees the problem and views it objectively and another whose instincts tell her to keep losing weight. As Karen confesses, "I don't feel I'm thin enough. . . . When I look in the mirror, what I see makes me feel I'm too fat. I still hate food—that's why I'm trying to live without it" (*U.S. News and World Report* 48). *Note period after parenthesis.*

Use of example.

Often these emotional disturbances become so intense that the anorexic begins to display acts of compulsive behavior. One young woman would chew half a raisin at a time to get two bites out of it instead of eating them by the handful (Seligmann 60). Another girl I went to high school with would bring only a cracker for her lunch, nibbling no more than a crumb at a time to make it last the full, 30-minute lunch period. In fact, there are a number of warning signs indicating the emotional disturbance typical of a person in the early stages of anorexia, including constant talk about food, with a sudden disinterest in once favorite foods; compulsive counting of calories; excessive exercise; a withdrawal from social activities; and such bizarre eating rituals as refusing to let food touch the lips or painstakingly organizing food on the plate (*U.S. News and World Report* 47–48).

Use of author's own experience.

Nevertheless, how does one initially distinguish between bizarre, self-destructive behavior and personal, yet relatively harmless, idiosyncrasies? Where does one draw the line between svelte and skinny? Questions like these make the diagnosis of anorexia very dif-

Use of questions.

Transition from psychological to physical.

ficult indeed. According to the authors of *Adolescence and Youth*, a patient must satisfy at least five criteria before anorexia may be diagnosed: (1) an intensive fear of being overweight, which does not diminish as weight is lost; (2) a disturbed perception of body image; (3) a weight loss of at least 25 percent of the original body weight; (4) a refusal to maintain body weight over the minimum normal weight; and (5) evidence of no other physical illness that may account for the weight loss (Conger and Petersen 667). Unfortunately, given that the initial causes and immediate effects of the disease are psychological and therefore not readily apparent, the detrimental physical effects of the disease may be well underway before the patient is even diagnosed.

Relevant to a consideration of these physical effects is the theory that a rapid weight loss, such as the one the anorexic experiences, can actually alter the chemistry of the brain. According to a 1983 *Health* magazine interview with Dr. Sarah Leibowitz, the brain cell receptors that control appetite may become chemically altered due to prolonged starvation. How does this happen? It involves cell receptors and certain chemicals. On the surface of the cell is a structure that binds chemicals flowing through the blood or bodily fluids. This structure is a receptor, and the chemicals it binds carry important messages to the brain from the rest of the body. If a cell does not capture all of the chemicals it needs, it can produce more receptors to bind the chemicals. Likewise, if there are too many chemicals available, the cell will destroy some of its receptors (10).

The chemical involved in appetite control is called norepinephrine, a substance that carries messages about eating to the the hypothalamus, the structure in the brain that controls appetite behavior. The messages that norepinephrine relays to the brain are either

Introduction to second category: "physical effects."

Use of question.

Personification: "chemicals carry messages."

Definition of hypothalamus inserted in sentence.

that more food is needed or that the body has consumed enough. It is thought that individuals with anorexia have a decrease or a total loss of chemical activity in the area of the hypothalamus associated with hunger signals. According to Dr. Leibowitz, "Young women with anorexia may be so desperate to control their appetites and refuse so consistently to 'hear' hunger signals that they actually end up changing their norepinephrine levels and thus the number of cell receptors on the hypothalamus." Or, she hypothesizes, "perhaps the hypothalamus reduces its receptors so efficiently that it can no longer respond to the call for food. Whatever happens, the feeling of hunger practically vanishes" (*Health* 10). Further research is necessary before these assumptions about the activity of norepinephrine and the hypothalamus can be confirmed.

Good integration of quotation.

Single quotes within double quotes.

These chemical operations occurring deep inside the brain are, of course, not easily detected. What is quite obvious, however, are the physical symptoms of a woman going through anorexia, which, unfortunately, appear only in the later stages of the disease. Some of these are dry skin, extreme emaciation, the ability to see the bones and veins through the skin, a complete halt in the menstrual cycle, low blood pressure, and a constant state of chill (Coleman and Butcher 259). Moreover, as Dr. Hyatt explained to me, since the anorexic has no fat to keep her body warm, she frequently becomes covered with soft, fine, downy hair reflecting her body's natural attempt to retain heat.

Transitional sentence.

Return to interview.

In contrast to these usually reversible effects, there is often permanent bodily damage as a result of anorexia. Often destroyed is the body's delicate balance of potassium, which may lead to serious cardiac abnormalities. In the 1983 *Newsweek* article cited earlier, Jean Seligmann noted of anorexics: "Their

Transition: from reversible effects to permanent ones.

Underlining for title of magazine.

bodies—starved for calories—eventually start feeding on the protein in the muscles. When the heart muscle weakens, it can lead to irregularities in rhythm or even congestive heart failure" (59–60). Indeed, it was due to heart failure that singer Karen Carpenter died of anorexia at the age of thirty-two. Then, too, as Dr. Hyatt explained, the disruption of the menstrual cycle noted earlier is occasionally permanent for severely anorexic women, leaving them forever unable to bear children. Indeed, just being underweight without any indication of anorexia can lead to such uncomfortable consequences as insomnia, irritability, and a lack of concentration (Seligmann 59–60).

Of course, the most detrimental physical side effect of any disease is death. The mortality rate for anorexia nervosa varies from source to source, but the one I encountered most frequently was that stated by Dr. Hyatt— 10 percent. This means that one out of every 10 individuals with anorexia progresses past the danger point of a 25-percent loss of body weight and dies from the disease. According to Dr. Hyatt, this is the highest death rate for any psychophysiological disease.

Because it is, therefore, a psychophysiological disease, the treatment of anorexia is threefold, consisting of nutritional therapy, psychotherapy, and family counseling. The most critical concern is to get the patient to eat again and to gain weight, which is encouraged in a hospital atmosphere. Physical therapy usually takes at least three months, and it includes a program for the redevelopment of muscles as well as a gradual daily increase in nourishment and calories. The patient starts out at about 1500 calories daily and slowly increases her intake until she arrives at her normal weight. During this time, many foods such as fats and dairy products must be carefully rationed because the anorexic has lost

Indicates familiarity, literature.

Note that numbers ten and over are written as numerals.

Transition: topic sentence moves on to three kinds of treatment.

the ability to digest them (Seligmann 59–60). Physical recovery is a long and traumatic process, but it is usually successful.

The complexity of the psychological disorders contributing to the development of the disease makes the psychological treatment for anorexia more complicated. Treating the patient psychologically involves approaches ranging from psychotherapy to techniques of behavior modification. It is essential that personal reorientation, self-identity, and self-respect are achieved. Psychotherapy is used to increase self-awareness, to encourage the patient to take an active part in social activities, to inspire self-direction, and especially to eliminate the disease from her mind. In behavior modification, the patient is rewarded as her weight gain progresses. Drugs such as antidepressants may be included in the therapy in cases of severe depression (Conger and Petersen 667). Finally, family counseling is encouraged in an effort to help the anorexic and her family eliminate or at least minimize the problems at home that contributed to the development of the disease in the first place.

Note parallel construction using infinitives.

Still, it is a sad fact that even though the disease can be treated and the patient eventually cured, there is today no known way that anorexia nervosa can be prevented. Once practically unknown, the horrors of this terrible affliction have recently gained the attention of a number of dedicated researchers, who may someday discover a way to insure that no one ever suffers from it again. In the meantime, we can only hope that the ever-increasing effort to educate young teenagers about the horrors of anorexia will help dissuade at least some of them from choosing like Jerry to waste their bodies and their lives.

Conclusion.

Return to Jerry in introductory illustration.

Works Cited

American Psychiatric Association. *Diagnostic Statistical Manual of Mental Disorders.* 3rd ed. Washington, DC: APA, 1980.

Note edition.

"Anorexia—The 'Starving Disease' Epidemic." *U.S. News and World Report* 30 Aug. 1982: 47–48.

No author so listed alphabetically by title.

Coleman, James C., James N. Butcher, and Robert C. Carson. *Abnormal Psychology and Modern Life.* Glenview, IL: Scott, 1980.

Three authors.

Conger, John Janeway, and Anne C. Petersen. *Adolescence and Youth: Psychological Development in a Changing World.* 3rd ed. New York: Harper, 1984.

Dove, Jody. *Facts About Anorexia Nervosa.* Bethesda, MD: National Institute of Health, n.d.

n.d. indicates there is no date.

"The Hungries: A Personal Interview with Sarah Leibowitz, Ph.D." *Health* Aug. 1983: 10.

Hyatt, Robert, M.D. Personal Interview. 25 Sept. 1984.

Person interviewed and date of interview given.

Seligmann, Jean. "A Deadly Feast and Famine." *Newsweek* 7 Mar. 1983: 59–60.

This author begins the paper with a vivid example that immediately brings the problem of anorexia to the reader's attention. Jerry is very real. The opening example is followed by a definition of the term *anorexia nervosa* and background information in the form of statistics and a description of the symptoms. The thesis or proposition is stated at the end of the third paragraph, and the paper develops the cause of the disease—certain psychological disorders—the physical results of these psychological disorders, and the types of treatment. The conclusion reverts to Jerry in the opening example and points to the hope of continuing research. The paper is carefully edited, easy to read, and presents a good first impression. Finally, the development of the ideas, the organization, and the coherence and clarity of the style all reinforce that initial impression.

Questions to Consider

1. Discuss ways in which the following subjects could be narrowed to subjects that could be developed in a five-to-seven-page research paper. Ask the questions of conjecture, definition, and quality suggested in Chapter 2 about each subject.

A. adjustment problems confronting college freshmen

B. drug abuse in high school

C. unethical advertising practices

D. foreign car sales in the United States

E. academic dishonesty

F. energy conservation

2. Discuss the ways in which the ideas you created above could be developed using narration, description, and the topics of definition, classification, comparison, illustration, and causal analysis.

3. Suggest what sources of information could be used to develop the subjects you generated above.

4. The following introduction is for a research paper written for a class studying the Bible as literature; the student's assignment was to research the meaning and use of the lottery in the Old Testament. Read the paragraph and the accompanying footnotes and perform the exercises that follow it.

Lottery Justice in the Old Testament

In mans historical quest for discovering the divine will of his deity, it is essential that some means outside human control be employed for determining that will. The Hebrew conception of the lottery as described in the Old Testament was considered as a reliable method of doing so. It was assumed that people could not manipulate the instruments of the lottery to produce an effect which they themselves desired. Such a method free from human manipulation would therefore indicate the desire of God.[1] The lottery was thus a religious ceremony in the Hebrew tradition of the Old Testament which was conducted by priests at the sanctuary, the outcome of which was regarded as the voice of the Lord (1 Samuel 10:20–24).[2] Usually accompanied by prayer, the lottery was a means of deciding an issue or of determining the devine will in a matter, was a common practice of ancient Isreal as a direct appeal to God.[3] As indicated in Proverbs 16:33, it was concieved that God was pleased to use the lottery as a method of revealing his will, "The lot is cast into the lap; by the whole disposing thereof is of the Lord."

Footnotes

1.   W.O.E. Oesterley and Theodore H. Robinson. *Hebrew Religion*, New York, Macmillan, 1949, pp. 200–201.
2.   The Interpreters: Dictionary of the Bible, Vol. K–Q, Abingdon Press, 1962, New York, p. 457.
3.   The *Living Bible Encylopedia*, Vol. 9, New York: H.S. Stuttman Company, Inc., 1968, p. 1157.

A. Recast the references with a list of works cited for this paragraph as suggested in this chapter and in the *MLA Handbook*.

B. Go to the library and find another kind of footnote style (psychology or linguistics). Recast the references and list of works cited accordingly.

C. What differences are there? Can you account for these differences? Which method do you prefer and why?

Suggestions for Writing

1. Write a five to seven page research paper using one of the subjects you generated during the class activity prescribed above or a subject of your own choice. In preparing your paper, be sure to follow the procedure prescribed in this chapter as indicated below:

A. Begin by choosing a subject that can be adequately developed in a five-to-seven-page research paper. Obtain your instructor's approval.

B. Submit to your instructor a working bibliography consisting of possible sources of information on your subject.

C. Compose a bibliography card for each source of information you find useful.

D. Use note cards on which you record information you intend to incorporate in your paper.

E. Once you have obtained all of your information, compose a tentative outline for your paper and submit it to your instructor for approval.

F. Prepare a draft of your paper from your revised outline.

G. Check your draft to make sure that you have established your credibility and good will, that you have appealed to your reader's interests, and that your arguments are valid and your premises acceptable. Finally, is your introduction and conclusion well stated and your organization clear and coherent?

H. Prepare a final draft for your paper in accordance with the recommendations provided in this chapter. Edit it carefully for spelling, punctuation, and typos.

Exercises in Revision

1. With your workshop group, answer the following question:

A. Does the first paragraph perform the function of an introduction? Does it contain the thesis? If not, revise it appropriately.

2. Some students when confronted with a long writing assignment, fall into unnecessary wordiness rather than concrete development to achieve the assigned length. Examine each sentence in the paragraph to determine whether this is the case with this writer and, if so, eliminate it in your revision.

3. Correct any grammatical, spelling, or typographical errors you can detect in the paragraph.

For a Commonplace Book

Determine now to sharpen your ability to extract information from published materials by periodically writing a paragraph in your commonplace book that summarizes something you've recently read. That "something" can be a scholarly article, an editorial in *Glamour* magazine, or an account of a tennis match in *Sports Illustrated*. The point is to practice picking out the author's main idea and the points he or she uses to develop it. After summarizing the content, write another paragraph responding to what you've read. Do you agree with the author? Admire the style of the article? Suspect that the writer doesn't know what he or she is talking about? Record your decision and try to account for your reaction. The more sensitive you become as a reader, the more sensitive you will become as a writer.

Chapter 14

Other Common Forms
of College Writing

THE SHORT PAPER ABOUT LITERATURE

    Selecting a Subject
    Rereading to Focus on Your Subject
    Providing Textual Support

A SAMPLE PAPER, "GESTURE IN *A DOLL'S HOUSE*"

THE ESSAY EXAM

    Preparing for an Exam
    Taking the Exam

Chapter 13 covered the research paper, a common kind of assignment in many courses such as English, history, political science, and psychology. This chapter covers other kinds of writing assignments that you may encounter before you graduate: the short paper about literature and the essay exam.

The first place to start in any writing project is with the assignment where directions and suggestions may be stated either implicitly or explicitly. Does the assignment pose a question or does it suggest a possible kind of development by asking you to compare or define? Does it suggest the use of examples or possible sources of information (library or interviews)? Often the assignment will suggest a length and format for your paper. Learn to take advantage of such suggestions.

College writing differs from other kinds of writing in two important ways: the audience addressed and the purpose of the communication. In essay exams, literature papers, or research papers, your audience is always your instructor, an important fact to keep in mind. Even when your professor tells you to imagine an audience, the final reader will be your instructor. So in some cases you may have to deal with a double audience—your imagined audience *and* your instructor (see the section on the multiple audience in Chapter 3).

In addition, the real purpose in college writing, is to demonstrate your knowledge of a subject. It will help you to remember this fact and make use of it. In an essay exam on Shakespeare, for example, you are well aware that the professor or grader who reads the exam knows more about Shakespeare than you do. The purpose in such cases is not to inform the reader but to demonstrate your knowledge of a subject and your ability to think critically and creatively and to adopt the conventions of the discourse of the discipline. Although that fact alters to some extent the nature of college writing, the lessons learned in such assignments can be transferred to writing in the professions as you write for multiple purposes to multiple audiences

THE SHORT PAPER ABOUT LITERATURE

You will encounter this kind of paper in your basic literature courses or possibly in your composition class. Any such paper starts with a careful reading of the original text. In addition, you will want to review any class notes that you may have. Some instructors specifically warn students against going to outside sources, but generalized articles about the literary work, such as introductions to editions and introductory material in literature textbooks, can sometimes help you gain a greater understanding of the text.

It is important to read your instructor's assignment carefully or to take careful notes if the assignment is given orally. Do not hesitate to ask questions about matters that are not clear. Assignments can suggest ideas and give guidance about ways to proceed in addition to giving obvious directions about due dates and length of the paper.

Selecting a Subject

The instructor may give you a specific assignment or require that you select your subject. A paper about literature can do one of a number of things: It may argue a position or offer an opinion. It may explain some limited aspect of the work. More ambitiously, it can evaluate or interpret the work. For example, the question of whether Hamlet's madness in Shakespeare's *Hamlet* is real or feigned is a commonly argued question by critics, which your instructor may point out to you. You may wish to take one position or another in your paper. On the other hand, you may wish to give your opinion that the issue of madness real or feigned is not an issue in the final outcome of the tragedy. You may wish to discuss the setting of a novel and its effect on the plot, or compare two characters in a play, or analyze the use of language in a poem explaining how sound—alliteration or assonance—reinforces the meaning.

Rereading to Focus on Your Subject

After you have selected a subject, it is a good idea to reread the work, focusing on your subject. As you read you will be focusing on your idea, testing its validity and searching for support from the text itself. If you can find such support your idea is likely a good one; if you cannot, you may wish to alter your direction. In this rereading you will be performing a number of tasks simultaneously.

1. You will be focusing your reading searching for material relevant to your subject.

2. You will be narrowing and directing your subject.

3. You will be forming and testing several ideas for a thesis.

4. You will be forming a workable thesis and looking for ideas to support that thesis.

5. You may wish to jot down appropriate quotations, being careful to record page and line numbers.

Somewhere in this process your pencil will find its way to the paper or your hands to the keyboard.

Providing Textual Support

The thesis must be supported and each subsequent point must be supported by evidence from the text itself. Thus in a paper arguing that Coleridge's use of language contributes to the poetic effect of "The Rime of the Ancient Mariner" you might cite as evidence his use of alliteration and support that point by reference to the use of "f" sounds to give the impression of blowing wind.

> The fair breeze blew, the white foam flew,
> The furrow followed free.

In papers based on written texts, the text itself—the play, the poem, the novel, the short story—is your data resource.

The following student paper makes ample use of textual support for the thesis that in Henrik Ibsen's *A Doll's House* Nora's gestures reinforce the picture of Nora maturing during the course of the drama from childhood to full adulthood. Note that after an introduction that states the issues and then narrows to the thesis, the author works through the play itself giving support in the form of specific references to actions or lines quoted from the play to support her main points.

This paper was written in response to the following assignment:

Paper One—500 to 800 words (2–3 pages typewritten)

A critic contends that gestures are part of the "language of drama." If this is so, they, like dialog, costumes, setting, lighting, and sound effects, make some kind of specific contribution to the meaning of the whole play. For this paper, consider the gestures of one of the main characters or one type of gesture of affection, for example, used by several characters.

Figure out what the gesture communicates. Then relate your analysis to the thrust of the entire drama.

GESTURE IN *A DOLL'S HOUSE*

It is often said that actions speak louder than words. Perhaps we are at a disadvantage then, when reading a play, since we can't see or hear but only read about the events. However, if one reads the stage directions, one may visualize the action according to how the character is portrayed. In *A Doll's House*, by Henrik Ibsen, the gestures of Nora seem to mature during the course of events, and, in the short time span of the story, her body language grows from that of a young, carefree child to a troubled adolescent and finally to a mature woman.

In the first part of the play, before the audience knows of any conflict, Nora seems to be a happy, almost mischievous girl. She eats a couple of macaroons (knowing her husband disapproves) and immediately checks to see if her husband is home. He is, and, when he comes out of his study, she quickly has to hide the evidence as she puts the bag of macaroons

Starts with broad general statement, then narrows it to plays.

Narrows to stage directions and then to gestures.

Statement of thesis predicts organization.

Topic sentence of part one that depicts Nora as a child.

Textual evidence that Nora is "happy, mischievous girl."

back in her pocket, wipes her mouth.* One can almost picture her wiping her mouth by drawing her sleeve across her face. This episode seems very reminiscent of a child stealing cookies before dinnertime, behind her mother's back, and then having to hide everything for fear of being discovered.

Compares Nora's actions to those of a child.

Another example of her little girlishness occurs when she is talking to Mrs. Linde. Nora is asking personal questions about her marriage—did she love her husband or not and why did she marry him. When she asks these questions she "sits down on a foot stool close to Mrs. Linde and puts her arms on her lap" (36, col.1). Nora is acting like a little girl sitting at the foot of her grandmother's rocker, asking for a fairy tale. It doesn't occur to Nora that perhaps this is a painful subject for Mrs. Linde to talk about or that she might appear a bit nosy. By her action of sitting at the feet of Mrs. Linde like a child, Nora treats the whole subject of Mrs. Linde's personal life as just another interesting tale.

More textual evidence to show Nora as a girl.

Again compares Nora's actions to actions of a child.

The second stage in Nora's development is while she is wrestling with the truth of the fraud she has committed as well as with Krogstad's bribery. Her gestures are not as childish as before, but she still seems to be unsure as to which world she belongs in—the playful child world or the harsh adult world. At one point during this turbulent "adolescence" she "nudges [the children] gently into the other room and closes the door. She sits down on the couch, picks up a piece of embroidery, makes a few stitches, then stops" (43, col. 2). She then calls for the maid to bring in the Christmas tree.

Topic sentence brings up second stage—Nora's adolescence.

Textual evidence of Nora's development as an adolescent.

By pushing children away, she pushes her own childhood away.

These actions seem to signify Nora's attempt to push out her own immaturity when she pushes the children out of the room. She then tries to do some embroidery, which is

This and all references are to: Henrik Ibsen, "A Doll's House" in Types of Drama *ed. Sylvan et al., pp. 32–66.*

what the nice adult ladies of her time did. This is her attempt to be an adult. Another interpretation could be that she is trying to "stitch" her life together in some meaningful way. But this attempt does not work. She calls for the Christmas tree to be brought in. This seems to be the only symbolic object that exists in both childhood and adulthood and gives pleasure despite one's age. This is her link to both sides, and she doesn't know quite where she belongs.

Embroidery is symbol of adulthood.

More textual evidence. Christmas tree seen as link between childhood and adulthood.

The last scene is when Nora finally grows up. Not only are her words mature, but she has ceased to be the jumpy girl or the dramatic teenager. After the letter comes and Helmer has forgiven her, her gestures all imply a cool, calm, and collected adult, something her gestures did not convey at the start. At one point she consults her watch and quietly sits down at the table (63, col. 1). Finally at the end, she is composed when she changes and returns with her streetbag, puts on her coat, and wraps a shawl around herself. She does this all in an adult-like manner. Had she still been childlike, the stage directions might have said, "runs into the room with streetbag, throws on coat and shawl and takes hat with her under her arm." But she is now an adult and proceeds with a quiet dignity.

Topic sentence introduces idea of Nora as an adult in the last scene.

Textual evidence.

Contrasts Nora's adult actions in last scene with those of a child.

When Nora is treated like a child, she invariably acts like one, but when she begins to understand the circumstances around her in an adult fashion, she sheds her immaturity and impulsiveness. She now begins to act her age. She also seems to understand that she is not yet an adult, but rather she has begun to become one and, indeed, a little late.

Concludes that Nora sheds her childishness during the play.

Nora understands that becoming an adult is a slow process.

Notice how well this student supports the points that she makes with evidence from the play's stage directions. In making the point that Nora's actions at the beginning of the play show her as a "happy, almost mischievous child" the writer demonstrates Nora's childlike behavior in stealing the macaroons and quickly hiding them from her husband. She also cites her childlike posture as she talks with Mrs. Linde. All of these actions drawn from the stage directions provide evidence for the point that the writer is making. She continues to cite similar textual evidence to support her thesis.

Notice that this writer does not summarize the plot of the play. You may safely assume that your reader knows the plot.

THE ESSAY EXAM

Essay exams are easier to tackle if you prepare yourself by studying the material and adopting a strategy for presenting that material. Remember that an essay exam tests a number of things besides the material in the course. It also tests your ability to prepare for the exam, to organize the material, and last but most important—to write creatively and critically about that material. Often the topics—definition, comparison, classification, causal analysis—and other inventional strategies are useful ways of developing an essay answer. Note how the following questions demand such development.

From a philosophy examination: *Compare and contrast* the Stoic and Epicurean philosophy as a way of life.

From an English examination: *Define* the epic form by showing how *Beowulf* and "The Nun's Priest's Tale" satisfy or do not satisfy its conventions.

These essay questions test not only your knowledge of the material, but also your ability to write clearly and coherently about that material by following the suggestions in the questions *define* and *compare and contrast*.

Preparing for an Exam

The best way to prepare for an essay exam is to be thoroughly familiar with the material that the exam will cover, including all classroom lectures and assigned readings. In reviewing you will be making connections in your mind as you define, compare, and classify ideas drawn from these sources. So in studying you not only review what you have already learned but you are examining your notes from different perspectives and putting ideas together in new ways. This kind of preparation not only helps you to absorb the material but will also help to generate ideas when you write the exam.

Lecture Notes Ideally, your professor will prepare lectures in the same way that you make an outline for a paper, speaking from main points and filling in with details and specific examples to develop those main points. Your notes will include the main points, omitting the details. For example, a professor may give a lecture on the child's acquisition of language and spend the class hour discussing the three stages of development that the child goes through. In the course of discussing those stages, the professor may give many examples. It is the examples and details that are the easiest to remember, so you need not record them. Note main points with just a word or two reminder of examples. In writing an exam or paper you will of course need to use the examples to support your points. Lectures, notes, and papers all follow these same principles of organization.

Textbook Material Similarly, in studying textbook material, it is important to recognize the writer's organization and seek out the outline from which the author works. Tables of contents, again, are helpful, as are chapter titles, subtitles, and section headings (see Chapter 12). Take notes from your textbooks, or use a highlighter. In taking notes the act of writing assists in retention of the material. Working out the organization in large bodies of material helps in understanding and retaining it and suggests possible questions that may be on the exam.

In taking lecture notes, in reading the textbook, in writing the essay exam itself, it helps to separate main ideas from supporting ideas, thesis statements from topic sentences, and topic sentences from details and examples. If you retain the main ideas; you can remember details and examples more easily.

Take special note in your text of words that are in boldface or italics. Usually such words are important and may be followed by definitions. All disciplines—English, political science, mathematics, and history— have their vocabulary, and knowing the discipline means knowing the vocabulary. It might help to make a list of special words in your discipline and their definitions. Learn how to spell the key words in a field that you will almost surely have to use on an examination. Misspelling of key words may destroy your credibility at the outset.

Taking the Exam

Before beginning to write you will want to read through the entire exam—underlining instructions such as "Answer one of the following," or "Answer only A and B." Consider the order in which you plan to answer the questions. When there is a choice, make the choice quickly and then stay with it. It is not wise to take too much time on such decisions.

Take special care that your handwriting is legible. An exam that is difficult to read will only irritate the grader.

Formulating an Answer   It is wise to make a short scratch outline of any ideas that occur to you as you read the questions before you start writing in order to organize your material and to prevent accidental omissions. You may not stay with the outline, but it provides a thinking period before you begin. Essay exams do not make allowance for multiple drafts.

Remember that your answer should be a self-contained essay that could stand alone, separate from the question. Your first sentence or two should restate the question in statement form and suggest your plan of organization. Note the following question:

> Explain why the Stoics believed that only moral *virtue* is good, and why nothing that befalls a man is ultimately bad.

The question with its two "why's" clearly calls for development from cause. The first sentence should restate the question:

> The Stoics believed that only moral *virtue* is good, because . . .

You may wish to restate key words in order to maintain focus and direction.

Allotting Time   Always wear a watch and allot your time as closely as possible. Try to allow some time, five to ten minutes, to reread and edit your answer at the end of the period.

Most examinations have indirect indications of the amount of time to allot to each question, such as a point value attached to it (ten points or twenty points). Thus, if your exam period is fifty minutes, a twenty point question should be given about ten minutes. Since it is worth one-fifth of the total points it should be given one-fifth of the time. A few rapid mathematical calculations at the start will help you plan your time. Sometimes instructors will simply state how much time should be spent on each question.

The following key words often used in essay exams also indicate how long to spend on each question.

The following terms usually indicate full, detailed answers:

> Explain
> Discuss
> Describe
> Trace

The following terms indicate shorter answers:

Enumerate
Outline
Name
Identify
List

If your time does not work out as planned and you run out of time on your last question, rather than leave an answer blank, you might outline your material indicating main points. Such an answer will not receive full credit, but your instructor may allow partial credit if you can indicate your knowledge of the material in such a way.

Key Words Familiarity with the following key words that you may encounter in essay exams will help you decide on a strategy to use in answering each question. These strategies involve the classical arguments or proofs already covered in detail. The terms are cross-referenced to chapters that give fuller explanations.

Compare	When you are asked to compare, you should examine qualities, or characteristics, in order to discover similarities. You are to emphasize similarities, although differences may be mentioned (see Chapter 5).
Contrast	When you are instructed to contrast, you should stress dissimilarities, differences, or unlikeness of associated things, qualities, events, or problems (see Chapter 5).
Criticize	In a criticism you should express your judgment with respect to the correctness or merit of the factors under consideration. You are expected to give the results of your own analysis and to discuss the limitations and good points or contributions of the plan or work in question.
Define	When you are asked to define something, try to give concise, clear, authoritative meanings. In such statements details are not required but boundaries or limitations of the definition should be briefly cited. You must keep in mind the class to which a thing belongs and whatever qualities differentiate the particular object from all others in the class (see Chapter 4).
Describe	In a descriptive answer you should recount, characterize, sketch, or relate in narrative form (see Chapter 7).
Diagram	For a question which specifies a diagram you should incorporate a drawing, chart, plan, or graphic repre-

	sentation in your answer. Generally you are also expected to label the diagram and in some cases to add a brief explanation or description (see Chapter 7).
Discuss	The term *discuss*, although a bit vague, directs you to examine, analyze carefully, and present considerations pro and con regarding the problem or items involved. This type of question calls for a complete answer with detailed examples.
Enumerate	The word *enumerate* specifies a list or outline form of reply. In such questions you should recount, one by one, in concise form, the points required.
Evaluate	In an evaluation question you are expected to present a careful appraisal of the problem, stressing both advantages and limitations. Evaluation implies authoritative and, to a lesser degree, personal appraisal of both contributions and limitations.
Explain	In explanatory answers it is imperative that you clarify, elucidate, and interpret the material you present. In such an answer it is best to state the "how" and "why," reconcile any differences in opinion or experimental results, and, where possible, state causes. The aim is to make plain the conditions which give rise to whatever you are examining (see Chapter 7).
Illustrate	A question that asks you to illustrate usually requires you to explain or clarify your answer to the problem by giving detailed examples (see Chapter 5).
Interpret	An interpretation question is similar to one requiring explanation. You are expected to analyze, exemplify, or comment upon the subject and usually to give your judgment or reaction to the problem.
Justify	When you are instructed to justify your answer you must prove or show grounds for decisions. In such an answer, present convincing evidence (see Chapter 6).
List	Listing is similar to enumeration. You are expected in such answers to present an itemized series or a tabulation. Such answers should always be given in concise form.
Outline	An outlined answer is organized description. You should give main points and essential supplementary materials, omitting minor details, and present the information in a systematic arrangement (see Chapter 13).
Prove	A question which requires proof is one which demands confirmation or verification. In such discussion you should establish something with certainty by evaluat-

<table>
<tr><td>Relate</td><td>ing and citing experimental evidence or by logical reasoning (see Chapter 6).
In a question that asks you to show a relationship, your answer should emphasize connections and associations in descriptive form (see Chapter 5).</td></tr>
</table>

Relate   In a question that asks you to show a relationship, your answer should emphasize connections and associations in descriptive form (see Chapter 5).

Review   A review specifies a critical examination. You should analyze and comment briefly in organized sequence upon the major points of the problem.

State   In questions which direct you to specify, give, state, or present, you are called upon to express the high points in brief, clear narrative form. Details and usual illustrations or examples may be omitted.

Trace   When a question asks you to trace a course or event, you are to give a causal analysis of progress, historical sequence, or development from the point of origin. Such narratives may call for probing or for deductions (see Chapter 5).

Sample Questions and Answers Notice how the following questions from essay exams determine the organization of the answer.

1. From Political Science

   Socialism and totalitarianism are often thought of as the same kind of political system. What differences exist between them? Are either or both inconsistent with democracy? In what ways?

   Outline of Answer

   I. Similarities between socialism and totalitarianism

      A.
      B.

   II. Differences between socialism and totalitarianism

      A.
      B.

   III. Similarities and differences between socialism and democracy

      A.
      B.

   IV. Similarities and differences between totalitarianism and democracy

      A.
      B.

2. From English Literature

Thoroughly define the epic form by showing how *Beowulf* and "The Nun's Priest's Tale" satisfy or do not satisfy its conventions.

Outline of Answer

   I.   Definition of epic: Three Characteristics

  II.   First Characteristic

     A. In *Beowulf*
     B. In "The Nun's Priest's Tale"

 III.   Second Characteristic

     A. In *Beowulf*
     B. In "The Nun's Priest's Tale"

 IV.   Third Characteristic

     A. In *Beowulf*
     B. In "The Nun's Priest's Tale"

It is fairly easy to visualize a general outline of the answer from the nature of the question in the essay exam.

The following question from an economics exam calls for a cause and effect answer.

Why have trucks gradually supplanted trains as carriers of freight?

Answer B received a higher grade than Answer A. Can you give reasons for the difference?

Answer A.

For one thing, trucks are relatively new because of the short history of the auto. But the trucks have become popular for other reasons. They are more flexible than trains. Also, they make door to door deliveries at any time, but a train has to follow its tracks. The truck does not encounter delays at terminals, as trains do, thus speeding up transit, which reduces loss of perishables. The truck is best for small hauls, but the train for longer ones. Small shipments can be sent by truck more economically. They can travel faster, then too the trucks get their roads free. They don't have to load and unload so many times, and that makes a difference. The truck is not damaging the train business of very long cross country hauls. Goods probably ride easier in a truck equipped with rubber tires and springs.

Answer B.

The one essential reason that trucks are gradually supplanting trains as carriers of freight is that for most hauling they are more economical. Let us say that a central Illinois farmer has a number of hogs to ship to Chicago. If he sends them by train, he usually must first load them into a truck, unload them at the local stock pens, have them loaded on the train, hauled to Chicago, and unloaded once again. These operations consume time and money. The truck, a more flexible unit, takes the hogs direct from the farm to the stockyards, perhaps in half the time, and consequently with less weight loss; for almost invariably truck transportation is more speedy than train. Truckers, because of lower taxes, smaller investment, and greater flexibility, perform for lower cost and give better service than trains. However, service, speed, flexibility, or whatever you choose to call the advantage of the trucker, really amounts in the end to economy for the person hiring the truck.

Answer A is not self-contained; it seems to start in the middle with an irrelevant introduction and is not governed by any main idea. The phrase "for one thing" does not have an antecedent. The student goes on to list a series of unconnected statements comparing trucks to trains which appear to support reasons why trucks are supplanting trains. But the second to last sentence seems to negate the other ideas. The use of "probably" in the last sentence leaves a note of uncertainty. The answer lacks direction.

Answer B, in contrast to Answer A, starts with a sentence that restates the question within the student's own main idea or thesis statement. The student focuses the answer around "one central reason" that puts the other reasons listed within a context. The second-to-last sentence summarizes and restates the reasons and the last sentence returns to the thesis stated at the beginning: "the advantage . . . amounts in the end to economy. . . ." Notice that the key words contained in the question— *trucks, trains, carriers of freight,* and *supplanted*—are repeated in the first sentence and carried throughout the paragraph.

The kinds of writing discussed in the last two chapters—the research paper, the short paper about literature, the essay exam—cover some important kinds of writing that you will be expected to do in your four years of college. All of them rely on the rhetorical strategies discussed in the preceding chapters in this book. In concentrating on the conventions of a good presentation, never forget that this final step of editing and revising still involves all of the important inventional strategies of establishing your own credibility, appealing to your reader, and presenting well-formed arguments. In addition to being well-organized, the paper must embody clarity and coherence, because, in the end, all of these elements are part of an effective presentation.

Questions to Consider

1. Bring in some essay exam questions that you have encountered in other courses and discuss how to organize and develop answers based upon an interpretation of the key words provided in the original questions.

2. Bring in copies of the original questions and the answers that you wrote for exams taken in other classes with your name deleted. Examine strengths and weaknesses with your classmates.

3. Examine Chapter 1 and suggest questions that could be answered in an essay.

4. Bring in an assignment for a paper in a literature class. Discuss how you might approach such an assignment.

Suggestions for Writing

1. Write an essay in response to one of the questions you generated about Chapter 1 above.

2. Taking your cue from the positive suggestions provided in this chapter, write a humorous essay in which you describe the *worst* way to prepare for an exam or to actually take it. Don't fail to rely on personal experience for developing your "recommendations."

Exercises in Revision

1. Choose an essay you wrote for an exam given in another class that you were dissatisfied with and rewrite it to eliminate as many of its shortcomings as you can. Append to your revision a paragraph in which you point out what makes the revision better.

2. Review your lecture notes for a given day in one of your classes, and then develop them into a coherent and organized essay. Be sure to make the connections clear between each point and to provide a thesis statement.

For a Commonplace Book

1. Get into the habit, if you aren't already, of reading something regularly that is totally unrelated to your course work. Keep a novel or a collection of short stories (your instructor would be happy to recommend some) by your nightstand to read for pure enjoyment. To continue to practice your writing skills, set aside some time once a week to write about your response to what you've read. Are you enjoying the novel you're reading? Why, or why not?

Epilogue

What follows are three excerpts from the writings of ancient philosophers on subjects that concern all rhetoricians. In the first, Plato, through the voice of Gorgias, an early teacher of rhetoric, extols the power of rhetoric and compares it to wrestling, insisting that both skills must be used justly.

In the second passage, Quintilian speaks of writing and gives students practical advice that has a ring of modernity, including when and where to write and how to revise. He concludes with words of encouragement, advising students not to be anxious about their revisions but to "let there be something in all our writing, which, if it does not actually please us, at least passes muster."

In the final passage, Aristotle speaks of friendship in Book Two of his *Rhetoric*, which contains long discussions of human emotions and passions. Following his belief that the rhetorician must be aware of the hopes and fears of his audience he discusses emotions such as happiness, pity, fear, and friendship. This book is often considered the earliest known treatise on psychology.

ON RHETORIC AND WRESTLING

PLATO

Rhetoric embraces, so to say, all the other arts! I shall give you an important proof of this. On many occasions in the past, in the company of my brother and other physicians, I have made calls on patients who were unwilling to take their medicine or submit to an operation or a cautery; and though their doctor could not persuade them, I did so, by no other art than rhetoric. And I make the further declaration that if a rhetorician and a physician should come to any city you please and have occasion to debate in the assembly or any other public gathering as to which of them ought to be elected public physician, the doctor would be utterly eclipsed, and the capable speaker would, if he chose, be elected. And likewise in a contest with any other craftsman whatsoever, the rhetorician would win his own election against all opposition of any kind; for not a single craftsman is able to speak in a crowd, on any subject in the world, more persuasively than the rhetorician. This is to show you how great and how splendid is the power of his art.

One should, however, Socrates, make use of rhetoric in the same way as one does of every other sort of proficiency. This, too, one should not employ against any and everybody. Because a man has learned to be so proficient in boxing or wrestling or the use of arms that he is superior to friend and foe alike, that is no reason for him to go about beating or stabbing and killing his friends! And if a man frequents the gymnasia, gets his body in first rate condition, becomes a prize-fighter, and then takes to beating his father and mother or his friends and relatives, that is no reason for detesting and banishing the trainers and teachers of the art of fighting! You can recognize that they imparted their instruction to be used rightly in self-defense against enemies and criminals; but the pupils perverted their own strength and skill to its wrong use. The teachers, therefore, are not evil, nor is their art responsible for these misdeeds, nor is it vicious in itself; those who misuse the art I hold to be responsible.

Exactly the same argument holds for rhetoric also. The rhetorician is capable of speaking against everyone else and on any subject you please in such a way that he can win over vast multitudes to anything, in a word, that he may desire. But the fact that he can rob doctors, or any other craftsmen, of the credit due them, is no reason why he should do so: he must use his skill justly, exactly as one should physical prowess. And if a man learns rhetoric, and then does injustice through the power of his art, we shall not be right, in my opinion, in detesting and banishing his teacher. For while the teacher imparted instruction to be used rightly, the pupil made a contrary use of it. Therefore it is only right to detest the misuser and banish and kill him, not his teacher.

Gorgias *456–57.*

ON WRITING

QUINTILIAN

It is the pen which brings at once the most labor and the most profit. . . . We must therefore write as much as possible and with the utmost care. For as deep ploughing makes the soil more fertile for the production and support of crops, so, if we improve our minds by something more than mere superficial study, we shall produce a richer growth of knowledge and shall retain it with greater accuracy. For without the consciousness of such preliminary study our powers of speaking extempore will give us nothing but an empty flow of words, springing from the lips and not from the brain. It is in writing that eloquence has its roots and foundations, it is writing that provides that holy of holies where the wealth of oratory is stored, and whence it is produced to meet the demands of sudden emergencies. It is of the first importance that we should develop such strength as will not faint under the toil of forensic strife nor be exhausted by continual use.

For it is an ordinance of nature that nothing great can be achieved in a moment, and that all the fairest tasks are attended with difficulty, while on births as well she has imposed this law, that the larger the animal, the longer should be the period of gestation. . . .

At first, our pen must be slow yet sure: we must search for what is best and refuse to give a joyful welcome to every thought the moment that it presents itself; we must first criticize the fruits of our imagination, and then, once approved, arrange them with care. For we must select both thoughts and words and weigh them one by one. This done we must consider the order in which they should be placed, and must examine all the possible varieties of rhythm, refusing necessarily to place each word in the order in which it occurs to us. In order to do this with the utmost care, we must frequently revise what we have just written. For beside the fact that thus we secure a better connexion between what follows and what precedes, the warmth of thought which has cooled down while we were writing is revived anew, and gathers fresh impetus from going over the ground again. We may compare this process with what occurs in jumping matches. The competitors take a longer run and go at full speed to clear the distance which they aim at covering; similarly, in throwing the javelin, we draw back our arms, and in archery pull back the bow-string to propel the shaft. At times however, we may spread our sails before the favoring breeze, but we must beware that this indulgence does not lead us into error. For we love all the offspring of our thought at the moment of their birth; were that not so, we should never commit them to writing. But we must give them a critical revision, and go carefully over any passage where we have reason to regard our fluency with suspicion. It is thus, we speak better than our nature will permit. For to make any real advance we need study, not self-accusation. And it is not merely practice that will enable us to write at greater length and with increased fluency, although doubtless practice is most important. We need judgment as well. So long as we do not lie back with eyes turned up to the ceiling, trying to fire our imagination by muttering to ourselves, in the hope that something will present itself, but turn our thoughts to consider what the circumstances of the case demand, what suits the characters involved, what is the nature of the occasion and the temper of the judge, we shall acquire the power of writing by rational means. It is thus that nature herself bids us begin and pursue our studies once well begun. For most points are of a definite character and, if we keep our eyes open, will spontaneously present themselves. That is the reason why peasants and uneducated persons do not beat about the bush to discover with what they should begin, and our hesitation is all the more shameful if it is simply the result of education. We must not, therefore, persist in thinking that what is hard to find is necessarily best; for, if it seems to us that there is nothing to be said except that which we are unable to find, we must say nothing at all. . . .

Everyone, however, will agree that the absence of company and deep silence are most conducive to writing, though I would not go so far as to concur in the opinion of those who think woods and groves the most suitable localities for the purpose, on the ground that the freedom of the sky and the charm of the surroundings produce sublimity of thought and wealth of inspiration. Personally I regard such an environment as a pleasant luxury rather than a stimulus to study. For whatever causes us delight, must necessarily distract us from the concentration due to our work. The mind cannot devote its undivided and sincere attention to a number of things at the same time, and wherever it turns its gaze it must cease to contemplate its appointed task. Therefore, the charm of the woods, the gliding of the stream, the breeze that murmurs in the branches, the song of birds, and the very freedom with which our eyes may range, are mere distractions, and in my opinion the pleasure which they excite is more likely to relax than to concentrate our attention. Demosthenes took a wiser view; for he would retire to a place where no voice was to be heard, and no prospect greeted the sight, for fear that his eyes might force his mind to neglect its duty. Therefore, let the burner of the midnight oil seclude himself in the silence of night, within closed doors, with but a solitary lamp to light his labors. But for every kind of study, and more especially for night work, good health and its chief source, simple living, are essential; for we have fallen into the habit of devoting to relentless labor the hour which nature has appointed for rest and relaxation. From those hours we must take only such time as is superfluous for sleep, and will not be missed. For fatigue will make us careless in writing, and the hours of daylight are amply sufficient for one who has no other distractions. It is only the busy man who is driven to encroach on the hours of darkness. Nevertheless, night work, so long as we come to it fresh and untired, provides by far the best form of privacy.

But although silence and seclusion and absolute freedom of mind are devoutly to be desired, they are not always within our power to attain. Consequently we must not fling aside our book at once, if disturbed by some noise, and lament that we have lost a day: on the contrary, we must make a firm stand against such inconveniences, and train ourselves so to concentrate our thoughts as to rise superior to all impediments to study. If only you direct all your attention to the work which you have in hand, no sight or sound will ever penetrate to your mind. If even casual thoughts often occupy us to such an extent that we do not see passers-by, or even stray from our path, surely we can obtain the same result by the exercise of our will. We must not give way to pretexts for sloth. For unless we make up our mind that we must be fresh, cheerful and free from all other care when we approach our studies, we shall always find some excuse for idleness. Therefore, whether we be in a crowd, on a journey, or even at some festive gathering, our thoughts should always have some inner sanctuary of their own to which they may retire. . . .

IV. The next point which we have to consider is the revision of our work, which is by far the most useful portion of our study: for there is good reason for the view that erasure is quite as important a function of the pen as actual writing. Revision takes the form of addition, excision and alteration. But it is a comparatively simple and easy task to decide what is to be added or excised. On the other hand, to prune what is turgid, to elevate what is mean, to repress exuberance, arrange what is disorderly, introduce rhythm where it is lacking, and modify it where it is too emphatic, involves a twofold labor. For we have to condemn what had previously satisfied us and discover what had escaped our notice. There can be no doubt that the best method of revision is to put aside what we have written for a certain time, so that when we return to it after an interval it will have the air of novelty and of being another's handiwork; for thus we may prevent ourselves from regarding our writings with all the affection that we lavish on a newborn child. But this is not always possible, especially in the case of an orator who most frequently has to write for immediate use, while some limit, after all, must be set to correction. For there are some who return to everything they write with the presumption that it is full of faults and, assuming that a first draft must necessarily be incorrect, think every change an improvement and make some alteration as often as they have the manuscript in their hands: they are, in fact, like doctors who use the knife even where the flesh is perfectly healthy. The result of their critical activities is that the finished work is full of scars, bloodless, and all the worse for their anxious care. No! let there be something in all our writing which, if it does not actually please us, at least passes muster, so that the file may only polish our work, not wear it away.

From Institutio Oratoria *10-3-4.4.*

ON FRIENDSHIP

ARISTOTLE

Let us now turn to Friendship[1] and Enmity, and ask towards whom these feelings are entertained, and why. We will begin by defining friendship and friendly feeling. We may describe friendly feeling towards any one as wishing for him what you believe to be good things, not for your own sake but for his, and being inclined, so far as you can, to bring these things about. A friend is one who feels thus and excites these feelings in return: those who think they feel thus towards each other think themselves friends. This being assumed, it follows that your friend is the sort of man who shares your pleasure in what is good and your pain in what is unpleasant, for your sake and for no other reason. This pleasure and pain of his will be the token of his good wishes for you, since we all feel glad at getting what we wish for, and pained at getting what we do not. Those, then, are friends to whom the same things are good and evil; and those who are, moreover, friendly or unfriendly to the same people; for in that case they must have the same wishes, and thus by wishing for each other what they wish for themselves, they show themselves each other's friends. Again, we feel friendly to those who have treated us well, either ourselves or those we care for, whether on a large scale, or readily, or at some particular crisis; provided it was for our own sake. And also to those who we think wish to treat us well. And also to our friends' friends, and to those who like, or are liked by, those whom we like ourselves. And also to those who are enemies to those whose enemies we are, and dislike, or are disliked by, those whom we dislike. For all such persons think the things good which we think good, so that they wish what is good for us; and this, as we saw, is what friends must do. And also to those who are willing to treat us well where money or our personal safety is concerned: and therefore we value those who are liberal, brave, or just. The just we consider to be those who do not live on others; which means those who work for their living, especially farmers and others who work with their own hands. We also like temperate men, because they are not unjust to others; and, for the same reason, those who mind their own business. And also those whose friends we wish to be, if it is plain that they wish to be our friends: such are the morally good, and those well thought of by every one, by the best men, or by those whom we admire or who admire

---

[1] In this chapter and elsewhere it is difficult to translate φιλεῖν (and its related words) by any single English equivalent; 'to be a friend,' 'to like,' 'to love,' may have to be used in turn. . . .

us. And also those with whom it is pleasant to live and spend our days: such are the good-tempered, and those who are not too ready to show us our mistakes, and those who are not cantankerous or quarrelsome—such people are always wanting to fight us, and those who fight us we feel wish for the opposite of what we wish for ourselves—and those who have the tact to make and take a joke; here both parties have the same object in view,[2] when they can stand being made fun of as well as do it prettily themselves. And we also feel friendly towards those who praise such good qualities as we possess, and especially if they praise the good qualities that we are not too sure we do possess. And towards those who are cleanly in their person, their dress, and all their way of life. And towards those who do not reproach us with what we have done amiss to them or they have done to help us, for both actions show a tendency to criticize us. And towards those who do not nurse grudges or store up grievances, but are always ready to make friends again; for we take it that they will behave to us just as we find them behaving to every one else. And towards those who are not evil speakers and who are aware of neither their neighbours' bad points nor our own, but of our good ones only, as a good man always will be. And towards those who do not try to thwart us when we are angry or in earnest, which would mean being ready to fight us. And towards those who have some serious feeling towards us, such as admiration for us, or belief in our goodness, or pleasure in our company; especially if they feel like this about qualities in us for which we es-pecially wish to be admired, esteemed, or liked. And towards those who are like ourselves in character and occupation, provided they do not get in our way or gain their living from the same source as we do—for then it will be a case of 'potter against potter':

Potter to potter and builder to builder begrudge their reward.[3]

And those who desire the same things as we desire, if it is possible for us both to share them together; otherwise the same trouble arises here too. And towards those with whom we are on such terms that, while we respect their opinions, we need not blush before them for doing what is conven-tionally wrong: as well as towards those before whom we should be ashamed to do anything really wrong. Again, our rivals, and those whom we should like to envy us—though without ill-feeling—either we like these people or at least we wish them to like us. And we feel friendly towards those whom we help to secure good for themselves, provided we are not likely to suffer heavily by it ourselves. And those who feel as friendly to us when we are not with them as when we are—which is why all men feel friendly towards those who are faithful to their dead friends.

[2]i.e., both wish to pass the time pleasantly.
[3]Hesiod, *Works and Days*, 25. . . .

And, speaking generally, towards those who are really fond of their friends and do not desert them in trouble; of all good men, we feel most friendly to those who show their goodness as friends. Also towards those who are honest with us, including those who will tell us of their own weak points: it has just been said that with our friends we are not ashamed of what is conventionally wrong, and if we do have this feeling, we do not love them; if therefore we do not have it, it looks as if we did love them. We also like those with whom we do not feel frightened or uncomfortable—nobody can like a man of whom he feels frightened. Friendship has various forms—comradeship, intimacy, kinship, and so on.

Things that cause friendship are: doing kindnesses; doing them unasked; and not proclaiming the fact when they are done, which shows that they were done for our sake and not for some other reason.

From Rhetoric. *2.4. 13 81a-81b.*

Glossary

The use of classical terms throughout this book is intended to give you a vocabulary for talking about writing. Every discipline has an established terminology, and rhetoric is no exception. In fact, these terms have a two thousand year history behind them. Understanding them will not only contribute to your knowledge of the vocabulary in other disciplines but can enhance your understanding of intellectual history, as old meanings are lost and new ones emerge.

The glossary provides you with a brief definition of the major terms in the text and gives the chapter where you can find a full discussion of the term. It also shows you how to pronounce the more difficult words. The capital letters *E, L,* and *G* indicate whether the word is English, Latin, or Greek. Since many of the terms appear in more than one place in the text, you can locate the different occurrences by checking the index.

PRONUNCIATION GUIDE

Below is a guide that will help you approximate the pronunciation of unfamiliar words.

Vowels

ay	pay, say
a	act, bad
ee	beet, meat
e	bet, bed
i	bit and bite
o	boat, open
u	*a*bove
uh	(end of syllable) antith*e*sis (an-TI-thuh-sis)
oy	boy
oo	boot

Consonants

p	pin, hip	s	seal, bus
b	bin, rib	z	zeal, buzz
t	tin, not	sh	shin, rush
d	din, nod	h	hen
k	cot, back	m	meat, ham
g	got, bag	n	neat, man
ch	chin, rich	l	leap, peal
j	gin, ridge	r	rue, peer
f	fine, leaf	y	you
v	vine, leave	w	win
th	thigh, thy		

GLOSSARY OF MAJOR TERMS

actio (AC·tee·o; L.): See PRESENTATION

ad hominem (ad·HO·mi·nem): A psychological fallacy which shifts the argument from the issue to a personal attack on the person involved. (Chapter 8)

alliteration (a·li·ter·AY·shun; E.): One of the most commonly used figures, alliteration is the repetition of the same sound at the beginning of successive words. (Chapter 11)

amplificatio (am·pli·fu·CA·tee·o; L.): See PROOF

anadiplosis (a·na·di·PLO·sis; G.): A figure that uses the last word of a phrase or clause as the beginning word in the following clause or phrase. (Chapter 11)

analogy (an·AL·o·gee; E.): A form of logical inference. Analogy is based on the assumption that if two things are known to be alike in some ways, they are presumed to be alike in other ways. (Chapter 11)

anaphora (a·NA·fo·ruh; G.): A figure which repeats the same word at the beginning of successive clauses or phrases. (Chapter 11)

anastrophe (a·NA·stro·fee; G.): A figure which inverts the usual word order. The original Greek means a "turning back." (Chapter 11)

appeal to authority: A psychological fallacy which uses a person who is an authority to influence the audience, whether or not the person is an authority in the area being discussed. (Chapter 8)

appeal to force: A psychological fallacy which influences by threatening the audience in some way. (Chapter 8)

appeal to humor: A psychological fallacy which uses humor to divert the audience from the issue. (Chapter 8)

appeal to ignorance: A psychological fallacy which argues that the proposition is true because it cannot be proved false. (Chapter 8)

appeal to pity: A psychological fallacy in which feelings of pity outweigh the logic or fairness of the argument. (Chapter 8)

appeal to tradition: A psychological fallacy based on the positive and influential feelings an audience may have toward tradition and precedent. (Chapter 8)

apposition: A figure in which a noun or phrase next to another noun describes or explains it. (Chapter 8)

appropriateness: A feature of style which matches the language, subject matter, occasion, and audience. (Chapter 10)

Aristotle: (384–322 B.C.) Greek philosopher and author of the *Rhetoric*. Aristotle was a pupil of Plato and teacher of Alexander the Great.

arrangement: The second of the five parts of rhetoric which concerns the ordering of the discourse. (Chapter 9)

artistic proofs: One of the two kinds of arguments or means of persuasion available to a speaker through the art of rhetoric; the other kind is called INARTISTIC. The artistic proofs are *logos* (appeal to reason), *pathos* (appeal to the audience), and *ethos* (appeal of the writer). (Chapters 3, 6)

assonance (AS-uh-nans; E.): A figure closely allied to alliteration, which involves the repetition of sounds within words. (Chapter 11)

asyndeton (a-SIN-duh-tun; G.): A figure that omits conjunctions between related clauses to quicken the pace of the prose. (Chapter 11)

Athens: Ancient Greek city-state; home of Socrates, Plato, and Aristotle. (Chapter 1)

average: In statistics, the term that describes the number obtained by dividing the sum of a set of quantities by the number of quantities in that set. (Chapter 7)

background: The second part of arrangement which provides the facts or history of the subject being discussed. (Chapter 9)

backing: In the TOULMIN MODEL of deductive reasoning, the *backing* provides additional reasons or supporting arguments for the WARRANT. (Chapter 6)

bandwagon: A psychological fallacy based on the assumption that the audience should do something because everyone else does it. (Chapter 8)

bibliography: A list of the works of an author or of the sources of information on a particular subject. (Chapter 13)

brevity: A quality of style in which material is presented succinctly. (Chapter 10)

categorical syllogism: A type of syllogism dealing with categories or whole classes; it is characterized by the words *all* or *every* in the major premise. (Chapter 6)

cause/effect: One of the topics. (Chapter 5)

chiasmus (ki-AZ-mus; G.): A figure which reverses the order of the first clause or phrase in the second clause or phrase. (Chapter 11)

Cicero: Roman orator, politician, and rhetorician, the author of *De Inventione* and *De Oratore*. (Chapter 1)

claim: The conclusion in the TOULMIN MODEL of deductive reasoning. (Chapter 6)

clarity: A feature of style which demands that words be selected and arranged with care for the meaning to be clear. According to Quintilian, *clarity* is the first virtue of style. (Chapter 10)

classification: A topic which places objects into a class or group. (Chapter 4)

cliché: A word or expression once fresh and vivid that has lost its original meaning because of overuse. (Chapter 10)

climax: A figure that arranges ideas in order from the least to the most important. (Chapter 11)

coherence: The logical linking of ideas in a discourse. (Chapter 10)

colloquialism: A word or phrase commonly found in spoken language or in informal written language. (Chapter 10)

commonplace book: A record of ideas and strategies for writing—words or phrases that you think might be effective in writing—or of anything to help you generate and locate ideas. (Chapter 1)

comparison: One of the common topics involving similarities. (Chapter 5)

conclusion: The seventh part of a discourse, which summarizes the arguments. (Chapter 9)

conformatio: (kon-for-MA-tee-o; L.): See PROOF

connotation: The implicit meaning(s) of a word. (Chapter 4)

contrast: One of the common topics involving differences. (Chapter 5)

Corinth: Ancient Greek city-state.

correctness: A feature of style which involves the proper use of language. (Chapter 10)

correlation: A particular kind of statistical probability in which two events frequently occur together. (Chapter 7)

data: Evidence in the TOULMIN MODEL of deductive reasoning. (Chapter 6)

deduction: A method of reasoning which works from a general statement to a particular instance. (Chapter 6)

definiendum (day-fi-nee-EN-dum; L.): In a definition, the term to be defined. (Chapter 4)

definition: A topic that sets bounds to and limits the meaning of a term. (Chapter 4)

definition of issues: The third part of a discourse, which defines terms and explains the issues. (Chapter 9)

De Inventione (DAY-in-ven-tee O-nay; L.): One of Cicero's works concerned with the rhetorical canon of invention. (Chapter 1)

deliberative: One of the three types of oratory, also called *political oratory*, which urges the hearer to do or not do something. It is concerned with the future. (Chapters 1, 9)

delivery: See PRESENTATION

Demosthenes: Greek orator and political leader. (Chapter 13)

denotation: The explicit meaning(s) of a word. (Chapter 4)

description: A topic that emphasizes what is seen or experienced from the writer's perspective. (Chapter 7)

dialectic: A method of searching for truth through dialogue. (Chapter 6)

differentia (di-fe-REN-shee-a; L.): Differences between members of the same class. (Chapter 4)

dignitas (DIG-ni-tas; L.): See EMBELLISHMENT

disjunctive syllogism: A type of syllogism concerned with contraries and contradictions, marked by words like *either, or, neither, nor*. (Chapter 6)

dispositio (dis-po-ZI-tee o; L.): See ARRANGEMENT

division: A topic that defines or clarifies by placing (dividing) into groups. (Chapter 4)

either/or fallacy: A logical fallacy which reduces a complex issue to only two unacceptable alternatives. (Chapter 8)

elocutio (el-o-KU-tee-o; L.): See STYLE

embellishment: One of the qualities of style which involves using the figures of speech. (Chapter 11)

enthymeme (EN-thi-meem): A truncated syllogism, based on probabilities, in which one of the premises is not stated but implied. (Chapter 6)

epideictic (ep-i-DIK-tik; G.): One of the three types of oratory, also called *ceremonial*, which praises or blames. This type of oratory is concerned with the present. (Chapter 9)

epilogus (e-pi-LO-gus; L.): See CONCLUSION

equivocation: A logical fallacy which uses the same term in two different ways. (Chapter 8)

essence: The question of what something really is; in classical rhetoric the question *quid sit* or "What is it?" helps the author explore the issue under consideration. Answering this question often involves defining the subject. (Chapter 2)

essential definition: The most basic definition of a concept or term, usually one sentence; defines the term by placing it in a class and differentiating it from other members of the class. (Chapter 4)

ethical proof: The good character and credibility of the writer which emerges from the discourse. (Chapter 3; see also ETHOS)

ethos (EE-thos; G.): The Greek term for one of the artistic proofs; it was borrowed directly from Greek by Latin rhetoricians. *Ethos* is the ethical argument of a discourse that depends on establishing the credibility and goodwill of the speaker. (Chapters 1, 3)

etymology: The historical roots of a word. (Chapter 4)

example: In rhetorical induction, the specific instance or situation that provides the proof of the argument. (Chapter 6)

exordium (eks-OR-deum; L.): See OPENING

explanatio (eks-pla-NA-tee-o; L.): See CLARITY

explicatio (eks-pli-KA-tee o; L.): See DEFINITION OF ISSUES

exposition: The second part of arrangement which defines the terms and issues being discussed. (Chapter 9)

fact: Something that is known to have happened. In the invention process, the question from classical rhetoric of *an sit* or "Did it happen?" is one way of exploring the topic. (Chapter 2)

fallacy: An error in reasoning. (Chapter 8)

faulty cause (*post hoc ergo propter hoc*): A logical fallacy which confuses chronological sequence with cause and effect. (Chapter 8)

faulty hidden generalization: A material fallacy in which the premise that has been omitted from the enthymeme is false. (Chapter 8)

footnote: A note placed at the bottom of a page, which comments on or provides the source for information used in the text. (Chapter 13)

forensic (also *judicial*): One of the three types of oratory which attacks or defends someone. Forensic discourse is concerned with past events. (Chapter 1)

genus (JEE-nus): A class or group of things sharing certain common characteristics. (Chapter 3)

Gorgias (GOR-jis): One of Plato's early dialogues, which discusses his view of rhetoric. In this work, Plato compares rhetoric to cookery and calls it a knack. (Chapter 1)

heuresis (hu-REE-sis; G.): See INVENTION

hyperbole (hi-PER-bo-lee; E.): A trope which involves exaggeration. (Chapter 11)

hypocrisis (hi-POK-ri-sis; G.): See PRESENTATION

hypothesis: Today the term usually means a provisional assumption; in classical rhetoric it concerned the specific case being discussed, whereas the thesis concerned the general case. (Chapter 2)

hypothetical syllogism: A sequential syllogism characterized by words such as *if, when, provided that.* (Chapter 6)

immediate cause: In examining a chain of causes, the *immediate cause* is the one closest in time to the effect. (Chapter 5; see companion term REMOTE CAUSE)

inartistic proofs: One of the two kinds of argument or means of persuasion available to the speaker (the other kind is *artistic proof*). Artstotle in the *Rhetoric* cited five kinds of *inartistic proofs*, which the speaker did not have to invent but could use: laws, witnesses, contracts, tortures, and oaths. (Chapters 6, 15)

induction: A method of reasoning which begins with particular instances and moves to a general truth. (Chapter 6)

Institutio Oratoria (in-sti-TU-tee-o or-a-TOR-ee-a; L.): A treatise by the Roman educator Quintilian which describes and prescribes educational and rhetorical principles.

insufficient sampling: A material fallacy resulting from a sample that is too small. (Chapter 8)

inventio (in-VEN-tee-o; L.): See INVENTION

invention: The first of the five parts of rhetoric which involves ways of finding the best possible proofs for developing a subject. (Chapter 2)

irony: A trope which uses a word or words in such a way that the meaning conveyed is the opposite of what is expressed. (Chapter 11)

jargon: The highly technical language of a specialized group. (Chapter 10)

judicial: See FORENSIC

latinitas (la-TI-ni-tas; L.): See CORRECTNESS

lexis (LEKS-us; G.): See STYLE

litotes (LI-to-teez; G.): A trope that intensifies by deliberate understatement. (Chapter 11)

localism: A word or phrase that is characteristic of a certain geographical area. (Chapter 10)

logical fallacy: A group of fallacies that result from faults in reasoning. (Chapter 8)

logical proof: The reasoned arguments used to persuade the audience. (Chapter 6)

logos (LO-gos; G.): The original Greek term (now Anglicized) which combines the meanings of thought and expression. In Aristotle's *Rhetoric*, *logos* is one of the artistic proofs. (Chapter 6)

major premise: One of the statements in a syllogism that states a generalization. (Chapter 6)

material fallacy: A fallacy which concerns the subject matter of the argument. (Chapter 8)

maxim: The statement of a general truth which can serve as either a premise or a conclusion of an ENTHYMEME. (Chapter 6)

mean: See AVERAGE

median: The middle number in a set of quantities. (Chapter 7)

memoria (me-MOR-ee-a; L.): See MEMORY

memory: The fourth of the five parts of rhetoric. (Chapter 12)

metaphor (ME-ta-for): The most important and widely used trope, implies a comparison between two unlike objects. (Chapter 11)

metonymy (me-TA-nuh-mee): This figure is closely related to SYNECHDOCHE and designates one thing by an object closely associated with it (e.g., the "King" is called the "crown"). (Chapter 11)

minor premise: One of the statements in a syllogism. (Chapter 6)

mode: In statistical analysis, the number that occurs most often in a set. (Chapter 7)

name calling: A psychological fallacy that uses emotionally loaded terms to influence the audience. (Chapter 8)

narratio (na-RA-tee-o; L.): See BACKGROUND

narration: The telling of a story, involving elements of time, place, actor, action, cause, manner. (Chapter 7)

necessary cause: The *necessary cause* is one without which the effect could not have occurred. A SUFFICIENT CAUSE is one that could produce the effect. (Chapter 5)

onomatopoeia (on-a-mat-o-PEE-uh): A trope which uses words that sound like what they mean, such as tinkle, rush, and whoop. (Chapter 11)

opening: The first part of the discourse which gains the audience's attention and interest. (Chapter 9)

oxymoron (oks-ee-MOR-on): A trope that joins two terms that ordinarily contradict each other, such as "wedded maid" or "sweet sorrow." (Chapter 11)

paradox (PA-ra-doks): A trope in which a statement that appears to be contradictory in fact has some truth, such as "He worked hard at being lazy." (Chapter 11)

parallelism: Expressing similar or related ideas in similar grammatical construction. (Chapter 11)

paraphrase: To recast an author's idea in different words. (Chapter 13)

parenthesis (pa-REN-the-sis; E.): A device that inserts a word, phrase, or sentence not syntactically related to the rest of the sentence. (Chapter 11)

partitio (par-TI-tee-o; L.): See THESIS

pathos (PAY-thos): The original Greek term (now Anglicized) for emotional argument. In Aristotle's *Rhetoric*, *pathos* is one of the artistic proofs or means of persuading the audience by appealing to the emotions. (Chapter 3)

percentage: In statistics, the quantity of a part with relation to the whole. (Chapter 7)

peroratio (per-or-RA-tee-o; L.): The term for the conclusion of the oration; it is the seventh part of the typical seven-part oration as described in the *Ad Herennium*. (See also CONCLUSION; Chapter 9)

personification (per-son-uh-fuh-KA-shun): A trope that attributes human qualities to an inanimate object. (Chapter 11)

Phaedrus (FA-drus; G.): A dialogue of Plato in which he describes the ideal orator and the possibility of a true rhetoric.

plagiarism: Knowingly using another person's words or ideas without giving credit to that person. (Chapter 13)

Plato: (429–347 B.C.) Ancient Greek philosopher and student of Socrates. Author of *Phaedrus* and *Gorgias*.

polyptoton (po-LIP-to-ton; G.): A figure which uses the same root word in different parts of speech, such as *psychology* and *psychological*. (Chapter 11)

polysyndeton (po-lee-SIN-de-ton; E.): A figure that uses many conjunctions (in contrast to *asyndeton*), slowing down the pace of the writing. (Chapter 11)

presentation: The fifth of the five parts of a discourse, sometimes called delivery. (Chapters 13, 14)

proof: The fifth part of a discourse which sets out the arguments that support or prove the thesis. These strategies are derived from the classical *topics* of definition, comparison, contrast, classification, and causal analysis, which are discussed in Chapters 4, 5, and 6.

psychological fallacies: Fallacies which play on the feelings of the audience. (Chapter 8)

pun: A trope that plays on words that sound alike but are different in meaning or that plays on different meanings of the same word. (Chapter 11)

qualifier: This element in the TOULMIN METHOD of deductive reasoning marks the limitations of the CLAIM. (Chapter 6)

quality: In rhetoric, the *quality* of a subject involves questions of right and wrong, good and bad. The classical question of *quale sit* asks "What is its quality?" and helps the author explore the nature of the subject. (Chapter 2)

Quintilian: (A.D. 35–95) A Roman rhetorician and teacher, head of the Roman School of Oratory, whose work *Institutio Oratoria* provides the best ancient summary of the classical tradition.

rebuttal: An element in the TOULMIN METHOD of deductive reasoning which allows for the exceptions, limitations, or special circumstances that may limit the CLAIM. (Chapter 6)

refutatio (re-fyoo-TA-tee-o; L.): See REFUTATION

refutation: The sixth part of a discourse which answers the opposing arguments. (Chapter 9)

remote cause: The first in a long chain of causes. (Chapter 5; see companion term IMMEDIATE CAUSE)

reprehensio (re-pre-HEN-see-o; L.): See REFUTATION

Rhetoric: This work by Aristotle is probably the most important early treatise on rhetoric and is the first systematic treatment of the subject.

Rhetorica Ad Herennium (rhe-TOR-ee-kuh od her-REN-ee-um; L.): A work, often attributed to Cicero, which provides the most complete synthesis of classical rhetoric.

rigged question: A logical fallacy that requires an admission of guilt regardless of the answer given. (Chapter 8)

schemes: The arrangement of ideas, words, or phrases that are stylistically effective. (Chapter 11)

sexist language: Language that privileges one gender (traditionally the male) over another, such as the use of the pronoun *he* to stand for all people. (Chapter 10)

simile (SIM-i-lee): Like METAPHOR, *simile* involves a comparison of two unlike things but the words *like* or *as*, make the comparison explicit. (Chapter 11)

slang: Colorful words and phrases often used by speakers to identify themselves with a particular group. (Chapter 10)

Socrates: (469–399 B.C.) A philosopher of ancient Greece who taught Plato. Although Socrates left no written texts, his influence was great.

Sparta: One of the ancient Greek city-states, known for its military prowess and rigid discipline.

species (SPE-shees): A class of individuals or objects grouped together but subordinate to a larger grouping (the GENUS). (Chapter 4)

statistics: Mathematical data which can provide evidence for an argument. (Chapter 7)

stipulative definition: When a term has more than one meaning, the *author stipulates or makes clear* the specific meaning being used in a discourse. (Chapter 4)

style: The third of the five parts of rhetoric. (Chapter 10)

sufficient cause: A cause that could produce a particular effect, but which is not the NECESSARY CAUSE. (Chapter 5)

summary: To restate the ideas of a text in briefer form without distorting the writer's main points. (Chapter 13)

syllogism: A form of deductive thinking consisting of a major premise, a minor premise, and a conclusion. (Chapter 6)

synecdoche (si-NEK-duh-kee; E.): A trope which substitutes a part of the whole for the whole, as in "I have wheels." Here *wheels*, a part of a car, stands for the car. (Chapter 11)

synonym: A word with a similar meaning. (Chapter 4)

tagmemic theory: A theory of invention developed by Richard Young, Alton Becker, and Kenneth Pike using the terminology and concepts of modern physics and linguistics. This theory focuses on the different perspectives from which an object can be viewed: as a particle, wave, or field. (Chapter 7)

taxis (TAK-sus; G.): See ARRANGEMENT

taxonomy: The science, laws, or principles of classification. (Chapter 4)

textual support: The evidence from a text being discussed which supports the points being made about the text. (Chapter 14)

Thebes: One of the Greek city-states.

thesis: In classical rhetoric the statement of the issue to be proved in an oration. (Chapter 2)

topics: The strategies for finding arguments that would persuade the audience. (Chapters 3, 4; see also TOPOI)

topic sentence: A sentence which serves to guide and control one segment of an essay, often a paragraph. (Chapter 2)

topoi (TO-poy; G.): Greek word for the topics, divided into special topics (*idioi topoi*) and common topics (*koinoi topoi*). (Chapter 2)

Toulmin model of deductive reasoning: Developed by Stephen Toulmin, a model of reasoning (with similarities to the syllogism) that has three primary elements: the DATA, the WARRANT, and the CLAIM. The data are the evidence, the warrant is the supporting argument, and the claim is the conclusion. (Chapter 6)

tracings: Information on the catalog card which guides the researcher to other subject headings that may provide additional information. (Chapter 13)

trope (trop): The unusual use of language which transfers expressions from their natural and ordinary meaning to another meaning. Falling under the canon of rhetoric-designated style, examples of tropes are metaphor, simile, metonymy, synecdoche, and pun. (Chapter 11)

truth: The term applied to an argument whose premises are generally agreed upon. (Chapter 6; see also VALIDITY)

unrepresentative sampling: A material fallacy resulting from a sample which does not represent the whole group or population being considered. (Chapter 8)

validity: The term applied to an argument which is well reasoned but which may or may not be true. (Chapter 6; see also TRUTH)

warrant: In the TOULMIN MODEL of deductive reasoning, the *warrant* is the supporting evidence. (Chapter 6)

works cited: A list of the sources of material cited in a text, which comes at the end of the paper. (Chapter 13)

zeugma (ZOOG-muh; G.): A figure in which one word governs several successive words or clauses, as in "It becomes a way of life, influencing perceptions, choices, and ideals." (Chapter 11)

SHERRY BOOTH
Texas Christian University

Acknowledgments (continued from p. iv)

Loren Eiseley, "The Brown Wasps," from *The Night Country*. Copyright © 1971 Loren Eiseley. Reprinted with the permission of Charles Scribner's Sons, a division of Macmillan, Inc.

Gary Goshgarian, "Zeroing in on Science Fiction" by Gary Goshgarian, in *The Bedford Reader*, First Edition, edited by X. J. Kennedy and Dorothy Kennedy. Copyright © 1982 by St. Martin's Press and used with permission.

Stephen Jay Gould, "Evolution as Fact and Theory," first printed in *Discover* magazine, May, 1981, pages 34–37. Reprinted with permission of Stephen Jay Gould.

Maxine Hong Kingston, "No Name Woman." From The Woman Warrior, by Maxine Hong Kingston. Copyright © 1975, 1976 by Maxine Hong Kingston. Reprinted by permission of Alfred A. Knopf, Inc.

Susan Lardner, "Notes and Comment" by Susan Lardner from The Talk of the Town. Reprinted by permission; © 1961 The New Yorker Magazine, Inc.

John Lempesis, from "Murder in a Bottle" by John Lempesis in The Bedford Reader, First Edition, edited by X. J. Kennedy and Dorothy Kennedy. Copyright © 1982 by St. Martin's Press and used with permission.

Russell Lynes, abridgment from "Weekend Guests," in *Guests, or How to Survive Hospitality*, by Russell Lynes. Copyright 1951, by Harper & Row, Publishers, Inc. Reprinted by permission of Harper & Row, Publishers, Inc.

Lenny Shulman, "In New Mexico: Visions Along the Amtrak Line." Copyright 1987 Time Inc. All rights reserved. Reprinted by permission from *Time*.

Adlai E. Stevenson, "The Hard Kind of Patriotism" by Adlai E. Stevenson. Copyright © 1963 by Harper's Magazine. All rights reserved. Reprinted from the July issue by special permission.

Judy Syfers, "Why I Want a Wife." Reprinted by kind permission of the author.

Dylan Thomas, "Memories of Christmas," from *Quite Early One Morning*. Copyright 1954 by Dylan Thomas. Reprinted by permission of New Directions Publishing Corporation.

Lewis Thomas, "Magic in Medicine." Reprinted by permission of *The New England Journal of Medicine*, volume 285, pages 1366–68, 1971.

James Thurber, "The Rabbits Who Caused All The Trouble," Copyright © 1940 James Thurber Copyright © 1968 Helen Thurber. From *Fables for our Time*, published by Harper & Row.

Virginia Woolf. From *The Death of the moth and Other Essays* by Virginia Woolf, copyright 1942 by Harcourt Brace Jovanovich, Inc.; renewed 1970 by Marjorie T. Parsons, Executrix. Reprinted by permission of the publisher.

The following translations have been used in this book:

Aristotle. *Rhetoric and Poetics*. Trans. W. Rhys Roberts and Ingram Bywater. New York: The Modern Library, 1954.

Cicero. *Cicero in Twenty-Eight Volumes: Vol. 2: De Inventione, De Optimo Genere Oratorum, Topica*. Trans. H. M. Hubbell. Cambridge: Harvard UP, Loeb Classical Library, 1976.

Cicero. *Cicero on Oratory and Orators*. Translated and edited by J. S. Watson. Carbondale: Southern Illinois UP, 1970.

[Cicero]. *Cicero in Twenty-Eight Volumes: Vol. 1: [Cicero] Ad C. Herennium: De Ratione Dicendi (Rhetorica Ad Herennium)*. Trans. Harry Caplan. Cambridge: Harvard UP, Loeb Classical Library, 1981.

Longinus. *On the Sublime*. Translated with Commentary by James A. Arieti and John M. Crossett. Texts and Studies in Religion, Vol. 21. New York and Toronto: The Edwin Mellen Press, 1985.

Plato. *Gorgias*. Trans. W. C. Helmbold. Indianapolis and New York: The Bobbs-Merrill Company, Inc., 1952. *Phaedrus*. Trans. W. C. Helmbold and W. G. Rabinowitz. Indianapolis and New York: The Bobbs-Merrill Company, Inc., 1956.

Quintilian. *The Institutio Oratoria of Quintilian*. 4 vols. Trans. H. E. Butler. Cambridge: Harvard UP, Loeb Classical Library, 1980.

Index

Boldface numbers refer to definitions in the glossary